72

Environmental Policy in an International Context

PROSPECTS FOR ENVIRONMENTAL CHANGE

ENVIRONMENTAL POLICY IN AN INTERNATIONAL CONTEXT

EDITED BY
Pieter Glasbergen and Andrew Blowers
Open Universiteit, The Netherlands, and Open University, UK

PERSPECTIVES ON ENVIRONMENTAL PROBLEMS
P. Glasbergen and A. Blowers

ENVIRONMENTAL PROBLEMS AS CONFLICTS OF INTEREST
P. B. Sloep and A. Blowers

PROSPECTS FOR ENVIRONMENTAL CHANGE
A. Blowers and P. Glasbergen

Environmental Policy in an International Context

PROSPECTS FOR ENVIRONMENTAL CHANGE

EDITED BY
ANDREW BLOWERS AND PIETER GLASBERGEN

Open University, UK, and Open Universiteit, The Netherlands

A member of the Hodder Headline Group
LONDON • SYDNEY • AUCKLAND

Copublished in North, Central and South America
by John Wiley & Son Inc.
New York • Toronto

© 1996 Open University of The Netherlands

First published in Great Britain in 1996 by
Arnold, a member of the Hodder Headline Group,
338 Euston Road, London NW1 3BH

Co-published in North, Central and South America
by John Wiley & Sons Inc.,
605 Third Avenue, New York,
NY 10158–0012

British Library Cataloguing in Publication Data
A catalogue record for this book is available from the British Library

Library of Congress Cataloging-in-Publication Data
A catalog record for this book is available from the Library of Congress

ISBN 0 340 65262 4   ISBN (Wiley) 0 470 23585 3

Typeset in 11/12 pt Times by GreenGate Publishing Services, Tonbridge, Kent
Printed and bound in Great Britain by
St Edmundsbury Press Limited, Bury St Edmunds, Suffolk and
J W Arrowsmith Limited, Bristol

Contents

BOOK 1: PERSPECTIVES ON ENVIRONMENTAL PROBLEMS

EDITED BY
Pieter Glasbergen and Andrew Blowers

BOOK 2: ENVIRONMENTAL PROBLEMS AS CONFLICTS OF INTEREST

EDITED BY
Peter B. Sloep and Andrew Blowers

About the contributors

Dr Susan Baker is Senior Research Fellow in European Social Research at the University of Wales in Cardiff, UK. Her primary research interest is in environmental policy and politics at the EU level and she is currently engaged in a study of the implementation of sustainable development policies in a European context. Another research interest of hers is the gender-specific dimension of environmental policy. Her most recent publications include *Protecting the Periphery: Environmental Policy in Peripheral Regions of the European Union* (edited with K. Milton and S. Yearley), published by Frank Cass, London; 'Environmental policy of the European Community: a critical review', *Kent Journal of International Relations*; and 'Environmental policy in the European Union: institutional dilemmas and democratic practice' (in W. Lafferty and J. Meadowcroft (eds.,) *Environment and Democracy*, Edward Elgar).

Professor Andrew Blowers is Professor of Social Sciences (Planning) at the Open University, UK. Most of his teaching, research and publications have been in the fields of environmental planning, politics and policy. He is particularly concerned with the politics of sustainable development and the problems of radioactive waste. Among the books he has written are *The Limits of Power*; *Something in the Air* and *The International Politics of Nuclear Waste* (as a co-author); he has also edited *Planning for a Sustainable Environment*. As a former Dean and Pro-Vice-Chancellor of the Open University, Professor Blowers is currently Chairman of the Interfaculty Studies Board. He is also a member of the government's Radioactive Waste Management Advisory Committee (RWMAC), a former Vice-Chair of the Town and Country Planning Association and has served as an elected county councillor in Bedfordshire since 1973.

Dr Gerrit Faber is Associate Professor of International Economics at Utrecht University, The Netherlands. His main research interests are trade policy issues related to European integration and Third World development. He has published widely on these subjects. He is a member of the Dutch National Advisory Council on Development Co-operation.

Dr Pieter Glasbergen is Professor of Environmental Studies (Policy and Management) at both the University of Utrecht, The Netherlands, and the Dutch Open University. He specialises in planning and policy issues, with particular reference to environmental policy, physical planning, water management and landscape and nature conservation. He has conducted research for various government bodies, including the Ministry of the Environment, the National Physical Planning Agency and the Ministry of Public Works and Water Management. Dr Glasbergen has authored, co-authored and edited 12 books. He recently edited the fourth edition of *Milieubeleid; een beleidswetenschappelijke inleiding* (*Environmental Policy: A Planner's Perspective*), Vuga Publishers, and *Managing Environmental Disputes. Network Management as an Alternative*, Kluwer Academic Publishers. He chairs the Environmental Policy Section of the Dutch Institute for Physical Planning and Housing.

Professor Kenneth Hanf is Royal Dutch Heidemij Professor of Environmental Management at Nijenrode University (The Netherlands School of Business) and a Senior Lecturer in Public Administration at Erasmus University, Rotterdam (both in The Netherlands). He is primarily interested in issues involving multilevel policy implementation. His current research activities range from an examination of changing governmentbusiness relations with regard to environmental regulation to a study of the formation and development of the international regime for the regulation of the long-range transport of air pollutants (otherwise known as 'acid rain'). Professor Hanf is one of the editors of *Environmental Policy and Administration in Europe*, published by Harvester Wheatsheaf.

Henk C. van Latesteijn is Deputy Staff Director of the Dutch Scientific Council for Government Policy. He has published on a number of environmental issues (including impact assessment, monitoring and policies), as well as on agricultural issues (such as land use policies and long-term analysis). He is particularly interested in methodological approaches to research and has also published on this topic.

Dr Pieter Leroy is Professor of Social and Political Sciences of the Environment at the Faculty of Policy Studies, University of Nijmegen, The Netherlands. His chief interest is in the spatial aspects of environmental problems and in the formulation and evaluation of environmental policy, particularly in relation to physical planning. He has published on environmental policy in both The Netherlands and Belgium. In 1994, he edited, with Professor K. Bouwer, *Milieu en ruimte: analyse en beleid (Space and the environment: Analysis and Policy)*, a book (in Dutch) on environmental policy and physical planning. He recently published a book entitled *Environmental Science as a Vocation*.

Dr Martin List is Assistant Professor of International Relations and Comparative Politics at Fernuniversität Hagen, Germany's Open University. His main interests include international environmental policy and public international law. Relevant publications of his include *Umweltschutz in zwei Meeren* (*Environmental Protection of Two Seas*), Tuduv, Munich ; 'Regime theory and international environmental management' (together with V. Rittberger) in A. Hurrel and B. Kingsbury (eds) *The International Politics of the Environment,* OUP, Oxford; and 'Nuclear safety in Eastern Europe and the former Soviet Union' (together with B. Connolly) in R.O. Keohane (ed.) *Institutions for Environmental Aid: Pitfalls and Promise*, Cambridge, Mass, MIT Press.

Dr David Potter is Professor of Political Science at the Open University in the UK. His current research interest is the advocacy work of NGOs in relation to the environmental policies of nation states and transnational corporations in Asia. He edits the *Journal of Commonwealth and Comparative Policies*. A recent publication of his is 'Democratization in Asia' in D. Held (ed.), *Prospects for Democracy*, Polity Press, Cambridge.

Dr Colin Sage is a Lecturer in International Environmental Policy at Wye College, University of London, UK. He currently has research interests in Indonesia, Mexico, Bolivia and China; these centre primarily upon issues of rural resource management and livelihood security. He recently co-edited (with Michael Redclift) *Strategies for Sustainable Development: Local Agendas for the South,* John Wiley & Sons, Chichester, UK.

Jan Schoonenboom is a senior member of the Dutch Scientific Council for Government Policy and part-time Professor of Future Research at the Agricultural University of Wageningen, The Netherlands. His publications cover a wide range of subjects such as immigration, the labour market, the mass media, future research and the environment.

Dr Gerrit H. Vonkeman is a chemist by training, with a long experience in international environmental policy. He is presently Director of the Institute for European Environmental Policy, Brussels, and part-time Professor for International Environmental Policy at the Environment Department of Utrecht University, The Netherlands. His publications cover a wide range of subjects. He is particularly interested in fundamental, long-term solutions for international environmental problems.

Richard Welford is Professor of Business Economics at the University of Huddersfield and Director of the Centre for Corporate Environmental Management, both in the UK. He has written widely on issues relating to business and the environment and is the editor of *Business Strategy and the Environment.*

Preface

Environmental Policy in an International Context or, to use its familiar acronym, *EPIC,* is a course that developed as a result of discussions between the Dutch and British Open Universities in 1991. Eventually a collaborative project emerged which now consists of three textbooks, a workbook/study guide and six video programmes. The course has been written by an international group of experts able to bring together the latest thinking on a subject area that is relatively new but of immense importance to our future.

The course takes a critical and analytical look at contemporary environmental issues building up a discourse around four key questions. In Volume 1, *Perspectives on Environmental Problems*, the key question is, 'What are international environmental problems, and why have they become important politically?' The question is examined from the different viewpoints of the natural sciences, sociology, politics, law and economics. It is emphasised that a multidisciplinary approach is necessary if we are fully to understand environmental problems. Volume 1 covers various themes. One is that environmental problems have both physical and social aspects and that, therefore, the social context must be understood. A related theme is that environmental problem solving is both a scientific and technical and an economic and political matter. There is a need to assess the relationship between scientific evidence and policy. The scale of contemporary environmental problems is such that policy must be addressed through international arrangements. Volume 1 focuses on conceptual and theoretical analysis, illustrated by a range of environmental issues. It adopts a critical perspective on the concept of *sustainable development*. It is stressed that sustainable development should be seen in terms of the conflicts of interest that arise out of development and distribution problems.

Volume 2, *Environmental Problems as Conflicts of Interest,* considers the interaction between political power, policy making and environmental consequences. The organising principle of Volume 2 is the question, 'What are the causes of international environmental problems, and what are the conflicts surrounding their definition and potential solution?' Volume 2 consists of case studies of specific environmental problems. The logic of the case studies is that they move from the local to the global, analysing the nature of problems in the western world, the former communist countries and the South, concluding with those problems that are truly global, such as the threat of nuclear proliferation, the onset of global warming, and the loss of biodiversity. In Volume 2 it is emphasised that conflicts of interest often have both local and global implications in relation to policy and that resolution of the conflicts must be related to the social context of the problems.

Volume 3, *Prospects for Environmental Change*, goes on to discuss the possibilities for influencing environmental policy at the international level. The question addressed here is, 'What are the major constraints and opportunities that influence environmental policy making in an international context?' The opening chapters consider the role of major international actors, the nation state, non-governmental organisations and the business community in setting the policy-making agenda. The following chapters examine the importance of international relations (trade; West and East; North and South) in setting the context for environmental policy making. From this analysis the book turns its attention to the prospects for achieving sustainable development. The key question here is, 'How far can international action achieve sustainable development and in whose interest is such action taken?' The problem of translating the concept of sustainable development into practical policy and its implementation is considered before, finally, the book speculates on the social changes that are necessary if a sustainable society is to be secured.

Although *EPIC* is designed as a course with integrated components, each of the course books is also freestanding so that it can be read by those who are not taking the course. The three books, both individually and together, are intended to provide a context and body of knowledge of interest and importance to both social and natural scientists and a wider audience beyond.

Andrew Blowers (The Open University, Milton Keynes, UK)
Pieter Glasbergen (Open Universiteit, Heerlen, The Netherlands)
Course Chairs – April 1996

Acknowledgements

The present book is part of a course which is taught by the open universities of both The Netherlands (Open Universiteit) and the UK (Open University). The course has been developed by a joint course team from both universities.

Particular thanks go to the senior administrators and staff in both institutions who made EPIC possible by providing the necessary funding and administrative support to permit the venture to go ahead.

The editors wish to extend their thanks to the members of the course team and to the many others who have in some way or other contributed to the present book. Without wanting to seem ungrateful to those who contributed in small yet important ways, we would like to thank a number of people explicitly:

John Bennett, Dr John Blunden, Ron J.M. Cörvers, Dr Bernard Eccleston, Professor David Potter, Dr Alan Reddish, Varrie Scott, Paul Smith, Dr Peter Sloep, René van Veenhuizen, Dr John Wright, Anke H. van der Zijl for their services rendered as members of the core course team.

Professor Michael Redclift, the course's External Assessor, is thanked for his comments on and assessments of the course materials. Also, the services of the Tutor Panel (Fenella Butler, Mike Gordon, Gordon Jones and Miles Litvinoff) in the UK and Dr Wim Westera and the Student Testers in The Netherlands were invaluable and indispensable.

We further thank Miek A.M. Wierts-van Helden for logistics support, Ommo E. Smit for editing the manuscript and Tony Parr for his editing of the English language. Finally we must thank Evelin B.A. Karsten-Meessen for typing up the manuscript and all the secretaries who provided their services over the years.

This book, *Prospects for Environmental Change*, is volume three of the series Environmental Policy in an International Context. First published in 1996, it is part of the Open University course N.22.2.1.2.

The following photographs were provided by:
○ ABC Press, Amsterdam, The Netherlands: 1.2
○ ANP-Foto, Amsterdam, The Netherlands: 1.1, 2.3, 3.1, 4.1, 5.2, 7.4, 8.1, 8.2, 9.1, 9.3
○ Bettmann, New York, USA: 1.3, 9.2
○ Blowers, Andrew, UK: 10.2, 10.4, 10.5
○ British Antarctic Survey, Cambridge, UK: 1.4
○ Camera Press, London, UK: 6.3

○ Commissie van de Europese Gemeenschappen, Den Haag, The Netherlands: 5.1, 5.3
○ Esperit Benelux bv, Amsterdam, The Netherlands: 3.2
○ Greenpeace, Amsterdam, The Netherlands: 2.2
○ Hollandse Hoogte, Amsterdam, The Netherlands: 6.1, 6.2, 10.3
○ Lineair/Derde Wereld Fotoarchief, Arnhem, The Netherlands: 2.1, 4.2, 4.3, 4.4, 7.1, 7.2, 7.3, 7.5, 9.4
○ Mercedes-Benz Nederland bv, Utrecht, The Netherlands: 8.3
○ Open University programme clip taken from a broadcast by the British Broadcasting Corporation, UK: 10.1
○ ZEFA Nederland bv, Amsterdam, The Netherlands: 10.6

Introduction

Andrew Blowers

The development of environmental policy confronts a basic, fundamental dilemma – the clash between the *long-term* aspirations of societies (which is, perhaps, expressed in the idea of sustainable development) and the *short-term* reality of the requirement to maintain or secure economic growth. What is required, then, is a way of adapting or changing social activities in the short term so that a sustainable form of development can be achieved in the long term.

This final book of the EPIC series focuses on the prospects for achieving policies that will contribute to sustainable development. Yet, as the first two books have made clear, sustainable development remains a vague, elusive, largely rhetorical concept. What becomes clear is that, in the present state of scientific knowledge and within the limits imposed by contemporary political conflicts, sustainable development will continue to be subject to varying interpretations depending on the interests involved.

Thus, the scientific community, concerned to protect its professional interests, will provide qualified advice, emphasising the problems of uncertainty both in defining the origins of problems and in preparing strategies for their solutions. The business community – and notably the multinationals – will undertake those aspects of 'greening' their operations that will both maintain their political support and ensure they retain their competitive strength. Environmental movements, in their efforts to attract the support of some sections of public opinion, will emphasise the problems created by contemporary production patterns. Nation states – and the international regimes to which they subscribe – will seek to devise policies that meet their main requirements, political feasibility and acceptability.

The problem of achieving sustainable development depends, at one level, on the prospects for achieving political solutions through effective policies. In seeking answers we have posed a question: 'What are the major constraints and opportunities that shape environmental policy making in an international context?' Our concern here is not so much with specific policies (some of which have been the subject of case studies in Book 2) but on the policy process itself. In a formal sense this covers the deliberate courses of action by an organisation (or organisations) which requires analysis of the separate but interrelated processes of policy formulation and implementation.

This leads to a further question we have asked ourselves: 'How far can international action achieve sustainable development and in whose interest is such action taken?' Given the series' focus on international policy, we are particularly interested in the results of international action. Also, although well-chosen actions may overcome constraints and seize opportunities, for a full evaluation of the extent to which such actions contribute to a sustainable development it is crucial to establish who stands to profit from them.

This focus on policy and action leads us, in the first three chapters, to focus on key agents or actors which shape policy: the nation state, non-governmental organisations (NGOs) and business. In the following four chapters we look at international relations, specifically international trade and at the relationships within the EU, between the EU and Central and Eastern Europe and between North and South. It is in the context of these relations that policies are negotiated and outcomes determined.

The problems encountered in seeking and reaching international agreements are considered in Chapter 8. A major problem is translating the concept of sustainable development into practical policies that can be applied in specific political contexts. This is the issue for Chapter 9 which looks at policy making in terms of policy scenarios which can form the basis for action.

Effective policy making is a necessary but not sufficient condition for realising sustainable development. Although policy can influence change, it is conditional upon the needs, aspirations and attitudes of society. This suggests that analysis of the prospects must also be conducted at the level of social change. The importance of social change, an emerging theme of this book, becomes the explicit focus of the final chapter. If sustainable development is to become attainable, very significant changes must come about in societies. Chapter 10 looks at the prospects for what amounts, in effect, to a social revolution. These two dimensions, policy making and social change, frame the subject of this book.

Policy making for environmental change

International policy making is different from state policy making in certain significant respects. First, unlike the nation state, the international community does not yet have the powers to establish policy, define targets, select instruments for implementation or apply sanctions for non-compliance. Agreements must be forged through negotiation and implementation and secured through voluntary agreements. Second, there is the immense difficulty of establishing policy goals and targets, particularly in areas where the scientific knowledge is incomplete and contestable. In conditions of such uncertainty and especially where the costs and benefits of action are difficult to calculate, agreement is very difficult to secure. Third, there are the underlying conflicts between interests and priorities over a range of policy areas (of which the environment is only one) which hinder collaboration. From this analysis it becomes clear that a basis for co-operation has to be found if international policy making is to make a contribution to a sustainable environment.

Co-operation requires certain conditions to be met. One is that the interests involved must recognise their mutual dependence, the fact that they can only realise their own interests through co-operating with others. It has long been recognised that transboundary impacts (imposing negative externalities such as pollution on neighbours) can only be remedied by international agreements. These are most likely to be forged where each participant gains some benefit or some relief of costs or where sanctions can be applied in some form on the polluter. It is difficult to gain agreement where, for example, pollution can be exported with impunity. But, in the case of global environmental problems such as ozone depletion or climate change, everyone potentially stands to lose unless precautionary action is taken. Solutions, therefore, are perceived to carry more benefits than losses. Since all will benefit from such action (although, initially at least, to different degrees) the argument therefore shifts to who is responsible and therefore who will bear the costs of prevention.

The constraints on achieving the necessary agreements at the political and institutional level are formidable indeed. They include, firstly, a range of political uncertainties and impediments. With the ending of the Cold War the international political context has become at once more fragmented and unstable. Nationalist and fundamentalist movements have threatened to undermine nation states and have precipitated wider regional conflicts in former Yugoslavia and within the former Soviet Empire. Problems of resource scarcity are at the heart of conflicts in parts of sub-Saharan Africa. The pressure of population, resource scarcity and environmental change has created the fear of widespread migrations. And, on top of all this, nuclear proliferation (with a number of countries already capable of producing nuclear weapons and several on the brink of doing so) has increased the prospect of regional wars turning into a more general – and possibly terminal – conflagration. In such conditions of uncertainty it is not surprising that global environmental problems create rather less immediate anxiety than the prospects for peace and security.

On the other hand, one of the outcomes of the ending of the Cold War has been the prospect of using the so-called 'peace dividend', through the switch from the arms race to other priorities. Though fragile, the rapprochement between East and West has introduced co-operation in many areas of mutual interest, one of which is the global environment.

A further constraint is that the world is fragmented into nation states who lay claim to sovereign territorial rights over specific parts of the land surface. Although this sovereignty is not absolute (and is compromised in various ways, as is made clear in the first chapter of this book), nevertheless international environmental policies must be agreed and administered by the nation states acting in co-operation and concert. Clearly, individual nation states and groupings of states will jealously protect their own interests and advantage and priorities will vary from place to place and from time to time. Reaching agreement in principle requires lengthy negotiation, trade-offs, compensation and compromises. Translating principles into practical policies is another stage of lengthy bargaining to achieve consensus. Beyond that there are problems of implementing policies in a world where the administrative capacity and control of states varies enormously and where there are opportunities for evasion, procrastination and free-loading which will be exploited by the less scrupulous states.

It is difficult enough to achieve agreement even among those states which appear to share mutual interests in environmental protection, such as the EU (Chapter 5). It is much more problematic when interests are sharply divided as they are between North and South (an aspect discussed in Chapter 7). These sharp differences of perspective have led to a polarisation which ramifies across the whole range of environmental and economic concerns that divide the rich from the poorer countries of the world. Inequalities between rich and poor remain a major barrier to compromise and agreement on the whole range of issues subsumed under the general terms of environment and development.

Against all this there has also been the vigorous development of international environmental regimes to deal with global environmental change. Although each of them is fraught with problems of agreement and implementation, their mere existence signals the emergence of supranational co-operation. Progress has gone much further in some areas – notably in the protocols on ozone depletion and the protection of the Antarctic – than in those where the issues are exceedingly complex and the interests diverse (such as global warming). The various conventions ensure a continuing process of societal learning, the building of confidence and the effort to achieve consensus by concessions, compromise and compensation which is the essence of policy development and implementation (Chapter 8). The idea of sustainable development, though still elusive, is beginning to be translated into policy scenarios that can lead eventually to more practical, implementable strategies (Chapter 9).

The globalisation of the economy also acts as a fundamental constraint on sustainable forms of development. The international market economy has now penetrated virtually everywhere. Barriers to trade have been progressively removed and, while there are divergent views about the immediate implications of trade liberalisation for the environment (as discussed in Chapter 4), the main motivation is to generate economic growth, not to secure environmental protection. The driving logic of the capitalist system is competition based on comparative advantage creating demands for goods and services, which inevitably results in the depletion of resources and the degradation of the environment. Indeed, Western efforts to help bring about environmental improvements in the East are largely motivated by the desire to capture markets and lock these economies into the international system (Chapter 6). In a similar way multinational companies, whose operations worldwide are the motor of the capitalist economy, emphasise the need for improving environmental standards, the so-called 'greening' of business (the subject of Chapter 3). Part of their aim is to ensure business as usual by retaining the favour of governments while at the same time seeing off any competition by erecting barriers to entry of rivals unable to meet the standards.

Through a process of uneven development environmental problems tend to become concentrated in the poorer parts of the world (Chapter 7). The association of poverty with environmental degradation is especially evident in the gross pollution of parts of the former Soviet empire, in the problem of desertification which affects large areas of sub-Saharan Africa and in the deforestation that has occurred in parts of Asia and Latin America.

Prospects for social change

Focusing on the constraints induces a pessimistic, even fatalistic attitude, an assumption that global environmental deterioration is inevitable. On the other hand it is possible, by looking at the opportunities for change, to feel a tentative, cautious optimism. This is especially true if attention is turned from the immediate problems of policy making to the prospects for adaptation through social change. Although social change is, to some extent, a guided process, it is not simply dependent on the actions and influence of organisations and institutions. It is also, probably predominantly, the product of a wide range of cultural as well as political influences. Whatever the influences at work, there are some signs that societies may be changing in ways that make the attainment of policies for sustainable development a possibility.

In the first place there is some evidence of greater openness and participation in policy making and implementation. With this comes a recognition of the importance of grassroots activity and local solutions which emphasise sustainability. This has already been recognised in some international regimes, notably the Convention on Desertification, which emphasises the part to be played by NGOs and by local communities in developing sustainable forms of production. This signals a growing recognition that change occurs from below, it cannot simply be imposed from above. Connected to this is the need for greater social equality. Co-operation can only occur if all parties perceive the outcomes to be broadly fair.

Social change is motivated by changing perceptions and values. Environmental issues often reinvigorate values that were supposedly annihilated by modernisation. In particular, the environment emphasises the importance of locality and community, the need to achieve quality of surroundings. Environmental value systems embrace such issues as defence of amenity, conservation of resources, prevention of risk and concern for survival which are fundamental aspects of both the material and spiritual quality of life. But environmental values are in competition with the materialist values that permeate modern society. They are values that are likely to influence those who have satisfied their material needs and desires. They are, therefore, luxurious values especially to those who struggle for daily survival. Vast areas – especially in the poorer countries – are as yet quite beyond the reach of these values.

Nevertheless, the problems of environmental change appear to be such that, unless there are fundamental shifts in values in the short term, there may be no survival in the long term. The shifts required will vary from society to society. In the North, where the problem is a high per capita consumption of goods, energy and travel, an emphasis on the reduction in demand and conservation of resources will be necessary. In poorer countries it is the increasing dominance of Western values and economic systems that has threatened the sustainability of traditional production systems. In all countries the connections between social and environmental change needs to be appreciated in its local, social and cultural context.

If social change favouring sustainability is to come about then the dominant value system must be challenged by countervailing forces promoting values that are able to penetrate at all levels of society and to subvert the prevailing power structures. The possibilities rest on two contemporary phenomena. One is the rise of the environmental movements which, apart from seeking to influence specific policies, are also intent on promulgating environmental values in society at large. The development of networks among these movements in both North and South (and sometimes linking North and South) has been a dynamic feature helping to shift values and influence decision makers (Chapter 2). Environmental movements operate at local, national and international levels and the activity they generate poses a challenge to centralised, closed decision making and to contemporary assumptions about economic growth. Their influence over policy making and implementation has been increasing and the potential impact of these movements on future social change is one of the subjects considered in the final chapter.

The influence of environmental movements has been enhanced by a second phenomenon – the spread of electronic means of communication. The ability to achieve instantaneous communication worldwide both through the media and through networks of organisations provides environmental movements (as well as governmental bodies and scientists) with immediate access to detailed information and analysis. This could have a major impact on raising environmental awareness and on the ability to monitor the process of environmental change and compliance with environmental policies. It would assist the process of 'social learning' whereby ideas and values and associated policy developments permeate the decision making process and eventually society at large.

It is impossible to predict which direction social change will take. But, at the end of this series, perhaps a tentative optimism on the prospects for change is permissible. A process of societal learning has begun. Networks have developed, international organisations have been established and negotiations have commenced over a whole range of international environmental issues. Institutions that are transnational, transmedia and trans-sectoral are beginning to develop. As the risks become more obvious, co-operation is likely to increase with the aim of finding solutions that are acceptable to people and which are politically feasible. They will be brought about by a shift in social values, imperceptible and restricted at first, but gathering momentum as people's attitudes and behaviour undergo the transformation necessary to usher in a sustainable society. If that transformation occurs society will have moved from a *conflict between* environment *or* development to a *concern for* environment *and* development. If it does not, then the limits of environmental tolerance may be transgressed and society's very survival will be imperilled.

1

Sovereign states and international regimes

Martin List

1.1 Introduction

The first underlying question for this book is, 'What are the major constraints and opportunities that influence environmental policy making in an international context?' In an attempt to answer this question we shall look at specific types of actors that influence or shape environmental policy. In this chapter, we shall concentrate on one particular type of actor: the modern state. The modern state is a ubiquitous form of political organisation assuming certain powers, roles and functions over a defined territory and the people who occupy it. Although the modern state is ubiquitous, it is not omnipotent. It must be seen in its societal context and special attention should be paid to the delicate balance between state and non-state actors of civil society. The state must concede certain powers and functions in the process of international co-operation. Here we shall focus on the relationship between the state and those international regimes concerned with the environment which modify or constrain its sovereignty. It will be convenient to analyse the domestic and international settings separately, although these tend to merge into what may be termed an international context. Accordingly, the state and civil society will be considered first (section 1.2) and then the state in its international context (section 1.3). Finally, attention will be given to regimes, societal learning and the redefinition of states' sovereignty (section 1.4).

Before beginning the discussion a brief word is necessary on the assumptions behind my argument. I am focusing attention on democratic regimes although it must be remembered that more than half the world's states are not democracies. I shall argue that democracies are the best forms of political organisation for ensuring the development of policies to protect the environment. That is not to say such policies are impossible in other regimes nor that all democracies succeed in developing appropriate environmental policies. I believe, however, that democracies provide the flexibility, openness and level of citizen participation to ensure understanding and responsiveness to the needs of the environment.

A second assumption follows from this, namely that policy is largely shaped through the influence and stimulus provided by non-state agencies within a flourishing civil society, characteristic of democracies. It must be recognised, of course, that this is only one view; others would include the opposing view that policy is driven largely by the state and the vested interests of the elites within it.

1.2 The state and civil society

Contrasting state-society relations

The modern state can be defined as an ensemble of political institutions (also referred to as a state apparatus) claiming superior authority, or sovereignty, over a particular territory and the population living within it. This is a very general definition; basically it involves (1) the underlying idea of a state apparatus that is distinct from but related to 'its' society and (2) the territorially delimited claim to sovereignty, i.e. a legal status with factual implications. We shall return to this latter notion, more specifically to external sovereignty, later. For the moment we shall focus on the idea of the state apparatus.

In a certain sense, the state, or state apparatus, is part of 'its' society. This is just another way of saying that states are social institutions. At the same time, they claim superior authority (i.e. internal sovereignty) over 'their' societies and are hence distinct from other, non-state or societal actors, to which they relate in various ways. Basically, according to modern political theory, there is a flow of legitimacy from society towards a democratically constituted state, which has in turn a legal competence to set and if necessary to enforce, certain rules. Society therefore exercises a degree of autonomy in relation to the state and vice versa. The state should not be owned by any particular societal group and hence should not promote its interests alone. On the other hand, societal actors should be free to act, within the limits of the rules set, in the interest of the common good. Theory thus requires an intricate balance between the state and, as it is called, civil society (Arato and Cohen, 1992; Keane, 1988; Perez-Diaz, 1993; Putnam, 1993). Practice has proved that achieving this balance is both a difficult and a permanent task. It has also proved that different types of states meet this criterion to different extents.

Western developed nations come closest to the theoretical model, which is hardly a coincidence given the fact that it was in the West that the model first developed historically. The state here guarantees what is called private autonomy, including such basic rights as freedom of speech, assembly and political activity (interestingly incorporating the freedoms both to participate in and to abstain from this activity), freedom of the press and of research and, last but not least, the right to private ownership. In doing so, the state opens up the space in which civil society can thrive. This holds notably for private economic activity, both in the unfolding domestic markets and across borders, out of which arises the phenomenon of international, or rather transnational, markets. Similarly, private activities such as journalistic and scientific gathering and dissemination of information occur both domestically and across borders, again creating transnational networks of communication. Private organisations such as religious communities, political parties and citizens' action groups add to the diversity of civil society.

A contrasting model of state-society relations was realised in the communist states such as those in Eastern Europe and is still in evidence in those that remain. State or, allegedly, public control, especially of economic activity, was and is the very essence of these systems. Neither domestically nor transnationally should there be any private economic activity on a major scale. The underlying ideology is that unchecked markets tend to outpace public control while at the same time producing unintended consequences, not all of which are as beneficial as those praised by Adam Smith as the doings of an 'invisible' and supposedly benign hand. The price for state control in these systems is high, however: civil society is deprived of the necessary freedoms, is

Plate 1.1 State power symbolised by a military parade in Red Square, Moscow. The celebrations in question were intended to mark the 70th anniversary of the October Revolution on 7 November 1987. Photo: ANP Foto

therefore unable to unfold and hence cannot play its beneficial role as a reservoir of countervailing elites and innovative ideas (Etzioni-Halevy, 1993). The ossification of power structures and an inability to recognise malfunctions in the system have been the results of and the reason for the collapse of this type of system in many countries.

Finally, there is the whole group of so-called developing countries. This group is in itself much too heterogeneous to justify any broad generalisation. Suffice it to say that in a number of cases the paradoxical situation exists of states that are at once too weak and too strong. They are too weak wherever they lack the autonomy to resist the overwhelming influence of particular powerful societal groups (Migdal, 1988). The state is then 'owned' by either the adherents of a state party, often modelled along communist lines, or, as in more recent cases, by a religious movement or by an ethnic group, allegedly or in fact favouring members of the in group and disfavouring other groups. There is finally the possibility that the state and such essential functions as the application of force and the administration of 'public order' are controlled by the members of a certain (generally wealthy) class.

The results tend to be similar in all such cases. The fear of potential miscreants and opponents deprives civil society of necessary freedoms, mismanagement is not checked and economies tend to be run down (although it is also true that the world market often contributes to the weakness of these economies). Forced industrialisation and forced obedience are then often seen by those in power as the sole remedies, which is where developing states tend to be, paradoxically, too strong. The means of force wielded and the potential for repression held by even weak governments is tremendous and democracy is all too often one of the victims.

The ugly face of these strong states may show even in their environmental policies as, for example, Peluso (1993) points out referring to Kenya (see Box 1). It seems that even an ecological dictatorship is, above all, a dictatorship. Such regimes are often assisted in the application of 'conservationist violence' by international nature protection organisations. This is a reminder that this kind of transnational activity, too, should not be accepted uncritically. It may serve to strengthen states which are already excessively strong *vis-a-vis* their local populations.

Why this excursion into political theory and a brief explanation of differing types of state-society relations in a chapter supposedly dealing with environmental policy? The answer is that only if the societal context of state action is taken into account is it possible to assess the potential role of state action in the process of solving environmental problems. States differ considerably in their capacities and limits for action and (perhaps even more importantly) state-civil society complexes differ in their potential for societal learning. Let us turn to state capacities and limits first and then discuss and assess the potential for societal learning.

Opportunities and constraints for state action

In order to examine briefly the limits and capacities for state action, we need to run through our list of types of state-society relations again. In developed Western countries the state apparatus itself, i.e. the administrative system, tends to be elaborate and relatively effective. In fact, it was the administrative sector which initiated some of the first steps towards environmental policy, e.g. in the field of water and air

---

Coercing conservation

I

In her article entitled *Coercing Conservation*, Peluso (1993) gives an example of the undemocratic consequences that may result from conservation efforts driven by the central authorities and affecting local populations. The example concerns the establishment of national parks and wildlife reserves in Kenya.

She writes:

> The traditional users of these lands, the Maasai, Somalis and pastoralists of other ethnic groups, have been excluded from access to these lands to various degrees over the past century. …Some Maasai were benefiting from the Park's existence, but not necessarily those who had the most to lose from the Park's creation. …The creation of national parks to protect wildlife has not only separated the Maasai from their livestock production base and created a mythical nature devoid of humans for tourist consumption, but also provided the government with the financial means to 'develop' and 'modernize' them.

In her view, anti-poaching measures demonstrate particularly well how a conservationist drive may produce harsh consequences:

> A great deal …has been left out of the international discussion of the poaching issue and neither the origins nor the implications of the proposed solutions to the poaching problem have received the critical analysis they merit. …Within two years of (Richard Leakey's) taking over (as director of Kenya's Wildlife Service), more than a hundred poachers had been killed, many of them with no chance for discussion or trial; the rangers are licensed, like military in a state of emergency, to shoot-to-kill.

Leakey defended himself in an interview by claiming that his rangers were in a difficult predicament, facing poachers armed with high-powered rifles.

---

pollution control. Indeed, with the establishment of special administrative bodies and ministries responsible for environmental protection, concern for the latter is now reflected in its own bureaucratic support. This is no minor factor in intragovernmental processes of decision making. However, there is a drawback as well: in making environmental protection the responsibility of a special branch of government, other branches tend to be (or to see themselves as) exempt from environmental responsibility. The Ministry of Trade can thus pursue its policies of (quantitative) growth, with environmental concerns being taken care of by 'the responsible ministry'. Environmental protection is thus broken down by bureaucratic sectors instead of being integrated in all public policy.

The dominance of the 'growth paradigm', i.e. economic growth actually being the stated goal of public policy in legal statutes such as the German 1967 (Economic) Stability Act and the dependence of the state on a flourishing economy as a source of revenue tend to tear the state between the two goals of economic growth and environmental protection and, to the extent that they are mutually exclusive, to force it to favour the former.

Plate 1.2 Western democracy in action: members of Bill Clinton's campaign team during the run-up to the US presidential elections in 1992. Photo: ABC Press/Sygma

The leeway left by Western states to the forces of civil society limits their steering capacity. The democratic process requires the state to convince rather than coerce societal actors to implement public policies, including environmental policies. The process of formulating the detail of these policies is open to all sorts of private interest intervention (such as lobbies). The steering capacity of the state meets its limits in the runaway activity (literally the shifting of investments to foreign countries, e.g. because environmental standards are lower there) of an almost unlimited, or at least borderless, capitalist economy.

It is precisely limits of the latter kind that a communist state would not meet. In principle, its steering or commanding capacity is unlimited. However, as has already been noted, there is a price to be paid for this. Economic success tends to be limited to heavy, severely polluting industrialisation. Once the stage of a 'postindustrial' economy has been reached, former communist states tend to lack the resources of information technology, free flows of information and of a population that is not only well educated but also allowed to make free and creative use of its formal skills. There are obvious reasons for this. In the past the communist regimes nipped in the bud all civil society activity that provides the very matrix of creativity (e.g. by giving both scientists and the general public only limited access to transborder flows of information and by deliberately restricting the freedom of international travel and exchange of ideas).

Finally, it is a combination of deliberate, politically imposed restrictions of the latter kind (i.e. lack of international freedom of movement and information) and involuntary restrictions, owing to a lack of money and technology for the purpose of transnational (and often even national) communication and hence of both economic and administrative capacity that severely limits the potential for state action in developing countries. These states tend to be poor, their administrative systems less effective, their access to information (even on the state of their own environment and potential countermeasures) limited and their elites often unwilling and unable to give any priority to environmental protection. The situation has often been made worse by external factors. International offers of public or private investment projects have often resulted in environmental damage (Rich, 1994).

This somewhat simplified analysis shows that different ways of organising state-society relations imply varying capacities for state action. These differences also affect the potential for societal learning and the capacity of states to deal with their environmental problems.

Societal learning and environmental problems

Societal learning relates to the extent to which individuals are free and able to acquire and disseminate knowledge (in this case about the environment) at all levels of society, including the state (Janicke, 1992). Knowledge about the environment means not only the results of scientific studies, but also the more informal organisational know-how and communication skills necessary for a lively public debate about the necessity of a transition to a more sustainable way of life and about the ways of bringing this about. It is argued here that this is what is required and actually already going on in many places. For example, this book, and the course to which it relates, is a very good example of the process of individual learning that contributes to the process of societal learning. Certainly environmental matters would not have aroused so much interest a few decades ago.

The need for a global learning process about the environment was recognised at the United Nations Conference on Environment and Development (UNCED) at Rio de Janeiro in 1992 and is contained within the 40 chapters of Agenda 21. The following are some of the processes of societal learning that may be identified:

○ recognition at an individual level of the urgency of the need for preserving a viable habitat for humans and the responsibility of each and every one to make a contribution to this
○ scientific assessment of the actual damage and potential risks and the development of skills by scientists (aided by journalists) for communicating their findings to both decision makers and the public
○ research into techniques for improving energy efficiency and creating closed production cycles (or at least low-waste production), i.e. technical solutions which go beyond add-on technology in making the necessary (but not in itself sufficient) technological contribution which is needed in order to solve environmental problems.
○ innovation in the organisation of economic activities so as to render business practices ecologically safer
○ reform of the public sector ('the state') so as to minimise its own detrimental environmental impact and to stimulate all of the above processes (e.g. by redirecting research funds, redesigning tax incentive systems and also regulating by imposing

strict environmental standards where necessary). In short, this means that the public sector should play a more proactive role in trying to prevent environmental damage instead of the mainly reactive approach that has characterised environmental policy so far.

As the final point shows, although the state has a role to play, it depends greatly on the influence and sometimes the 'push' exerted by actors from civil society. As should be clear from the above discussion, the opportunities for this kind of fruitful interaction between state and civil society that results in societal learning vary across the globe and it is here, i.e. in its aptness for societal learning, that democracy shows its efficacy. It is the only way of organising state-society relations that inherently provides channels both for the flow of information and for enabling opposing viewpoints to be arbitrated. For example, there have been many cases of local opposition to centrally planned projects and, in some cases, the central government has had to withdraw or at least change its plans. This has been particularly true in the case of unwanted land uses such as nuclear power plants, toxic water incinerators, refugee camps, new road proposals and so on. But, the tendency is for the more powerful groups in society to protect and enhance their environments often at the expense of the weaker groups. (This point will be discussed in more detail in the final chapter of this book.)

The democratic state is also sufficiently flexible and open to enable the integration of new members into the political elite (witness the rise of Green Party politicians in several Western countries). The two main mechanisms of societal learning, which we could briefly describe as an openness to new ideas and to new leaders, are thus built into the very fabric of democratically organised state-society complexes. But, it must be recognised that certain qualifications about the efficacy of democratic states should be made, as Box 2 demonstrates.

Whatever the internal organisation of state-society complexes (which are often simply referred to as states, countries or nations), none of them exists in isolation. Rather, they are closely entangled in the increasingly global net of transnational and international relations. Nowhere is this clearer than in the field of environmental policy and it is to the ensuing changes in the system of states that we now turn.

1.3 Co-operation between states in a transnational societal context

Sovereignty and transnational interdependence

Let us start with a paradox. On the one hand, the Western model of political organisation, the sovereign state, has spread all over the world, not least due to the process of decolonisation. On the other, the actual autonomy of states is being undermined by the ever tighter web of transnational relations, i.e. relations between the various national civil societies, notably in the field of economics.

The global system of states today comprises more than 180 members, each one formally sovereign in terms of legal status. It is worth emphasising that this is not a mere formality. The status of sovereignty is a legal fact with real significance in that

A discussion of various objections

2

A discussion such as the foregoing must of necessity simplify many complicated relationships. Various additional points may be highlighted by means of a fictitious exchange between the author and a critic.

Question: Isn't your picture of Western 'state–civil society complexes' overly simplistic? Don't these countries differ considerably in their approaches to environmental policy? And doesn't societal involvement often also mean the blocking of environmental progress?

Answer: Of course, you are right on these points. Western systems do differ considerably, for example as a result of differing political cultures and institutions. Take the case of Green Party electoral success and failure in Germany and the UK respectively. This has much to do with differences between electoral systems that make it more or less easy for new parties to win representation. Germany's federal structure also helped to bring the Green Party into government participation. Such aspects must be taken into account in any detailed political scientific research into (comparative) environmental policy. Although the above discussion is more abstract, it is not entirely misleading. As to the potential for anti-environmental obstruction, one of the costs of democracy is the need to take account of differing viewpoints. This takes time but the benefit is that decisions, once taken, tend to have sufficient support and hence legitimacy.

Question: There are still a lot of authoritarian regimes in the world. Are they not also confronted with environmental problems? And couldn't one say that an authoritarian ruler might be able to take 'more drastic action' to encourage conservation than a democratic government?

Answer: You are certainly right about the number of authoritarian regimes. However, few, if any, of them have turned out to be ecologically benign. Unless you believe in a naturally benign 'Green dictator', there is always the question of motive. What reason would a military dictator, for example, have to protect the environment if protest and criticism, as well as constructive proposals, from affected and concerned citizens are stifled? There is a potential for dictatorial technocratic environmental policy, but this potential has been largely unexploited. Certainly, some enforcement of environmental standards is necessary. That is why a certain degree of state autonomy is necessary. But no authoritarian regime is needed simply for this reason.

Question: What about large countries like China? How they behave in environmental terms is very important for the rest of the world, on account of the sheer size of their population. Is the global environment doomed if they don't become democratic enough to allow the sort of societal learning which you propose?

Answer: That's an important question. Let me remind you, first of all, that what counts is not only the size of population, but also the amount of energy and resources which they use. In that respect, any Westerner is much more of an ecological burden than anyone from a developing country. But looking into the future, you are certainly right; unless we learn how to achieve sustainable development (and the traditional Western model is heading in virtually the opposite direction), we will run into big problems. International assistance in rendering development more sustainable is certainly required. We must bear in mind, however, that external 'inducement' towards ecological reform is required not only with regard to non-democratic states in the South. Even Western countries sometimes need external pressure, from both other states and non-state actors. The UK, for instance, has been pushed forward both by EC regulations and by the North Sea regime.

political elites can and do make use of it. This is something which needs careful formulation, because the legal fact of sovereignty has two implications which are often not sufficiently recognised.

The first is that sovereignty is a legal principle or status which can be used or abused by actors. Overlooking this often results in what might be called mistaken categorisation: sovereignty is blamed for being an impediment, e.g. to an effective global environmental policy. Blaming the principle of sovereignty is of no avail. If anyone is to be blamed, it is the actors for the use they make of the principle. Holding state actors responsible for the way they exercise sovereignty may in fact lead them to reassess their position and, for example, to change their conception of sovereignty. It is precisely this kind of change that is currently occurring in the international system under the pressure of transnational interdependencies.

The second implication is that sovereignty is a legal fact with real-world consequences. With the exception of so-called state-free spaces such as the high seas and their subsoil, the globe is divided into the areas of jurisdiction of the 180 or so individual states. This division does not take into account the interdependencies of ecosystems cutting across formal state boundaries. This is important, because it is the main reason for transnational ecological interrelations. However, there is another side of the coin. For every territory, there is a legal entity (i.e. the respective state) which may be held responsible for the environmental damage both occurring within this territory and emanating from it.

The necessity for states to deal with transboundary environmental problems results in transnational interdependence. The concept of interdependence has been the subject of much discussion in the discipline of international relations and beyond, especially since the early 1970s (Keohane and Nye, 1989). In such discussions, the term 'interdependence' has been used mainly to describe the increasing mutual dependence of highly industrialised nations in their economic relations. High volumes of trade and foreign direct investment among these countries and their dependence on an uninterrupted flow of these goods and capital have been said to make these states interdependent. It now seems that the concept can and must be broadened, in both its substance and its geographic scope. Interdependence should now be taken to refer to the way in which any state is affected by events occurring anywhere else in any substantial field. Ecological interdependence, e.g. in the field of global warming, is thus truly global, since the greenhouse effect potentially affects all the world's people and is being caused by processes occurring in every country. In the light of the virtually instantaneous flow of information around the globe, one might well broaden the concept to include the interdependence of knowledge, i.e. the fact that ever more people are affected by knowing what is going on elsewhere in the world. Given this wide definition of interdependence, two facts become clear:

1 Most of these various types of interdependence actually result not so much from actions taken by states, but from societal activities.
2 These activities transcend the boundaries of nation states either directly or indirectly, through their effects and hence have a tendency to slip out of public political control.

Both aspects can be grouped together under the heading of transnational interdependence, which has demanded a response from the state system. The response has been to establish a variety of institutions in order to deal with transnational environmental problems. This has come to be known as the process of international regime formation.

The formation and operation of international regimes

According to the consensus reached in the discipline of international relations (e.g. Haas *et al.*, 1993; Krasner, 1983) international regimes possess the following common elements:

○ They are mostly formal (i.e. treaty-based) schemes of international co-operation.
○ Each regime specifies rights and obligations by means of internationally agreed standards and rules.
○ Implementation (which remains mainly the responsibility of individual nations) is overseen by internationally organised working bodies (secretariats, commissions, etc.).

There has been a considerable increase in the number of these co-operative ventures during the past few years, especially in the field of international environmental policy. In the remainder of this chapter, we shall look at the formation of such regimes, their

Plate 1.3 International co-operation between sovereign states. In 1945, the United Nations Charter was unanimously adopted in San Francisco by the heads of delegation of 50 allied nations. The aim was to create a global organisation that would be dedicated to keeping the peace, if necessary with the aid of force of arms. Photo: UPI/Bettmann

operation and their relation to societal learning. This will enable us to reach some conclusions on the relationship between regimes and sovereignty.

The emergence of international environmental regimes has seemed to be an automatic response by 'the system of states' to the problems of dealing with transnational ecological interdependence. This is a shorthand way of putting it and is certainly not a complete explanation. To the extent that regime formation is demand driven, this demand must be articulated and it is not nature as such that does so. Rather, in any particular case, it is a politically articulated demand which may come from various sources, both state and non-state.

One source is the administrative system of individual states. Examples are the mid-19th century commission established to govern the River Danube, the mid-twentieth century efforts to improve water quality in the River Rhine (an international commission was established in 1950 and reorganised in 1963) or the International Conventions on Oil Pollution and Dumping in the North Sea and North East Atlantic area, dating from 1969 and 1972 respectively. However, the latter case also showed that purely interadministrative negotiations in the framework of the so-called Oslo Commission would not lead very far.

Another source of regime demand comes from the pressure of public interest groups. This was partly responsible for the creation of the International North Sea Conferences in 1984 to speed up the process of international rule making. As a more visible international political institution, the Conference also became the focus of transnationally organised public interest groups.

Concerned scientists, too, played a role in articulating the need for action, though their role was more visible in cases such as that of the international regime for protecting the ozone layer. Here, the potential threat to the environment only became clear through scientific research, the results of which were used to alert the public. In fact, the importance of transnational networks of experts in various fields (marine sciences, atmospheric sciences, etc.) as a factor contributing to the formation of regimes has been so prominent in the field of international environmental policy as to earn them their own, rather ugly, designation in the jargon of political science: they are referred to as 'epistemic communities' (Haas, 1989, 1992). The phase of agenda setting for regimes clearly shows the involvement of both state actors and societal actors, at a domestic as well as an international level.

Constraints and opportunities for regime formation

While regime demand is a necessary condition for regime formation, it is certainly not a sufficient one. In most cases, actual regime formation is the result of prolonged international negotiations and the conditions for their success are not easy to spell out. The following factors indicate the constraints and opportunities that are experienced in many negotiations leading to the formation of international regimes.

Leadership

A first group of factors may be gathered under the heading of leadership (Young, 1991). This may be exercised by individuals, such as the former executive director of the United Nations Environment Programme (UNEP), Mostafa Tolba, who promoted both UNEP's Regional Seas Programme and the negotiations leading up to the international regime for the protection of the ozone layer. Leadership may also be exercised by international organisations, of which UNEP is again a prominent example. Finally, individual states or groups of states may play a leading role, either under the pressure of domestic environmental action groups or because they are threatened by specific environmental damage. Sweden and Canada and later also Germany, led the efforts to prevent damage from acid rain. The United States was a leading force in the case of ozone depletion, partly because it had a lead in the substitute technologies. Again, the interaction of state and societal actors plays a vital part in leadership.

The power of veto

However, certain states can also obstruct or hinder the formation of regimes by using what has been termed veto power. Without their participation, co-operative efforts by others may be doomed to fail. Interestingly, it is not only leading industrialised countries like the USA (or the members of the European Union, who are more and more frequently party to regime negotiations) whose participation is vital due to their potential financial and technical contributions. Given transnational ecological interdependence, the participation of large developing countries, such as China, India and Brazil, is just as important, due to their potentially large contribution to future pollution. There are grounds for serious contention over the actual share of current global pollution contributed by different countries. The conflict is especially divisive between North and South since, in principle, responsibility for pollution carries responsibility for clean-up. In most cases, however, the North is clearly dominant in pollution output owing to its much higher per capita levels of energy and resource consumption.

International assistance

It is this latter situation which has, in fact, given rise to one of the more original mechanisms for overcoming negotiating stalemates and a reluctance to participate in regime formation. To the extent that such reluctance genuinely results from a lack of capacity or a fear of overwhelming costs among less developed countries, it has been recognised that the more developed states need to provide international financial and technological assistance (see the contribution in Keohane, 1996). An example of this has been the establishment of a special fund for this purpose under the ozone layer protection regime (a similar mechanism is described in Article 11 of the Climate Convention arising from the Rio Conference).

Sanctions and exemptions

Other mechanisms for encouraging negotiations to move ahead are less benign. They include: linking agreements with other issue areas to facilitate a 'tit-for-tat strategy' of concessions; exerting pressure such as threatening to close markets to products from non-regime members that continue to use ozone-depleting technologies; and exempting members from obligations agreed upon in principle, such as the exemption granted to the UK in relation to the dumping of waste in the North Sea. This kind of concession tends, of course, to weaken the effectiveness of international regimes and is therefore rightly anathema to all those who are concerned for the state of the environment.

Self-regulation

At least concessions are only made under conditions which oblige states to submit to peer review, i.e. collective self-control by the states. Peer review is also the main mechanism for overseeing the implementation of the obligations under international environmental regimes, which otherwise remains a largely national affair. Peer control may take the form of a duty to report regularly on measures taken and progress made at a domestic level. Actual on-site inspections by international bodies or their staff are still an exception. When undertaken, inspections such as those of nuclear plants by the International Atomic Energy Authority may occur only with the consent of the visited state (a tribute to the still prevailing principle of sovereignty).

International monitoring

States may be criticised for not living up to internationally agreed standards, both behind the closed doors of regular commission meetings and sometimes even in public. As in international law in general, the critics attempt to use a country's concern for its reputation as a lever to influence its behaviour. On the whole, though, there is a tendency among governmental representatives not to throw stones from inside glass houses and hence to suppress criticism of 'sinning' states. Consequently, the monitoring and, if necessary, denunciation of state policies by national and transnationally organised environmental action groups is absolutely vital (and sometimes even welcomed by states who share their views). This situation is analogous to that which can be observed in the field of international human rights protection where non-state actors, such as Amnesty International, play a similar role.

Administrative capacity

However, there is the problem of domestic non-implementation which results not so much from an unwillingness on the part of the respective states, but from a lack of administrative, technical and financial capacity. International co-operation and the pooling of state capacities under international regimes is a partial remedy for this problem. International efforts to build administrative capacity (e.g. by assisting with the creation of nuclear inspectorates in Eastern Europe), to disseminate relevant knowledge (e.g. on the combatting of oil spills) and, as has already been mentioned, even to transfer financial and technical resources are undertaken under many regimes, both from West to East and from North to South.

Development of regimes

Finally, in order to understand the operation of international environmental regimes, it is also important to take their dynamic nature into account. These regimes do not come ready-made once and for all. Rather, the regular meetings and working bodies serve constantly to adapt, revise and, if necessary, toughen internationally agreed prescriptions and proscriptions (Gehring, 1994). Supplementing framework conventions with more easily revisable protocols has turned out to be a useful legal device in this respect. Yet again, this is a legal innovation which has grown out of the experience of organising international co-operative ventures. Given the often rather limited bite of initial regime requirements, the further development (or, as it has been called, evolution) of regimes leaves at least the hope that they will in due course come close to an adequate international reaction to environmental needs.

There are certainly limits to what can be done for the environment by means of internationally negotiated agreements. This is due to the fact that the changes in patterns of production and consumption which are needed for environmental reasons are probably beyond what is internationally negotiable. This holds both for single issue area regimes (the relatively easy success in relation to ozone depletion may not be reproducible in the much more complicated case of global warming) and for comprehensive negotiations in a forum like UNCED.

1.4 Regimes, global learning and the re-definition of sovereignty

What, then, is the relation between international regimes and societal learning? Firstly, regimes depend on societal learning; witness the non-state, societal input at all stages in the life of regimes (i.e. agenda setting, negotiation, implementation and revision). Secondly, by pooling existing capacities and transferring some of them, as well as by making explicit the (interim) goals which the participating states are expected to achieve, regimes may actually stimulate societal learning processes. They do so by spreading environmental awareness, by stimulating technological progress, e.g. via the obligation to use the best available technology and by empowering pro-environmental societal actors. Thirdly, regime formation and evolution is itself the expression of learning on the part of state actors in the international system. After all, environmental policy is a relatively new international field and, since the beginning of regime formation in the 1960s, there have been improvements both in the process of negotiating environmental agreements (Susskind, 1994) and in the design of regimes. This has come through learning from experience. For instance, the lessons learned from the early regime for protecting the marine environment of the Baltic Sea have been applied in UNEP's Regional Seas Programme. (Another example of learning from experience is given in Box 3.)

Finally, in creating regimes, states are also learning to redefine sovereignty. Let us begin by saying what redefining sovereignty does *not* mean. It does not imply the merger of states into a supranational entity, a world state. So far, the only example of this kind of merger has been that of the European Union. This is indeed a process of transferring sovereignty and it is all the more remarkable for the fact that it is taking place peacefully. However, it is also clear that this process is not driven by environmental concerns (if environmental concerns are indeed involved at all) and its actual

Reduction of international oil pollution

The traditional practice by tankers of discharging waste oil overboard has regularly accounted for far more of the oil that enters the ocean than have accidents. Attempts to control international oil pollution from tankers started in 1926. Since then, learning narrowed the range of positions that actors could reasonably take on alternative strategies, thus fostering co-operation. Some examples of this learning process were: the recognition that crude oil pollution could persist over long distances; the need to recognise what discharge standards and regulations were necessary; and the knowledge of what equipment standards could be adopted. In the meantime, industry learned how environmental goals could be achieved at lower cost. They were able to discard strategies that had been shown to fail while successful strategies could be built upon. This confirms the view that the initial rules established to attack environmental problems are unlikely to solve the problems for which they are designed. Learning as the regime developed created a bias towards certain goals and means of achieving them. Learning can be seen as a process that promoted effective regulation of oil pollution.

Source: Mitchell (1955), pp. 223–251.

impact on environmental policy has so far been somewhat mixed. Co-operation under international regimes is not a renunciation of sovereignty either but, in some cases, there is a renunciation of the exercise of sovereign rights. For example, under the regime concerning the ocean seabed and its resources, as laid down in the Law of the Sea Convention of 1982 (which has still not been legally ratified), the deep seabed and its resources are to be regarded as the 'common heritage of mankind' and hence not subject to the sovereignty of any single state (or group of states). However, the Convention has been rejected by some of the leading Western states, mainly due to the redistributive implications of the prospective regime. States have been more eager to extend the limits of their national jurisdictions through the declaration of 'exclusive economic zones', a practice so widespread that it must by now probably be regarded as customary international law. In the case of the other terrestrial state-free space, Antarctica, the states participating in the Antarctic regime in 1991 at least agreed to suspend the exploitation of Antarctic resources for 50 years.

So what does participation in international regimes, both environmental and otherwise, amount to with respect to sovereignty? It amounts to a recognition that the right of sovereignty implies duties as well. It is not an absolute right, without any restrictions, but a relative right to be exercised within the limits of international law, including such obligations as not to cause environmental damage to others and to co-operate where this is necessary for the preservation of transnational ecosystems. There is a parallel to be drawn here with the successful treatment of private property rights in Western states. These, too, are recognised in principle, but are restricted where this is necessary for the common good. Similarly, the right to sovereignty must henceforth be exercised within the framework of international environmental law and is limited by the obligations under various environmental regimes. As has already been said, this must be accompanied by increased international assistance to improve capacities where they are lacking and by the spread of democracy to improve conditions for societal learning globally.

2

Non-governmental organisations and environmental policies

David Potter

2.1 Introduction

Most environmental problems are caused by human interferences in physical and biological surroundings, including interferences caused by the policies of government agencies or business enterprises. Environmental policies can and do change, of course, because policy-making processes occur in dynamic political contexts involving an array of more or less powerful organisations and groups with conflicting interests and values. Environmental NGOs (non-governmental organisations) are part of such political contexts and engage in advocacy work to try to change policies that they perceive as damaging to the environment. Sometimes NGOs are more or less successful. Sometimes they try but fail to make much of an immediate impact on policy. Why? Part of the answer to any such question about influence always involves some agency – the initiatives, choices and *actions of the actors involved* – and some structure – the *constraints and opportunities* within which the actors act.

This is the broad context for this chapter on NGOs and their influence on environmental policies. The chapter concentrates on trying to:

1 characterise briefly the nature, diversity and growth of environmental NGOs throughout the world
2 identify major constraints and opportunities within which NGOs work to try to influence environmental policies
3 identify major aspects of NGO action that can affect the extent to which they are influential
4 consider a variety of factors that need to be borne in mind when trying to assess the influence of NGOs on environmental policies.

The four main sections of the chapter deal with each of these subjects in turn.

2.2 The nature, diversity and growth of environmental NGOs

What are environmental NGOs?

An environmental NGO is an *organisation* that is *non-governmental* and *non-profit-making* and engaged with an *environmental problem or problems.*

An NGO is an organisation in the sense that it has at least several full-time people involved, some sort of hierarchy, a budget, an office (although with local NGOs this can sometimes mean little more than someone's house or flat). In Europe, NGOs as organisations are registered for VAT, non-organisations are not. The boundary between organisations and non-organisations can sometimes pose problems. For example, is Earth First! an NGO? It has only very limited organisational features; it only has a place, not permanent staff, in Montana (USA) from which a journal is produced.

An environmental NGO is non-governmental. Boundary problems can also arise here. There are QUANGOS (quasi non-governmental organisations), for example, that the government appoints to advise it on an environmental issue, but these are usually not classified as NGOs because they are too closely involved with the state. But then, there are NGOs clearly outside the state in civil society that are almost exclusively financed by the government – does that make them an arm of the state?

An NGO is non-profit-making. An example of a boundary problem here is an NGO that is a non-profit-making environmental research organisation sponsored entirely by profit-making business enterprises. Normally there are legal distinctions that establish a boundary. In the UK and the USA, for example, most non-profit-making organisations are registered as such; surpluses can be made and distributed, but not to themselves. There are anomalies; religious institutions and party political organisations are non-profit-making and non-governmental, but they are conventionally not considered NGOs.

An environmental NGO is engaged with an environmental problem or problems. Such a problem is defined as a change in the physical environment brought about by human interferences which are perceived to be unacceptable with respect to a particular set of commonly shared norms (Sloep and van Dam, 1995, p.42). Many NGOs have broader remits than just the environment, e.g. OXFAM. This is particularly true in the South, where nearly all environmental NGOs direct their attention more broadly at development problems within which a particular environmental aspect may be only one of several concerns.

Despite such boundary problems, the definition of environmental NGOs as non-governmental, non-profit organisations engaged with environmental problems works reasonably well in identifying a distinct category of actors in the arena of environmental policy-making.

NGOs and the environmental movement

NGOs as organisations are distinct from movements. The famous Chipko movement in India, for example, involves village people in the Garwhal Himalaya, especially women, who hug trees when loggers arrive to cut them down; but it is not an NGO because although there are leaders and followers there is no formal organisation.

More broadly, there is an environmental movement made up of diverse NGOs, groups and individuals who generally share a set of beliefs about the environment and what should be done about it, for example as set out in Agenda 21 and who seek through collective action to convert – to *move* – people to action and new consciousness consistent with those beliefs. The individuals and groups may be mobilised from time to time by NGOs to contribute money or, more unusually, engage in political action like demonstrations or letter writing campaigns. The movement also continually tries to mobilise new constituents to the collective enterprise from amongst the silent multitude of people who may share the beliefs of the movement and are anonymously recorded as doing so by periodic opinion polls.

The collective enterprise of the environmental movement in localised settings will be galvanised every now and then to try to change environmental policies impacting adversely on the environment. Perhaps even more importantly in the longer term, the work of the environmental movement can gradually transform public environmental consciousness. (This is a subject taken up later in this chapter and in the final chapter of this book.) The size and strength of the environmental movement can wax and wane through time; and the fortunes of environmental NGOs, embedded in the movement, can rise and fall correspondingly.

Diversity of NGOs

There are various ways to classify NGOs within the environmental movement. A quick way to appreciate their diversity is to note differences of size, level and links.

Size

Environmental NGOs are far smaller, generally speaking, than organisations of either the state or the business world in terms of numbers of full-time staff, size of budgets, extent of record keeping and so on. Large NGOs like Greenpeace UK have an office building and attached warehouse in London, a multi-million pound budget, over 100 paid employees and so on. But this is exceptional. At the other end of the scale are NGOs that are so small that they occupy a very borderline position in terms of their organisational characteristics. An example is Spandana Samaja Seva Samudaya, near Sirsi in the remote rural district of Uttara Kannada in the state of Karnataka, in South India. Spandana aims at sustainable agricultural development in a small rural area and its 60 members (in 1994) engaged in activities to promote environmental awareness, the use of alternative sources of energy and so on. There is a membership fee of Rs 100 and a managing committee consisting of a president, secretary and four co-ordinators. They keep rudimentary records mainly regarding Spandana's several sources of funding, but there are no full-time or part-time paid employees. It may not be quite a formal organisation, but it is a little environmental NGO.

It is mistaken to assume that Northern environmental NGOs are usually larger than Southern ones. There is no such pattern. BRAC (Bangladesh Rural Advancement Committee) is one of the largest NGOs in the world, with a paid staff of 2000 (WRI, 1992, p.224). Some Northern NGOs with international operations like Greenpeace are large but others can be surprisingly small. JATAN (Japan Tropical Forest Action Network), well known in Japan and abroad, had only four staff members in 1992.

Level

Environmental NGOs can operate at a very local level indeed. Spandana in rural Karnataka is an example. Other NGOs are international. An example is the European Environmental Bureau (EEB), with corporate-like offices in Brussels which, at the beginning of the 1990s, was an organisation linking over 100 national-level environmental organisations with a combined membership of 20 million located within member states of the EU. The EEB worked on EU environmental policy issues that had implications for both European and global environmental problems.

There are NGOs also at various intermediate levels. There are national-level environmental NGOs, e.g. Vereniging Milieudefensie in The Netherlands, ANADEGES (Análisis, Desarrolo y Gestión) in Mexico. There are regional-level environmental NGOs, e.g. Sierra Club of Western Canada. Any one country will have NGOs at different levels, e.g. FOE (Friends of the Earth) Scotland, SCOTTIE (Society for the Control of Troublesome Industrial Emissions) in Stirlingshire and a local SCOOT (Scottish Community Organization Opposed to Toxics). The NGO 'coverage' at different levels is not uniform. In the state of Karnataka in South India, for example, some rural districts have numerous NGOs, others have very few. In the early 1990s, the Philippines had more than 2000 development cum environmental NGOs at various levels, whereas there were virtually no environmental NGOs in Vietnam.

Links

Nearly every environmental NGO is linked to others. The linkages can involve only a few NGOs at a local level; they can include numerous NGOs within any one country; and linkages can be truly global, bypassing the nation state. There are perhaps four types of NGO linkages, as set out in Table 2.1.

Networking is part of any environmental NGO's life, even if it is only in the form of an occasional telephone call to a neighbouring NGO. The new information technologies have helped to make networking possible on a far wider scale. Most NGOs,

Table 2.1 Types of linkages between environmental NGOs

Type of linkage	Methods/characteristics
Networking	Access to information flow from elsewhere; passive, occasional,unpredictable use of information technology 'nets'.
Networks	More active exchange of information, sometimes involving a secretariat (which can itself be an NGO); more regular personal contacts; more emphasis on information sharing on more general matters (including morale boosting), less on joint campaigning on specific issues.
Coalitions	Single event joint campaigns often by fairly diverse NGOs; limited life recognised and accepted.
Alliances	Long-term allegiance to common ideals among trusted partners; regular consultation by post, fax, IT and personal meetings.

Source: based on Eccleston (1996)

including many in the South, had by the mid-1990s access to information relevant to their environmental work through some form of APC net: in the USA there was Econet; in Europe there was Greennet and there were other nets elsewhere. Most NGOs are rather passive in relation to such nets.

A network exists when there is more active, regular networking between NGOs. Many networks have no name, many others do and some of these may have a small secretariat which is itself an NGO. Examples include FEMNET (African Women's Development and Communications Network), PAN (Pesticides Action Network), APPEN (Asia-Pacific People's Environment Network). Such networks can sometimes convert to a coalition on a particular campaign of limited duration.

Coalitions come and go. They can form from networks and alliances. An example is ASOC (Antarctic and Southern Ocean Coalition) through which about 200 NGOs from 49 countries linked up for some years in relation to a campaign to make Antarctica a World Park; for most of the time it had only one staff member (Clark, 1994, p.165). Most NGO campaigns involve some sort of NGO coalition.

Alliances come in various shapes and sizes. One type is the North–South confederation; some of these are global in scope. Friends of the Earth International is an example comprising in 1993, 50 national-level NGOs (each with local branches) from around the world with a total membership of over 1 million. These national FOE organisations are basically autonomous but do meet annually to agree certain priorities for the coming year and co-ordinate strategy. Other examples include Greenpeace International, WWF (Worldwide Fund for Nature; see Figure 2.1) and the World Conservation Union (IUCN).

Another type of alliance is the long-term (although not indefinite) formal allegiance between a Northern NGO and Southern NGO partners. The Northern end of these alliances can be financed largely by subscriptions, like Save the Children and OXFAM in the UK. In other cases the Northern NGOs are dependent on funding from the governments in which their headquarters are located, like CARE in the USA, Médicins sans Frontières in France and most of the large development NGOs in The Netherlands and Scandinavia. Some sustain environment and development projects directly in Southern countries. Others work indirectly, that is, they fund and give technical assistance to indigenous Southern NGOs. There are four mechanisms used in India, for example (Farrington and Lewis, 1993, pp. 95–96):

1 An intermediary organisation or umbrella organisation in India identifies local NGO projects on behalf of the Northern NGO and monitors the work done.
2 An Indian intermediary pools incoming resources from a consortium of Northern sources and distributes them to local NGO projects.
3 A Northern NGO (e.g. NOVIB in The Netherlands) has an office in India staffed by Indian nationals and with a high degree of autonomy, through which its funds are channelled.
4 A Northern NGO (e.g. Christian Aid) works directly with a local NGO, periodically visiting it.

Many other alliances are not North-South. There are Northern alliances, e.g. ANPED (Alliance of Northern People for Environment and Development), based in Amsterdam. There are Southern alliances, including NGO umbrella organisations, e.g.

29

IN THE FORESTS OF PAKISTAN, THE AXE IS MORE DANGEROUS THAN THE GUN.

In the Suleiman mountains of Pakistan, conservationists find a wedding is no cause for celebration.

It's a tradition that the bridegroom must first cut down 125 chilghoza trees to raise enough money to provide a payment to the bride's parents. This year, 40 men want to get married and they don't intend to let 5,000 trees stand in their way.

The real price, however, is paid much later. The forests protect the soil and water of wildlife feeding grounds. They provide a vital watershed for the local rivers. Without the trees, water from torrential rain funnels down valleys, smashing houses and bursting river banks.

The consequences are no less ruinous for the local economy. Mature trees offer a rich harvest of nuts and oils that earn vital rupees in the markets of Karachi, Lahore, Quetta, Peshawar and Islamabad.

So what can be done to protect them?

In this part of the Baluchistan, some 15 warring tribes own 70% of the forests.

Into this troubled land walked the local WWF organiser. At their first meeting the tribesmen still had their rifles slung across their shoulders. They listened as the WWF representative explained that the forests were their future. That reforestation was possible. That they could profit from sustainable development of nuts, berries and fruit.

"Hawk-eyed and tough looking," they may have been. But he met with success. An agreement was reached to limit the cutting down of trees. All based on a WWF feasibility study.

This, however, is not the end of the story. Merely the beginning.

The education programme goes on. More efficient uses of fuel wood and alternative energy sources are needed.

And not just here.

This is just one of over 100 WWF forest projects in 45 different countries.

Of course, this costs money. If you want to help, you can make a donation or a legacy to WWF's work.

Armed with that, we can achieve anything.

World Wide Fund For Nature
(formerly World Wildlife Fund)
International Secretariat,
1196 Gland, Switzerland.

WWF

Fig. 2.1 WWF advertisement: informing people all over the world about nature conservation and environmental degradation.

COICA which in 1991 formally co-ordinated the work of NGOs in five Amazon basin countries representing the interests of indigenous minorities living there. Alliances can disintegrate; ANEN (African NGO Environment Network) linked 530 NGOs in 45 countries in 1990, but it became moribund for a time subsequently, due to internal problems. Communication within some of these alliances can from time to time be all irregular and the umbrella may at times be more adequately described as a network. WALHI in Indonesia is perhaps an example; at times the relations between the more than 300 environmental NGOs under this Indonesian umbrella have been fairly quiescent, then a certain campaign can make a part of the alliance into a temporary coalition.

Growth

The growth in the number of environmental NGOs has been striking, most of them coming into existence since about 1980. For example, it has been estimated that there were more than 6000 NGOs in Latin America and the Caribbean at the beginning of the 1990s, most of them having been formed only in the previous ten years (Tolba *et al.*, 1992, p.728). The story is repeated in other regions of the world. Numerous NGO directories have recently appeared to cope with the development.

Plate 2.1 Bombay, India. Demonstrators protest against the Narmada Valley Dam project, one of the largest and most controversial water resource developments undertaken anywhere in the world (and financed by the World Bank). Over the next 50 years or so, 30 major dams, 135 medium-sized dams and 3000 smaller dams are to be built on India's Narmada River and its tributaries. Once the project has been completed, the dams will provide 50,000 sq km of land with irrigation and generate 2700 megawatts of electricity. The protesters' main objections are directed at the negative externalities of irrigation (i.e. waterlogging and salination), the displacement of people, the danger to public health (e.g. the spread of schistosomiasis) and the loss of forests and cultivated and grazing land. Hindus have also objected to the project because they regard the river as a holy site. Photo: Roderick Johnson/Lineair

Another indicator is the phenomenal growth in size of some individual NGOs. Greenpeace, for example, originated in a small committee hastily formed in Vancouver, Canada, in 1969 to organise an environmental demonstration at the US-Canada border between Seattle and Vancouver. Various radical students, draft dodgers, yippies, housewives, a few professors and one or two ministers (religious) showed up and managed briefly to close the border. The committee turned itself into Greenpeace in 1971. By 1992, Greenpeace International was an alliance of national offices in 30 countries with thousands of full-time and part-time staff, about 4.5 million supporters in 143 countries and annual revenues in excess of $100 million (Bergesen *et al.*, 1992). Top people from national offices now jet in grey suits from science conferences to international banks, to advertising agencies, to government departments, to campaign meetings. While they quietly confer and lobby inside, other Greenpeace people actively demonstrate outside in the streets and at sea. Other major Northern-based NGOs and North-South NGO coalitions have similarly come a long way in the last two decades.

There has also been a burgeoning in the number and resources of Northern-based NGOs linked financially to Southern NGOs partners. A prompting factor was Northern governments channelling some of their international aid for environmental and development projects in the South through such NGO links. In 1970 such North–South NGO arrangements handled less than $0.9 billion, but between 1975 and 1985 the financial resources deployed in this way roughly doubled in real terms (at 1986 prices). By 1989 Northern NGOs were shifting $6.4 billion to their Southern partners, about 12% of all public and private Northern aid – in terms of net transfers, more than was provided by the World Bank (Clark, 1991, p.47). This development helped to spawn the growth of tens of thousands of new NGOs in the South formed in the expectation of having access to the funds pouring through from the North.

An important reason why the role of NGOs increased quickly in the 1980s and early 1990s in terms of growth of numbers and resources was the advance of neoliberal economic ideas in the 1980s about minimising the role of the state in the functioning of the market – an upheaval in thinking drastic enough to be called a 'counterrevolution' by Toye (1993). In the new orthodoxy of 'public-bad, private-good', NGOs were viewed as part of a private non profit sector and therefore 'good news'. One must be careful not to exaggerate the extent to which NGOs moved in as governments cut back. For one thing, governments did not cut back very much. But the new economic ideology was congenial to the growth of the NGO sector.

The activity leading up to and immediately following, the UN Conference on Environment and Development in Rio de Janeiro in 1992 also energised the environmental movement. Environmental NGOs, being part of that movement, grew in size and numbers as part of that wave of interest. Such interest seemed to taper off somewhat by the mid-1990s and NGO growth appears to have slowed down.

Environmental NGOs are non-profit-making, non-governmental organisations, many of which are now linked to each other in various ways throughout the world. Their rapid growth up to the early 1990s made them highly visible, even trendy. However, one needs to be careful, in making such observations, not to jump to the conclusion that NGOs generally became more influential in relation to environmental policy-making. Sometimes NGOs have some influence, frequently they have little or no impact on policy. Why the difference?

2.3 Constraints and opportunities

Part of the answer to the question about more or less influence involves understanding the constraints and opportunities within which NGOs act. A structural constraint can severely limit what an NGO can do. However, constraints for NGOs should not be seen as cast in concrete, irremovable obstacles that forever determine what NGOs can and cannot achieve. Although structured constraints tend to carry on through time, their features can and do change slowly and sometimes not so slowly. Changing structures can provide opportunities for NGOs. Even essentially unchanging structures offer opportunities in some circumstances. For these reasons the structural context in which NGOs act must be analysed in terms of *both* constraints *and* opportunities. This basic point is illustrated in this section with reference to four structures with which NGOs must contend.

First, any NGOs attempting to influence an environmental policy inherits *the particular environmental issue* to which the policy relates. This is a 'given' in the situation they confront, about which they can do very little in the short term; but certain environmental issues tend to be more amenable to NGO influence than others. For example, it is harder to influence an environmental policy where the proposed policy changes can be shown by opponents to involve the sacrifice of economic benefits for significant sections of society. An environmental policy where proposed policy changes by NGOs would affect the vital interests of powerful organisations is also less likely to be accepted; examples are NGOs campaigning to end commercial logging in tropical moist forests when the interests of government are served by land concessions as political favours to large wood-producing firms or when policy proposals would involve agrarian reform detrimental to powerful landed interests. Similarly, proposed environment policy changes advocated by NGOs that are self-evidently grounded in ideas about intergenerational equity are also more difficult to bring to fruition. These examples are instances where the content of environmental issues and policies can make a difference to the success or otherwise of NGO advocacy work.

NGOs usually work on one particular environmental issue at a time and if it happens that the issue is intrinsically less amenable to NGO influence, then that is a major *constraint* on their advocacy work. But there are also *opportunities* here. For example, certain environmental issues can become more amenable to NGO influence if they advance on the global environmental agenda, in terms of international agreements reached. Of the ten global environmental issues identified in 1992 by the long-time Executive Director of the United Nations Environment Programme (UNEP) (Tolba, 1992), ozone depletion (in the stratosphere) was furthest advanced in terms of the international conventions and protocols agreed, which regulated environmental policies on this problem. By contrast, five issues had hardly been advanced at all in this sense – climate change, deforestation, land degradation and desertification, water resources and water quality, environmental disasters. The other four issues – atmospheric pollution, marine pollution, loss of biological diversity, management of hazardous and radioactive wastes – may be said to have fallen between these two extremes in that there were some international agreements. On the whole, NGOs can be more influential on global environmental problems where there are conventions and protocols with nation states agreed on certain policies or courses of action.

There are perhaps three reasons for this. First, an internationally agreed convention or protocol amounts to a public commitment by parties to the agreement (i.e. governments) to pursue policies meant to deal with an environmental problem and such public commitments provide points of leverage for NGOs when lobbying governments that are slow about meeting their commitments. Second, meetings of the parties provide avenues of access for NGOs to important policy networks related to global environmental problems, access which in the absence of such agreements may be lacking. Third, once such international agreements have been reached and meetings of the parties have begun to occur, the focus of attention shifts somewhat from agenda setting to issues of policy implementation, a matter on which NGOs can have considerable leverage. The reason for this is that in implementing environmental policies, governments frequently depend to some extent on NGOs for the public support needed in such administrative activity, for monitoring and so on.

A second major structural constraint on NGO advocacy work is the character of the *target organisations* whose policies are affecting the environmental problem. There are three main types. First, there are organisations within the state, e.g. a Ministry of the Environment, of Industries, of Forests, a Nuclear Inspectorate, an Overseas Aid Agency. There are also different state organisations at national, state/provincial and local levels. These different organisations within the state sometimes do not agree about environmental policies and some of them may be more amenable to NGO influence than others. Second, NGOs target business organisations whose policies use or abuse the environment. Many do abuse it but a few are beginning to move towards more sustainable business policies (e.g. Business Council for Sustainable Development, 1992; Hawken 1993). Third, NGOs target IGOs (intergovernmental organisations) whose policies have important environmental consequences. These range, for example, from the World Bank to various organisations within the UN, from GATT to the ITTO (International Tropical Timber Organisation), from the G7 to the G77, from relevant agencies within the EU to the secretariats and meetings of the parties for international environmental conventions and protocols.

NGOs not only target organisations directly, they also seek to influence certain target organisations in order indirectly to influence others. For example, environmental NGOs in the USA have directly lobbied congressional committees which make decisions about US government funding for the World Bank, in order indirectly to put pressure on the Bank to build environmental considerations into the Bank's lending criteria.

Basically, certain target organisations are more amenable to NGO influence than others. If the 'opposition' for an NGO is a particularly tough target organisation, then that is a major *constraint* on their advocacy work which profoundly affects their attempts to influence policy. But there are also *opportunities*. Targets which are, or are becoming, more accessible can be more amenable to NGO influence. Accessible targets are open to the arguments of others, they may even be quite favourably disposed towards environmental NGOs. NGOs may be invited to the meetings of such target organisations from time to time and the proceedings of the organisation may be more or less known rather than kept secret behind closed doors. GATT, for example, was never accessible; NGOs were never allowed into the meetings and their influence on the organisation was virtually non-existent.

More vulnerable target organisations are also more amenable to NGO influence. Vulnerability in this context means that the organisation is accountable to some constituency or 'public'. Where there is such accountability, then political leverage can be brought to bear on the target organisation by NGOs. For example, commercial firms whose policies impact adversely on the environment can be vulnerable to consumer boycotts, organised by NGOs, which can hurt sales and profit margins. Target organisations can also be vulnerable if their sources of funding are accessible to NGO lobbying.

A third major structural constraint for NGOs is the character of the *policy network* involved (Smith, 1993). One target organisation may publicly enunciate an environmental policy and take responsibility for implementing it, but the policy may actually have been fashioned by a policy network. Changing that policy may require dealing with a network rather than just the front organisation. Certain types of policy networks are more amenable to NGO influence than others. For example, closed and fairly settled policy networks made up of a set of powerful organisations may be less amenable to NGO influence than more open and changing networks of organisations between which there is more or less severe conflict over environmental policy issues. Once again, both constraints and opportunities are involved here. NGOs try to stay well informed about the state of policy networks relevant to their environmental policy concern and whenever networks are changing, NGOs can try to move to take advantage of this opportunity. Richard Sandbrook, head of IIED (International Institute of Environment and Development) in London, summed up (in a personal interview in 1992) the NGO view of network watching: 'Don't trust target organisations; track them'.

Some policy networks include environmental NGOs while others do not. An important example of the former was the 'Tuesday Group' in the USA in the early 1990s which brought together each month in Washington DC representatives of the main government agencies involved in current environmental policy issues at a national level and leaders of 20 major environmental NGOs in the country. In other political contexts, NGOs cannot gain access to environmental policy networks, e.g. in an authoritarian regime like Indonesia. Sometimes NGOs deliberately stay outside. An example is Greenpeace UK and its relations with the comparatively closed policy network that deals with radioactive waste. When, in October 1993, Greenpeace was described by a High Court judge as an 'eminently respectable and responsible lot' during a court action by Greenpeace to try to stop British Nuclear Fuels at Sellafield from proceeding with the THORP Reprocessing Plant, Peter Melchett (Executive Director of Greenpeace) was quick to deny that the organisation was now becoming part of the establishment or of the relevant policy network. 'Our role,' he said, 'is to be as independent and uncompromising as possible to achieve success in protecting the environment [...] Government's role appears to be to admit the problem [...] while carrying on as before. Our role is to say that's crap – we say shut down [THORP] and find alternative, clean technologies' (*Guardian*, 2 October 1993, p.23).

Consideration of the relationship between NGOs and policy networks points straight at a major conundrum all NGOs face in their advocacy work. If an adversarial NGO is part of a policy network, then it has in a sense joined the opposition and its capacity to speak out forcefully against a policy on the environment may be compromised. If an NGO stays outside or cannot gain access to the policy network, then its advocacy work in relation to environmental policies it opposes may be marginalised.

Fourthly, policy networks are part of broader institutional structures of politics and government and the *political structures* that an NGO confronts can affect the influence it has on environmental policy. NGOs in Britain, for example, have to contend with a unitary state with power heavily concentrated in London (with the exception of Scottish and Welsh Offices in Edinburgh and Cardiff which do attract regional lobbies), an electoral system which tends to produce exaggerated majorities in Parliament and strong governments, ministers more or less dependent for advice on generalist civil servants who tend to depend a lot on specialist advice from outside the government department (including sometimes specialists in NGOs), unusually centralised media dominated by national newspapers and London-centred broadcasting which also assist the centralisation of power, both in terms of agenda setting and policy formulation. NGOs therefore tend to concentrate their main energies in Whitehall (Richardson, 1993, pp.89–90). NGO advocacy work *vis-à-vis* government policy is not easy in such an institutional context. It has been said that 'Because many policy makers think of themselves as custodians of the public interest and feel that they understand the best interests of the public with minimal reference to the public itself, environmental policy in Britain continues to be made in closed policy communities' (McCormick, 1993, p.269).

Environmental policy-making in the US government, by contrast, is much more open. NGOs and other lobbies are much stronger in relation to a more divided state (divided between executive, bureaucracy and legislature), with multiple points of access at national, state and local levels. NGO advocacy work in this context is quite different from the UK. Japan is different again. So one could go on from one institutional context to another.

It is widely assumed that NGOs have more opportunities to be influential when operating in more democratic political structures. NGOs cannot choose the political structure in which they find themselves. Such structures shape NGO advocacy work. In countries with more authoritarian forms of rule, NGOs may have a much tougher time influencing environmental policy; indeed in some repressive regimes, there are virtually no NGOs anyway.

On this issue of the importance of democratic political structures, there are perhaps four general points that can be made. First, NGOs are more likely to be influential where the target organisations whose environmental policies they are trying to change are accountable to voters or members of a 'public'. Second, NGOs are more likely to be influential where there is a plurality of conflicting and changing power centres within the state providing points of leverage for NGO lobbying. Third, NGOs are more likely to thrive and be influential in political contexts where relevant civil and political liberties prevail, especially freedom of expression and association. Fourth, NGOs are least likely to exist or be influential in communist party mobilisation regimes, where mass organisations of citizens are mobilised by a political party to participate directly in making binding rules and policies relating to their environment. NGOs can thus be said to have their *raison d'etre* within liberal democratic politics; if such regimes move towards more participative forms of direct democracy, then NGOs may wither or take different forms.

Such general propositions stating relations between features of liberal democratic regimes and NGO advocacy work are perhaps worth bearing in mind at a general level of analysis. Their limitation is that they can obscure particular non-democratic structures of power within liberal democracies. For example, local NGOs campaigning on an environmental issue in a liberal democracy may make little headway if they are up against powerful and united 'triangles of accommodation' between bureaucrats, politicians and local 'strongmen' (Migdal, 1988).

Structures of power that shape what NGOs can and cannot achieve by way of influencing environmental policies are not confined to local and national political arenas. Such structures can also be global in scope. Transnational economic processes of global capitalism and uneven North–South development are powerful forces about which NGOs can do nothing in the short term. For example, Cubatao in Brazil is one of the most polluted areas on earth, but local or even national NGOs are unable to make much of an immediate impact on the policies producing that pollution because the Cubatao zone has been occupied and developed mainly by multinational industrial and pharmaceutical firms, including the French petrochemical giant Rhone-Poulenc. Development in the North has had adverse environmental consequences in the South.

Major conflicts of interest between the North and the South can develop from such relationships. Such conflicts are publicised particularly by NGO people in the South. For example, Anil Agarwal, of the Centre for Science and the Environment in New Delhi, has argued:

> The North works on the warped assumption that population and not consumption, leads to environmental degradation. But if the world's population were to survive on average Indian standards of consumption, global consumption would be much lower than at present, significantly reducing the strain on the environment. One American child consumes as much as thirty-three Indian children or 477 Ethiopians. And this is precisely the root of the problem. The rich countries want to reduce the population of the developing world so that they can continue to enjoy their 75 per cent share of the world's natural resources, but the developing countries want the rich to reduce their consumption so that the poor can have better access to these resources. (paraphrasing Agarwal, 1994)

Many Southern NGOs broadly share this view. Such North–South conflicts can reverberate in the NGO world and can have adverse effects on attempts by Northern and Southern NGOs to engage effectively in common endeavours to influence global environmental policies.

Various structures that shape NGO advocacy work in relation to environmental policies have been briefly considered – the nature of the environmental issue being worked on, the nature of the target organisation and the policy network being confronted, aspects of the particular political context in which the NGO finds itself. Structures can be constraints for NGOs; they can also provide opportunities. Examples other than the ones already mentioned include the changing structures of public opinion about the environment which can provide an opportunity for NGOs to strengthen their political base within the environmental movement. The ending of the global superpower conflict in the late 1980s and the prospect of using the peace dividend for major programmes of sustainable development may be another opportunity which NGOs can use when advancing their arguments. Whether or not an NGO takes advantage of an opportunity will depend on their capability as agents or actors.

2.4 NGOs as agents/actors

NGOs act as agents within structured constraints and opportunities to influence environmental policies. Their actions may be said to involve a combination of advocacy work directly aimed at changing an existing environmental policy and a much longer term effort to shift ideologies and other structural constraints taking advantage of structural opportunities. This latter aspect of NGO work involves what Gramsci called a protracted 'war of position'.

NGOs may be engaged in the 'war of position' without exactly seeing it that way or being conscious of it on a regular basis. But their normal work, year in and year out, may gradually have the consequence of transforming public consciousness and, in so doing, shifting environmental policies. For example, a small NGO in British Columbia may be opposed to the government policy of clear-felling of the temperate rainforest there by logging companies and its direct advocacy work of trying directly to lobby relevant people in these target organisations to change their policies may have been completely unsuccessful. But this little NGO, doing its normal thing of going out into the forest on a regular basis from year to year to monitor and map what is going on, trying to make this public, forms part of a long 'war of position' in which gradually the sheer existence of this NGO, what it does and might do, together with its allies and supporters in the environmental movement, begins to figure in the calculations of policy makers.

NGOs can also more deliberately engage in what they know will be a protracted 'war of position'. An example is the decision by a group of NGOs in the early 1980s in North America, including the National Wildlife Federation and the Environmental Policy Institute, to work on the major 'underlying causes of the accelerating degradation of natural resources in developing countries' involving (in their view) problems of external development finance and pressure to pay mounting international debt. MDBs (multilateral development banks), including the World Bank, were targetted because they were seen as 'effective levers for eventually modifying development theory and practice globally' (Bramble and Porter, 1992). Environmental issues hardly figured at all in MDB policies. Shifting priorities at the World Bank especially, it was believed, would in the long run affect the policy priorities of many other organisations engaged in development policy affecting the environment. The NGOs began to lobby the House and Senate Appropriations Subcommittees on Foreign Operations as a way of getting at the World Bank, because the USA government is the single largest shareholder in the Bank, giving these legislative committees important leverage to which the Bank must pay careful attention. The NGOs brought people from the South affected by Bank policies to testify, including Chico Mendez from Brazil. Over the years, these efforts gradually had some effect. By 1993 the Bank had built environmental concerns into its policies to some extent (World Bank, 1993) and by 1994 the Bank was involved in 118 environmental projects involving about $9 billion in loans and credits (World Bank, 1994).

The literature has comparatively little to say about the 'war of position' aspect of NGO work. Most of the attention is on deliberate advocacy campaigns by NGOs aimed directly at changing an environmental policy. What do NGOs do in such campaigns? They lobby policy makers within target organisations, brief journalists, work together in the field to monitor the implementation of environmental policy, engage in litigation, go to conferences and meetings, produce publications and engage in direct action (from handing out leaflets in shopping malls to filming lawbreaking whaling ships at sea and putting sand in chainsaws). There are at least six criteria for assessing the effectiveness of NGO action.

First, *political expertise allied to a clear strategy and sense of purpose* is important in NGO advocacy work. For example, having the skill and political intelligence to pick the right target organisation at the right time can be crucial. It is also important to be able to identify political support and political opponents. A campaigner with Indonesia's WALHI said some years ago: 'we do not generalise among government officials, but try to identify those who have mutual objectives and democratic attitudes and

Plate 2.2 On 30 April 1995, Greenpeace protesters occupied a disused oil platform in the North Sea. The Greenpeace campaign proved a success and Shell, the owner of the Brent Spar, was forced to abandon its plan to scuttle the platform. Later, however, it emerged that Greenpeace had miscalculated the amount of toxic substances which it had alleged were present in the Brent Spar. Photo: Greenpeace/Sims

co-operate with them. It is actually a matter of identifying the "good guys", targeting the "bad guys" and educating the "ignorant guys" ' (Witoelar, 1984, p.417). Political expertise is also about having advance intelligence of proposed policies damaging to the environment before they are publicised and having clear and workable alternative policies ready for use. Implied in all this is the capability to organise swiftly to exploit chance events favourable to advancing an NGO's cause. Being able to move quickly is one of the distinctive advantages NGOs can have over a larger, more bureaucratic target organisation. 'Influencing the BERD' (see Box 1) is an example.

The overall importance of political expertise was summed up (in a personal interview, in 1993) by Tony Juniper, forest campaigner at FOE in London, when he was asked why his work in trying to influence policies damaging to the forests was sometimes successful. He paused, then said, 'Essentially it comes down to being able to intervene effectively as a catalyst in a developing political opportunity'.

A second important asset for NGOs trying to influence environmental policy is having, or having ready access to, relevant *professional, technical and scientific expertise*. This is well recognised in interest group research. A characteristic remark in this literature is that the most successful organisations lobbying the EU, 'will be those which exhibit the usual professional characteristics – resources, advance intelligence, good contacts with bureaucrats (and with parliamentarians when the occasion arises) and particularly the ability to put forward rational and technical arguments which will

39

Influencing the BERD

I

NGOs sprang into action in the early 1990s when the proposed Bank for European Construction and Development (BERD) was being set up. Twelve EU members, 14 other developed countries and eight Central and East European countries had agreed to take part in BERD. Within two weeks of its formal announcement an international coalition of NGOs moved swiftly to try to ensure that the statutes and byelaws of the BERD would have an environmental mandate more friendly than that of the older World Bank. The coalition comprised the Polish Ecological Club, the Danube Circle (Hungary), ARCHE (German Democratic Republic), FOE (USA), Greenpeace, WWF, Sierra Club and Natural Resources Defence Council. They drafted model language for the BERD statute, translated it into the languages of the various parties to the agreement and used it for lobbying purposes. BERD eventually became the first multilateral development bank to have clear environmental language in its legal statute, byelaws and operating manual. It is impossible to say for certain that the lobbying of the NGO coalition produced that outcome, but it seems likely the NGOs had some influence. (Sands, 1992, p.28)

---

assist in the formulation of practical policy' (Mazey and Richardson, 1992, p.105). Another student of interest group politics in the North asserts that 'organisations without a strong and professional staff have great difficulty in influencing politicians, civil servants and industrialists' (Willetts, 1982, p.111). NGO campaigners engaged in effective policy advocacy work are also usually known to be exceptionally well informed about the technical and scientific aspects of the environment problem with which they are concerned. To be able to deploy an argument about what 'the science' says regarding an environmental problem can be a distinct advantage in advocacy work. The problem, of course, is that usually 'the science' is not at one; target organisations can have their scientists, NGOs theirs.

Third, the role of *the media* at crucial junctures in a campaign can be very important. Most NGO campaigners try to stay regularly in touch with 'their' journalists and broadcasters. Coverage of environmental issues by the press and electronic media can build public awareness which can be a factor in shifts in environmental policy by governments and business organisations. However, newspapers are frequently owned by conservative businessmen and the electronic media are almost always owned or at least controlled by the state. Their coverage may not be particularly supportive of an NGO campaign and indeed, may be hostile to it. This can be the case particularly for NGOs working in authoritarian political regimes in the South. For NGOs, the media can be a mixed blessing.

A fourth important consideration is *political support*. NGOs can command more influence in their advocacy work when they can draw upon political support, thereby enhancing their bargaining power. Isolated NGOs with small memberships and few resources are rarely influential. This is obvious enough, but surprisingly underdiscussed in the literature. Political support can come from other large organisations, e.g. trade unions or professional associations. For an NGO to be able to say that they speak for a large membership or body of supporters can also be advantageous. More generally,

NGOs will refer to the environmental movement, that large collectivity of actors who express ideas about nurturing and preserving the physical environment on which human societies depend (Eyerman and Jamison, 1991). One thing about the environmental movement is that it has NGOs 'of all shapes and sizes, but you don't have to join one to become part of it' (Anderson, 1987, p.285). So NGOs are both part of the environmental movement and purport to speak and act for it but the relationship between the two is a complicated and uncertain one. Critics will dispute the claim that NGOs represent accurately the views of such an amorphous constituency. The argument has been even further advanced, particularly by target organisations in democratic governments, that NGOs are not elected by or accountable to anyone and therefore what NGOs advocate can be dismissed as of marginal importance because they are small elitist organisations who speak only for themselves.

Fifth, the undoubted importance of political support has been an important motivation leading NGOs to form *coalitions* and build *networks and alliances with other NGOs*. Clearly, to be able to demonstrate to a target organisation that you are part of a larger advocacy formation can increase your influence on environmental policy. For Northern NGOs, to be allied with Southern NGOs and 'the grassroots' has been an advantage for some time. Southern NGOs also can increase their influence locally by 'going international', alerting their foreign friends in Northern NGOs to put pressure on leaders in Northern institutions that have political clout in relation to Southern target organisations. Southern NGOs are also beginning to ask what their Northern partners are doing to educate Northern publics about environmental problems affecting the South. The Southern end of some global coalitions and networks are becoming assertive in another way. In 1993, within FOE International and the World Rainforest Movement more generally, a move began, orchestrated from the South, to shift campaigning strategy from 'tropical forests' to 'forests', including boreal forests in the North. This was because Southern NGOs insisted they wanted to campaign on both Southern and Northern forest issues to overcome charges from their opponents in the South that they were merely tools of Northern interests. Such moves can strengthen the advocacy potential of North–South NGO coalitions and alliances.

A sixth important factor is that *complementarity of NGOs acting together* can add more to a campaign than mere increases in numbers of NGOs. One NGO may lack the technical expertise needed to campaign effectively, but it may have exceptionally good relations with the media. Another NGO may have the former and not the latter. Together, the quality of their shared argument can be enhanced. For example, it is claimed that, in the NGO advocacy work in the USA in the period prior to the 1990 London Conference on Ozone, the Natural Resources Defence Council took 'the pivotal role of providing information and analysis and a legal approach to the negotiations. Friends of the Earth organised boycotts and media campaigns. Neither would have sufficed alone' (Bramble and Porter, 1992, p.352). Complementarity can also work globally, giving extra strength to NGO advocacy work. In the case of Barito Pacific's flotation on the Jakarta Stock Exchange (see Box 2), a variety of NGOs in Asia, Europe and North America with different expertise combined to try to change Barito's environmentally damaging policies by actions in London and elsewhere.

The Barito Pacific example not only suggests that North–South groupings of NGOs with complementary expertise can be effective in lobbying on global environmental

41

2

Barito Pacific's flotation

In 1993, a North–South network of environmental and human rights NGOs engaged in co-ordinated environmental lobbying by sending letters to fund managers in London, New York and elsewhere in the North urging them not to invest in an Indonesian wood products company called Barito Pacific, which was planning a £179 million flotation on the Jakarta Stock Exchange.

The letters made specific allegations about a vast array of environmental and social abuses associated with Barito business practices, made public in Indonesia by SKEPHI, an Indonesian NGO working on forest issues. For example, Barito was fined $4.2 million in July 1991 for logging in a restricted area of East Kalimantan but the company refused to pay the fine and no legal action was taken; and according to the UK-based NGO Forest Monitor, Barito had logged the traditional lands of indigenous people in East Kalimantan and South Sumatra, replaced the forest with fast-growing trees for pulp and paper production and used transmigrants from East Timor as labourers who had since 1992 been actively protesting about having been deceived by Barito about wages and living conditions (RAN, 1993, p.8).

In London, according to the *Financial Times* (18 August 1993), the response was mixed: One leading fund manager – who did not want to be named – was impressed with the environmental arguments and said he believed most of the allegations. He would not be subscribing. 'If there is an environmental cloud hanging over this issue then I think it will sink it. This campaign could be quite effective.'

Simon Fraser, Investment Director at Fidelity Investment Services, said: 'I have been in the business over 10 years and this is the first time I have been confronted with a situation like this. It is difficult to know how to react.'

Michael Hanson-Lawson, Managing Director of Crosby Securities UK, the flotation's international co-ordinator, said the project was environmentally sound and he would not be swayed by the campaigners' arguments. He was, however, impressed with the efficiency of the campaign. 'They targeted the fund managers very well – this could be an inside job.' He considered the environmental campaign to be nothing more than a 'minor irritant'.

James Robinson of Henderson Administration found the campaigners' document too emotive. 'They would do their cause more good if the language was less emotive. They use phrases like unacceptable political connections. Unacceptable to whom?' He said this was one of the first times he had been approached by a group of environmental campaigners. In future he would pay more attention to similar approaches if their arguments were presented in a better way.

Simon Counsell of FOE in London said NGOs would continue to target fund managers and would attempt to use the City as a lever in bringing about change. He admitted the campaigners had much to learn in dealing with the City. 'In the past we have, for example, successfully persuaded investors away from Fisons over their policy on peat extraction. We are relative novices in the use of City language, but we intend to improve,' he said.

issues. It also shows that NGOs individually and collectively can improve their political skills. The relationships between NGOs and target organisations are dynamic; over time, the influence of NGOs can increase because they can grow in confidence, become more knowledgeable about the political and other contexts they are facing and become more practised in the skills of advocacy campaigning. Of course, over time, the influence of NGOs can also decline due to internal disputes, decrease in financial and other support, the growing strength of their opponents and other causes.

It has been suggested that the influence of NGOs on environmental policy can be enhanced if NGO action is marked by political expertise allied to a clear strategy and sense of purpose, technical and scientific expertise, good relations with the media, political support from memberships and publics, strong alliances in the form of enlarged coalitions and networks and complementarity of NGOs working together. These are not the only considerations. They are important ones, however and one indication of this is that these same considerations crop up also when NGO people are asked why they are *not* influential. Edwards (1993), in an analysis of the weaknesses of UK NGOs in relation to international advocacy, draws attention to the problems of an overall absence of clear strategy, a failure to build strong alliances, a failure to develop credible alternatives to current orthodoxes and the loss of advocacy edge due to becoming too cosy with donor agencies. Colchester (1993), speaking about NGO advocacy work on forests, identifies lack of co-ordination between NGOs due to divergent constituencies, inconsistent objectives and conflicts over fund raising (turf wars); he also names lack of appreciation of the nature of the environmental problem, including its technical and scientific aspects and an inability (due to faulty political analysis) to identify clearly 'the real enemies'.

2.5 Assessing NGO influence on environmental policies

NGOs try to *influence* the policies of target organisations. Influence is a complex concept. A standard definition (Knoke, 1990) in this context says that NGO A is influential when it intentionally transmits information to target organisation B which alters B's policies. The definition is useful as far as it goes, A can also intentionally influence B in order indirectly to influence C. Further complications arise upon consideration of the fact that A may influence B's policies without A intentionally transmitting information. The mere existence of A may shape B's policies because of B's belief in what A could or would do if certain policy options were adopted. Such influence is structural; it is part of the broader structure of power in society which shapes the interrelationships between A and B and helps to determine their relative power. The analysis of NGO advocacy work in relation to specific environment policies of particular target organisations involves both intentional transmissions of information directly or indirectly, from one to the other and other interdependencies that are structural in character.

The world of target organisations, environmental policy and NGO influence is marked by dynamic processes of collaboration and conflict. NGOs are not 'outside' this world. They are part of what amounts to a *public sphere* that produces environmental policies (Wuyts *et al.*, 1992).

Are NGOs influential within this public sphere? It is widely assumed that sometimes they are but can we be sure? Answer: not completely. NGOs frequently claim that they have changed policy here or been successful there but if they are asked about this privately and if they are candid, they will reply that it is actually difficult to say for sure whether, or to what extent, they have been influential. The best indicator, they say, is their honest evaluation of a particular campaign, or clear 'sense' of their achievement, together with an indication from a disinterested party that their advocacy work had an effect on the outcome. Sometimes a spokesperson in the target organisation will concede publicly that an NGO campaign affected their policy choice or that the presence of NGOs shaped their agenda. Sometimes such corroboration by the 'opposition' can be believed by the NGO, but sometimes what target organisations say may be deliberately misleading. They may say the NGO was very influential in the hope that the NGO will go away satisfied and not bother them any more. Also, sometimes target organisations change policies because of NGOs but make no mention of NGO influence. An NGO rule of thumb in advocacy work is always to be cautious about what the opposition is saying.

Such uncertainty about assessing influence is part of a more general problem in interest group research: an organisation advocates a change in policy, the policy then changes, but there is no connection between the two events (the policy may have changed because of pressure from other organisations or other factors like sheer chance). *Correlation has been mistaken for causation.* Such problems do not mean that determinations of NGO influence are impossible, but there is no doubt that one needs to be careful about public claims by the parties involved. And even when care is taken there is still an element of uncertainty.

Why are NGOs influential? A number of factors have been considered. Some involve agency – the actions of NGOs and others involved. Some involve structure – constraints and opportunities that shape what NGOs can and cannot do and the content of their demands. Each factor throws some light on why NGOs are influential. There are also more general theories of interest group influence which draw upon a number of such factors and they do so in different ways. Any assessment of NGO influence will draw on some sort of theory, if only implicitly and different theories tend to produce somewhat different general assessments of the extent to which NGOs are influential.

For example, one standard explanation of NGO influence on environmental policy by state agencies is set broadly within pluralist theory. The basic premise in pluralism is that the driving forces that produce state policies are interest groups in civil society and, roughly speaking, the more powerful the interest group the more influence it will have (e.g. Dahl, 1961). A general pluralist explanation of environmental policy would tend to see NGOs as quite influential, or at least worthy of careful attention. A Marxist explanation of environmental policy would give much less attention to NGOs and more to class alignments and the structure of the state. Other explanations emphasise the importance of policy elites in environmental policy-making. For example, Grindle and Thomas (1991, p.33) argue that:

> Specific policy choices are the result of activities that take place largely within the state and that are significantly shaped by policy elites who bring a variety of perceptions, commitments and resources to bear on policy content, but who are also clearly influenced by the actual and perceived power of societal groups and interests that have a stake in [policy] outcomes.

The perceptions of policy elites within the state are shaped by their personal attributes and goals, ideological predispositions, professional expertise and training, memories of similar policy experiences, position and power resources and institutional commitments and loyalties. The lesson is that different explanations of policy-making can lead to different assessments of NGO influence.

Some explanations work better in the North than in the South. For example, a pluralist explanation used in an authoritarian political regime in Southern Africa would lead to an overestimation of the influence of NGOs on the environmental policies of the state. The importance of particular factors that help to explain NGO influence can also be affected by North–South differences. It has been argued, for example, that scientific and technical expertise is very important in the broadly middle-class politics of NGOs advocacy work in relation to environmental policies in the North, whereas such expertise is less important in India than NGO-led direct action and constructive work, the NGOs there tending to be lodged in 'a peasant movement draped in the cloth of environmentalism' (Gadgil and Guha, 1994).

The complications of competing explanations and North–South differences need to be borne in mind when trying to assess NGO influence. Beyond that, there are two broad, not necessarily contradictory generalisations that should be built into one's thinking about such assessments. The first is that NGOs usually do not have as much direct influence on environmental policy changes as they would like or that they tend publicly to proclaim. The second is that environmental NGOs have four unusual features which can give them sometimes more influence than standard interest group analyses would suggest.

First, assessments of the influence of NGOs on environmental policies can be faulty because insufficient attention is given to the *time lag* that can be involved between NGO activity and subsequent policy change. Earlier, a distinction was made between direct advocacy work and a 'war of position'. The latter involves a prolonged effort to change values in society, the intention being to change the perceptions of significant portions of society such that environmental problems are brought to the top of the political agenda. It is a feature of environmental NGOs as protest groups that they all, more or less, engage in such work aimed at society generally rather than only at specific targets and their policies (Rochon and Mazmanian, 1993). The indirect impact of such societal work by NGOs on changing environmental policies can be underestimated if the time lags are ignored.

Second, environmental NGOs may have more influence than a conventional analysis of their power would suggest because, in comparison to their targets, they can focus persistently on a *single issue*, enabling them to concentrate their (limited) resources for maximum effect. By contrast, political leaders and top government officials are compelled to take into account 'the complex interdependence of policy issues' (Kitschelt, 1993, p.250), to weigh environmental requirements with others. NGOs are also distinct from that other main target, the business organisation. The two are similar in that both are usually motivated by a single interest and pursue their 'partisan' advantage in the wider society. But NGOs, although engaged with a single issue, may be said to position themselves as representatives of the public's interest about an environmental problem that potentially affects everyone; the interest boundaries of environmental NGOs are unusually broad, taking in a wide range of people who have a stake in environmental policies (Princen and Finger, 1994). Environmental

NGOs can benefit from this unusual position when arguing for access to policy-making fora within the state.

Third, as we saw earlier, NGOs engage with a problem defined uniquely in terms of *physical and biological properties*. This particular feature can be both a constraint and an opportunity for NGOs. It can profoundly shape the policy-making arena in which environmental NGOs work, but it can shape it to the NGOs' advantage. The case of the pollution problem in the Great Lakes area of North America makes this important point (see Box 3).

3

Environmental NGOs and the Great Lakes Water Quality Agreement *(from Manno, 1994, pp.69–73)*

The world's largest system of fresh surface water, draining nearly 200,000 square miles of land, is shared by people in Canada and the United States. The region is made up for the most part of the Great Lakes and St Lawrence River. The two national governments began to co-operate this century, first to recognise each other's rights to peaceful navigation, more recently to respond to large-scale problems of water pollution in accordance with the Canada-US GLWQA (Great Lakes Water Quality Agreement), agreed in 1972.

A complex array of organisations and individuals involved in Great Lakes Water Quality now forms an evolving governance structure or international regime made up of bilateral institutions, federal, state and provincial agencies, professional and informal networks of scientists, native activists, environmental advocates, financial and industrial and tourism interests, hunters and anglers, the press and others.

A major development since the 1980s has been the increasing importance of environmental NGOs in the negotiations that periodically attend GLWQA. Particularly prominent has been GLU (Great Lakes United), the Sierra Club and the National Wildlife Federation. In the negotiations leading to the 1987 amendments, these three were invited by the State Department to be observer-members of the US delegation and the Ministry of External Affairs invited two representatives of GLU onto the Canadian delegation. The NGO representatives did far more than observe. For example, they placed on the agenda and won requirements for public participation in GLWQA implementation. They argued for stricter and narrower definitions of 'point source impact zones', arguing that no industry exceptions be made in the commitment to virtual elimination of persistent toxic substances throughout the Great Lakes. They successfully insisted on a redefinition of critical pollutants and the elimination of gender-specific language from the GLWQA. They were instrumental in expanding the range of subjects covered under the Agreement to include airborne pollutants, pollution from agricultural and land use activities, contaminated ground-water and wetlands protection.

Environmental NGOs have clearly played a major role in the development of environmental policies affecting this region. Not only is it impossible to understand US and Canadian environmental relations without considering the strategies and actions of the NGOs but, even more important, the activities of neither the NGOs nor the nation states can be understood apart from the geographical realities and the changing ecological characteristics of the Great Lakes Basin ecosystem itself, which ultimately shape the region's economies, demarcate its political boundaries and affect all enterprises within its realm.

The Great Lakes example shows how the biophysical properties of an environmental policy can set up unusual political arrangements which can enhance the power of environmental NGOs in policy-making contexts. The examples also illustrate, once more, the importance of technical expertise. As the author dramatically states:

> The issues on the table were highly technical and difficult to understand for almost everyone in the negotiations except the environmental agencies and the NGO representatives. The environmentalists, both the government professionals and the NGO representatives, shared a common vocabulary and certain assumptions drawn from their shared understandings of the environmental sciences and their political implications. Career diplomats and bureaucrats from such organisations as the US Office of Management and Budget were likely to defer to those who were fluent in the language of environmental science and regulations. The NGO representatives involved in this case, all highly articulate and knowledgeable, had an influence in the negotiations perhaps disproportionate to what, according to conventional measures, might have been considered their actual political clout. Their particular skill was an ability to translate the language of environment into the language of politics. (Manno, 1994, pp.106–107)

Finally, the environmental NGO sector is distinct from others in the policy-making arena because of its striking *transnational* dimensions. The prevalence and variety of such linkages between NGOs has already been noted. To be able to draw upon such widespread support can enhance the influence of environmental NGOs beyond what one would normally expect. That this would be so when NGOs are trying to influence intergovernmental negotiations related to an international environmental problem is obvious enough. The Great Lakes case is an example. Other examples would include the intergovernmental negotiations related to ozone, global warming, biodiversity, toxic and radioactive wastes. But transnational linkages can also figure importantly in NGO efforts to influence the policies of agencies within nation state boundaries. Northern NGOs will call on the support of Southern NGOs in their coalitions or alliances when campaigning against a state-level policy-making body in the North. Southern NGOs send 'action alerts' directly to foreign NGO friends, who then alert their members to write letters to environmental policy makers in a Southern country.

Even very local level NGOs will 'go global' when campaigning against policy-making targets in their own country. For example, a local NGO in British Columbia campaigning to preserve the remaining temperate rainforest there was making no headway against the forest policies of the provincial government and Macmillan-Bloedel (the main business enterprise logging the forest for pulp and paper products) until it 'went international' by urging Greenpeace UK and other European NGOs to enter the campaign, which led later to certain European companies cancelling contracts with Macmillan-Bloedel, thus putting pressure on the policy makers back in British Columbia. Another example: a local environmental NGO in Karnataka (South India), called Samaj Parivartana Samudaya, was working to try to change the policies of an agency in the Karnataka government whose major programme adversely affected the environment and was being funded substantially by the ODA (Overseas Development Agency) of the British government. They thought nothing of communicating

Plate 2.3 The parallel conference held by NGOs during the UNCED in Rio de Janeiro, 10 June 1992. A giant chainsaw-shaped blimp floats in front of the National Library in downtown Rio as environmental organisations stage a protest against the deforestation in Brazil's Amazonian jungle. Photo: ANP Foto

directly with supportive NGOs in London, urging them to 'educate' ODA about what was happening on the ground in Karnataka, thereby hoping that ODA would put pressure on the Karnataka government.

The way people think and act within the NGO sector generally in the 1990s can be strikingly international. Once again, one sees how an assessment of the influence of NGOs on environmental policy needs to bear in mind their unusual characteristics. These can sometimes give environmental NGOs more political clout than the normal social science analyses of interest groups would suggest.

2.6 Conclusion

NGOs have been defined, their diversity noted, their growth remarked upon. Two sets of factors have been considered which together can help to explain why NGOs have more or less influence on environmental policies. First, there are structural constraints and opportunities within which NGOs act, e.g. the particular environmental issue concerned, the target organisations and policy networks confronted, the nature of the political structure in which an NGO finds itself. Second, there are various actions an NGO engages in, with criteria for assessing their effectiveness, including political expertise, scientific and professional expertise, use of the media, political support and complementarity of NGOs working together in coalitions, alliances and networks.

All that may appear reasonably straightforward. However, various difficulties are involved in reaching an unambiguous assessment of NGO influence. Reasons for this include the absence of clear objective measures of influence, the problem of mistaking correlation for causation, competing theoretical explanations of NGO influence, explanations used in the North not working in the South and unusual features of the world of environmental NGOs that can affect an assessment of influence, e.g. time lags, special characteristics of environmental problems, transnational links between NGOs. In short, assessments of NGO influence on environmental policies require making informed judgements based on incomplete evidence, bearing in mind the unusual complexities involved.

3

Business and environmental policies

Richard Welford

3.1 Introduction

There can be little doubt that environmental concerns have become so great that legislators, regulators, policy makers and some polluters have given environmental considerations a higher priority amongst competing policy areas. It is difficult to assess precisely when the new environmental emphasis which we observe in contemporary society first began to impinge directly on business. It was clearly a phenomenon of the 1960s. Rachel Carson's book *Silent Spring* published in 1962 had a major impact on the environmental movement with its unequivocal argument that much of the pollution in the world emanated from business:

> For the first time in the history of the world, every human being is now subjected to contact with dangerous chemicals, from the moment of conception until death. In the less than two decades of their use, the synthetic pesticides have been so thoroughly distributed throughout the animate and inanimate world that they occur virtually everywhere. They have been recovered from most of the major river systems and even from the streams of groundwater flowing unseen through the earth. Residues of these chemicals linger in soil to which they may have been applied a dozen years before. They have entered and lodged in the bodies of fish, birds, reptiles and domestic and wild animals so universally that scientists carrying on animal experiments find it almost impossible to locate subjects free from such contamination. They have been found in fish in remote mountain lakes, in earthworms burrowing in soil, in the eggs of birds - and in man himself. For these chemicals are now stored in the vast majority of human beings, regardless of age. They occur in the mother's milk and probably in the tissues of the unborn child. (Rachel Carson, 1965, p.31)

Very little has changed in the three decades since such views were first expressed. Moreover, the situation has probably been compounded many-fold such that we now face a real crisis which may ultimately affect the very existence of human life on the planet.

By providing the goods and services demanded by the public, businesses fulfil many vital social needs and many not so vital social wants. The investments and innovations of industry drive economic growth and satisfy the demands of the consumer. However in doing so, as a result of the resources they consume, the processes they apply or the products they manufacture, businesses are major contributors to environmental destruction. Unless change occurs rapidly, environmental degradation brought about by resource depletion and pollution created by industry may become irreversible.

Protecting the environment involves meeting the needs of both current and future generations. In part, there is a need to develop new technologies and to develop more efficient methods of production. However, this potential technological solution cannot be relied upon to cure the problems of the past and present. Many would also point to the need for a change in attitudes towards both consumption and production.

This chapter examines the ways in which international environmental policy can be used to get businesses to improve their environmental performance and how business itself influences that policy. In relation to business it is possible to identify three contemporary approaches to environmental policy and one more radical alternative approach. In terms of the first three approaches, the ongoing debate revolves around the question as to whether businesses should be left alone to regulate themselves; whether we should introduce taxes, subsidies or other incentives to encourage more environmentally responsible behaviour; or whether there is a need for stricter legislation, applied internationally, to bring about environmental improvement within the time-scale demanded. However, the more we examine the increasingly international nature of business, issues of world trade and the power of transnational corporations, the more we must begin to question whether the international capitalist system within which business operates can, in fact, deliver a sustainable future. A more radical solution which challenges the very nature of the way we do business within the capitalist system therefore represents our fourth approach to policy.

It is by examining these four approaches, which are not necessarily mutually exclusive, that I shall consider the role and possible implementation of environmental policy. After considering and comparing these approaches in Section 3.2, the chapter goes on to examine the constraints and opportunities introduced as a result of policy, focusing on the range of stakeholder interests relevant to business activity and associated policy (Section 3.3). Section 3.4 considers the key debate over whether industry should be allowed to regulate itself through codes of conduct. Finally, in Section 3.5, the chapter examines environmental policy within the context of sustainable development, international trade and the global economy and points to an urgent need for a reassessment of the way we do business.

In examining these four approaches to business-related environmental policy, we look closely at the constraints and opportunities that influence environmental policy in an international context. We also consider the extent to which international action can achieve sustainable development. The focus will be on Northern industries and interests since these have a dominant influence on the global economy and environment. The argument applies to pluralistic societies where policy-making can be influenced by the relative power of different interests acting in a relatively open and democratic political context. Business is a powerful influence in any society and an underlying assumption of this chapter is that business is a powerful operator on a world stage and will clearly want to see environmental policy implemented in a way which will do least harm to its own interests.

3.2 Alternative approaches to business-related environmental policy

The four approaches

One of the most important debates which we will return to again and again in this chapter relates to the style and approach of environmental policy which may be pursued in relation to business. Four broad approaches can be recognised. The first three are, to varying degrees and in different contexts, applied in the development of international environmental policy-making. The fourth stands alone as an approach that would require fundamental social and economic change.

I The free market approach and self-regulation

This stance would be taken by those who believe that markets work well and can deliver the desired outcomes of citizens through the desire of businesses to remain profitable. Thus it might be argued that when consumers put more emphasis on the environment, then businesses will follow since their customers will prefer environmentally responsible goods. Not to provide such goods and services will mean a company losing market share, profitability and eventually going out of business. Equally, at an international level, those companies with 'environmental credentials' will find themselves with a new competitive advantage. Environmental policy, it is argued, should therefore be directed at allowing the free market to operate, whilst providing education and information to consumers to allow them to make more informed choices. A common view amongst businesses is that they will 'go green' when their customers demand it of them. In addition, we see the development of voluntary schemes and codes of conduct for businesses which allow them to respond to the environmental challenge in a flexible way over a time-scale which most suits them, bearing in mind the many competing objectives facing the enterprise (profits, sales, public relations, employee protection, etc.).

2 The reformist approach and financial incentives

Whilst still accepting that the market mechanism has a very strong role to play and that environmental management strategies can be a source of competitive advantage, the reformist approach suggests that firms, consumers and markets need incentives in moving towards more environmentally superior outcomes. In this approach the market mechanism is supplemented with appropriate financial incentives for businesses to make better decisions. The emphasis here is on the use of taxes and subsidies to encourage environmentally responsible behaviour by both companies and consumers. The more agreement there is between governments about appropriate fiscal arrangements and the more codes of conduct can achieve international recognition, the more it will be possible to affect the activities of a wide range of businesses. That, of course, relies on the development of an international consensus on environmental issues.

3 The interventionist approach and legislation

Whilst not wishing to throw away the improvements which can be made through market instruments, interventionists would also want to see direct controls on businesses. They would argue the need for legislation to force the most polluting branches of industry to improve their performance. They would argue that this approach to environmental policy is superior to other forms because it is legislation which has been primarily responsible for companies integrating environmental considerations into their activities. At the international level, interventionists recognise that there needs to be a 'level playing field' and that a lack of environmental legislation in one country may give that country's companies an unfair relative cost (and therefore competitive) advantage. They would therefore argue for increased international regulation, co-operation between governments and, where necessary, a degree of protectionism against countries not adhering to agreed international standards.

4 The radical approach

A rather different approach to the way we frame environmental policy is provided by more radical thinkers. Ostensibly this approach argues that we need to re-examine the fundamental ways in which we do business, the way the capitalist system forces businesses to operate and the way we organise enterprises (and the people within them) which are responsible for so much environmental damage. Radicals would put an increased reliance on co-operation and partnership (rather than competition and individualism). They emphasise the gross inequalities between countries that are a major impediment to the achievement of sustainable development. They are also concerned about the long-term impacts of contemporary industry on future generations. Their approach is one which questions whether the present structure of capitalism is capable of bringing about sufficient environmental improvements on an international scale to reverse current destructive trends.

Each of these generalised approaches has its advantages and disadvantages, which are discussed below. The first three are not, however, mutually exclusive and we can see elements of one or more of these in some of the environmental policies introduced recently. The major debate surrounds which style of policy is most able to bring about the outcome of sustainable development. On the face of it, the debate is not about ends since most will accept the aim of sustainable development, although there will be different conceptions of what it means in reality. At this stage the debate is over the means by which the elusive goal of sustainable development may be achieved.

Policy approaches compared

The free market approach

Like most free market solutions, the first approach to improving the environment relies very much on full information. Thus, to rely solely on this approach, we would have to assume that consumers had perfect information about the products and services they were buying and all the alternatives available and that firms had full information about the activities of competitors and were also scrupulously honest. This is clearly difficult to achieve and particularly so when we consider firms and markets in a more international context. Such a *laissez-faire* policy towards business also relies on consumers consistently preferring environmentally responsible solutions, not being tempted to buy (perhaps cheaper) imports where environmental concerns may have been neglected and having the time to weigh up different alternative products and different prices.

The free market approach is often used as an excuse for businesses when they decide not to follow a particular course of action. 'When our customers demand us to be more environmentally responsible, then we will respond' is a common excuse made by senior managers when under pressure from campaigners and commentators. This approach puts the emphasis on the consumer to change and, implicitly, puts the blame for inaction at the feet of the individual. However, it ignores the wider social responsibilities which the business has as a major institution in a pluralist society. In other words, as a major actor and source of influence in society, businesses should make a more positive contribution to the environmental problem.

With its emphasis on providing consumers with education and information to make better informed judgements, the free market approach to environmental policy assumes that such unbiased information is available and internationally transferrable. Certainly, one of the roles of the European Environmental Agency, established in the European Union in 1994, is to collect and disseminate information about the activities of companies so that consumers and other customers can make better informed judgements. The extent to which that will be successful remains to be seen, but it is impossible that it can hope to provide information about all product categories to all consumers very quickly. Moreover, the dishonest and misleading environmental claims made by some companies are still able to distort the market either by confusing consumers or by making them increasingly cynical about environmental claims.

The reformist approach

Reformists would not disagree with using the market to influence the behaviour of consumers and firms. They would want to introduce incentives to achieve a swifter response. They would argue therefore that, if harnessed correctly, the market mechanism can be utilised to develop the solutions which are so vital if the environment is to be protected. This requires co-operation between governments, who must provide fiscal incentives for environmental improvement which may be applied directly on industry or aimed at influencing consumer behaviour. This means, for example, using the fiscal system to impose taxes on the most damaging products and services so that their consumption (and consequent production) falls.

Within the European Union the European Commission has proposed shifting fiscal arrangements in member states away from taxes on work (income taxes and National Insurance contributions) towards carbon taxes (on energy sources and other environmentally damaging raw materials and processes). To date, however, governments have been unable to reach agreement on such a course of action, mainly because it would mean substantial increases in indirect taxation which may be politically unpopular.

Critics of this sort of approach can often take a very radical position. They often argue that reformist efforts tinker with the market mechanism and merely forestall the impending collapse of the industrial economies, a collapse which may need to occur before the real work of reconstruction can begin (Tokars, 1987). Reformers are often optimists who still put a great deal of trust in both the market mechanism and the willingness of firms to react. They rarely consider any action appropriate which forces change outside the market system or which envisages alternative economic systems. Elkington and Burke (1987), who we might consider as representatives of the reformist approach, argue that:

> [...] what we are seeing is the emergence of a new age of capitalism, appropriate to a new millennium, in which the boundary between corporate and human values is beginning to dissolve. It is now clear from the results who won the nineteenth-century argument about capital and labour. Socialism, as an economic theory, though not as a moral crusade, is dead. The argument is about what kind of capitalism we want. (Elkington and Burke, 1987, p.250)

Such an approach represents the view that we can adjust the system to bring about our desired objectives. It suggests that we should introduce new 'eco-friendly' codes of conduct and appropriate taxes and that we can use the price mechanism to bring about desired change. Theirs is a view which sees 'business as usual', supplemented by changes in business operations to bring about incremental environmental improvement.

The interventionist approach

The trust which reformists put in both the market mechanism and the altruism of companies is challenged by those who would see a role in intervening through increased legislation. It is argued that only by the introduction and enforcement of legislation will we be able directly to control, regulate and prevent the environmentally harmful effects of production and consumption. Indeed, within most industrialised countries this sort of approach has dominated environmental policy to date. For example, within the European Union, up until 1987 environmental policy was centred on the application of nearly 200 command and control directives in areas as diverse as lead in petrol, industrial emissions and aircraft noise.

The objectives and nature of EU environmental policy have since been expanded within the Single European Act and the Fifth Environmental Action Programme. Realising that environmental policy is of little use unless enforced, EU environmental policy has given increased emphasis to the improved enforcement of existing legislation rather than the rapid adoption of new legislation. Emphasis has also shifted from the use of command and control instruments in environmental policy to the application of (reformist) economic market-based instruments such as the proposed carbon tax and voluntary (free market) agreements such as the eco-labelling and the eco-management and audit scheme (see below). It is argued that the aim of such measures is to encourage change in all sectors of industry and society in a more general way than can be achieved through the use of tightly defined legislative instruments. However, within the EU

Fig. 3.1 The EC developed its 'eco-label' in 1992. It is awarded to those products which are regarded as being more environmentally friendly than others in a given category and which comply with the latest environmental regulations.

context, the use of economic instruments and voluntary measures is seen as a complement to rather than a substitute for the more traditional application of command and control measures.

The radical approach

The first three general approaches to environmental policy can and do, sit quite happily side by side with each other. Encouraging consumers to make more informed choices through information provision such as eco-labelling, taxing non-renewable raw materials and legislating against air pollution are all examples of policies from the first three approaches which are fully consistent with one another. The arguments between the different 'camps' will relate to their *relative* effectiveness. At the root of all of these approaches, however, is the acceptance that the current form of capitalist system and its associated model for the organisation of industry is the most advantageous arrangement. More radical approaches to environmental policy would argue that this view, no matter the extent to which it integrates environmental costs, is still largely alien to the sustainability of the planet. They would argue that we need to recognise that human life and economic activity are an interdependent part of wider ecological processes that sustain life on Earth. We must therefore operate within those ecological processes or they will, in turn, bring about the demise of industry. That requires fundamental reforms of the structures and processes which have caused the problem in the first place. That means finding new ways of doing business, of emancipating workers, of protecting the developing countries and indigenous populations and of sustaining all other life forms on the planet. The argument made here is that the dominant ideology of capitalism, based on the exploitation of valuable resources (including people), needs to be fundamentally reassessed.

Radicals would also argue that we cannot rely on established structures to bring about change because they have not done so to date. Change has been slow and piecemeal. Radicals would argue that we can no longer rely on science and technology to dig us out of the holes which we have created. Although in 1798, Thomas Malthus warned that the population was growing so fast that it would eventually outstrip food supply, technology eventually rescued us in the form of fertilisers and refrigeration. Now, as the population rises exponentially, Malthusian voices are raised again. Faith

Plate 3.1 Two children keep watch over their grandfather, who has been blinded by poison gas. The photograph was taken in a camp near the Union Carbide pesticide plant in Bhopal, India. Over 2500 people died and tens of thousands were injured as a result of a poison gas leak in December 1984. Photo: ANP Foto

in the technological fix has become more tentative. The science and technology which initially provided deliverance can lead to sick plants with inadequate resistance to pests, to water contaminated by pesticides and to consequent loss of biodiversity, desertification and erosion.

3.3 Constraints and opportunities

Environmental policy as a constraint and an opportunity

The rapid growth of public environmental awareness in recent years has placed constraints on both industry and policy makers. These pressures can take many forms as individuals collectively exercise their environmental conscience as customers, employees, investors, voters, neighbours and fellow citizens. At the same time, this environmental awareness has opened up opportunities for the development of international policy-making and for the development of enviromentally friendly industrial processes and products.

Throughout the world the approach of governments has been to respond to increasing public concern for the environment by developing policy frameworks for environmental protection. Environmental policies and any associated legislation obviously impose new constraints on activities but also generate new opportunities for industry as they change the competitive climate in economies. In the market place, profits and survival are often linked to the ability of companies to be flexible and to respond to the new pressures put before them. Rather than being seen only as a significant contributor to environmental degradation, industry can also respond and show itself to be part of the solution to the problem.

Companies often strive to minimise the costs of their operations and in doing so they may transfer the burden of environmental degradation from one area to another. This is especially relevant in the case of the production of wastes. As the ability of the environment to supply raw materials and accept waste is diminished, industrial costs will rise. Faced with increasingly stringent legislation and higher charges for landfilling and incineration, waste generators may look for the cheaper option of exporting it. For example, prior to German reunification, waste was often transported from West to East so that the environmental damage done as a result of increased consumption was simply traded across borders. Such trade still occurs, however, with many underdeveloped countries finding that foreign currency can be earned from accepting waste. This is just one example of the need for more co-ordinated, international approaches to environmental legislation.

An alternative response to cost increases and tighter legislation has been to increase industrial efficiency. A more efficient use of raw materials and a decrease in the amount of waste generated will allow industry to minimise its environmental impact. If waste is viewed both in terms of physical waste generated and the less tangible losses experienced through an inefficient use of resources, then avoiding these losses improves both the business and environmental performance of a company. Indeed, many companies have found it profitable to pursue a strategy of waste minimisation for a number of years and have experienced short payback periods on investment in waste management. Legislation has often provided the impetus for improved environmental performance from which companies have eventually achieved commercial benefit.

At the same time, however, we must recognise that in other areas costs may have to increase to bring about the more efficient use of resources and new technology may have to be introduced to reduce emissions. Increased costs in a competitive international market place may therefore act as a constraint to businesses wishing to improve their environmental efficiency. Indeed, there is often a perception amongst businesses that 'going green' will cost money and managers are therefore reluctant to move forward on their own, especially where they are already facing competition from developing countries where wages are significantly lower. By working together and perhaps even sharing some research and development costs, firms will be less likely to feel the constraints of a 'go it alone' strategy. However, for many, such co-operative strategies are hardly consistent with the essentially competitive strategies to be found within modern capitalism.

Roberts and Wheale (1991) argue that companies are unlikely to innovate and introduce 'clean technology' within such a competitive environment if they feel that competitors will bring in better innovations before they have achieved payback. Thus there exist so-called 'cartels of refusal', consisting of firms waiting around for someone else to move first. Being a leader in industry is often not nearly as attractive as being a follower. Such cartels will often continue to exist until they are broken by governments decreeing particular standards to be achieved within a set time period. It will be national governments and international agencies, such as the European Union, the United Nations and other intergovernmental institutions (for instance, the World Trade Organisation), which will have a role in shaping the rules, regulations and norms which steer and influence business activity.

To date, the main impact of government on the environmental performance of industry has been through the development of environmental legislation. Environmental considerations have been built into the legislative framework for many years. Initially, in feudal times, establishing rights of ownership over natural resources led to the development of a legal system to protect those rights and subsequently, the impact of industrial activity on the health of employees and the surrounding community led to the creation of public health and safety legislation. Arising from industrialisation, measures have also been introduced to control the use of products, processes and wastes which may harm the environment.

As the strain placed upon the environment mounts and knowledge of the causes and effects of environmental degradation becomes more complete, the extent and impact of environmental policy will continue to develop. The relationship between governments and industry is a two-way process. On the one hand, industry responds to legislation by planning to meet the demands of current and forthcoming environmental policies. On the other hand, industry also seeks to influence policy-making by becoming part of the process that formulates policy. Thus, although governments have power over industry through legislation, industry also exerts its power over governments. Indeed, there is a mutual dependence between governments and businesses; they need each other to carry out their own respective tasks. Unlike environmentalists who, much of the time, must rely on pressure applied on governments through the media, public protests and lobbying, business often has a privileged, routine access to government because of its power within the domestic economy. It can exert its power in various ways, ranging from persuasion to the threat or application of sanctions. Direct threats by business to move out of one country to another with fewer environmental regulations and warnings that more environmental legislation will affect costs (reducing profits and tax paid to the government, as well as having an impact on domestic unemployment) will make governments themselves think very carefully about just how far they can go, particularly without international co-operation. Thus the worries about the socioeconomic impacts of more direct regulation of business have encouraged governments to explore other, more market-based approaches to environmental policy.

Thus, in parallel with the development of environmental legislation, governments are increasingly applying market instruments to achieve environmental objectives. Examples include the imposition of taxes on environmentally damaging goods, subsidies on new 'clean' technology or the provision of information relating to the environmental performance of companies or products (e.g. through eco-labelling schemes). Market instruments are intended to channel the choice of consumers towards better environmental options. Through a combination of legislative and market instruments, aimed at encouraging certain activities and discouraging others, governments seek to bring about improved environmental efficiency in the economy as a whole.

The stakeholder approach to environmental policy

Individual businesses interact not only with their customers and governments but also with a range of other 'stakeholders'. These stakeholders include individuals, groups or institutions which have an interest in the performance of that company in one way or another. Each stakeholder imposes its own constraints and opportunities on the firm, but these are often contradictory. Traditionally the main focus of stakeholder interest has been upon the financial performance of the company because of the prominent position given to shareholders. Increasingly, however, businesses are recognising their wider responsibilities and attention is being paid to the environmental performance of the company. From the perspective of environmental policy, it is possible to use the growth of this environmental concern to influence the activities of the firm. The range of stakeholders which can be encouraged to demand high environmental standards from companies is displayed in Figure 3.2 and it would be useful to deal with each one in turn.

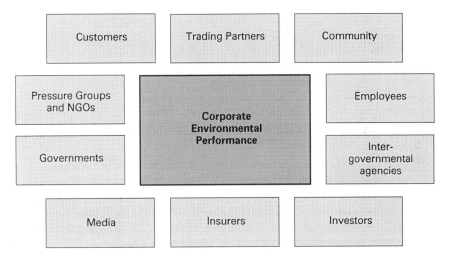

Fig. 3.2 Stakeholder pressure and environmental performance

Customers

The relationship between a company and its customers is obviously of paramount importance. In relation to environmental considerations, the potential importance of green consumerism cannot be overstated and once again provides both constraints and opportunities for the firm. The range of factors that underlie the purchasing decision are a fundamental consideration for all businesses. The environment is being accepted as one such factor by consumers, although its precise degree and form will vary from one country to another, being influenced, in part, by cultural differences.

According to surveys by MORI (Worcester, 1994) 'green' issues were nominated as being the most important issue facing Britain by over one-third of the population in 1989. However, by 1991 this percentage had fallen to under 10%. Nevertheless, 73% of the public suggest that 'pollution and environmental damage are things that affect me in my day-to-day life'. Sixty-five per cent of the population believe that manufacturers need to provide much more information to assess environmental damage or impacts of their products.

Plate 3.2 Esprit ecollection:'Esprit baby', Spring 1996. The Esprit clothing company decided in 1992 to apply environmentally friendly principles to its manufacturing process. These include the use of organic cotton and low-impact dyes. Photo: Vicky Pearson

At present, however, the influence of green consumerism on most businesses is marginal. Of the myriad products that each consumer buys, very few are chosen on the basis of their environmental credentials alone. Nevertheless, it is certain that credible claims relating to environmental performance constitute one positive element amongst the many characteristics upon which consumers base their purchasing decision. Helping customers to make more informed decisions through the provision of accurate information about a product's environmental attributes can therefore be an effective policy. Successful eco-labelling initiatives have been operating for some years in countries such as Germany, Canada and Japan. However, many companies have gone further than this in trying to educate their customers about environmental issues.

Leaflets and briefings about products and production processes are a common feature within The Body Shop's outlets, for example.

Trading partners

Many businesses do not sell into 'end-consumer' markets and may therefore perceive themselves to be remote from any consumer pressures to improve their environmental performance. Particularly for smaller businesses who may be quite dependent on one larger trading partner, the pressure to improve environmental performance often comes from larger companies rather than the ultimate consumer. In efforts to improve overall environmental performance, many companies are exercising their own rights both as purchasers and vendors and are demanding that all the companies within their supply chain seek to reduce their own environmental impacts. Companies such as the UK-based do-it-yourself retail chain B&Q send out questionnaires on environmental policies and environmental performance to all their suppliers. In using suppliers with the best environmental credentials, they are able to improve their own environmental performance.

Demands to improve environmental performance at all stages in the supply chain are therefore being diffused beyond companies that are directly exposed to the pressures of green consumerism. This is particularly true of companies operating in international markets where environmental standards are often quite different. In order to cut down on needless duplication, the obvious strategy is simply to adopt the highest standards in existence anywhere. Thus, the standards imposed in one country can often become the norm for another. For a long time, for example, IBM has had a policy of adopting the highest environmental standards in existence (usually regulatory-driven US ones) wherever they operate. Forcing (or encouraging) the largest companies to have high environmental standards therefore can often have the effect of improving environmental performance right along their supply chains.

The community

Industry shares its surrounding environment with the local population. This local community often demands a high level of environmental performance from its industrial neighbours and seeks some degree of reassurance that people are not being exposed to significant environmental risk from a company's operations. This concern has been recognised for many years and was initially recognised in public health legislation. Trends towards freedom of access to environmental information will give greater power to local communities when they question the activities of local industrial cohabitants. A policy of providing information to interested parties can be a powerful motivator for change. It is often asserted that more participatory styles of industrial organisation, where employees have a greater say in the direction of the company, result in greater productivity and lower absenteeism (Welford and Prescott, 1994).

Employees

The community surrounding a company often includes the workforce of that company. The pressure to provide a healthy living environment is magnified within the workplace.

63

Employees seek healthy and secure working conditions and can draw on an established framework of health and safety legislation in this respect. The concern about the environmental performance of their company may go beyond the impact of operations on the working and living environment. Increasingly, people wish to work for ethical and responsible companies. Many would argue that companies that reflect the environmental concerns of the public will find it easier to attract, retain and motivate a quality workforce.

Investors and insurers

The rapid growth of ethical investment schemes in recent years reflects the desire of many investors to invest only in companies which behave in a responsible manner. There are also a number of very good business reasons why investors prefer to work with companies that have a proven track record of environmental integrity. The structure of legal liability for environmental damage dictates that any party that causes environmental damage may be fined and required to bear the costs of repairing that damage and to compensate the affected parties for any associated losses. It is increasingly difficult and expensive to obtain insurance to cover such issues. Consequently, companies associated with a significant environmental incident may suffer significant financial losses. These losses are then translated into reductions in the share price and the associated dividends. Therefore, policies aimed at making the polluter pay for damage done (central to the policies of most countries) can be very effective.

Some banks and other financial institutions have found a profitable market niche in providing services to customers committed to what may be deemed socially responsible corporate policies. Thus the UK based Cooperative Bank promises not to invest any money in companies involved in experiments on live animals or in those which are major polluters.

Media, pressure groups and NGOs

A combination of increased public awareness of environmental issues and freedom of access to information on the environmental performance of companies will serve to magnify media and pressure group interest in the environmental performance of industry. In order to manage media and pressure group attention, companies must be able to state that they have made a commitment to reduce their environmental impact. However, while it may be tempting to allow the public relations or marketing departments to lead the way in convincing all stakeholders of this effort, any shallow or spurious claims will soon be uncovered. Claims which cannot be substantiated are likely to be seized upon and will be very detrimental to a company's public image.

Governments and intergovernmental agencies

One of the key roles for any government is to attempt to maintain a stable and healthy economy. To some extent it can only achieve that by promoting a partnership with industry. The largest employers, investors and even purchasers in any economy are often found in the private sector. Any destabilising situation in a world of free trade and easy capital movements can lead to companies simply moving out of certain countries.

An environmental policy which is so restrictive that it forces industry to move to other parts of the world where policy (or its implementation) is weaker might simply translate an environmental problem into a social crisis based on unemployment. Moreover, its effect is that global environmental damage might actually increase as firms do not even have to bother with minimal environmental standards in the unregulated economy.

Increasingly larger companies (particularly those operating at a transnational level) influence and are influenced by intergovernmental organisations, set up to represent interests which are not related only to the nation state. Many of these organisations would like to see environmental policies in all countries brought up to the best standards prevailing. Others would even go as far as to challenge free international trade, preferring local production, purchasing and consumption. There is often tension, therefore, between the transnational corporations and intergovernmental organisations operating across national boundaries.

The relative power of stakeholders

Whilst we have laid out the idea that there are many stakeholders whose demands constitute differing constraints and opportunities to which the firm must respond, it is also important to recognise that those stakeholders will have differing amounts of power. Within the capitalist system common in the Western world, where the state does intervene, the two most important groups influencing businesses are governments who have the power to legislate and shareholders to whom managers are ultimately responsible for the operation of the company.

Through their ability to withhold funds, dismiss senior management and their ability to shape the overall strategy of the firm, shareholders have enormous amounts of power. Senior management knows that without the support of shareholders, the operation of the firm is impossible. In a worst case scenario, where shareholders lose confidence in a company, they can sell their shares, depressing the price of the company and leaving it open to a hostile takeover. However, since embarking on this (almost suicidal) strategy would inevitably mean them losing money, shareholders are more likely to dismiss boards of directors. Institutional shareholders such as pension funds and insurance companies have enormous amounts of power because of their often significant shareholdings. Such institutions may have representatives on boards of directors, forcing the strategy of a single company to be consistent with the strategy of the large institution itself.

Governments and their agencies, on the other hand, may impose completely different constraints on the company. Their aims will, in part, reflect environmental concerns. This will involve meeting the requirements of international environmental conventions and, through the use of the fiscal system, redirecting economic activity away from the most polluting branches of industry towards less harmful ones.

At the same time governments will have pressure put upon them by industries, industrial associations and other international organisations. These are likely to push for less legislation and more voluntary action by businesses, for example. Governments are particularly influenced by transnational corporations which can exert enormous power over policy makers and challenge their environmental strategies.

Particularly in the Third World, the investment decisions of transnational companies will often be based on doing deals with governments to reduce the amount of legislation to which the company is subject.

3.4 The debate over self-regulation

Although there has been an increasing amount of legislation, covering a range of environmental issues, there has been a tendency, partly resulting from the power exerted by industry, to put more and more emphasis on market-based and voluntary measures. Coupled with this, the introduction of widespread deregulation by more right-wing governments to appease industry has meant even more emphasis being put on voluntary codes of conduct and standards. Industry, in general, prefers a voluntary approach based on self-regulation because of the flexibility it offers.

The Business Charter for Sustainable Development

One of the best known codes of conduct relating to business and the environment has been drawn up by the International Chamber of Commerce (ICC) and boldly named the *Business Charter for Sustainable Development* (see Box 1). Given that the ICC is an international agency funded by businesses and best known for its campaigning work on free trade and deregulation, the development of an environmental charter has been seen by many as an attempt to move debates away from command and control instruments, such as legislation and towards voluntary action and broad codes of conduct.

The Business Charter for Sustainable Development is the most widely supported code of conduct of its kind with over 1200 corporate signatories worldwide. Companies who sign up to the Charter are expected to express their commitment to the ICC and the wider public, work towards improved environmental performance and demonstrate and communicate progress.

Since there is no established mechanism for monitoring or ensuring compliance, those who recognise the Charter are therefore putting trust in industry to adhere to its principles. However, whilst Principle 16 asks organisations to measure environmental performance and conduct regular audits, there is no strict requirement to report this to the public. Background notes to the Charter suggest that the role of environmental auditing is to serve as 'an internal tool, the results of which are for company use'.

The Eco-Management and Audit Scheme

Another voluntary approach to environmental improvement adopted within the European Union is the Eco-Management and Audit Scheme. In 1990 the Environment Directorate of the (then) European Community began discussions about a scheme which would provide a benchmark for the assessment of environmental performance in industry. Initial proposals were that over 50 industrial sectors would be covered by a mandatory scheme whereby companies within those sectors would be required to undertake annual environmental audits and publish a detailed environmental statement. However, after considerable pressure from industry, which claimed that the

The 16 principles of the ICC Business Charter for Sustainable Development

1. **Corporate priority** – to recognise environmental management as among the highest corporate priorities and as a key determinant to sustainable development; to establish policies, programmes and practices for conducting operations in an environmentally sound manner.

2. **Integrated management** – to integrate these policies, programmes and practices fully into each business as an essential element of management in all its functions.

3. **Process of improvement** – to continue to improve corporate policies, programmes and environmental performance, taking into account technical developments, scientific understanding, consumer needs and community expectations, with legal regulations as a starting point; and to apply the same environmental criteria internationally.

4. **Employee education** – to educate, train and motivate employees to conduct their activities in an environmentally responsible manner.

5. **Prior assessment** – to assess environmental impacts before starting a new activity or project and before decommissioning a facility or leaving a site.

6. **Products and services** – to develop and provide products and services that have no undue environmental impact and are safe in their intended use, that are efficient in their consumption of energy and natural resources and that can be recycled, reused or disposed of safely.

7. **Customer advice** – to advise and, where relevant, educate customers, distributors and the public in the safe use, transportation, storage and disposal of products provided; and to apply similar considerations to the provision of services.

8. **Facilities and operations** – to develop, design and operate facilities and conduct activities taking into consideration the efficient use of energy and raw materials, the sustainable use of renewable resources, the minimisation of adverse environmental impact and waste generation and the safe and responsible disposal of residual wastes.

9. **Research** – to conduct or support research on the environmental impacts of raw materials, products, processes, emissions and wastes associated with the enterprise and on the means of minimising such adverse impacts.

10. **Precautionary approach** – to modify the manufacture, marketing or use of products or services to the conduct of activities, consistent with scientific and technical understanding, to prevent serious or irreversible environmental degradation.

11. **Contractors and suppliers** – to promote the adoption of these principles by contractors acting on behalf of the enterprise, encouraging and, where appropriate, requiring improvements in their practices to make them consistent with those of the enterprise; and to encourage the wider adoption of these principles by suppliers.

12. **Emergency preparedness** – to develop and maintain, where appropriate hazards exist, emergency preparedness plans in conjunction with the emergency services, relevant authorities and the local community, recognising potential crossboundary impacts.

13. **Transfer of technology** – to contribute to the transfer of environmentally sound technology and management methods throughout the industrial and public sectors.

14. **Contributing to the common effort** – to contribute to the development of public policy and to business, governmental and intergovernmental programmes and educational initiatives that will enhance environmental awareness and protection.

15. **Openness to concerns** – to foster openness and dialogue with employees and the public, anticipating and responding to their concerns about the potential hazards and impacts of operations, products, wastes or services, including those of transboundary or global significance.

16. **Compliance and reporting** – to measure environmental performance; to conduct regular environmental audits and assessments of compliance with company requirements and these principles; and periodically to provide appropriate information to the board of directors, shareholders, employees, the authorities and the public.

GOOD ENVIRONMENTAL MANAGEMENT AWARD

TECHAGRI M., S.R.L.
Via Manzoni 5
60032 Castelplanio
Statzione (Ancona)
ITALY

AWARD WINNER

Techagri M. Srl., Italy

The company has orchestrated associations of arable farmers, beef stock farmers, poultry farmers, an animal fodder manufacturer, meat processors and a fertilizer company in such a way as to achieve organic farming methods on a large scale.

The end product of the integrated system is the production of high quality foodstuffs, including chicken and turkey meat, that is free of risks caused by chemical residues. The integration goes through to special labelling and marketing, so that the consumer is aware of the nature of the products being bought.

Techagri M, which created the project on its own initiative, developed the scientifically advanced technological and management steps involved. The company itself checks the processes involved in the agricultural and processing stages, using its own laboratories, so that it is able to provide the final guarantees of quality that it targets.

The project started in 1990–91: it involves a surface area of 160 000 hectares, in a region with a population of 270 000 inhabitants. The location of the project is the Marches region, on the Adriatic coast in central Italy.

Techniques involved include crop rotation, recycling waste-products (such as animal excrement, slaughter-house products, animal bedding straw, etc.) to provide organic fertiliser, use of this fertiliser (plus limited use of synthetic fertilisers), appropriate harvesting methods, and technically advanced waste-water treatment.

The technology and systems involved are thought to be highly transferable to other regions in Europe.

Fig. 3.3 Good environmental management award, awarded by the European Community in 1992 to Techagri M. Srl., Italy.

costs of imposing such a scheme would make them uncompetitive in relation to competitors outside the European Community, the requirements were relaxed and the mandatory nature of the scheme was abandoned.

Thus at the end of 1991 the European Commission approved a proposal for a Council Regulation to establish the Eco-Management and Audit Scheme and the final details were published in 1993. The scheme provides a framework for companies to assess their own environmental impacts and commit themselves to a policy of reducing them. It also requires firms to keep the public informed by regularly making statements and reporting progress (see Box 2).

The problem of self-regulation

The ability of firms to set themselves targets that are honest and realistic yet challenging and attainable and which result in significant improvements in environmental performance will ultimately be the benchmark against which the efficacy of this voluntary approach is measured. Self-regulatory approaches are backed by industry, possibly because voluntary action is perceived to be less costly than compliance with regulations and they are considered to be more easily achievable. Moreover, when other corporate objectives (e.g. profits) are under pressure, the voluntary approach allows for a loosening up of other (perhaps secondary) objectives (Shayler *et al.*, 1994)

Environmental policy based on codes of conduct such as the ICC Charter and voluntary standards such as the Eco-Management and Audit Scheme provide industry with the opportunity of demonstrating its commitment to the environment whilst not imposing the rigid constraints more associated with legislation. However, the adoption of codes of conduct and standards within any organisation necessarily raises a number of questions. The most obvious one concerns the type of subculture which a standard brings with it. Does it represent a piecemeal attempt to placate demands from pressure

The EU's Eco-Management and Audit Scheme

2

The objective of the Eco-Management and Audit Scheme is to promote improvements in the environmental performance of industry by requiring companies to:

○ establish and implement environmental policies, programmes and management systems on a site-specific basis
○ carry out periodic, systematic and objective evaluations of activities through an environmental audit
○ provide information about environmental performance to the public.

The purpose of the scheme is not to confirm compliance with legislative requirements, although this must be achieved. The scheme aims to recognise efforts to improve environmental performance over time, given a baseline established by an environmental review of the firm. Thus the scheme highlights the need for a continuous cycle of improvement.

Essentially, there are seven stages to be undertaken by those sites wishing to register with the scheme. The firm must:

1 adopt an environmental policy
2 undertake an environmental review
3 establish environmental programmes
4 install an environmental management system
5 undertake an environmental audit
6 prepare an environmental statement
7 seek verification.

All of these steps (except verification) can be internal to the company if there is sufficient expertise available to perform the various tasks adequately. Indeed, the intention of the Eco-Management and Audit Scheme is that the discipline of having to follow these steps should help the company to manage its own environmental performance better. The scheme requires that an environmental statement is prepared based on the findings of the audit or initial review. Validation of this statement must be made by external accredited environmental verifiers. The validation will confirm that the statement has covered all of the environmental issues relevant to the site in enough detail and that the information presented is reliable.

There are of course criticisms which can be made of this voluntary standard. The most common criticism is that basic environmental performance requirements are not specified. Instead, compliance with the standard is centred on each firm specifying and reaching its self-imposed performance objectives. In other words, the only requirement seems to be to demonstrate a capability for marginal environmental improvements within a self-determined framework of policies, targets, systems and assessment methodologies. Moreover, we should recognise that industry often acts defensively, anticipating changes in attitudes and making marginal adjustments to 'business as usual'. It rarely acts in a proactive way, adopting the highest possible environmental standards.

groups and consumers or is it a more serious attempt at ethical behaviour? We ought also to ask how effective the codes are in promoting what they stand for. Taken together, these questions provide a measure of the extent to which the standards are genuine and operational, rather than cynical and self-deluding.

Codes of conduct and particularly standards, which become accepted across firms in an industry or even across industries, are very powerful and we often see them written into contracts between organisations. We might be inclined to think that a standard promoting some sort of environmental improvement is a huge step forward and that companies who follow others in adopting such standards should be congratulated. But rather more analysis of the content and purpose of such a standard is necessary before we can judge whether they are really effective. If codes of conduct are set up as 'smoke screens' which hide environmental damage whilst purporting to be effective remedies then they are clearly misleading.

There is very little research on the generation, operation, monitoring and amendment of codes and standards. However, it is argued forcefully by Donaldson (1989) that because codes tend to be expressions of mixtures of technical, prudential and moral imperatives and because they tend to vary in the extent to which they are or can be enforced, they cannot be regarded as the major vehicles for identifying and encouraging the practices which will improve the environmental performance in business and industry. Moreover, codes and standards are defined outside the normal democratic framework which determines laws. They are constructed by agencies (often professional bodies or representatives of senior management in industry) with their own motivations, values and interests. On this subject Donaldson and Waller (1980) point to a statement of Bernard Shaw when he asserted that professions can be conspiracies against the laity and their codes are widely held to be primarily aimed at the protection of the members of the profession, rather than the public. Much the same accusation might be levelled against industry standards. Moreover, the matter of the development of codes and standards is bound up with the matter of enforcement. Codes which are not enforced or which fail to deliver their expected outcomes, for whatever reason, might be thought of as little more than expressions of pious hopes.

The Responsible Care Programme

Much of what has been discussed here can be illustrated by reference to the Responsible Care Programme, which provides a standard for firms in the chemicals industry. The Responsible Care Programme can be seen as one of the earliest environmental management standards used across companies. It is a voluntary code where performance is measured in terms of continuous improvement. Responsible Care is unique to the chemical industry and originated in Canada in 1984. Launched in 1989 in the UK by the Chemical Industries Association (CIA), the cornerstone of the system is 'commitment' (see Box 3). Chief executives of member companies are invited to sign a set of guiding principles pledging their company to make health, safety and environmental performance an integral part of overall business policy.

A company operating the Responsible Care Programme is required to have a clear company policy and the communication of this is seen as vital. The key principle being

The Chemical Industries Association's Responsible Care Programme

3

Adherence to the principles and objectives of Responsible Care is a condition of membership of the Chemical Industries Association (CIA). All employees and company contractors have to be made aware of these principles. The guiding principles also require companies to:

○ conform to statutory regulations
○ operate to the best practices of the industry
○ assess the actual and potential health, safety and environmental impacts of their activities and products
○ work closely with the authorities and the community in achieving the required levels of performance
○ be open about activities and give relevant information to interested parties.

used in the Responsible Care Programme is self-assessment. However, the CIA does assess the effectiveness of the programme across all firms by collecting indicators of performance from the firms. Companies are encouraged to submit six classes of data to the Association. Individual company data are not published but a national aggregate figure is published annually. This shows industry trends and enables individual companies to assess their own placing accordingly. The six indicators of performance are:

1 environmental protection spending
2 safety and health (lost time, accidents for employees and contractors)
3 waste and emissions: discharges of 'red list' substances; waste disposal; an environmental index of five key discharges by site
4 distribution (all incidents)
5 energy consumption (total on-site)
6 all complaints.

A key element of the Responsible Care system is the sharing of information and participation of employees and the local community. Local Responsible Care 'cells' operate for the exchange of information and experience between firms. Employee involvement is also encouraged and the CIA has established training programmes which set targets for appraisal. Firms are also encouraged to have community liaison groups and initiatives recognising the continuing need to forge improved relationships with the public.

In its three-year report of the Responsible Care Programme (ENDS, 1993), the CIA was implicitly forced to admit that the programme was not functioning in accordance with its aims. The main reason for this is that sites claiming to adhere to the Responsible Care standard were simply not adhering to its principles. Over the three-year reporting period only 57% of firms made returns for all three years and only 74% made any returns at all. Even more importantly, the third indicator of performance deals with waste and emissions where firms are supposed to present an environmental index by site designed to give a composite picture of gaseous, liquid and solid releases. Only one-third of the total firms supposed to be operating Responsible Care reported these data in full and of those who reported the index, over 30% reported a worsening environmental impact.

Codes of conduct are therefore nothing if they are not adhered to and voluntary approaches often slip down a list of priorities when other pressing issues arise. It is perhaps not surprising that the lack of response from the chemical industry over Responsible Care occurred during a particularly bad economic recession. However, at the core of any strategy for environmental improvement has to be commitment and no standard or code of conduct will survive without that commitment. Whilst some chemical companies are clearly committed to improving their environmental perform-ance it seems that too many are not adhering to the spirit of Responsible Care. Indeed, whilst some make efforts to follow the guidelines of the programme many more seem to treat Responsible Care as a smoke screen. Many of those managers in the chemical industry who appear confident of their procedures to improve environmental perform-ance are either unaware of the environmental impacts or are deliberately trying to hide their environmental impact in an attempt to hang on to market share and profitability.

That raises two questions. The first relates to whether legislation which forces companies to be more environmentally responsible is therefore superior to voluntary approaches. The second, more fundamentally, relates to whether in the capitalist system, where the number one priority is the maintenance of profitability, the environ-ment can ever be sufficiently important to an individual firm to give it the priority which it needs. To answer both of these questions we need to look at the international dimension of both business activity and environmental policy.

3.5 Sustainable development, international trade and the global economy

The conditions for sustainable development

The continuing ability of the environment to supply raw materials and assimilate waste whilst maintaining biodiversity and environmental quality is being increasingly undermined. The concept of sustainable development implies that, as a minimum, all human activity must refrain from causing any degree of permanent damage through its consumption of environmental resources. Sustainable development stresses the inter-dependence between economic growth and environmental quality. The achievement of sustainability requires policy makers to tackle the problem of inequality throughout the world. In part, this requires a proper consideration of the future impacts of present activities.

For industry, policies for sustainable development have several implications. Firstly, the environment must be valued as an integral part of the economic process and not treated as a free good. The environmental stock has to be protected and this implies minimal use of non-renewable resources and minimal emission of pollutants. Ecosys-tems have to be protected so the loss of plant and animal species has to be avoided.

Secondly there is a need to deal with the issue of equity. One of the biggest threats facing the world is that the developing countries want to grow rapidly to achieve the same standards of living as those in the industrialised countries. That in itself would cause major environmental degradation if it were modelled on the same sort of growth experienced in postwar Europe and North America. Therefore, there needs to be a greater degree of equality and the key issue of poverty has to be addressed. But equity applies not only to relationships between the North and South, but also within countries between people. A major source of inequality exists between those who are employed and those who are unemployed and this must also be tackled within the context of sustainability.

Thirdly, in an economy based on sustainable development society, businesses and individuals should operate on a longer time-scale than is currently the case. This is the issue of futurity. While companies commonly operate under competitive pressures to achieve short run gains, long-term environmental protection is often compromised. To ensure that longer term, intergenerational considerations are observed, longer planning horizons need to be adopted and business policy needs to be proactive rather than reactive.

The Brundtland Report concludes that these three conditions are not being met (WCED, 1987). The industrialised world has already used much of the planet's ecological capital and many of the development paths of the industrialised nations are clearly unsustainable. Non-renewable resources are being depleted, while renewable resources, such as soil, water and the atmosphere, are being degraded. This has been caused by economic development but is also undermining the very foundations of that development.

International interdependence and the capitalist economy

One of the characteristics of postwar Europe has been the growing integration associated with European economic union. But that trend, more recently, has been mirrored in other parts of the world. International trade is dominated by the global triad of Europe, North America and Japan and all the OECD countries have found their economies becoming more interdependent and interrelated through the growth of trade, technology transfer and global communications networks. In the decade between 1980 and 1990 the Worldwatch Institute estimated that gross world output of goods and services grew from US$4.5 trillion to US$20 trillion and international trade grew by approximately 4% per year (Brown, 1991). Through the mass media models of Western consumer culture have been relayed across the planet. This reinforces the perception of gross and persistent inequalities between the higher income and lower income countries and the considerable differences within the lower income countries themselves.

The global spread of industrial activity along with the expansion of information systems means that no country can insulate itself from its external economic climate. Neither can countries insulate themselves from the growing pollution flows caused by industrialisation and consumerism. Perhaps most intrusive, however, are the activities of the transnational corporations (TNCs) who bring with them their own corporate cultures, dominate international trade and production and are therefore to be held responsible for significant levels of transnational environmental damage.

The rapid evolution of an international economic system has not been paralleled by international political integration or international laws to regulate that system. The consequence is that many transnational corporations operate above the law, beyond national boundaries and are able to set their own international economic agenda. Moreover, by creating a situation where many countries in the South are dependent on their patronage, employment and technology, they often wield considerable political power as well.

Since the 1980s we have seen an increasing move towards the liberal market version of the capitalist economy. By the beginnings of the 1990s there were many former communist countries putting radical and austere policies in place to introduce a market mechanism into their economies and to privatise previously state-run companies. However, the process of reform has taken much longer than expected, has resulted in significant costs associated with human suffering and in some countries has resulted in a nationalist backlash. Foreign investment in Central and Eastern Europe has also been disappointing and is still blocked by political uncertainty, environmental degradation and infrastructural backwardness.

Governments in the developing countries have also been attracted towards the liberal free market model, seeing it as the system which is able to deliver the goods and raise general levels of material prosperity. They have often been encouraged along that path by institutions such as the World Bank and the IMF who link the provision of loans to conditions relating to structural adjustment. This has meant that financial support and advice have been linked to the implementation of market-friendly structural reform in the economy in question.

Despite all the pains of transition, however, it is likely that the countries in the South and in the former Eastern bloc will continue to move towards liberal capitalism, attracted by Western levels of prosperity and consumption. Whilst the time-scales for achieving such targets are uncertain there seems little doubt that some countries will achieve greatly increased levels of national output and per capita income. But, as Carley and Christie (1992) point out, ironically the drive for economic growth and hunger for Western levels of consumption in the newly industrialising countries and the ex-communist world are developing precisely at the point at which consumerism in the West is beginning to appear socially self-defeating and ecologically unsustainable.

The impact of trade

The enormous expansion of world trade has been a characteristic of the spread of capitalism and is fundamental to the internationalisation of the industrial system. The central institution which lays out the terms of engagement in the international trade system and which monitors trade is the World Trade Organisation, formerly the General Agreement of Tariffs and Trade (GATT). The Uruguay round of GATT negotiations on removing trade barriers began in 1986 and was completed in 1993. Environmental considerations were largely ignored during this process, reflecting the fact that issues of international trade and environmental management are seen as separate and discrete. Indeed, whilst at the Rio Summit governments and other agencies made declarations in support of the principles of sustainable development, when involved in the GATT negotiations, they were making decisions which could undermine progress towards sustainability.

The GATT has consistently acted in favour of free trade and against environmental protection. It has consistently linked environmental issues to the issue of protectionism and has ignored issues of sustainability. For example, in 1991 the GATT overruled an American ban on imports of tuna fish from Mexico (claimed to be fished in such a way as to kill an unacceptable number of dolphins) on the grounds that such a restriction would violate free trade (see Chapter 4). Indeed, the GATT view is that restrictions on trade, claimed on environmental grounds, would be more likely to be mere excuses for protectionism, rather than real attempts to reduce environmental damage.

Thus when we consider the activities of business in a wider context we must question the ability of nationally-based environmental protection policies to make a significant difference. More legislation and higher taxes might drive some companies out of one country, where tough environmental policies have been introduced, into another where they do not exist (although there is little evidence of this having occurred in the past). Tough policies in one country may lead to a competitive disadvantage to domestic companies and replace an environmental problem with an unemployment problem. Moreover, in their constant attempt to keep prices down, large, transnational corporations can often find ways of doing business in developing countries where environmental legislation is weak. Such arguments might be a justification for leaving any change solely to free market forces and to voluntary action by individual firms. Indeed, it is often argued that the liberalisation of trade will encourage the more efficient use of factors of production through comparative advantage, thus helping to prevent environmental degradation (an argument which will be explored in detail in the next chapter). Other, more sceptical commentators would simply see the need for a radical change in the way we do business.

Business strategies for sustainability: the radical agenda

The key question posed by the more radical school of thought relates to the extent to which current environmental policy based on a mixture of environmental legislation, financial incentives and self-regulation can actually deliver sustainability. Certainly, if we rely on free market approaches and broad codes of conduct, sustainability may take a very long time to achieve. Moreover, voluntary standards such as the Eco-Management and Audit Scheme are dominated by self-imposed objectives and targets which may be very marginal. Many firms are embracing voluntary standards and codes of conduct because they are easily achievable, highlighting the idea that an organisation is doing something rather than nothing in order to satisfy the competing demands of stakeholders.

There is a contradiction which arises when organisations commit themselves to sustainable development and then opt for an approach which does not necessarily achieve these fundamental aims, as so many firms have done by signing the ICC Charter. One of the key problems that has arisen, is that by adopting narrow environmental management strategies, firms believe that they are adopting principles of sustainable development. They seem to be of the view that environmental improvement equates to sustainable development. This is clearly not the case, as a closer look at the sustainable development concept reveals.

To begin to deal with the broad issues of sustainable development, many would argue that we need to see a new style of management based on a holistic approach and predicated on a clear world view and an understanding of the need for further 'paradigm shift' in business culture (Commoner, 1990; Welford, 1995; Wheeler, 1993). Organisations committed to sustainability must be committed to integrating environmental performance and wider issues of global ecology (the maintenance of biodiversity, prevention of pollution, etc.) into their business planning.

Thus, as a starting point, energy efficiency should be focused on the need to minimise NOx, SOx and CO_2 emissions and avoid nuclear waste. Waste minimisation, re-use and recycling should be driven by the need to conserve non-renewable resources. Product design should incorporate the use of renewable resources wherever possible. The extraction and processing of raw materials should have no negative impacts on global biodiversity, endangered habitats or the rights of indigenous peoples. Overall corporate policies should examine the business's impact on both the developed and underdeveloped world, both now and into the future.

A radical approach to environmental strategies designed to achieve sustainability would involve significant changes in management attitudes and objectives. Businesses must begin with real commitment on the part of the whole organisation to deal with the wider issues associated with sustainability. This may mean a change in corporate culture and therefore management has an important role to play. In leading that commitment and laying out the organisation's corporate objectives with respect to the environment, management has to be the catalyst for change. Indeed, it needs to rethink its whole rationale and reassess the very structures in its own organisation which act as impediments to change. Moreover, change has to be ongoing and management must be ever mindful of the full range of (often competing) objectives to which it is subject. Management has to find compromise between these objectives if they conflict and design corporate strategies which are operational, consistent and achievable. Change will have to be addressed in a systemic way, dealing with the company as a whole rather than in a compartmentalised way. There is also a need to look towards the 'larger picture' rather than focusing on product-specific considerations. This may involve changes in corporate structures and the abandonment of attitudes that insist on the continuation of 'business as usual'.

When it comes to the integration of environmental considerations, co-operative strategies also need to be considered. All too often competition has been the dominant ideology in business, but increasingly co-operative strategies between businesses and involving the public and regulatory agencies can bring about benefits which are environmentally sustainable. Single-minded competitive strategies run the risk of isolating businesses from new developments, expertise and public opinion which are invaluable to the environmentally aware company.

Companies are faced with a challenge of integrating considerations based on the elements of sustainable development into their production and marketing plans. There is always an incentive, however, for profit-maximising firms seeking short-term rewards to opt out and become a free rider (assuming that everyone else will be environmentally conscious such that their own pollution will become negligible). To some extent, environmental legislation is able to plug the gaps which allows this to happen and firms attempting to hide their illegal pollution are now subject to severe penalties. However, more radical thinkers argue that what is really required is a shift in paradigms towards an acceptance by industry of its ethical and social responsibilities. In the short term this may require a legislative stance to push companies into action, but in the longer term firms must look at their overall impact on the environment, on equity and on futurity and construct a social and ethical balance sheet. It challenges firms to give greater priority to ecological considerations even if it means some lowering of profits, at least in the short term.

Such a change in ideology is, of course, difficult to achieve because environmental policy in relation to business is increasingly self-regulated. We have seen that environmental management standards and codes of conduct have been set by industry itself. They have been designed to be voluntary and not to conflict with the ideology associated with profit maximisation in the short to medium term. Arguments such as the ones outlined above, suggesting that industry has not gone far enough, will be treated with derision by many in industry and sidelined. The power which industry has in the current economic system may therefore be a barrier to further development of the concept of sustainable development. Thus, radical commentators would argue that the only way to bring about a change in this dominant ideology is to challenge the very basis of that power. Without a fundamental revolution in the way we organise our society, such a challenge can only come about through a legislative process. Not, however, at the level of the nation state, but across the whole world. It is not clear how that might be achieved.

3.6 Conclusion

I began this chapter by exploring four different ways in which international environmental policy might be applied to businesses. We have seen that the traditional approach of imposing command and control instruments on industry through legislation is increasingly being replaced by instruments which attempt to use the market mechanism to bring about a desired outcome. That approach recognises that to leave the market mechanism completely to its own devices is unlikely to bring about environmental improvement in the time-scale required.

The contemporary debate amongst policy makers surrounds the relative merits of the unhindered free market as against a market constrained either by financial incentives or by legislation. These three approaches are not mutually exclusive. Indeed, the use of taxes and subsidies relies on the operation of the market. There is nevertheless considerable tension between those who favour the reformist market-based approach and those who wish to see a more interventionist legislation-based regulatory stance. The former implies using the fiscal system to redirect expenditure and investment decisions, although we have seen very little use of environmental taxes anywhere in the world to date. It also means allowing industry to adopt voluntary codes of conduct and environmental standards based on self-defined objectives and targets. Such approaches are supposed to give the company competitive advantage in the international market place. Once again, there is little evidence to date that such non-regulatory approaches do work and some limited evidence that they do not.

However, we have seen that the biggest constraint to achieving environmental improvement is often the very system in which business operates. This is particularly true when we look at the wider international dimension of capitalism with its emphasis on free trade. If our ultimate aim is sustainable development, then it is difficult to see how we will achieve our desired outcomes without international co-operation over legislation and without a significant change in the way we organise industry. This is consistent with the more radical approach to environmental policy.

4

International trade and environmental policies

Gerrit Faber

4.1 Introduction

The linkages between the environment and international trade have been the subject of much debate in recent years. At the same time, as a result of experience and growing research, it has become clear that the relationship between trade and the environment is extremely complex and characterised by contradictions, painful dilemmas and trade-offs. This makes it impossible to make simple generalisations such as 'trade is beneficial for the environment'.

International trade is, by definition, a set of economic relationships between countries. These relationships are regulated by international policy. Trade has impacts on the environment and, in terms of policy, there is a consequent relationship between trade and environmental protection. Three types of interrelationship between trade and the environment can be identified and each of these demonstrates the problem of trying to assess whether trade is beneficial or detrimental for the environment.

The first is that trade is based on comparative advantage. That means that production of specific commodities tends to be concentrated in countries where the factors of production (resources, labour or capital) are cheapest for the production of those commodities. Production will lead to trade in those goods in which countries have comparative advantage. But this may result in exhaustive and polluting production, such as mining minerals and the growing of cotton in certain countries. On the other hand, international trade also fosters a more efficient use of resources, which means less environmental damage per unit of product.

The second interrelationship arises as a result of the impact of national policies on trade. Instruments of domestic environmental policy such as prohibitions, levies, taxes and subsidies have an influence on the international competitiveness of industries. As a consequence, industrial pressure groups lobby their governments and international organisations in order to secure what they believe is the optimum policy. Indirectly, this may have different outcomes for the environment. In extreme cases, a 'green' policy may be advocated in order to achieve greater protectionism. Conversely, the adoption of liberal economic policies may lead to the attraction of industries that deplete resources or pollute the environment.

Thirdly, there are those interrelationships that are created by the impact of action by one country (or countries) on others. Action may be taken to limit the trade undertaken by a certain country in order to force that country to adopt environmental measures that one or more other countries deem necessary. The United States, for example, banned imports of tuna from Mexico in order to make Mexico adopt US rules for the protection of dolphins. The economic and environmental consequences of this measure were controversial, as we shall see later in the chapter.

A major objective of this chapter is to describe and clarify the relationships between trade and the environment in order to see how trade can be made to contribute to the sustainable development of the world economy. The relationship between trade and the environment cannot be isolated from the unequal distribution of wealth over the globe. The fight against poverty necessitates more production, as well as a more equitable distribution of income, both within many countries and among countries (see Box 1). As it is not likely that rich countries will cut back their levels of production and consumption, the growth of world production is unavoidable. This will put more pressure on the environment. One of the major challenges of the coming decades will be to eradicate poverty and simultaneously to protect the environment in order to enable future generations to satisfy their needs. International trade has an important role to play in this respect.

Section 4.2 will discuss the role of trade in relationship to its environmental impact. It will present some basic facts about international trade and then examine the theoretical arguments about whether or not trade is beneficial to the environment. The relationship between the development of poor countries, trade and the protection of the environment is the subject of Section 4.3.

The chapter then goes on to consider issues of international policy. The protection of the environment is complicated by the existence of a large number of national jurisdictions. An international environmental policy requires national jurisdictions to adapt to internationally agreed measures; this entails a generally time-consuming process of compromise and negotiation. Most of the multilaterally agreed rules on international trade are to be found in the General Agreement on Tariffs and Trade

The Rio Declaration on Trade

The fifth principle of the Declaration on the Environment and Development adopted at the UN Conference in 1992 reads as follows:

> All States and all people shall co-operate in the essential task of eradicating poverty as an indispensable requirement for sustainable development, in order to decrease the disparities in standards of living and better meet the needs of the majority of the people of the world.

(GATT) incorporated in the new World Trade Organisation (WTO). These rules will be discussed in Section 4.4. The question is whether the GATT rules form a constraint on or an opportunity for the realisation of the objective of making trade contribute to sustainable development.

Section 4.5 gives a review of the criteria which an optimum international environmental policy needs to meet with respect to international trade. Various international environmental agreements that incorporate trade measures are reviewed in Section 4.6. Section 4.7 presents a review of the main conclusions of the chapter.

4.2 International trade and resource use

Trends in trade

International trade in goods has grown at a very rapid rate since World War II. Its real value (i.e. discounting rises in prices) increased by a factor of more than ten between 1950 and 1990 (French, 1993, pp.6 *et seq.*). On a global scale, trade has increased faster than production. Figures 4.1 and 4.2 show that this conclusion also applied in the turbulent 1970s and 1980s to the world as a whole and to East Asia and the Pacific,

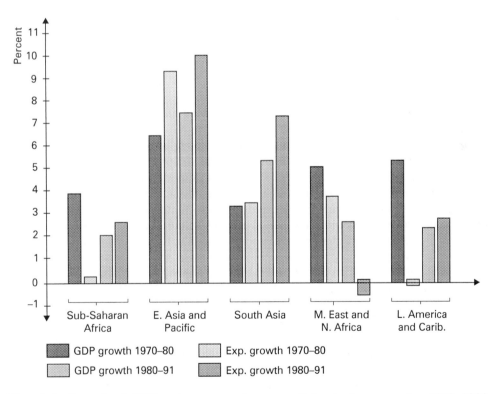

Fig. 4.1 Growth of GDP and exports of groups of developing countries, 1970–1980 and 1980–1991. Source: French, 1993

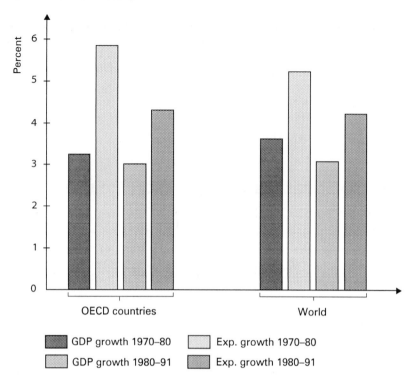

Fig. 4.2 Growth of GDP and exports of OECD countries, 1970–1980 and 1980–1991. Source: French, 1993

South Asia and the OECD in particular. After 1980, Latin America and sub-Saharan Africa showed the same tendency. The transition to a market-based economy of the centrally planned closed economies of Eastern Europe and China will undoubtedly increase the gap between the growth rates of trade and production.

To the extent that trade grows faster than production, economies become more open and interdependent. Open economies also appear to achieve more rapid economic growth. Conversely, measures which reduce imports and exports have an adverse effect on growth in developing countries (Faber, 1990, p.32). Some developing regions are showing extremely high rates of export growth (i.e. East Asia and the Pacific and South Asia; see Figures 4.1 and 4.2) in combination with relatively high rates of production growth. East Asia and the Pacific are narrowing the wealth gap with the industrialised countries. Export-based industrialisation is the strategy that these countries are following.

The first consequence of this growing interdependence is that international trade is increasingly determining what is produced and where and how production takes place. This also has an impact on the site, nature and intensity of the environmental effects that result from production. The second consequence of growing interdependence is that the competitiveness of a country's economy is a crucial condition for stable economic growth. National environmental policies that may undermine competitiveness have a political cost, as economic interest groups will put pressure on politicians.

At the same time, we should stress that, in many large trading areas, such as the European Union and the United States, the share of GNP that is traded internationally has remained relatively stable at 12% and 10% respectively. This means that of every US$100 that are earned from the production of goods, US$90 are consumed domestically. In the case of the services sector, an even higher share is consumed at home. As a result, there is scope in these trading areas for a relatively autonomous environmental policy.

The environmental impact of trade: conflicting views

Observers of the relationship between trade and the environment often have conflicting views. Looking at the extremes, one may distinguish two schools of thought on the issue. The first school believes that international trade and international specialisation give rise to a concentration of production and consumption of goods that have been produced in a resource-intensive manner in different countries. As a result, consumers have no idea of the environmental cost at which these goods are produced; after all, these costs are incurred in the exporting country. International trade is said to enable the importing industrialised countries to appropriate a disproportionate share of the world's natural resources. As world market prices do not reflect the relative scarcity of environmental goods in the present or in the future, the exhaustion of the environment is accelerated above an economically justified rate (Ritchie, 1990; Shrybman, 1990, 1991).

The second school of thought stresses the gains that can be earned from free international trade. Such trade is said to lead to maximum production (given the limited amount of resources) and to the highest possible level of prosperity in the participating countries. International trade is said to force producers to use resources as efficiently as possible and this helps to save natural resources. This school claims that restrictions on international trade are an inferior way of protecting the environment and are often counterproductive.

In short, it is not possible to make one simple statement about the effects of international trade on the environment. There is no clear-cut answer. There are examples where international trade has had a beneficial effect on the environment, such as when the success of Japanese car imports forced American car manufacturers to reduce the excessive fuel consumption to which their models were prone. However, there are also plenty of instances of adverse effects: the deforestation of Sarawak and Sabah in Malaysia as a result of the export of tropical timber is one such example. Nor may it be claimed that the manufacturing sector in countries with a relatively closed economy, i.e. a low ratio of trade to their gross domestic product (GDP), is generally less environmentally damaging than in countries characterised by an open economy. The former centrally planned economies of Eastern Europe provide perhaps the most obvious illustration of this point. They were relatively isolated from world trade but experienced much higher pollution levels per capita than in Western Europe with its much higher production levels.

The theory of international trade

The environmental impact of international trade depends on several factors. In order to understand these factors, we need first to discuss a general theoretical approach to international trade and then to turn to individual cases afterwards.

83

The general theory that explains international trade, the theory of comparative advantage, is based on a number of assumptions. Among the most important are perfect competition, which means that no single market party can exert influence on prices in a particular market; the absence of market interventions by official bodies; and the equality of private and social costs and benefits. The latter assumption implies that the costs and benefits on which private economic subjects (i.e. individuals and privately owned organisations such as firms) base their behaviour should be equal to the costs and benefits as perceived by society. It can be shown that, if these conditions are met, free trade gives rise to a maximum level of prosperity in the trading countries (see, for example, Lindert, 1991, Chs. 2 and 3). The reason for this is that each country specialises in the production of those goods in which it is most efficient and imports those goods which it produces least efficiently. The general presumption is that any limitation of international trade will reduce the wealth of the countries concerned.

In specific real-world situations, however, the general presumption may have to be modified. This is the case if there is a significant diversion from the assumptions underlying the theory. It may be that production (or consumption) gives rise to environmental damage and that the producer (or consumer) is not required to pay for this damage. In this case, the private cost of production (or consumption) may be lower than the social cost because the cost of the 'services of Nature' is not reflected, or not fully reflected, in the prices that producers (or consumers) have to pay for their inputs and for their harmful byproducts (e.g. emissions of polluting gases). In this situation, market prices do not reflect the true scarcity of products and resources. This implies that exporting countries do not receive full compensation for all the resources that have been used to produce the exported products concerned, whilst importing countries pay a price that is too low.

Attempts to introduce a more realistic pricing policy unilaterally may protect the environment while damaging the economy. Let us assume that the government of an exporting country introduces an environmental policy that increases the cost of production to a level that incorporates the social cost, thus including the cost of unpriced services of Nature. This increases the price that the producers need to charge in order to stay in business. The consequence will probably be a fall in exports. As long as there is trade, the country's social prosperity is still higher than it would be in the absence of trade. The exports may not be competitive on world markets any more; this means that the comparative advantage ceases to exist if the unpriced services of Nature are taken into account.

The upshot of this argument is that, even in the case of an environmentally damaging production process, international trade in the commodity thus produced will increase the social prosperity of an exporting country, even if the government takes steps to include the cost of unpriced services of Nature in the market price. This is illustrated in Box 2. For the importing country, the gains from trade are reduced as the import price increases. At the same time, however, the level of prosperity is higher than it would be in the absence of international trade (Anderson, 1992). So, for all countries concerned, international trade is still advantageous, as long as there is government intervention to equalise private and social costs. A second conclusion is that the exporting country's government should intervene to equalise social and private costs in domestic production in order to maximise the nation's social prosperity. A third

---

2

Exporting shrimps in Asia

A good illustration of the inequality of private and social cost is provided by the production and export of shrimps. Many countries in Asia have expanded their production and exports of shrimps. This has led to the clearing of large areas of coastal mangrove swamps (e.g. in the Philippines). It has recently become clear that mangrove ecosystems play a critical role in protecting coastlines and serving as spawning grounds for oceanic fisheries, as well as providing food for local people (French, 1993, p. 17). Thus, the clearing of mangrove swamps gives rise to higher public spending on coastal defence works, lowers the catch and probably the income of fishermen and forces local people to turn to alternative foodstuffs that are probably more expensive.

Selling shrimps (on both the domestic and the international markets) without taking into account the adverse effects on the prosperity of non-market parties means selling shrimps below their social cost. The public authorities can translate this social cost into private cost, for example by limiting the clearing of mangrove swamps and by setting up a licensing system for shrimp production in designated areas. The proceeds earned from the distribution of licences can be used to finance coastal defence works and to compensate local people.

---

conclusion is that the degree of scarcity of natural resources differs from country to country and that different countries attach different social values to them. It is precisely this type of difference that gives rise to comparative advantages and disadvantages in international trade. Equalising these values and the environmental policies based upon them would take away comparative advantages and mitigate the beneficial effects of trade on the environment. However, where the international commons are at stake (e.g. the climate), international co-operation is needed with respect to protection levels and measures, a point I shall return to later.

The environmental implications of trade policy

An optimum policy is both effective, i.e. in the sense that its objectives are achieved, and efficient, i.e. in the sense that the objectives are achieved at minimum cost. A policy that does not achieve its objectives is basically pointless. A policy that squanders scarce resources (i.e. is inefficient) will lose the support of society. In practice, it may be difficult to design and implement a policy that is both effective and efficient. Nevertheless, optimality is a good yardstick for evaluating policies and for ranking alternative policies and instruments on a scale from best to least good.

In the case of environmental policies, the objective is to reduce certain kinds of pollution or to lower the level of exploitation of a natural resource. Which instruments are chosen depends partly on the objectives. A rule of thumb is that an intervention that is made in order to redress distortion in the economy, i.e. the inequality of social and private cost, should be made as close as possible to the source of the distortion. An intervention that is made away from the source is likely to produce indirect effects or side effects that lower the efficiency of the policy. An example may serve to clarify this point. The large-scale production of pork in intensive cattle breeding areas may cause emissions of substances that lead to acid rain. This is the case if the manure that is the by-product of pork production is distributed over an acreage that is too small fully to absorb the manure and to convert it into vegetable growth. These substances are also emitted directly from pigsties. In order to lower the emissions of substances producing acid rain, the government could limit the production of pork. Cuts in production will also reduce the personal wealth of the producers (in the form of lower profitability, lower wages and perhaps more unemployment) and of consumers (in the form of higher prices). These adverse, indirect effects can be avoided, at least partially, if the government takes measures that limit the level of emissions in a direct way, e.g. by taxing emissions, by introducing a system of tradeable emission permits or by prohibiting emissions beyond a certain level. These measures will induce producers to invest in emission-decreasing devices and pigsties in order to keep production as high as possible within the emission limits. Thus, the objective of the policy will be realised at a lower cost in terms of social prosperity.

The key question is: 'What is an optimum environmental policy and how is it related to international trade?' Governments have a wide range of instruments at their disposal for achieving their goals: rules (i.e. prohibitions, limits and standards), taxes, subsidies, etc. For our purposes, it is useful to make a distinction between instruments that intervene primarily in the domestic economy and instruments that operate at the country's borders. The latter heading includes import and export levies, quantitative restrictions, technical standards for products and downright prohibitions on trade. The main focus of our attention is import measures which are aimed at limiting trade flows in general terms. Trade policy measures, such as levies, quantitative restrictions and import prohibitions, are less efficient as they do not meet the criteria of optimality indicated above. Trade is the link between production and consumption. Environmentally detrimental effects are almost invariably the result of production or consumption. As a result, policy measures that seek primarily to influence trade do not tackle the problem at its source and are thus seldom efficient or 'first best'. A number of specific cases will now be discussed to illustrate this argument.

○ It has occasionally been proposed that the exploitation of the environment should be reduced by means of an export tax or a quantitative limitation of exports. It is doubtful whether this measure would be effective, as the price of the product affected would fall on the domestic market, as would the value of the natural resources on which the exports rely (see Box 3 on the ban on ivory exports). Additionally, production for the domestic market would not be directly affected. This is irrational, as production for the domestic market is just as harmful as production for the world market. A side effect is that domestic demand would probably grow as a result of the price decrease and this would boost production again after some time.

○ In the case of a large number of products, the same countries are both importers and exporters. This phenomenon is particularly common in the industrialised countries. This is called intra-industry trade, in which industrialised countries export certain products (e.g. cars) of which they are also importers. If a country introduces an environmental policy to solve a purely local environmental problem, this will increase the private cost of production, so that the country's domestic industry will become less competitive with respect to the same imported products. The domestic industry will probably demand that the government levy a tax on imported products that have been produced in countries where the environmental policy is less strict.

It is probably inefficient to yield to these demands. First, the competing country may have sound reasons for not introducing an equally strict environmental policy, which means that there is already an optimum situation of social prosperity before the introduction of import levies. It may be, for instance, that the competing country is exploiting its resources without compromising sustainability whereas the importing country has already gone beyond the limits of sustainability.

Secondly, the introduction of 'green' import tariffs offers pressure groups of industries an additional opportunity to lobby for protective trade measures. It is very difficult to fix a tariff that exactly taxes away the difference between the two sets of environmental policies and this may induce politicians to fix the levies at a 'safely' high level. Thirdly, the import tariff does not tackle the environmental problem, as the trade flow concerned only represents part (and perhaps only a small part) of total production. But it may take away the comparative advantage of an exporting country based on a more abundant supply of natural resources relative to the importing country.

Plate 4.1 The illegal trade in endangered animal species. On 5 June 1992, customs officers at Amsterdam's Schiphol Airport came upon a consignment of 81 African elephant tusks and 20 rhinoceros horns during a routine check of a container bound from Malawi to Taiwan. Photo: ANP Foto

---

The African elephant and trade in ivory

3

In the framework of the Convention on International Trade in Endangered Species (CITES, see Section 4.6), an international ban was imposed on the trade in ivory. It was thought that this ban would make the 'harvesting' of ivory unattractive and that this would save the African elephant from unlimited shooting. However, a number of former exporting countries complained that this ban made it very difficult for them to bring about or maintain a policy for the sustainable management of their elephant herds. A regulated culling programme may make it possible to carry on a trade in ivory, while maintaining a viable population of elephants. Zimbabwe had already implemented such a policy before the ban came into effect. The problem is that a ban on ivory trade decreases the economic value of elephants. The opportunity to sell ivory brings a wealth gain to the exporting country and this is an incentive not to destroy the source of the export. The ban takes away this incentive. As a result neglect, poaching and smuggling may lead to an even faster deterioration in the elephant population than was the case before (Barbier *et al.*, 1990).

❍ A trade policy measure may be used in order to force a country to adopt certain environmental measures. Examples may be found in US trade law. The US Congress adopted legislation in 1987 under which unilateral sanctions were threatened against countries that did not enter into international agreements to monitor drift net fishing practices or that did not enforce their own drift net fishing laws (Charnovitz, 1993). The problem that arises here is that most international environmental problems can be solved only by international co-operation. This requires, first, that the problem is perceived by all countries concerned in more or less the same way. Secondly, there has to be agreement on the way the problem should be tackled and on the distribution of the policy's gains and costs over the various countries. It is doubtful whether an effective international agreement can be realised by an individual country forcing other countries into it. If a government is not convinced of the existence of an environmental problem or thinks that the distribution of gains and losses is unfair, the country in question is likely to cheat and to obstruct an efficient and effective implementation of the 'agreement'. A more adequate strategy is to negotiate an agreement that is acceptable to all countries concerned (Sebenius, 1991). The potential role of trade policy measures in the framework of such an agreement is discussed in the following sections.

4.3 Development and trade

Poor countries are often referred to as developing countries. Development is, however, a much broader concept than simply poverty reduction or economic growth. Development is defined by Todaro (1981) as 'a multi-dimensional process involving major changes in social structures, popular attitudes and national institutions, as well as the acceleration of economic growth, the reduction of inequality and the eradication of absolute poverty' (p.70). Nevertheless, for our purposes, we shall concentrate on

Plate 4.2 Coffee beans being washed and peeled on a coffee plantation in San Juan Laguna, Guatemala. The beans are destined for the export market. Photo: Sean Sprague/Lineair

economic development. Since the Second World War, a large number of countries in Asia, Latin America and Africa have tried to increase their domestic output of goods and services in order to arrive at a higher level of prosperity. Some countries have achieved spectacularly high rates of growth (e.g. the so-called newly industrialising countries, including the four Asian 'tigers': South Korea, Taiwan, Hong Kong and Singapore), while others have not succeeded in attaining such a rapid rate of economic development. Figure 4.1 (page 81) clearly indicates these differences. Some of these fast-growing countries are approaching levels of prosperity that can be found in industrialised countries. Most developing countries have serious environmental problems, caused by poverty, population pressure and the process of urbanisation and industrialisation (World Bank, 1992). We shall discuss these problems only insofar as they are trade related.

Generally speaking, economic development is characterised by industrialisation and increasing urbanisation. At a later phase of development, the services sector becomes the fastest growing part of the economy. The exports of developing countries diversify during this process. It is in the early phases of development that primary products are the main export products; in later stages of development, industrial products become more important. Many developing countries that have recently become industrialised are affected by serious environmental problems; however, these do not fundamentally differ from the environmental problems in traditionally rich countries. We shall concentrate here on the trade-related environmental problems of the poorest countries.

Developing countries at a very low level of development are often dependent on only one primary product, or a very limited number of primary products, for their

Table 4.1 Developing countries earning 60% or more of their export receipts from one commodity (excl. oil), 1989–1990

Name of country	Commodity	% of exports (value)
Burundi	coffee	76
Cuba	sugar	77
Dominica	fruits and nuts	60
Guinea	base metal, ores	84
Jamaica	base metal, ores	63
Malawi	tobacco	66
New Caledonia	pig iron	63
Niger	radio active material	80
Réunion	sugar	75
Rwanda	coffee	69
Uganda	coffee	90
Zambia	copper	82

Source: UNCTAD, *Handbook of international trade and development statistics* (New York, 1993), p. 195 et seq.

export earnings. Table 4.1 shows the developing countries which in 1989–1990 earned 60% or more of their export receipts from the trade in one single commodity. If oil were included, the table would double in length. Such a high level of dependency makes these countries vulnerable to falling world market prices. Insofar as certain trade-related environmental problems are typical of developing countries, these are largely to be found in situations of dependency on one, or a few, primary export products. The production of primary products is by its very nature resource-intensive. Agriculture is based on the fertility of the soil, which may be depleted by overproduction and the use of chemical substances. Irrigation may cause salinisation of the soil. Obviously, the production of minerals depletes the stocks of the mineral resources concerned; additional harmful effects may consist of pollution in the vicinity of mines, particularly as a result of the first stage of the processing of ores. The production of tropical timber may lead to deforestation and erosion. An additional problem often associated with the large-scale production of primary products is that the environmental effects are greatly concentrated in certain regions and in the form of damage to particular environmental resources.

Many of these countries have been forced to restructure their economies in order to service their debts. These structural adjustment programmes may give rise to environmental effects: these countries badly need every unit of foreign exchange, so they have strong incentives not to make their primary products more expensive or less profitable by levying taxes on producers or by limiting the use of scarce natural resources. On the other hand, structural adjustment will probably increase the domestic prices of agricultural products, which is likely to induce farmers to invest more in soil conservation and land improvement (Heerink and Kuyvenhoven, 1993).

Trade-related environmental problems in developing countries exporting primary products are closely linked to the problem of development as such. This means that they can only be solved in a structural manner by development in general. As has already been indicated, development will bring about a diversification of production and this means less one-sided environmental effects and more environmentally friendly production. This will lessen dependency on one or a few primary products. The abolition of trade barriers imposed on processed products would be one way in which developed countries could stimulate this. A more generous debt restructuring programme (including debt relief) for the poorest countries would also relieve the pressure placed on such countries to exhaust their environmental resources for the sake of export production, although it is no guarantee that the natural resources concerned will receive full protection. Proposals have also been made for including environmental tasks in commodity organisations and agreements, for instance by compensating producers who use environmentally friendly production techniques or by transferring clean technologies to developing countries in combination with eco-labelling by the exporting country (French, 1993, p.19; Kox, 1991, 1993). Development generally enhances governments' ability to adopt and implement policies for realising objectives of social justice and environmental protection.

So far this chapter has considered the relationship between trade and the environment and the impact of trade on development. Now, we shall turn to the application of international trade policy in practice.

4.4 The international trading order: GATT/WTO

The world trading order is based on the principles and rules that have been agreed by a process of multilateral negotiation. Rules and principles are intended to guide the behaviour of states and stimulate the orderly development of an international market economy. These principles and rules have been laid down in the General Agreement on Tariffs and Trade (GATT), which was recently incorporated in and expanded to form the World Trade Organisation (WTO) by the signature in Marrakech (Morocco) of the Final Act of the Uruguay Round of trade negotiations in April 1994. The organisation is referred to as the GATT/WTO in the rest of this chapter. The WTO has reached agreement on a large number of trade-related issues and services and on a dispute settlement system. The guiding principles of the GATT/WTO are non-discrimination, transparency, national treatment and reciprocity.

Non-discrimination

The principle of non-discrimination is fundamental to the GATT/WTO legal order. It is implemented by most favoured nation (MFN) treatment, which means that a concession agreed between two parties is automatically extended to all parties to the GATT/WTO. As a result, competition between producers in different countries is distorted to the least possible extent.

Transparency

In order to make trade policies transparent, the parties to the GATT/WTO have agreed to use tariffs as the only instrument of trade policy (art. XI). This instrument has several advantages: price competition among exporting countries remains intact, while the protective effect of a given *ad valorem* tariff may decline over time as the loss of comparative advantage in the importing country continues. Moreover, a tariff is easiest to apply in a non-discriminatory fashion. Tariffs have the additional practical advantage that they are very easy to negotiate.

National treatment

This entails the equal treatment of domestically produced and imported goods (with the exception of agreed trade policy measures). This makes it difficult or impossible for governments to introduce all kinds of prescriptions and rules that discriminate against goods produced in foreign countries.

Reciprocity

The principle of reciprocity is used as a means of balancing the rights and obligations and costs and benefits of the countries that are party to the GATT/WTO.

The GATT/WTO interferes with domestic policies only in a small number of cases, viz. those that have a particularly marked influence on trade (e.g. subsidies). Although the Uruguay round of multilateral trade negotiations has extended the impact of GATT to some new areas of domestic policy (such as rules on intellectual property rights and on direct foreign investment), it may be said that the GATT/WTO does not interfere with most domestic policies. GATT/WTO rules are applicable when goods cross borders. Basically, the way in which they are produced is not a concern of the GATT/WTO; the GATT/WTO does not relate to production processes. This entails, first, that

Plate 4.3 Street trade in Western products, Maputo, Mozambique. Photo: Ron Giling/Lineair

governments are not constrained by the GATT/WTO as to enact rules with respect to the way in which goods are produced within their jurisdiction. Conditions in the workplace, the prohibition of the use of certain inputs and, generally, limitations on the freedom of producers to choose inputs, technologies and the scale and geographical site of production may form part of the environmental policy of the nation concerned. The GATT/WTO does not limit national sovereignty in this area. The second implication is that countries are not allowed to introduce prescriptions with respect to the production processes of imported goods. As a result, an individual GATT/WTO member state is not allowed, for example, to require that imported wooden furniture should be produced from timber produced by environmentally safe production methods, even if this requirement is also applied to domestic production. This would constitute a process standard. As will be discussed below, process standards play a significant role in international environmental agreements and conflicts (for instance, in the dolphin case which is discussed below in this section).

Non-governmental organisations working in conjunction with private firms may offer a suitable alternative to official process standards. By monitoring production at the place of origin, conducting information campaigns and using targetted labelling, they can make consumers aware of their role and responsibility in environmental protection.

The contracting parties to the GATT/WTO enjoy a high degree of sovereignty over product standards that prescribe the technical specifications (i.e. quality) of goods, as long as these are implemented in the same way in relation to both domestically produced and imported goods alike. For instance, the parties are allowed to require that cars, both imported and home produced, should be fitted with catalytic converters.

Although these rules would appear to be unambiguous, they cannot preclude conflicts in the practice of international trade policy for two reasons. The first is that it is not always possible to make a clear distinction between a product and a process. This applies particularly to food and beverages, where the production process affects the taste and physical composition of the products, although they serve the same purpose and have most properties in common. A good example of this, which has a bearing on environmental matters, is the dispute between the EU and the US on the use of hormones in beef production. The EU wishes to ban all imports of beef produced with the aid of hormones. The US maintains that the hormone residues in the beef pose no threat to the health of consumers.

The second reason is that an unambiguous, non-discriminatory product standard may discriminate in practice, given that domestic producers are in specific circumstances that make compliance with the standards easy, while foreign producers may find it extremely costly to do the same. Denmark, for example, requires all soft drinks to be sold in returnable containers. The European Commission considered this to be discriminatory in relation to producers exporting to Denmark, for whom it is more costly to set up a collecting network for empty bottles. The regulation was therefore deemed to be a barrier to the free movement of goods in the EU and was forbidden. However, the European Court of Justice ruled in favour of Denmark; one of the considerations was that the protection of the environment may take precedence over free trade (Sorsa, 1992b). The contracting parties to the GATT/WTO have tried to solve such problems by drawing up an Agreement on Technical Barriers to Trade which sets rules with respect to technical standards which products may be required to meet. The basic rule is that a technical standard should serve a legitimate objective (environmental protection is explicitly cited as being one of these) and that it should distort trade as little as possible. The Agreement prefers harmonised, international standards (Sorsa, 1992a). From 1980 to 1990, the signatories to the (former) Code on Standards notified 211 technical regulations to the GATT Secretariat which were intended to protect the environment (GATT, 1992). Examples of such regulations are those relating to the composition of exhaust gases emitted by cars and the composition of pesticides and herbicides.

The general trend is that trade policy measures are not permitted to be used as instruments of environmental policy, which is in line with the general conclusion drawn in the previous section based on economic reasoning. At the same time the

---

4

The dolphin case

The most important issue with respect to the application of article XX of the GATT is whether trade policy measures may be used in one country to force other countries to adopt certain environmental policies (this is called the extraterritorial effect of domestic laws). In the dolphin case, Mexico lodged a complaint in 1991 against the US, as the US had banned imports of tuna from Mexico. The problem is that, in the eastern Pacific Ocean, shoals of yellowfin tuna often swim under schools of dolphins. When tuna is fished, dolphins may be killed in the nets, unless they are released in time. The US Marine Mammal Protection Act sets limits on dolphin catches for the domestic fishing fleet. This act also prohibits the importation of tuna from countries that have a higher rate of dolphin mortality in the catching of tuna than 25% above the US level (Charnovitz, 1993). The US claimed that, as art. XX does not state where the object of protection has to be, the exception constituted by this article could used in an extraterritorial way, which meant that US laws could be implemented in order to influence behaviour in foreign countries, i.e. to adapt Mexican rules and practices to US standards. The GATT panel that investigated the complaint and reported to the GATT Council concluded that:

1 the US was using a *process criterion* (i.e. the way tuna has been caught), which was not in conformity with GATT rules
2 an embargo was not *'necessary'* in the terms of art. XX; the US could have done more to bring about an international agreement on the protection of dolphins
3 article XX (b and g) could not be used *extraterritorially*
4 article XX could not be invoked in order to limit imports for the reason of differences in environmental regulations applied to producers (Sorsa, 1992b).

The upshot of this panel report is that a country is not allowed to use trade policy measures in order to force its trading partners to adopt the same internal policies, in this case measures to protect dolphins. The panel was of the opinion that, if dolphins were to be protected, this should be brought about by international co-operation; the US could not demonstrate to the panel that it had exhausted all options that would have been consistent with the GATT. Interestingly, the US received very little support from other contracting parties to the GATT.

GATT/WTO does not limit national sovereignty in terms of a nation's ability to pursue domestic environmental objectives with the aid of other instruments.

In particular circumstances, however, the contracting parties are allowed to deviate from these rules by virtue of article XX of the GATT '... nothing in this Agreement shall be construed to prevent the adoption or enforcement by any contracting party of measures ... (b) necessary to protect human, animal or plant life or health ... (g) relating to the conservation of exhaustible natural resources if such measures are made effective in conjunction with restrictions on domestic production or consumption ...'. The measures should be necessary and implemented in a non-discriminatory manner. It is generally accepted that 'necessary' means that other measures which do not have the effect of distorting trade are not available. The dolphin case is a good illustration of the disputes that may arise about the interpretation of this article (see Box 4).

Although some countries continue to contemplate the extraterritorial application of their laws, the dolphin panel report has clarified this issue to a very great extent. However, other questions remain with respect to the definition of the concept of 'necessity' and the scope of art. XX. In both theory and GATT/WTO practice, trade measures are deemed to be less than 'first best', which means that they become necessary only in the absence of 'first best' measures. Other trade-distorting environmental measures, including product standards, should also be 'necessary', which entails making some very difficult judgements about the relative distorting effects of alternative measures. Germany obliges car manufacturers to dispose of old cars in order to reduce waste and resource use. Is this the least distorting way of tackling the problem? With respect to the scope of art. XX, the question remains as to what is covered by the phrases 'the protection of human, animal or plant life' and 'exhaustible natural resources'. In the dolphin case, experts stated that the dolphins that were the object of protection were not members of an endangered species. The question therefore arises as to why dolphins should be protected and why tuna may be caught freely for commercial purposes.

4.5 Criteria for an optimum policy

In the above sections, we have discussed effectiveness and efficiency as criteria for an optimum policy. In this section, the discussion will be extended to various other principles that may be taken to underlie optimum policies: the principle that the user of an unpriced natural resource, e.g. a polluter, should pay for the exploitation of the resource (the polluter pays principle or PPP) and the principle of equity. These concepts warrant discussion in the context of international trade, as they may give rise to a number of specific issues and suggest solutions to international environmental problems. The PPP states that the user of a scarce service of Nature should pay the collective owners of nature, i.e. society, in order to rectify the damage caused or to compensate those whose welfare has been affected by the use of the natural service. The result should be that the scarcity of unpriced natural resources is a factor that is included in the market price. The principle of equity entails that the costs of environmental protection should be borne by those who profit or have profited from environmental degradation, bearing in mind their capacity to pay.

The application of these principles may pose difficult questions in the case of international environmental problems. Climatic change, the depletion of the ozone layer and acid rain are examples of international environmental problems where these questions arise.

The protection of the ozone layer necessitates a complete prohibition of the use of CFCs. In a purely technical sense, it is feasible to replace CFCs with other materials in almost all their applications. A complicating factor is, however, that the technical know-how has been developed by private enterprises in industrialised countries. Developing countries have argued that the decrease in the use and production of CFCs, as proposed by the industrialised countries, is not equitable. This is because, first, the latter countries have in the past emitted a large quantity of CFCs and are thus largely responsible for the problem. The second argument is that developing countries need all their scarce resources to improve their level of prosperity and cannot allow some of them to be diverted in order to buy ozone-safe technologies from private enterprise in industrialised countries (Vorlat, 1993, p.147). A number of large developing countries (such as Brazil, China and India) refused to sign the Montreal Protocol in 1987 for this reason, even though the period for phasing out the use of CFCs had been prolonged by ten years for these countries. They continued to demand additional concessions and financial and technological assistance in order to facilitate compliance. In the end, a CFC fund was created for this purpose and Brazil and India accepted the Protocol. The example shows that, in order to realise an agreement that is acceptable to all parties, the PPP may have to give way to the principle of equity. The alternative would have been to use the trade measures in the Montreal Protocol against countries that are not party to it. The parties to the Protocol may ban trade in CFCs and related products with non-parties. Given the fact that a number of large developing countries producing over 20,000 tonnes of CFCs each year refused to accept the Protocol, it is not likely that this strategy would have had much success.

The same problem occurs with respect to the issue of global warming. The UN Framework Convention on Climate Change differentiates between developed and developing countries and Article 3 states that the former 'should take the lead in combating climate change and the adverse effects thereof' (a more detailed discussion will be found in Faber, 1993). The industrialised parties recognise explicitly that their responsibilities differ in view of their historical contribution to global environmental degradation.

Developing countries weigh up the costs and benefits of participation in international environmental agreements, just as the rich countries do. The difference between the two groups of countries is that the immediate benefits of protecting global environmental resources (such as the climate) have a lower social value in developing countries than in rich countries. The opposite applies to the costs. This means that the option of staying outside an international agreement to protect certain elements of the environment, i.e. becoming a free rider or not solving the problem in hand, is more attractive for developing countries than it is for developed countries. The solution to the free rider problem in international environmental agreements may be found in the incorporation of special facilities for certain parties for which the agreement as such is not attractive. This may be a deviation from a strict application of the PPP, but is necessary on grounds of equity in order to bring about a viable agreement. The options that have been presented for protecting tropical forests (see Box 5) are a good example of the choice of instruments that has to be made.

It may prove impossible to solve the free rider problem by means of co-operative solutions. For this reason, many environmental agreements have trade provisions, in order to impose sanctions on parties to the agreement who do not comply with their obligations or to make it unattractive for non-parties to behave like free riders. A total of 127 multilateral environmental agreements were signed during the period between 1933 and 1990. Of these agreements, 17 included trade provisions, such as the above-mentioned Montreal Protocol (GATT, 1992, p.11). The question is whether the discrimination between parties and non-parties violates the non-discriminatory principle of the GATT/WTO and whether these trade provisions can be enforced under art. XX of the GATT. This is doubtful at the very least as this article was not formulated in

---

5

How should tropical forests be protected?

There are good reasons for protecting tropical forests: biodiversity is very high, they provide a means of livelihood for indigenous peoples and they absorb a massive amount of greenhouse gases. However, industrialised countries generally attach a higher value to these factors than developing countries. As a consequence, industrialised countries have sought ways to encourage developing countries to give a higher level of protection to their tropical forests. It has been suggested that a ban should be imposed on imports of tropical timber that is produced in a non-sustainable manner. This would force the developing countries concerned to harvest their forests in a careful and sustainable manner.

If one takes the facts of tropical timber production into account, however, it is very doubtful whether a ban on imports would be effective. A ban on the import of logs produced in developing countries would not have much effect, as only about 0.5% of log production in these countries is exported (GATT, 1992). If the ban were extended to cover sawn wood and wood panels made from tropical logs, this would amount to about 1% of the trees felled in developing countries, which is again insufficient to be effective. Approximately 80% of the trees felled in developing countries are used for fuel or simply disappear in the process of clearing land for agricultural production. A ban on the import of tropical timber could even reduce the incentives to manage tropical forests in a sustainable way, as the price of tropical timber would fall as a result of declining import demand.

More positive measures could create better results. If rich countries wish to maintain tropical forests, they may have to pay the developing countries for this service. It has been suggested that development contracts should be signed for the sustainable management of tropical forests and that these should include the provision of financial and technical assistance. Another proposal involves eco-labelling. If this increases the price of tropical timber produced in a sustainable manner, there will be more of an incentive to protect the forests. Given the pressures on forests that flow from poverty and land scarcity, a combination of development-related strategies is necessary.

At best, trade measures can be used as a sanction in clearly defined situations, i.e. where timber exports are the dominant cause of deforestation (which is not generally the case). A sanction is implemented after other, more efficient instruments have failed.

order to change the policies pursued by other countries, as should be clear from the dolphin case (see Box 4). Using it for this purpose might encourage its use outside the multilateral framework, perhaps for protectionist purposes.

A better solution would be to change the GATT/WTO rules. This could be done either temporarily by a waiver or permanently by amending the GATT/WTO itself. Waivers of specific GATT/WTO obligations may be granted 'provided that any such decision shall be approved by a two-thirds majority of the votes cast and that such a majority shall comprise more than half of the contracting parties' (art. XXV of GATT). However, waivers are granted in 'exceptional circumstances' only and the prevailing view is that they are of a temporary nature (GATT, 1992). A change of GATT/WTO rules will therefore be necessary in order to accommodate trade measures in environmental agreements that are of a permanent or long-term nature. This can only be brought about by unanimity.

The relationship between trade and the environment will be an important issue in the new WTO. The first paragraph of the preamble of the Agreement establishing the WTO reads:

> Recognising that their relations in the field of trade and economic endeavour should be conducted with a view to raising standards of living, ensuring full employment and a large and steadily growing volume of real income and effective demand and expanding the production and trade in goods and services, while allowing for the optimum use of the world's resources in accordance with the objective of sustainable development, seeking both to protect and preserve the environment and enhance the means for doing so in a manner consistent with their respective needs and concerns at different levels of economic development.

At the request of the countries of the European Free Trade Association (EFTA), the GATT Council decided in 1991 to convene the Group on Environmental Measures and International Trade in order to look into the compatibility of trade measures in existing multilateral environmental agreements, the multilateral transparency of national regulations which are likely to have trade effects and the trade effects of new packaging and labelling requirements aimed at protecting the environment (GATT Focus, October, 1991, p.1). This Group has been preparing the way for negotiations on these issues in the period from 1992 to 1994 (GATT Focus, No.105). In 1994, a subcommittee of the WTO PrepCom was established to take up the issue of trade and the environment.

4.6 International environmental agreements

The GATT/WTO is not a serious constraint on the introduction of domestic and international environmental policies. Whether individual countries are pursuing adequate domestic environmental policies and whether there is sufficient co-operation among the states in order to preserve the global environment are two entirely different questions. The answer to both questions has to be in the negative. With respect to international co-operation, although a large number of international agreements have been concluded in different areas of the environment (on which more will be said below), a great deal has still to be done.

A number of international environmental agreements, incorporating trade measures, have now been signed. Table 4.2 indicates the number of such agreements that have been made. The most important of these are reviewed below (Sorsa, 1992b, provides a more detailed review).

Table 4.2 Multilateral environmental agreements by subject, 1933–1990

Subject	Total	With trade provisions
Marine pollution	41	0
Marine fishing and whaling	25	0
Protection of flora and fauna	19	10
Nuclear and air pollution	13	1
Antarctica	6	0
Phytosanitary regulation	5	4
Locust control	4	0
Boundary waters	4	0
Animal cruelty	3	1
Hazardous wastes	1	1
Other	6	0
Total	127	17

Source: GATT (1992)

Whaling

One of the oldest agreements is the International Convention for the Regulation of Whaling, which came into force in 1948. Its objective is to secure the proper conservation and development of whale stocks. The agreement was ratified by 24 countries, including the most important whaling states. The International Whaling Commission, the managing body of the Convention, introduced a moratorium on whaling from 1986 onwards. Despite this, countries were allowed to continue to catch whales for 'scientific' purposes and Japan, Norway and Iceland made particular use of this opportunity. These countries have tried to persuade the International Whaling Commission to reopen the whaling grounds to normal fishing. Whaling has decreased considerably since the 1970s. In the spring of 1994, it was decided virtually unanimously (with only Japan voting against the motion) to prohibit all whaling south of the 40th parallel of the Southern hemisphere in order to create a safe haven (i.e. a reserve) for whales.

Endangered species

The Convention on the International Trade in Endangered Species of Wild Fauna and Flora (CITES, which came into force in 1975) specifically limits international trade in species that stand to become extinct. Three lists of species have been drawn up to this end. The species on the first list are in acute danger of extinction; trade is very strictly regulated and allowed only in exceptional circumstances. The parties to the Convention are required to take measures to enforce the Convention and in particular to penalise trade in these species and to return any specimens impounded to their country of origin. The Convention has been effective to a certain extent (some species have been moved from the first to a lower list as the threat of extinction has receded). Yet efficient solutions can be achieved only by internationally co-ordinated domestic policies that protect and improve the ecosystems of which these endangered species are part, as has been demonstrated by the ban on the ivory trade. At best, trade policy measures can support domestic policies. They are not substitutes for an adequate domestic policy that directly addresses the problem. The impending international agreement on biological diversity that was signed at UNCED in 1992 may be a step in this direction if it is given effect on a sufficiently wide scale.

The ozone layer

The Montreal Protocol on Substances that deplete the Ozone Layer is associated with the Vienna Convention for the Protection of the Ozone Layer. The Protocol came into force in 1989 and was renewed in 1990. The objective of the Protocol is the progressive elimination of the production and consumption of substances that deplete the ozone

Plate 4.4 A boy selling monkeys in the centre of Parimaribo, Surinam. As a result of lax law enforcement, people are more or less free to catch any animals they like in the enormous Surinam jungle and then sell them for a profit. Photo: Ron Giling/Lineair

layer (i.e. CFCs and halons). A large number of countries, representing 90% of global consumption and most of the production capacity, have ratified the Protocol. Annex A of the Protocol lists the substances that are the object of control. Trade measures are highly restrictive: trade with non-parties is completely banned.

Hazardous wastes

The Basel Convention on the Control of Transboundary Movements of Hazardous Waste and their Disposal (which took effect in 1992) is aimed at protecting countries from the dumping of hazardous waste by controlling its trans-border transportation. A number of important net importers and net exporters of waste (including the EU) are not party to the Convention. Parties are entitled to prohibit the import of hazardous waste and are bound to prohibit its export if the importing country does not consent in writing to the specific import. It is prohibited to trade in hazardous waste with non-parties and exports are allowed only if the exporting country itself does not possess the technical means of disposing of the waste. In March 1994, 64 countries (including Australia, Canada, the EU, Japan and the US) agreed on an immediate prohibition of exports of hazardous waste to developing countries. Waste that is intended for recycling in developing countries is exempted from the prohibition until 1997.

The definition of hazardous waste is fairly broad. There are many borderline cases, such as scrap metals. It is expected that the Convention and the agreement prohibiting exports of hazardous waste to developing countries will affect the trade in various scrap metals, making the recycling of metals more expensive, particularly by non-member parties. The reason for this is that the Convention makes clear that hazardous waste should be disposed of in its country of origin. Where least-cost solutions for the disposal of waste (including scrap metals) are located in foreign countries, the costs will rise.

The trade measures will be beneficial to developing countries. These countries can save the cost of setting up and maintaining the staff and infrastructure which are needed to monitor imports of potentially dangerous substances.

This brief review shows that international co-operation has led to agreements in various areas of environmental policy. The Whaling Convention and the Montreal Protocol are agreements that address narrowly defined problems for the solution of which both technical means and public support are available. Under these conditions, international co-operation has the best prospects. For broad and complex problems such as climate change and the management of the oceans, effective international co-operation is much more difficult to organise. The interests of states and pressure groups are diverse and this may make it difficult to formulate coalition-building compromises. Public support is not easily forthcoming in very complex matters. The Framework Convention on Climate Change that was signed in Rio de Janeiro in 1992 addresses such a difficult and complex problem. The mitigation of the growth of energy use and its transformation is far from costless and the distribution of gains and losses over countries and individuals poses very sensitive political problems.

A second conclusion which may be drawn from the above review is that trade measures are used as a supportive device and are necessary in order to make free riding unattractive to non-parties to the agreements. The exceptions to this rule are CITES and the Basel Convention that were formulated expressly with the aim of regulating the international trade in endangered species and in hazardous waste. Neither of these agreements, CITES in particular, has proved to be very efficient.

4.7 Conclusion

I have argued that international trade as such may stimulate production that causes environmental damage. However, international trade and competition may also contribute to the economic use of scarce natural resources. Production processes often exploit the environment at a rate that is not sustainable and is incompatible with social preferences. The consumption and transport of traded goods may have the same effect. I showed that it would not be wise, in terms of environmental policy goals, to curtail international trade. This would be both ineffective and inefficient. Both economic theory and the GATT/WTO would assert that trade policy measures are not the best instruments of environmental policy. Policy measures that directly address sources of environmental damage in production or consumption are more effective and more efficient.

Developing countries wish to grow and to export goods in order to achieve higher levels of prosperity. The challenge of sustainable development is to bring about growth without causing environmental destruction. As far as trade is concerned, the diversification of exports by improving market access and the transfer of 'clean' technologies have been suggested as means of contributing towards sustainable development. It may be necessary to have trade policy instruments at hand as a last resort in the framework of international environmental co-operation, in order to forestall free riding by countries that do not accept reasonable obligations.

Most industrialised countries and many developing countries have introduced environmental policies that attempt to reduce the environmental pollution caused by production and consumption. The GATT/WTO is not much of a constraint as long as no trade measures are used. Specific instruments can be implemented in exceptional cases and if certain conditions have been met (see art. XX of GATT and the GATT/WTO Agreement on Technical Barriers to Trade). The fact that international environmental policies have not yet succeeded in bringing about sustainable development throughout the world cannot be blamed on restraints imposed by the GATT/WTO. The divergent needs, interests and insights of countries and groups within countries have apparently prevented the states of the world from tackling the global and continental environmental problems in a more effective manner.

It has been decided to start negotiations in the new World Trade Organisation (WTO) on the relationship between trade policy and environmental policy. In the preceding sections, a number of issues where international agreement does not exist or is incomplete were discussed. One issue is the problem of the interpretation of the concepts of 'necessity' (i.e. have potential alternatives to trade measures been fully exploited?), 'proportionality' (is the damage to international trade worth the environmental benefit that is generated?) and 'transparency' (are the measures clear, simple and is information readily available?). Clarification is needed. A second issue relates to the meaning and role of scientific evidence and methodologies for risk assessment and risk acceptability. Another issue is whether the trade provisions in a number of multilateral environmental agreements are compatible with the GATT/WTO.

The issue of the protection of the environment by the use of trade barriers will be hotly debated during the remainder of this decade. Uncompetitive industries will use environmental arguments to obtain protection. Developing countries need growing exports for their development and cannot be expected to apply standards which the industrialised countries have only recently introduced. The governments of large countries will try to get their way by taking unilateral action in order to achieve political success. The risk is that the multilateral world trading order will be the victim of such action. This would be detrimental to the opportunities for fostering the development of poor countries and for creating a climate conducive to international environmental co-operation.

5

International co-operation: the European Union

Gerrit Vonkeman

5.1 Introduction

International policy making is a complex and time-consuming business. At a national level, in a democratic system, people are accustomed to well-defined decision-making bodies like governments and parliaments, exercising full jurisdiction over their territories and taking decisions in accordance with carefully defined, consistent rules and procedures. Decision making on these lines is both open and accessible and allows interest groups and citizens to exercise their rights of public participation and to make use of the opportunities for lobbying politicians and governments. As a rule, these activities receive plenty of attention in the media. The criterion in the decision-making process is clear: the decision taken should be in the interests of the country as a whole. Moreover, those who bear ultimate responsibility for such decisions, i.e. the elected politicians, have to face their constituencies from time to time in order to defend them. Once decisions have been taken, there is likewise a well-defined system of implementation and enforcement to ensure that they are made effective.

Internationally, however, the situation is entirely different. There is a wide variety of regimes, each of which covers a limited territory and deals with a limited range of subjects. In a large number of cases, such regimes have no powers in their own right and are instead dependent on the unanimous agreement of the participating states. These states, in turn, are generally eager to maintain unlimited jurisdiction over their own territories. Self-interest is paramount. Hence the criterion for decision making in a regime is the maximisation of the aggregate benefit to all participants. The process is one of negotiation, characterised by confidentiality. It is a closed system, which defines its own rules, based on unanimity. There is little scope for incorporating any checks and balances. As a rule, systems of implementation and enforcement are inefficient and sometimes totally absent. It is difficult, therefore, for citizens and interest groups to interfere with the process and media coverage is limited. International negotiations are the work of governments, seldom of elected politicians, and the result is a lack of proper public accountability.

This chapter discusses the decision-making process in relation to environmental policy under the regime of the European Union. In many respects, this regime is quite extraordinary. When it was established in the 1950s under the name of the European Community, the six founding member states agreed to create a well-equipped supranational regime with its own institutions, administration, court and sources of funding, that could in principle be endowed with its own supranational powers. These would override national sovereignties. Given the sensitivity of nation states to any diminution of their powers, it was agreed at the outset that all important decisions and particularly those that would entail the transfer of sovereignty, would be taken only on the basis of unanimity.

The European Community has gradually expanded over the years, not only in terms of the number of member states, but also in terms of the areas covered by common policies and in the systems, procedures and competencies in relation to decision making. Although the European Community was not created for the purpose of producing an environmental policy, the environment has emerged as an important policy area. This chapter provides a historical perspective on the development of process of environmental policy making within the European Union, breaking it down into four separate periods.

Plate 5.1 Brussels, 16 December 1994. A preparatory meeting of the new European Commission chaired by Jacques Santer. Photo: European Union

The first period (Section 5.2) covers the period from the Treaty of Rome (1957) until 1972. Environmental policy was non-existent during this period. The second period (Section 5.3) begins with the first Environment Action Programme and runs through until 1986, covering the second and third action programmes. During this period an official environmental policy was developed but progress was slow, geared to the most reluctant member states. The third period (Section 5.4) starts with the Single European Act (SEA) of 1987 and ends in December 1993 when the Maastricht Treaty came into force, creating the European Union. This period embraced two major additions to the original treaties and was affected by the globalisation of environmental policy, encompassed in the Brundtland Report of 1987 and the Rio Conference of 1992, which is reflected in the EC's Fifth Environment Action Programme, *Towards Sustainability* (Commission of the European Community, 1992). The fourth period runs from late 1993 and continues at the time of writing (Section 5.5). Various developments such as the Fifth Environment Action Programme are examined and possible future trends in the environmental policy of the European Union are presented, leading to the final summary of constraints and opportunities (Section 5.6).

5.2 The first period: 1957–1972

During the Second World War, not only were the allied governments in close contact with each other but several of them also lived in exile in the same city: London. It was there that the idea of some form of close post-war co-operation was first conceived. Immediately after the war, the United Nations was founded as a global forum and the Benelux (consisting of Belgium, the Netherlands and Luxembourg) was created as a customs union in Europe.

Ten years later, once the Marshall Plan had had its intended effect of placing Western Europe on the road to economic recovery, further steps were considered. These were based partly on a desire to intertwine the national European coal and steel industries so closely as to virtually rule out the possibility of one of them being instrumental in preparing for a new war and partly on a wish to improve the economic position of the Western European countries by creating a common European market.

The first European community, established in 1951 by France, Germany, Italy and the three Benelux countries, was the European Coal and Steel Community (ECSC), the aims of which were to modernise the industry, increase production and create a common market for coal and steel.

The European Economic Community (EEC) was founded in 1957 under the Treaty of Rome. Article 2 of the Treaty formulates its aim as 'the creation of a common market … the harmonic development of economic activities, a continuous and balanced expansion, an increased standard of living …'

At the same time a third community, the European Community for Atomic Energy (EURATOM) was established, designed to promote the rapid development and expansion of the peaceful use of atomic energy. It was based on the commonly held notion of the time that nuclear energy would be the most important resource for ensuring the development and modernisation of production.

Looking at the aims of the three communities, it is clear that economic development was the main priority. Environmental protection was not an issue at this time. Not surprisingly, therefore, no environmental protection measures were taken by the communities during the first 15 years of their operation. Whilst it is true that a number of the measures taken during this period had environmental effects, they were initially taken with the aim of harmonising national product legislation.

The treaties created various institutions and defined their responsibilities and competences. Many of these remain unchanged and for easy reference the institutions as they exist within the European Union are set out in Box 1.

5.3 The second period: 1972–1986

In the late 1960s, awareness of environmental deterioration was growing. The United States adopted a National Environmental Policy Act (NEPA); the United Nations prepared for a new conference and convened it in Stockholm in June 1972. In the same

---

1

The institutions of the European Union

The decision-making body of the European Union is the Council of the European Union (the Council), in which each member state is represented by one person. For general, political affairs, the ministers of foreign affairs form the Council; for more technical areas (such as agriculture and the environment), the Council is made up of the competent, national ministers. The European Summit consists of the President of France and the Prime Ministers of the other member states.

Council decisions must be based on proposals made by the European Commission (the Commission), except in relation to a number of new policy areas. The Commission acts as one coherent body and is the only institution with a right of initiative. Each member state nominates one Commissioner, the four larger ones (Germany, Italy, France and the United Kingdom) an additional one each. Each Commissioner is responsible for one or more of the Directorates-General and/or Staff Departments, of which there are over 20.

The European Parliament (EP; an elected body since 1979) originally had only limited (if far-reaching) decisive powers: it could dismiss the Commission as a whole and reject the budget. For the rest, however, it was merely an advisory body. Its powers have gradually increased in the course of time, although it is on no occasion empowered to overrule a unanimous Council decision.

The Economic and Social Committee (ECOSOC) is an advisory body of tripartite composition: employers, trade unions and 'the public interest'. Its members are nominated by the member states, which have so far refused to nominate representatives of environmental interests. There is one exception: one German member out of 185 represents a federation of environmental groups.

Any conflict between the institutions and/or the member states and/or EU citizens regarding activities performed under the treaties may be brought before the European Court of Justice. Until recently, the Court had no sanctions available to it by which it could enforce its verdicts.

The Court of Accounts and the European Investment Bank complete the list of institutions.

context, the European Community also decided to embark on an environmental policy. The European Commission had already published a 'First Communication' on 22 July 1971 and this was followed by a draft First Action Programme on 24 March 1972.

The decision to embark on a common environmental policy was taken formally at the European Summit Meeting of October 1972, in Paris. The first 'Environmental' Council meeting was held on 19 July 1973 and the principles of a common environmental policy were agreed. On 22 November 1973 the Council passed a resolution adopting the First Action Programme of the European Communities regarding the Environment (see Box 2). It was agreed that the action programmes would cover a five-year period, the first of which was to end on 31 December 1976.

During this period three new members joined the Community: Denmark, Ireland and the United Kingdom.

2

The First Action Programme

Although the programme is too complex to be discussed in its entirety, there are a number of principles which are worth mentioning.

In the first place, the programme stresses the importance of prevention rather than cure. The idea is that this should apply to both technical and political decisions: any measure which is under consideration at a national or Community level should be preceded by a study of its impact on the environment. This notion was clearly inspired by the introduction of environmental impact assessments under the NEPA in the United States and was strongly recommended by the Organisation for Economic Co-operation and Development (OECD).

Secondly, it refers to the polluter pays principle, under which the cost of any measures taken to prevent or abate pollution and nuisances should be paid for by the polluter and not by the state. The programme does, however, leave open the possibility of ignoring this principle during the first stage of environmental policy, provided that this does not result in a distortion of competition between manufacturers in the member states.

Another important principle rules that member states should neither cause transboundary problems nor create problems for the economic development of Third World countries.

Although not explicitly formulated, the programme implies that there is a need to respect the so-called 'stand-still' principle, i.e. the overall situation should not worsen in the future and problems should not be 'solved' by shifting pollution from problem areas to relatively clean areas.

The programme also stresses the importance of public participation, although the need to inform and educate the public is given much more attention than the need to involve the public in decision making.

Finally, there are two principles that are particularly interesting in the light of recent discussions and to which we shall be returning later on in the chapter. The first is that the level of action (i.e. local, regional, national or Community) should be determined carefully, in order to secure maximum efficacy and efficiency. In fact, this is what has since been referred to as the principle of 'subsidiarity'. Secondly, the programme underlines that Community policy should be based on a long-term strategy.

Source: *Official Journal* C 112, 20 December 1973.

The First Action Programme

When considering European environmental policy, it is important to remember that its introduction was not formally written into the original treaties (i.e. the ECSC, EURATOM and EEC treaties). Environmental policy therefore remained subordinate to the basic goals of these treaties and had to be based on existing articles in these treaties.

Two of these in particular were usually cited as grounds for environmental measures. Article 100 mandates the Council to *harmonise national measures* regarding production and products which might distort competition. The other, article 235, is a general mandate under which the Council is empowered to take measures which, although not provided for by the treaties, contribute to the promotion of the treaties' basic goals. In both cases, decisions have to be unanimous.

As article 100 could be applied only when a member state had taken the lead in initiating new legislation, one of the earliest actions was the creation of an Information Agreement on 5 March 1973. This agreement compels the member states to inform the Commission immediately of all drafts of national legislation, administrative measures or international initiatives such as may directly influence the functioning of the common market or have an effect on the Community's environmental legislation or programmes. The Commission is subsequently bound to inform all other member states (see Box 3).

Additional general rules and clarifications were published during the course of the First Action Programme, for example on the polluter pays principle, but formal legislation remained thin on the ground. The legislative instruments include directives, regulations and decisions. Directives are a form of binding legislation that is directed at all the member states. In order to become effective, a directive has to be implemented, i.e. the member states have to adopt national legislation that complies with all the demands contained in the directive. As a rule, a maximum period of two years is

---

3

The consequences of the Information Agreement

The member states are obliged to postpone the decision in question for two months in order to allow the Commission to consider Community-wide measures. If the Commission then announces an intention to draft measures at a Community level, the member state in question must postpone its decision for a further five months, in order to give the Commission enough time to submit the necessary texts.

Similar procedures apply to the way in which member states should take positions on international initiatives, the intention being that the Commission can try to forge a common position.

Formally, the Information Agreement is not a Community measure, but a voluntary agreement between the member states and the Commission, made during an Environment Council (outside an official session and without full Council status).

Source: Agreement (...) on information for the Commission and for the Member States with a view to possible harmonisation throughout the Communities concerning the protection of the environment. Official Journal C9, 15 March 1973, p. 1; supplemented by Official Journal C86, 20 July 1974, p.2.

allowed for implementation. A regulation is also a form of binding legislation but is directly applicable, while a decision is similar to a regulation but has more limited scope (for example, it may address a specific group (such as farmers) or be of limited duration).

Although a directive on waste was adopted in the course of 1975, most texts have concerned water only and have been issued in part in order to enforce international conventions. Among the earliest measures were the directives on the quality of bathing water and of surface water intended for the abstraction of drinking water. Both directives have caused problems and feature on the British 'hit list for repatriation' (see Section 5.5). They are presently under revision.

A third problematic directive is that on 'pollution caused by certain dangerous substances discharged into the aquatic environment of the Community'. This directive provides a framework for 'subsidiary directives' on the release of more than 100 substances into inland waters and the territorial seas and is intended to ensure that international conventions are implemented consistently throughout the Community.

Before this directive could be adopted, however, there was a fierce debate on standard setting between the United Kingdom and the continental member states. As an island in the Western part of the Community, the UK did not suffer from transboundary water pollution (and suffered relatively little from air pollution). It felt that its manufacturers and farmers should be able to benefit from this situation by being allowed to discharge certain substances into the rivers and the sea as long as this did not cause any problems. It hence opted for the use of *quality standards*.

Most of the continental member states and the Commission, on the other hand, preferred the use of *emission standards*. The environmental argument was that 'black list' substances were so dangerous that they should not be allowed to enter the environment at all and that any quality standard other than zero would therefore be unacceptable. This meant that uniform emission standards would have to be applied, based on the best available technologies. In addition, emission standards had the advantage of not distorting competition.

As a compromise, the member states accepted the possibility of using both types of standard and the conditions and mutual relationships were formulated on complex but non-committal lines. Hence the debate simply continued when the first subsidiary directive was published in draft form and it took another six years before it was adopted. Although further progress has been made since then, standard setting has remained a much debated issue.

The Second and Third Action Programmes

In the light of the above, it is hardly astonishing that the Second and Third Action Programmes neither reflected any spectacular successes nor announced any challenging new initiatives. During the Second Action Programme, which ran from 1977 to 1981, guidance was given on the evaluation of the cost of pollution control to industry. The first substantial air quality directive was adopted in 1980; it concerned sulphur dioxide and suspended particles. With regard to water quality, directives on the quality of fresh water needed to support fish life, shellfish water and drinking water completed the already existing set, together with legislation on sampling, monitoring and information exchange. The Community also implemented several international conventions and adopted a directive on groundwater protection. With respect to waste, a directive on dangerous waste was added.

Chemical substances in general became a major issue in EC policy making. This was partly due to the fact that the United States had produced a Toxic Substances Control Act (TSCA), under which manufacturers were required to submit pre market notifications of all new chemicals, for which purpose they were obliged to produce the results of a number of tests. It was accepted that the Community would have to consider adopting the American approach in order to avoid creating a need for a further series of different, costly tests. Yet, it was only after protracted debate that it finally proved possible to agree on some form of EC legislation. This took the form of an amendment to an existing directive originally issued in 1967; for this reason it became popularly known as the 'Sixth Amendment'.

In the meantime, a number of serious accidents with chemical plants had occurred both in Europe (at Flixborough in the UK, Geleen in the Netherlands, Basel in Switzerland and Seveso in Italy) and elsewhere (Bhopal in India being the most notable example). The Commission responded by issuing a directive on major accident hazards, usually referred to as the *Seveso Directive* that was eventually ready for implementation in 1982. The slow development of EC environmental policy making during the second stage was neither unusual nor limited to pollution-related issues.

Plate 5.2 'Dead march for the River Rhine'. The Sandoz disaster in 1986 heightened international awareness of industrial pollution and gave rise to fierce protests. Photo: ANP Foto

Two examples illustrate the tardiness of the policy process: environmental impact assessments (EIAs) and bird protection. Though very different as environmental issues, they have a great deal in common in terms of the problems they have caused in the decision-making procedure. It was felt by some member states that legislation on bird protection and EIAs could well restrict the extent to which they would be able to make use of their own territories and thus affect domestic physical planning. It was particularly difficult to relate the interests of bird protection to the basic goals in the treaties. More importantly, however, any new legislation on bird protection would have to include rules on the protection of habitats. Several member states, Denmark in particular, were extremely reluctant to extend the jurisdiction of the Community to this domain. The bird directive was agreed in 1979, albeit without a section on habitats. It was not until more than ten years later that this was added. In the case of EIAs, France feared considerable national and transboundary problems in the event of EIAs having to be applied to the large number of nuclear plants it was planning to build, many of which were to be located in border areas. It therefore took many years and over 20 (internal) drafts before a formal Commission proposal was formulated in 1985.

The Third Action Programme, covering 1982–1986, also lacked inspiration. In the meantime, Greece had joined the Community, which meant the accession of another poor member state (after Ireland) and the need to pay more attention to typically Mediterranean problems. The Community's economic position was poor at this time, with high rates of unemployment. For this reason, the programme emphasised the possibility that environmental protection might create jobs.

It also became clear that the adoption of Community measures was no guarantee that they would automatically become effective. Implementation and enforcement were often poor. Beside stressing the importance of timely and complete implementation, the programme also underlined the necessity of integrating environmental concerns into other policy areas.

In addition, two areas of increasing concern underlined the need for new areas of Community action. Firstly, it became apparent that a process of acidification was causing serious damage to the forests of the Northern part of the Community, particularly in its most powerful member state, the Federal Republic of Germany. Germany itself reacted immediately. Its budget for environmental research was considerably increased, to a level above that of the United States; resources were targeted primarily at studies on air pollution problems (Vonkeman, 1989). The Federal Republic also drafted powerful legislation on emissions from large combustion plants and became a strong supporter of the installation of catalytic converters in cars.

Secondly, it was a time when waste scandals mushroomed all around the world, resulting not only from irresponsible dumping in the past (such as the seepage of chemical wastes in residential areas at Love Canal in the United States and in Lekkerkerk in the Netherlands), but also from the dubious practice of 'waste tourism', often involving developing countries as the hosts (these problems of hazardous wastes are covered in Blowers, 1996).

Despite the attention which the Community gave to environmental problems, such as air quality and waste management, the results were disappointing from an environmental point of view (see Box 4).

4

Conflicts over waste control, and air and water pollution

Progress was slow in the domain of air quality. On the one hand, the United Kingdom was very reluctant to accept sulphur dioxide legislation for its many coal-fired power stations. On the other hand, the Mediterranean states regarded acidification as a problem affecting primarily the Northern (i.e. rich) part of the Community. For a while, the Commission attempted to put together a package deal, combining acidification abatement with forest fire control in one draft directive. However, it was later forced to drop this approach. Ultimately, a directive on large combustion plants was agreed in 1984. Air quality standards for nitrogen dioxide were set in 1985. As far as car exhaust emissions were concerned, although a directive on the lead content of petrol was likewise agreed in 1985, it was not until after the introduction of voting by qualified majority that emission standards were adopted that required the installation of catalytic converters.

In the field of dangerous waste, a directive on transfrontier shipments within the Community was agreed at the end of 1984. The problems of 'waste tourism' had to be tackled at a higher level, in the framework of the Basel Convention that was agreed much later (see Chapter 1 and Blowers, 1996).

In the water sector and again after difficult and lengthy negotiations, subsidiary directives were agreed for cadmium, mercury discharges outside the chloro-alkali industry, hexachlorocyclohexane and various other substances.

The situation in the mid-1980s

It is clear from the above that, up to the mid-1980s, the European Community failed to demonstrate any significant leadership qualities in the field of environmental protection. To a large extent, this was a deliberate choice.

As in the United States, European scientists and businessmen began to meet in the late 1960s in order to discuss the future of the environment. Although the first meeting place was in Greece, the group later came to be known as the Club of Rome. Its first publication, entitled *The Limits to Growth* (Meadows, 1972), received more attention in Europe than in the United States (see Box 5).

The Community remained devoid of any vision for a further ten years. In the meantime, there were a number of reports including 'Global 2000' (US Council on Environmental Quality and Department of State, 1980) in the United States, the Interfutures Report of the OECD (US Council on Environmental Policy and Department of State 1981), the Brandt Commission's report on the development of the Third World (Independent Commission on International Development Issues, 1980) and a 'World Conservation Strategy' produced by the World Wildlife Fund (WWF), the International Union for the Conservation of Nature and Natural Resources (IUCN) and the United Nations Environment Programme (UNEP) (IUCN, UNEP, WWF, 1980). None of these documents, all of which were aimed at building a long-term strategy, had much of an impact on Community policy.

5

A vision of the future

The late Dr Sikko Mansholt, a European Commissioner for agriculture and vice-chairman of the Commission, developed a great interest in the ideas of the Club of Rome. In February 1972, he sent his fellow Commissioners a letter in which he suggested that the Commission should draw up a 'last will and testament' for its successors, in which it addressed a number of major problems of global importance. (The term of the Commission was due to expire at the end of that year.)

Noting that no single government in the world was apparently capable of coping with the current economic problems of employment, inflation and monetary control, Mansholt wrote that even more fundamental and formidable problems were emerging: the growth of the world population, food scarcity, industrialisation, pollution and the depletion of natural resources. Among the solutions to these problems were meaningful employment, true democracy, equal opportunities for all and the rapid development of the Third World. Mansholt felt that neither the United Nations nor the United States would provide the necessary leadership: this would have to come from Europe.

He then went on to suggest that:

1 priority be given to food production and investments also made in 'uneconomic agricultural production'
2 resource consumption per capita be considerably reduced and offset by an increase in non-material consumption
3 the lifetime of products be increased, resource wastage prevented and the production of 'non-essential products' stopped
4 pollution and the depletion of the stock of raw materials be reduced.

He concluded that society could not be based on material growth alone and proposed the replacement of the gross national product as a key indicator of prosperity by the 'gross national happiness' (Bonheur National Brut, BNB). The Community, he said, should develop a strict 'European economic plan' directed at maximising BNB and a five-year programme for developing a production system that was clean, based on the recycling of raw materials and which yielded products with a long lifetime. Economic and financial incentives should be used as additional instruments.

Mansholt raised these important issues 20 years or more before they were recognised as fundamental to economic and environmental health. He was given little support at the time. In fact, the only response which he initially received from his colleagues was a question as to whether he wished 'to transform them all into hippies' (Mansholt, private communication).

Only one of the French Commissioners, Raymond Barre, reacted. In a letter dated 9 June 1972, he expressed fierce opposition to Mansholt's scheme. Barre made clear that he believed firmly in technological innovation, including the massive introduction of fast-breeder nuclear reactors and in the ability of the market to provide the right response in the event of certain problems becoming too serious. Mansholt's initiative was ignored.

This lack of vision and inertia was not restricted solely to the domain of environmental policy. In fact, most Community policies came under increasing criticism and the Community found itself labouring under an almost complete lack of decisiveness and progress. When it gradually became apparent, in the early 1980s, that the planned accession of Portugal and Spain, which were recognised as being 'difficult' countries, might bring the decision-making process to a complete standstill, the Commission finally took measures to break the deadlock and create a new momentum. In the first place, it commissioned a study of 'the costs of non-Europe' or rather, the advantages of a single, open, internal market. The resulting, 17 volume Cecchini Report sketched a very rosy picture of an 'open market' (see Box 6).

Taking the Cecchini Report as its starting point, the Commission then produced a 'white paper on the internal market' (EC, 1985). It summarised the advantages of a single market, listed the almost 400 Community measures which would be needed in order to give effect to a single market and highlighted the inadequacies of the decision-making system. It identified the legislation that would be needed to remove the physical, technical and fiscal barriers to an open internal market. The Commission urged the member states to make firm commitments towards completing the single market and to changing the rules on decision making. The latter would clearly necessitate a change in the treaties. The occasion should also be used, the Commission argued, to 'legalise' a number of existing Community policies, notably in the area of environmental protection and research and technology. Initially, the completion of the single market and the amendment of the treaties formed the subjects of two separate texts. These were later combined in the European Act, referred to in some countries as the Single European Act or the Acte Unique.

The second period, during which the first Community-wide environmental legislation was drafted, was characterised by slow progress and poor results. The former was due to the fact that all Council decisions were required to be unanimous, which implied that reluctant member states could block any decision to which they were opposed. Negotiating a compromise which was acceptable to all and yet still had some force therefore became a lengthy process.

The need for unanimity was also the cause of the ineffectiveness of the legislation. Given the fact that several countries (most of them from the Mediterranean region) had not developed any environmental legislation of their own, the Council usually preferred weak legislation to no legislation at all. In these circumstances and in spite of the criticism of the (powerless) European Parliament, the Commission generally drafted legislation which already took account of a possible final compromise.

The Cecchini Report

The report concluded that the present, fragmented state of the European market represented an annual loss of at least ECU 200 billion. If all the major barriers were swept away and firms and organisations in the EC made full use of the new opportunities, the result would be an average increase of 4.5% in the EC's gross domestic product, in combination with an average reduction of some 6% in consumer prices, a reduction in public expenditure, an improvement in the EC's overall balance of trade and the creation of nearly 2 million new jobs. The Report barely mentioned the word 'environment'.

Source: Cecchini, P. 1992: *The European Challenge*, Børsen International Publishers.

Another constraint was that all legislation had to be based on the original treaties, which did not contain any provisions in relation to the environment. For this reason, reluctant countries could easily claim that environmental legislation was hampering their economic development and hence threaten to lodge an appeal at the European Court.

5.4 The third period: 1987–1993

The Single European Act

The inception of the third period is marked by the coming into force of the Single European Act (SEA) on 1 July 1987. The member states (which now also included Portugal and Spain) committed themselves to completing an open internal market by the end of 1992 (although this was not a legally binding date). Article 13 of the SEA defines the open internal market as follows (via an amendment to article 8a of the EEC Treaty): 'The internal market shall comprise an area without internal frontiers in which the free movement of goods, persons, services and capital is ensured in accordance with the provisions of this Treaty'.

Most of the measures included in the SEA are subdivided into further categories. Further on in this chapter, we shall discuss their possible effects on the environment. These may be either direct or, where they result in a shift in economic activities, indirect.

The SEA has affected the environment policy of the Community in at least three ways:

1 directly, by giving environment policy a legal basis and creating a number of instruments for implementing it
2 semi-directly, by defining changes in the decision-making procedures of the EC institutions in relation to points that had previously formed important stumbling blocks for environmental decisions
3 indirectly, since environmental policy in an open internal market was bound to differ from that in the former situation.

Basically, the SEA makes environmental protection a Community goal in its own right. The main objectives and principles of an environmental policy are listed in article 130R: environmental policy is intended to preserve, protect and improve environmental quality, contribute towards the protection of human health and realise a prudent and rational utilisation of natural resources. It is to be based on the principles of preventive action, the rectification of damage at the source and the polluter pays. Environmental protection requirements should become a component of other EC policies (particularly with respect to the common agricultural policy and the regional, social and development policies); this is a process known as 'external integration'. EC environmental policy should take account of scientific and technical data, regional environmental conditions, the potential benefits and costs of both action and the absence of action and economic and social development. Finally, the principle of *subsidiarity* (already introduced in the First Action Programme) was now formally extended to environmental policy, implying the necessity of taking action at the most appropriate level.

The main obstacle with regard to decision making on environmental matters has traditionally been the demand for unanimity. In practice, this has meant that legislation has always been a compromise and that it has tended to gravitate towards the slowest-moving country in the Community. This is frequently referred to as the 'convoy principle'. Under article 130S, the SEA has the effect of prolonging this situation in relation to measures based on environmental protection in its own right. However, the Council may now decide to vote by qualified majority, although such a decision has to be taken unanimously.

A second point is that many environmental protection decisions are now considered as harmonisation measures, in the framework of the completion of the single market. One of the articles in the SEA, article 100A, is intended to speed up such measures. It states that such decisions are to be taken by qualified majority, which means that one single member state can no longer block a decision. A further aspect of this particular point is that the European Parliament has a crucial role to play in these cases. The European Parliament has traditionally been more 'environmentally friendly' than the Commission or the Council. This should not be seen as some sort of value judgement, for there are very practical reasons for this. As the Commission has to propose realistic legislation, it always starts by making a proposal that is somewhat tougher than the final compromise which it expects will ultimately be reached. The demand for unanimity in the Council usually weakens this carefully worded Commission proposal. In the past, the European Parliament used to demand stricter standards than the Commission. It was often said that the Parliament could easily afford to be environmentally friendly because its attitude had no direct consequences. It has now become clear, however, that the Single European Act has not changed the Parliament's attitude towards environmental protection.

The European Parliament's new powers are as follows. If the Council wishes to decide on a Commission proposal and in doing so to ignore a recommendation made by the Parliament, it is obliged to make its decision provisional and then return it to the Parliament for a second reading. The Parliament is then entitled to draw up a formal amendment based on its views. If it does so, the Commission has to set out its own position on such an amendment, because the Commission is the only body that can make proposals to the Council. In such a situation, however, the Commission is under pressure to be at least as 'environmentally friendly' as the Parliament. The final decision rests with the Council. However, if the Parliament has amended the proposal in question, the Council may reject the amendment only by unanimous vote. This is a very important point, as is illustrated by the case of car exhaust emissions (see Box 7).

Article 100A is likewise important in that it states that, where health, safety or the protection of consumers and the environment are concerned, the Commission will base any decision on a high level of protection. Article 100A's field of application is not limited to the proposals listed in the White Paper alone. All other harmonisation measures, including those in the field of environmental protection, may be based on it. Once it has been decided to base a decision on article 100A, it then follows that voting is by qualified majority and that the European Parliament is guaranteed a strong role.

The case of car exhaust emissions

Emission demands for car exhausts in Europe may be divided into three categories. As far as large cars are concerned, it was accepted that, as from a given date, American standards would apply and that the cars would have to be equipped with three-way catalytic converters.

The case of cars in the medium-size range had already been dealt with before the Single European Act came into force. There was a large majority in Council in favour of standards which were weaker than those applying in the US, with only Denmark, the Netherlands and Germany in favour of stricter standards. Unanimity had to be reached and the choice was between weak standards and no standards, as it was obvious that there would not be any unanimity on strict standards. The Netherlands and Germany decided to go for a compromise, but Denmark blocked the decision until the Single European Act came into force on 1 July 1987. In the same month, the question of car emission standards was again placed on the Council agenda, this time actually under the Danish presidency, but Denmark was outvoted under the new rules.

As a next step, the European Commission proposed standards for small cars. Again, these were much more lenient than those imposed by the United States government. This time, the European Parliament opted for much tougher standards during its first debate on the issue. After lengthy negotiations, the Council finally decided to adopt lenient standards, in a procedure in which Denmark, the Netherlands and Greece were outvoted. A number of other countries which were theoretically in favour opted for the compromise, since the choice was again between a compromise on lenient standards and no standards at all. Now, however, because the views of the European Parliament had been ignored, the European Parliament was entitled to give the Council's decision a second reading. It maintained its original position and formally amended the compromise with the effect that the standards imposed were effectively equivalent to those applying in the US.

Once the European Parliament had given its verdict, the Commission had to adopt a standpoint; it decided to back the European Parliament. This placed the Council in a difficult position. It could reject Parliament's amendments only by a unanimous vote and this was impossible because of the attitude taken by Denmark, the Netherlands and Greece (as well as Germany, in principle). On the other hand, it could accept the amendments by a qualified majority vote, but this would have required a handful of countries to change their minds. The third alternative was not to arrive at any decision at all within three months. In this case, the proposal would have been automatically rejected. If this had happened, there would have been no standards for small cars, a situation which would have met with strong opposition from the motor car manufacturers. In the event, the Council reached a compromise on American equivalent standards, which meant that, as from 1993, all new cars would have to be equipped with regulated three-way catalytic converters. Obviously, this also implied that the decision previously taken on medium-sized cars would have to be adapted.

The importance of the new Single European Act in this field has been in changing the nature of the alternatives facing the Council. Whereas, in the past, the Council had to choose between lenient standards and no standards at all, the options now are either tough standards or no standards at all. It is clear that the European Parliament has played a very important role in this respect in promoting the interests of the environment in Europe.

The Fourth Action Programme (1987–1992)

The Fourth Action Programme was drafted at the same time as the SEA was completed. It took advantage of the new opportunities offered by the SEA and listed five priority areas:

1 the implementation and enforcement of Community legislation
2 a substance-oriented and source-oriented approach to environmental policy, in particular in respect of pollution prevention
3 the dissemination of information, which meant in concrete terms the production of a kind of 'freedom of environmental information' directive and a thrice-yearly Community Report on the state of the environment
4 the relationship between environmental protection and the creation of jobs
5 the creation of new policy instruments (such as financial and economic incentives and communicative instruments) in addition to legislation.

The SEA not only created an atmosphere of economic 'Europhoria', but also fostered a revival in environmental thinking. During the European Year of the Environment, which lasted from 1 March 1987 to 1 March 1988, the Commission made a considerable effort to polish up its environmental image and create better links with both citizens and non-governmental organisations (NGOs) in Europe. The Commission also began to draft more and more of its own policies instead of simply responding to trends in the member states. Among the White Papers published were those on waste policy, traffic and transportation and industrial development.

The environmental consequences of the single market constituted a special problem. As we have already stated, whilst the Cecchini Report painted a very bright picture of the economic benefits of 1992, it did not devote any space to the environmental consequences. Not only were the economic forecasts the subject of some fierce criticism, some people also claimed that, however impressive the figures might look, they could only be achieved in a once-only setting and over a period of several years, which implied that they were of the same order of magnitude as common oscillations in the economy caused by cyclical and other factors. Unfortunately, no review or official study of the environmental consequences of the single market was available at the time. During 1988 a 'task force' was formed and, although there were problems and delays, it published a report towards the end of 1989 (Task Force Environment and the Internal Market, 1992). This swept away much of the euphoria caused by the Cecchini Report, but the Commission decided not to publish it as a Commission document. In spite of requests from the Council and the European Parliament, it also refused to formulate an opinion on the findings of the report.

Other important developments

As has already been stated, the Commission was very active during the period under review. It was widely recognised that many member states performed badly in implementing Community legislation, let alone enforcing it and so the question of implementation and enforcement became an important issue in EC environmental policy. The Commission itself concentrated its efforts mainly on implementation, i.e. the obligatory transformation of EC directives into national legislation in the member states. The Commission's activities led to an increase in the number of infringements which were brought before the European Court and both citizens and NGOs were requested to notify the authorities of any infringements (European Environmental Bureau, 1994). How Community legislation was actually applied in practice (i.e. the problem of enforcement) was a more difficult issue.

During this third period the Community was active in environmental matters on a variety of fronts including the establishment of an Environmental Agency, the introduction of new policy instruments, the deployment of funds, the problem of communication, the identification of responsibility, the conservation of Nature and research and development, each of which is discussed briefly below.

European Environmental Agency

The discussions on the establishment of a European Environmental Agency had shown clearly that there was still great reluctance on the part of the member states to allow inspections by Community officials. The Commission therefore had very little room for manoeuvre and this problem was taken on board during the Dutch presidency of 1991. The Dutch Environmental Inspectorate commissioned a study on enforcement in all the member states; the issue was then placed on the agenda of the informal Environment Council meeting in Amsterdam (Ministry of Housing, Physical Planning and Environment of the Netherlands, 1991). A year later, the UK presidency followed up the meeting by inviting the national enforcement agencies to a meeting with the Commission. Regular contacts have been maintained since then.

Before the decision to create a European Environmental Agency was taken, lively discussions took place on its competences. It was decided that the work of the Agency should initially be limited to the collection of data and the co-ordination and standardisation of monitoring. The extension of its activities to countries of the European Free Trade Association (EFTA) or of central Europe was a matter which could be considered at a later stage, as well as a possible role in policy studies and recommendations. It was a long time, however, before the decision to create the Agency was formally taken, owing to the fact that France blocked any decision on the location of Community institutions as long as it had not been given a firm assurance that the European Parliament would continue to convene at Strasbourg. The affair was settled at the Edinburgh Summit of October 1993 in the wake of the creation of the European Union, where the location of a number of different institutions was presented in the form of a single 'package' and it was decided to base the Agency in Denmark.

The importance of reliable and standardised data was clearly demonstrated when the Commission published its State of the Environment Report (Commission of the European Communities, 1992). Although it was presented as part of the Fifth Action Programme, it was too late and too outdated to play a role in the preparation of the Programme itself. Interestingly, a number of the data used in this publication are taken not from official publications but from a study carried out by the Institute for European Environmental Policy in Brussels (IEEP-B) (Vonkeman and Maxson, 1991).

Additional policy instruments

The poor record of implementation and enforcement of Community legislation and the success of the application of strict principles of responsibility and liability in the

8

Different types of environmental policy instruments

1 Legislative instruments, designed to set minimum levels of environmental protection, to implement wider commitments and to provide Community-wide rules and standards, where necessary, to preserve the integrity of the single market.
2 Market-based instruments, geared towards the internalisation of external environmental costs through the application of economic and fiscal incentives and disincentives and civil liability and aimed at encouraging the responsible use of natural resources, the avoidance of pollution and waste and 'getting the prices right', so that environmentally-friendly goods and services are not at a commercial disadvantage *vis-à-vis* polluting or wasteful competitors.
3 Horizontal, supporting instruments, including improved baseline and statistical data, scientific research and technological development, improved sectoral and spatial planning, public/consumer information and education, professional and vocational education and training.
4 Financial support mechanisms, including progressive insistence on the sustainability of development programmes and projects covered by the Community Structural Funds, support from the Community Financial Instrument for the Environment (LIFE) for practical demonstration models of sustainable measures and activities, for strengthening administrative structures, etc. and a new Cohesion Fund for the environment and the infrastructure, designed to deal with specific problems in the less prosperous countries of the Community, in the framework of the Maastricht Treaty.

United States, together with a growing lack of confidence in government action and a demand for deregulation, were among the factors that triggered the demand for additional policy instruments. These instruments are often divided into three categories: legal, economic and communicative. The Commission initially adopted these same headings. However, its Fifth Action Programme introduces a breakdown into four categories (see Box 8).

It has been the market-oriented instruments (see Box 9) which have been most in the public limelight during the past few years, not least because the possibility of a future climate change may lead to the introduction of a global or Community-wide tax on energy use. These instruments are by no means a panacea, however. Not only has a study, carried out on behalf of the European Commission (Huppes *et al.*, 1992), revealed that even the most promising of such instruments would be neither universally applicable nor without practical problems, the protracted and heated talks in the Council on the possible introduction of a Community energy tax have also shown how formidable the political resistance is to such taxes.

Structural funds

Right at the very outset of its existence, the Community created the Structural Funds with the aim of promoting the development of less prosperous regions. There were initially

Market-oriented instruments

Market-oriented instruments take a variety of forms:

Effluent charges	Charges paid on discharges into the environment and based on the quantity and/or quality of the pollutants discharged
User charges	Tariffs to cover the cost of collective or public treatment of effluents
Product charges	Fees imposed on products which pollute the environment
Administrative charges	Payment for authority services, for instance for the registration of certain chemicals or for the enforcement of regulations
Tax differentiation	Used to encourage the use of environmentally friendly products (such as unleaded petrol)
Subsidies	Grants, soft loans and tax allowances are used to provide an incentive for polluters to alter their behaviour or to assist firms facing problems in complying with standards
Deposit-refund systems	A surcharge is paid on potentially polluting products; it is refunded if the product or its residuals are returned to a collection system
Emissions trading	Artificial markets can be created, with the establishment of environmental standards and permits for polluters; pollution rights can be traded
Market intervention	The instrument of price intervention can be used to create a market in potentially valuable residuals
Liability insurance	Premiums reflect the probable damage or clean-up costs; the risk of incurring penalties or fines is transferred to insurance companies
Financial enforcement	Such fees are levied when polluters emit or discharge pollution in excess of levels permitted by regulations.
Non-compliance fees	These are refundable payments to regulatory authorities
Performance bonds	

Source: IEEP, Brussels/DRI McGraw-Hill.

three funds: a Regional Fund, a Social Fund and an Agriculture Fund (FEOGA). Other, more specific funds for such areas as environmental protection were added at a later stage. Even when taken together with the total budget for environmental protection, these funds are negligible compared with the Structural Funds and represent far less than 1% of the total Community budget.

When the SEA was negotiated, the peripheral member states expressed a concern that the economic benefits of '1992' would flow mainly to the central part of the Community, which was already the wealthiest region. As a compensation measure, the Structural Funds were virtually doubled in the framework of the SEA negotiations. An additional financial compensation followed in the framework of the Maastricht Treaty (to be discussed later), when a Cohesion Fund was created to support environmental and infrastructural developments in those member states whose gross national product was under 90% of the Community average, i.e. Greece, Ireland, Portugal and Spain. In the meantime, the environmental funds had been combined to form one 'Financial Instrument for the Environment', abbreviated as LIFE on the basis of its initials in French.

Attempts have frequently been made, throughout the life of the Structural Funds, to use them for the purpose of environmental protection. Unfortunately, the extent of their use for this purpose has been far outweighed by that for infrastructure projects and the drainage of wetlands. During the term of the Fourth Action Programme, the Commission issued an order to the member states instructing them to draft an Environmental Impact Statement for projects for which support from the Structural Funds had been requested. However, the Commission does not have the requisite legal authority or instruments with which to put a stop to damaging projects or even to refuse to award grants from the Funds; it can at best delay their allocation.

On the other hand, various environmental protection measures would not have been accepted without the existence of the Structural Funds. The agreement on the Waste Water Treatment Directive, which will require the investment of billions of ECUs in sewer systems and treatment plants in the Mediterranean region, is a clear example of this.

Communication

The European Community is in many respects a closed, almost inaccessible and undemocratic system. As the Chairman of the European Parliament's Environment Committee, Ken Collins, put it during a seminar organised by the Centre for European Policy Studies in Brussels in April 1992, 'If the European Community had been a state, it would never have been accepted as a Community member, because of its lack of democracy'. Both its legislation and the attitude of its bureaucracy reflect many tendencies of the Franco-German systems. This is entirely contradictory to the principles of environmental policy: the environment is everybody's concern, decision making on the environment should be open and accessible and the fact that decisions usually result in irreversible effects and irreparable damage necessitates both an open debate on all available data and the application of the precautionary principle: in other words, it is best to err on the safe side.

In the light of this situation, it is no surprise that it took such a long time to reach agreement on the above-mentioned Environmental Impact Assessment directive and that the same thing happened with regard to the directive on access to environmental information, which had been announced in the Fourth Action Programme. Although the initiative for the latter came from the European Parliament, the draft text from the Environment Committee failed to pass its plenary reading. The Commission subsequently drafted a much weaker proposal and this was adopted by the Council in 1993.

Concurrently with this, the Commission started work on eco-labelling and environmental auditing. After lengthy discussions, legislation to create a (voluntary) EC eco-label was adopted in 1993. As several member states had in the meantime introduced their own, national labels, it remains to be seen whether the EC label will have a positive impact on consumer information and behaviour. Whatever the case, it is already clear that its success will require considerable manpower and finance.

When they were introduced, *environmental audits* were designed to be compulsory, the intention being that each audit should become a public document. Since there was not a single member state which had such a compulsory system in operation, however, the scheme was doomed to fail. In fact, making such a system obligatory would have contravened the basic principles of environmental auditing. An environmental audit is an instrument which forms part of a company's internal system of environmental quality care, as promoted for some time now by the International Chamber of Commerce (ICC), which has designed an outline Code of Conduct for this purpose (International Chamber of Commerce, 1991). Where the management of a company has adopted an environmental quality care system, the company in question is committed to 'good environmental housekeeping'. Environmental audits are then used to identify any weak spots, either in the company's management and organisation or in its practical behaviour. Not surprisingly, companies do not want such audits to be made public.

The industrial lobby put a great deal of pressure on the Commission during the drafting phase. The result was the formulation of a proposal which made environmental auditing a voluntary system. Companies that adopt environmental auditing and publish acceptable results are entitled to display a special EC label on their buildings, letterhead, advertisements, etc. Here too, the environmental benefits as compared with the cost and effort have still to be proven. The relevant regulation was likewise agreed in 1993.

Responsibility and liability

The Commission has placed great emphasis during the past five years on the fact that the responsibility and liability of producers extends from the cradle to the grave. This is reflected, for example, in the lengthy talks that took place before a directive on packaging waste was adopted. The desire to adopt a 'cradle to grave' approach is also reflected in the recent directive on integrated pollution prevention and control (known as the IPCC Directive). In issuing this proposal, the Commission acted in accordance with the recommendations previously made by the OECD environment ministers.

With respect to liability, the Commission has produced a directive on liability for water pollution and has formulated a more general strategy in close consultation with the Council of Europe (Devos, 1991).

Nature conservation

The SEA greatly facilitated Community activities in the area of nature conservation by providing them with a legal basis. Until then, most European activities in this field had been initiated by the Council of Europe. A habitat directive has now finally been agreed. Under the Dutch presidency, the Dutch Minister of Agriculture, Nature Management and Fisheries, after examining the results of a study performed by the Institute for European Environmental Policy (Bennett, 1991), suggested creating a

European Ecological Network. This proposal was followed up within the EC by the Nature 2000 Project. A European Centre for Nature Conservation was set up at the University of Tilburg, the Netherlands, as a national nature conservation centre under the aegis of the European Agency.

Research and development

Although the Directorate-General for the Environment, Nuclear Safety and Civil Protection (DG XI) has supported its work with its own research programmes, most of the Community research and development budgets are funnelled through the Directorate-General for Science, Research and Development (DG XII). Not all funds and programmes with environmental relevance are DG XII programmes, but it is becoming increasingly common for them to be co-ordinated through the so-called Framework Programmes.

In 1990, IEEP Brussels reviewed the budgets and programmes of the member states in relation to the two leading environmental research programmes of the day: Science and Technology (STEP) and European Programme on Climate and Natural Hazards (EPOCH). It concluded that almost all funds were being spent on research projects in technology and the natural sciences and, more particularly, on conventional research in support of existing policies. It therefore strongly recommended that there should be a shift in emphasis towards socio-economic research. The Commission responded by creating a programme for socio-economic environmental research (known as the SEER Programme), which was endowed with a substantial budget and was later continued in the Fourth Framework Programme. It is now up to the scientific world to use the funds which are available for innovative research into the real causes of environmental problems: our social and economic structures and our culture.

Summary

The third period was characterised by the removal of major barriers and constraints in relation to both the legitimisation of EC environmental policy and decision making on environmental matters. The role of the European Parliament was significantly strengthened during this period. The time was evidently ripe for the adoption of key legislation, much of which had been under discussion for many years. The Commission took advantage of these new opportunities both to propose new legislation and to formulate its own policies and standpoints in a series of White Papers.

5.5 The fourth period: from 1993 to the present day
The globalisation of environmental problems

The last five years of the third period may be described as the years of the globalisation of environmental problems. The Brundtland Report, *Our Common Future,* which stresses the interdependence of the environment and development, had a tremendous impact. It introduced the concept of sustainable development, which was accepted all over the world, albeit perhaps because it was suitably vague. The United Nations (UN) decided to organise a world conference on the environment and development (UNCED) and this was held in Rio de Janeiro in 1992. The UN members committed themselves to drafting national reports before that date.

An important element of *Our Common Future* was the emphasis it placed on public participation and the involvement and support of all societal actors. Environmental and developmental NGOs, businesses, scientists and many others took part in the preparation of the report and staked out their positions. Although UNCED did not produce many tangible results, its impact is easy to underestimate (Vonkeman, 1992). Agenda 21 is a remarkable inventory and analysis of the global problems that are facing us; the Rio Declaration is an important guide for future policies. The big problem, however, is that few firm commitments were made and no in-depth analysis was presented of what sustainable development was actually intended to mean in practice (Vonkeman and Maxson, 1994). The relative success of the Rio conference can be attributed in part to the slackening of the tension between the West and the East power blocs that had dominated and frustrated international decision making for such a long time. The disintegration of the communist system has, however, produced unexpected problems. It has placed the deplorable environmental situation in Central and Eastern Europe firmly on the agenda of the Western world and it has replaced the East–West security conflict with the problem of environmental security.

In other words, intolerable situations with regard to the environment and economic development may yet cause international armed conflicts, either directly or indirectly via massive, environment- or development-induced migrations (Perelet, 1994), thus creating a genuine threat to global security. The importance of principle 25 of the Rio Declaration, which states that the environment, development and peace are interdependent and indivisible, cannot be sufficiently stressed. Both the developments in Central and Eastern Europe and the Rio conference have had a profound impact on EC environmental policy.

The EC and Central and Eastern Europe

Immediately after the fall of the Berlin wall, a number of Central European countries sought contact with the EC. The reunification of Germany even brought the considerable environmental problems of the former GDR directly within the Community. To a certain extent, this meant that justice had finally been done, as the EC member states had been exporting hazardous waste to the GDR for many years. Various initiatives were taken and/or supported by the Community. In 1990, environment ministers from Central Europe attended the Environment Council in Dublin. This was followed up in June 1991 by a similar conference in Dobrics, in Czechoslovakia as it was then called. There it was decided that further activities would be developed within the framework of the UN Economic Commission for Europe (UN ECE), on which both the United States and Canada have a seat. This resulted in a third conference held in Lucerne, Switzerland, in 1993 and a fourth held in Sofia in October 1995.

In the meantime, the EC had started providing bilateral environmental support to countries such as Poland and Hungary (under the Phare Programme), had added an eastern European branch known as Tempus to its teacher and student mobility programme (Erasmus) and had co-founded the East European Development Bank and the Regional Centre in Budapest. (The next chapter explores relations between the EU and Eastern Europe in more detail.)

In the long term, a number of Central European countries seem likely to join the Union. Commitments have already been made to the Czech Republic, Hungary, Poland and the Slovak Republic (known as the Visegrad countries), as well as the Baltic states of Estonia, Latvia and Lithuania. Before these countries can actually join, however, various fundamental changes will have to be made in both the Union and the countries involved. It is evident that decision making in a Union with over 20 member states will not work under the present rules. In addition, institutions like the Commission and the European Parliament will become unmanageable if the existing rules of representation are maintained. The costs will also become a barrier, not only because of the excessive size of the Community institutions (and a virtual doubling of the number of official working languages), but more particularly because the Common Agricultural Policy will cost a fortune if it is extended to the Central European countries.

As new member states have to respect all existing Community legislation and rules (under a principle known as the 'acquit communautair') and can at best only negotiate a state of temporary absolution, the process of adaptation will require a huge effort on the part of all those involved (see Box 10).

The EC and developing countries

Although we cannot go into any great detail, it is worth mentioning at this juncture that the EU maintains close relations with its member states' former colonies in Africa, the Caribbean and the Pacific: these are known as the ACP countries (there are about 70 of

---

10

Incorporating Central European countries into the EU

A strategy for preparing Central and Eastern European countries for future accession to the European Union was formulated by the General Affairs Council and adopted at the 'Essen Summit' of government leaders of the member states in December 1994. It contains provisions for a structured relationship with the presently associated C&EE countries and announces a long series of meetings that are planned to take place at regular intervals from 1995 onwards. Naturally, the document concentrates on the consequences of these countries entering the single market. Regarding the environment, the document stresses the importance of the 'Environment for Europe' process and the 1995 Sofia conference and states that Central and Eastern European countries should work in close co-operation with the Environment Agency. The need to ratify and implement the UN Framework Convention on Climate Change and further extend its commitments is also emphasised, as is the 1996 UN ECE Conference on transport and the environment. The document assumes that the central and eastern European countries will continue to receive assistance from the Phare Programme, which should also be financially supported by other donors.

them). These relations have been formalised in the Lomé Treaty and are supported by a number of special financial facilities.

In parallel with the general trend, environmental considerations have found their way into later texts of the treaty, particularly into the present one, Lomé IV and its recent amendment following a mid-term review. There is a complicating factor in that vital elements of the Lomé Treaty cannot be maintained in the future due to their incompatibility with the new rules of the World Trade Organisation (the successor to the General Agreement on Tariffs and Trade, GATT). The relations will therefore have to be reconsidered fundamentally when Lomé IV expires at the end of this decade.

Towards a European Union: the Maastricht Treaty

Important developments have also taken place within the EC during the period under review. During 1991, the basic treaties were again adapted, on this occasion with the aim of creating a European Union (EU). The goals of the Community were fundamentally expanded in the Maastricht Treaty, which incorporated a Common Foreign and Security Policy and a Home Affairs and Justice Policy. All decisions affecting the new domains will be decisions taken by the European Union. Although new decisions taken under the (amended) Treaty of Rome remain decisions of the European Community (EC; the Maastricht Treaty states that 'EEC' is no longer the correct term), they are at the same time EU decisions.

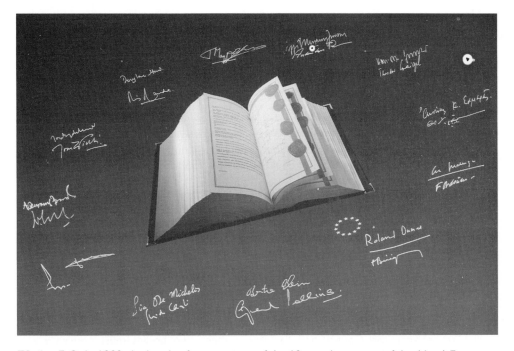

Plate 5.3 In 1992, the heads of government of the 12 member states of the (then) European Community signed the Treaty of Maastricht, the aim of which was to bring about a political, economic and monetary union in Europe. Photo: European Union

The new names of the European institutions are formally set out in an amended article 4 of the Treaty of Rome and include the 'Council' and the 'Commission'. However, the Council has decided to call itself the Council of the European Union and the Commission has decided to call itself the European Commission.

As was the case with the SEA, additional funds have been made available for the least prosperous regions, this time through the Cohesion Fund. The subsidiarity principle has now been extended to all EU policies. This should not affect environmental policy, because the principle was already mentioned in the First Action Programme (although the word 'subsidiarity' was not actually used to describe it) and was introduced formally in the SEA. However, the Maastricht Treaty triggered a great deal of anti-Community feeling in several member states and there is now a current of opinion in favour of 'repatriation', i.e. the restitution of EC competences to the member states coupled with the abandonment of existing Community legislation. In this context, a number of countries, notably the United Kingdom and France, have argued for the 'repatriation' of certain environmental legislation.

Important changes have also been made in the decision-making procedures and in the role of the European Parliament. However, each member state has retained its right of veto on key issues (see Box 11).

Procedures for environmental decision making

Environmental protection was not initially one of the EC's formal policy areas. The EC was, however, able to give effect to an environmental policy through one of two roundabout routes. The first was article 100 of the Treaty of Rome, which empowered the Council to take decisions in areas that were not mentioned in the treaties, provided that such measures were in line with the spirit of the treaties and did not counteract any official goals. Secondly, where any domestic measures inspired by a country's national environmental policy damaged that country's domestic industry by reducing its international competitiveness, the Council could use article 235 to harmonise legislation at a Community level.

In both cases, the Council had to decide unanimously and the European Parliament fulfilled a purely advisory role (i.e. there was a consultation procedure). The Single European Act contains a provision, included in article 100A, to facilitate decisions that had to be taken in order to create a single market. These decisions could be taken by a qualified majority, in a so-called co-operation procedure with the European Parliament. Environmental decisions that have no impact on the single market are based on article 130S and remain subject to the consultation procedure.

The Maastricht Treaty further extended the opportunities for decision making by qualified majority and stepped up the role played by the Parliament by introducing a so-called co-decision procedure. The latter implies in principle that, if there is a prolonged dispute between the Council and Parliament, these two bodies must nominate a conciliation committee that must try to arrive at a compromise (see also Verhoeve *et al.*, 1992).

The Fifth Action Programme: Towards Sustainability

The Fifth Environment Action Programme was drafted in parallel with the preparation of the UNCED conference. It was decided to use the Dutch National Environmental Policy Plan (NEPP) as a model (Ministry of Housing, Physical Planning and Environment, 1988). An important characteristic of the NEPP, which covers a period of five years, is that it is based on an independent study of the state of the environment, focusing on the expected trends during the next 20 years and the probable effects of existing policies. This study is updated every five years.

The Commission tried to follow the same approach, but its State of the European Environment was published too late to influence the contents of the Programme and was also hampered by a marked lack of sufficiently recent data.

The Programme itself, entitled *Towards Sustainability*, is built on a philosophy which is entirely in keeping with the spirit of the Brundtland Report and Agenda 21. As such, it is an interesting and important document. It stresses the need for sustainable development and major change in all areas of society and personal lifestyles. This need requires the integration of environment policies and goals in all other common policy areas. Agriculture, energy, industry, transportation and tourism are cited as being crucial sectors in this respect. Given that legislation will not be the most effective instrument for inducing such changes, there will be a need to adopt market-oriented policy instruments to complement and partly replace the traditional instrument of legislation.

Although the Programme stresses the need for formulating long-term goals, which should be achieved via concrete, short-term and medium-term intermediate stages and formulated in such a way that they can be checked and evaluated, very few such goals are actually specified in the Programme. The Programme proposes that the formulation of concrete policies should be postponed to a later date; these would then be published in a separate document. In spite of the good intentions of the Programme and its much more fundamental approach to the problem, the absence of concrete policies was generally viewed as a regrettable omission. Although previous programmes were often described as incoherent shopping-lists, drawn up by individual sections of the Environmental Protection Department, these lists did contain concrete information on what could be expected in the coming years. In spite of this, the importance of *Towards Sustainability* as a fundamentally new approach to the Community's environmental policy should not be underestimated.

New developments

There have been a number of important new developments in the recent past in both the Community and its environmental policy; some have been favourable, others detrimental. The single market has been completed and the establishment of a full European Union is well under way. Austria, Finland and Sweden joined the Community on 1 January 1995 and other potential new members are waiting on the doorstep. Several of these are former members of the former communist bloc of Central and Eastern European countries. Of course, this process is the subject of regular criticism and not all developments will have a beneficial effect on the European environment. Yet it is beyond doubt that the Union will become an increasingly important factor in environmental policy decisions.

On the other hand, it is hard to deny that the political focus is moving away from the environment, particularly because of the worrying employment situation in Europe. A clear example of this shift was the publication in December 1993 by the then Commission President, Jacques Delors, of a White Paper on Growth, Employment and Competitiveness (European Commission, 1993). This document not only contains a strong plea for the promotion of economic and industrial growth and the enhancement of the competitiveness of EC industry on the international market (without stopping to wonder whether this is in line with the demands of sustainability). It also suggests that these goals should be attained by a multibillion ECU investment programme in both the conventional infrastructure and the new information infrastructure. Needless to say, it is precisely the infrastructure that generally remains in place for decades, if not centuries and hence determines the long-term development of the many sectors that make use of it. In this way, it actually militates against fundamental change. Another, equally worrying factor is that the high unemployment rate in Europe is not a temporary phenomenon caused by a dip in the economy, but the result of a trend which has been in evidence for many decades now. As a recent OECD study shows, competition from the low-wage countries outside the OECD has only a marginal effect: it is the Western industrial and market system itself that lies at the root of the problem (OECD, 1995). Like earlier Commission papers, the White Paper contains a powerful argument in favour of the use of market-oriented instruments. However, the ongoing problems that have been encountered in connection with the proposed introduction of a Community-wide energy or CO_2 tax show how difficult this process is. At the same time, the use of the Community's traditional instrument, i.e. legislation, remains at least as difficult (see Box 12).

The Molitor Report   **12**

In mid-1995, an 'independent' commission dominated by representatives with commercial and industrial interests produced a document which became known as the Molitor Report. Although it does not contain any analysis of the development of unemployment and its causes, it assumes that many new jobs will be created if the competitiveness of EU firms on the world market is improved and that it is necessary to both reduce and simplify EU legislation (including environmental legislation) on a significant scale. Although the report has met with severe criticism, it is illustrative for the pressures under which national and international decision makers have to work.

Source: Commission of the European Communities. Report of the group of independent experts on legislative and administrative simplification (Molitor Report). COM (95) 288 fin., Brussels, 21 June 1995.

5.6 Constraints and opportunities on environmental policy making

Owing to the economic recession and the overriding concern about the level of employment, a paradoxical situation has developed. Ever since a number of major constraints on environmental policy making were removed and a fundamental strategy was formulated in *Towards Sustainability*, the Commission has refrained from taking any initiatives whatsoever that would lead to the industrial, agricultural or transport sectors having to make sacrifices for the sake of the environment. Almost all recent Commission texts have been either White Papers without any tangible impact or draft legislation introducing voluntary measures such as eco-labelling and environmental auditing.

Even if the member states had the political will to move 'towards sustainability', the road would still be very difficult. Very few member states have developed legislation and instruments which would allow them to interfere with production, products, the use of capital, access to markets, competition, etc. At an international level, even the regimes that could consider the introduction of such measures are virtually non-existent. This is an extremely serious problem, because of the complete internationalisation, if not globalisation, of industrial production, production factors, markets and capital flows.

An even greater problem is that it is difficult to imagine how the Western world's ever-increasing production and international market share could be reconciled with the demands of sustainability, let alone with those of equity and the redistribution of wealth. It is often argued that these problems will be solved by technology. Yet studies on 'sustainable technology' (Weterings and Opschoor, 1992) indicate that this implies the introduction of entirely new technologies and infrastructures, with ten-fold to 50-fold efficiency improvements; these are not available yet and will take many decades to develop. In these circumstances, it is not surprising that several recent studies have asked whether the present 'psychosis' of growth and competitiveness can continue much longer and have also suggested that there is an urgent need for an entirely new set of international regimes.

Whatever the case, the problems caused by the Western economic system will not easily be solved and high unemployment will remain with us for a very long time. In a general sense, this means that we should not rely on measures that support the existing systems and sectors, which have consistently reduced the role played by labour as a production factor, but that we should reconsider the redistribution of labour and its role in both the manufacturing sector and other sectors, particularly as the service and information sectors are displaying the same tendency of reducing the role played by labour. As far as environmental policy is concerned, we shall remain in a situation in which the unemployment issue overshadows all other concerns. The best policy here might be to try and link employment and environmental problems as much as possible and to develop creative solutions which are beneficial to both (see also Vonkeman, 1995a, 1995b).

This chapter has described the development of a unique, supranational regime, now called the European Union and the position of environmental policy within it. More and more decision-making powers have gradually been transferred from the member states to the Union, although the debate as to whether the final structure should be a federation or should remain an intergovernmental co-operation framework will probably continue for a long time. We have also noted that the area covered by the Union's activities has constantly expanded during the period under review, although its basic character remains that of an economic community, geared to the creation of a common market. This is particularly evident from the allocation of the Community's budget and the staffing of the Community's institutions: only a few per cent of both are devoted to environmental protection.

In spite of this, an impressive body of Community environmental legislation has been developed, whose impact on the Community as a whole is easy to underestimate. In a number of member states, 80% or more of domestic environmental legislation is based on Community texts, without which there might not have been any such legislation at all. In addition, the Community funds play a key role in assisting the poorer member states, as well as Central and Eastern European and developing countries, to improve their environmental situations. On the other hand, poor results in the implementation and enforcement of legislation and the counteractive effects of the much larger Community funds for economic development have unfortunately reduced their impact.

Global problems relating to the environment and development overshadow and affect the situation within the Community. They have led to an awareness that the environment, development and peace are interdependent and indivisible. In the context of the Community, this implies that the combination of the degradation of the environment and a paucity of economic growth will lead both to an unacceptable situation in society and to political instability.

Given this situation and particularly the continuing high rates of unemployment in the member states, the spotlight will continue to be focused predominantly on economic rather than on environmental problems in the Union during the coming decades. As a consequence, environmental policy will have to be positioned in the context of economic development. In other words, innovative strategies and instruments will have to be designed which make full use of the facilities offered by the Community's research programmes and funds.

Potentially, the regime of the European Union and its resources offer opportunities for the development of an international environmental policy of unprecedented dimensions that could act as a model for the rest of the world. An important precondition, however, is that the citizens of Europe and their political, governmental and non-governmental representatives not only learn to think at least at a European level, if not globally, but continue to act locally as well.

6

The scope for East–West co-operation

Susan Baker

6.1 Introduction

This chapter examines the international character of environmental policy by focusing attention on the role of the European Union (EU) in shaping environmental policy in countries that lie outside its own borders. The EU is playing an increasingly important role in environmental quality management in the newly emerging democracies of East and Central Europe, which have been left with a legacy of large-scale environmental devastation following the prolonged period of communist rule. While at first glance the EU's role may appear to be of a benign, even altruistic nature, closer analysis reveals the presence of a complex array of motivations guiding its involvement. These in turn are deeply rooted in the EU's desire to preserve its own interests.

This chapter addresses a series of important questions surrounding EU involvement in shaping the environmental polices of former Soviet bloc countries. What are the environmental problems facing East and Central European countries and why did they arise? Why is the EU interested in ensuring more effective environmental management in these countries? What are the consequences of this involvement, for the EU, the beneficiary countries and the environment itself? What opportunities does this involvement give rise to, for both the EU and the beneficiary states? What are the problems facing the EU in this task? What are the constraints acting on the EU? Do the countries' own political and economic structures inhibit or enhance effective environmental policy management? The chapter will attempt to link the answers to these questions back to a wider question, namely the nature of the relationship between the EU's involvement in environmental policy and the process of economic and political reform currently under way in these countries.

Historically, one of the motivations for the development of European integration and the setting up of the European Economic Community (EEC), later to become enlarged and eventually known as the European Union (EU), was the perceived threat to European peace and security posed by the Soviet Union after the Second World War. This led to the belief among key elites that the only way to counteract this threat was to develop a strong Europe, united politically as well as economically. The construction of a strong and unified Europe was financially and politically supported by the United States, via the Marshall Aid Plan. This acted as one of the primary stimuli for economic integration and the foundation of the EEC. The original founders of the EEC were also Christian Democrats who were strenuously opposed to communism. During the regime of Stalin in the early 1950s the Soviet threat was viewed with renewed concern and the Cold War became a haunting political reality. However, the original rationale for the unification of Western Europe became less important in the 1960s, particularly with the emergence of *détente* between the two blocs.

The system of international relations built around the Cold War encouraged the development of a new phase in capitalism, based on the growth of a large-scale military-industrial complex. During the Cold War, this enabled the superpowers to conduct an ideological and sometimes military struggle for supremacy. The arms race and the unchecked development of military-industrial capitalism had very serious environmental consequences for both sides of the Cold War and environmentalists in both the West and the East began to criticise this model of economic development. However, the two sides responded differently. While continuing to experience severe environmental stress, the West slowly began to incorporate some of the critiques of environmentalists, while the East regarded this criticism with hostility. As a consequence of this and other factors (discussed in more detail below) environmental damage in the East became much more severe.

From 1988 onwards the Soviet system began to collapse from within. The political superstructure of the Soviet bloc proved to be less robust than had been believed in the West and the regimes were shown to have commanded little popular support. Equally seriously, the economic costs of maintaining the Cold War were to prove unsustainable. The collapse of the Soviet system was initially expressed through the struggle for democratic rights by Soviet bloc citizens, beginning in countries like Poland but rapidly spreading throughout the region. Another main strand of criticism was based around the problem of environmental degradation and in particular the associated threat to health and the worsening of daily living conditions that this brought.

When the Soviet system eventually collapsed, the scale of environmental damage was revealed and the nuclear power accident at Chernobyl came to be seen as a symbol of the environmental irresponsibility of the old regime. Since the revolutions that swept the countries of the former Eastern bloc, the countries of East and Central Europe have been experiencing a series of highly complex adjustments. As with all other policy areas, environmental policy is situated within the context of radical reform of the previously existing economic, political, cultural, social and legislative structures. The transition to a market economy and pluralist democracy dominates all aspects of current social, political and economic processes in these countries. However, since environmental problems do not respect political borders, the West has been obliged, in its own interest, to respond to the environmental degradation of the former Soviet bloc by measures of support. But its involvement does not stop there. As we will see below, faced with the power vacuum arising from the collapse of the old Soviet system and the prospect of deepening political crisis on its own doorstep, the EU has become involved in managing the wider process of transition in the newly emerging democracies of East and Central Europe.

It is interesting to note that the same forces of economic transformation that are operating on a global scale, referred to as 'the process of globalisation', have affected the West as well as the East, but with radically different consequences. Western Europe is witnessing an increasing economic and political convergence, as seen for example in the deepening and widening of the EU. At the same time, in the Eastern bloc the same forces have contributed to economic collapse and political fragmentation.

For the sake of simplicity, in this chapter the term 'Central Europe' is used to refer to Hungary, Poland and the Czech and Slovak Federal Republics. 'East Europe' is used to refer to Albania, Bulgaria, Romania and the states of the former Yugoslavia. Both together are called 'Eastern Europe'.

The chapter is divided into three main parts. Section 6.2 looks at the environmental legacy of communist rule. It begins by painting a brief portrait of the environmental problems facing East and Central European countries. It then looks at the response of internal, domestic actors, including environmental groups, to the growing environmental crisis. Having set the stage, as it were, the remainder of the chapter explores the EU's involvement in shaping the current policy responses to this environmental crisis. Beginning with Section 6.3, the EU's interests are examined, an outline of the nature of the reforms needed is then provided and finally we look at why the EU has a specific interest in shaping environmental policy. Section 6.4 looks at the actual policy content and the variety of problems associated with their implementation. In the light of the importance of the Phare Programme, specific attention is given to examining the underlying aims, the procedures and the difficulties of this programme. The environmental dimensions of the Phare Programme are explored and the shift from *ad hoc* crisis management to strategic EU involvement in environmental policy in East and Central Europe is examined. Implementation is a crucial stage in the policy process and the EU is encountering difficulties in the effective implementation of its policies in East and Central European countries. These difficulties reflect wider problems which are in turn explored, both at the EU level and within the beneficiary countries. The conclusion of the chapter (Section 6.5) returns to the original questions specified in the introduction and provides some tentative answers.

6.2 The environmental legacy of communist rule

Environmental damage

There is a good deal of uncertainty surrounding the extent of environmental damage in the former Soviet bloc countries. However, as the liberalisation of these countries progresses and research findings are published and made available to a wide audience, it is becoming increasingly evident that these countries experienced a great deal of environmental stress during the period of communist rule. Problems in relation to poor air and water quality, inadequate treatment and disposal of hazardous, including radioactive, waste, contamination of land, particularly agricultural land and deforestation are among the most severe negative environmental legacies of communism.

However, while environmental damage can be seen in all parts of East and Central Europe, commentators are agreed that there are quite massive variations in the levels of air, water and soil/vegetation pollution across the former Eastern bloc (Carter and Turnock, 1993, p.4). High pollution rates are particularly noticeable in the so-called 'black triangle' covering the Czech and Slovak Republics, Poland and the former East Germany. Other areas of especially high pollution concentration include the Black Sea and Danube River basin. The emission of atmospheric pollutants correlates closely with thermal power stations and units or concentrations of heavy industry. Further to this, research has found that large cities are significant contributors through motor traffic and environmentally damaging domestic heating systems (Carter and Turnock, 1993, p.5). For example, in the former East Germany and in Czechoslovakia, the use of lignite as a major source of energy has led to the deterioration in air quality through increased sulphur dioxide emissions. Soil deterioration has also been found, especially in agricultural areas, following widespread use of chemical fertilisers and pesticides. Transboundary pollution has also emerged as a problem in East and Central Europe. Poland, for example, has unwillingly 'imported' pollution from the eastern parts of the

Plate 6.1 A power plant not fitted with filters for abating air pollution, Chorzow, Upper Silesia, Poland, 1991. Photo: Peter Hilz/Hollandse Hoogte

former East Germany and Bulgaria's own pollution problems have been added to by emissions from Romanian factories.

Numerous explanations have been put forward to account for the poor state of the environment in East and Central Europe (an issue that is also discussed by Tellegen in, 1995). On a general level, their underlying Marxist ideology emphasised economic growth, industrialisation and technical progress. In this world view, Nature and the natural world were seen as obstacles to technical progress, to be overcome through scientific and technical advancements. While differing in emphasis, this ideology holds much in common with Enlightenment thinking in the West, a dominant ideology which was important in shaping the development of Western capitalism (Baker, 1993a).

Specifically, in East and Central European countries under communist rule, there was a dogmatic assumption that environmental damage could never be caused by the state, as it had no profit interests (Baumgartl, 1993, p.158). Environmental degradation was seen as a product of capitalist, profit-orientated modes of production. This assumption blinded the authorities to the reality of their own environmental degradation and prevented an effective and early response to environmental deterioration.

However, when environmental damage became so serious that the state was forced to intervene, efficient policy responses were prevented by the nature of the communist, planned economy. The centralised economic planning system encouraged continuous waste of natural resources and highly inefficient use of energy in the production process. Furthermore, a single authority was often both the source of pollution and responsible for its prevention. Thus the system often lacked an independent authority to oversee environmental management. To add to this, even if polluters were detected, the solution was often not to address the source of environmental damage but to impose a fine, which was frequently disproportionately low. Setting unrealistically low fines was by and large due to the wish of authorities not to impose conditions that would restrict production. Further, in the late 1960s and 1970s attempts to redress environmental destruction, especially at the factory level, were often hindered by the fact that management preferred meeting its production quota rather than adhering to pollution control standards. As a consequence, projects aimed at pollution control were (and still are) often delayed or postponed. For example, according to a 1987 report of the official newspaper of the Bulgarian Communist Party, in 98% of the cases that were brought to the courts polluters were not fined – as managers had circumvented environmental laws in order to fulfil their plan targets and this was considered a more important goal (Spetter, quoted in Baumgartl, 1993). Agricultural production, to take another area, aimed at achieving sufficiency for the Soviet bloc as a whole, was also given priority over sustainable land use and environmentally sound cultivation practices. Furthermore, in many of the countries urbanisation was rapid and, while ideologically acceptable, was poorly planned, with inadequate zoning, poor design of housing and neighbourhoods and more often than not resulting in degradation in the local environment (The environmental legacy experienced in Eastern Europe is summarised in Box 1.)

While it is true that the communist regime in Eastern Europe has given rise to severe negative environmental consequences, it would be unwise to assume from this that either communism is inherently bad for the environment or that non-communist countries, particularly those in Western Europe, have escaped environmental problems.

The environmental legacy in Eastern Europe

○ **Communist ideological constraints**
   Marxist industrial ideology
   Collapse of civil society and closure of policy process
   Overambitious planning goals
   Promoting of prestigious industries irrespective of costs
○ **Hypercentralisation of decision making**
   Bureaucracy
   Corruption
   Lack of local level input in environmental policy decisions
   Delay in response to pollution problems
   Lack of flexibility
○ **Rapid industrialisation**
   Extensive growth
   High, inefficient and wasteful natural resource utilisation
   Mega industrial projects
○ **Inherited Soviet technology**
   Applied regardless of local/regional ecosystem capacity
   Resource wasteful and high energy use
   Little if any technology available to reduce pollution at source
○ **Free or underpriced consumption of environmental resources**
   Regarded as 'people's property'
   Unrealistic energy prices and inefficient use
   Use of air, water and soil not costed
   Domestic reliance on low quality, high pollutant lignite
○ **Limited application of economic incentives**
   Soft financial constraints on waste and pollution
   Low raw material prices
   Low/free waste disposal charges
   Low levels of pollution fines
○ **Low priority for environment**
   Managerial concern with meeting production quotas
   Managerial neglect of environmental issues
   Centrality of economic issues over environmental protection
   Concentration on *ad hoc* responses to environmental crisis
   End-of-pipe solutions over integrated environmental management
○ **Underinvestment in environmental protection**
   Lack of administrative capacity
   Lack of scientific capacity
   Financial limitations
   Systematic postponement of and delays in environmental projects
○ **Information scarcity**
   Lack of information on pollution
   Quality of data unreliable
   Quantity of data limited
   Lack of public access
○ **Rapid urbanisation**
   Poor housing quality and neighbourhood design

Source: modified from Georgieva (1993), p.72.

First, we should be aware of the argument that environmental deterioration in the East stemmed not so much from socialism *per se,* but arose as a consequence of the particular model of communist party rule that was adopted in the East, with its over-reliance upon the achievement of progress through industrialisation. (Perhaps what is needed is not so much the abandonment of Marxist ideology as the adoption of a different form of socialism in answer to the need for the management of environmental problems.)

Second, the West, as well as the East, has experienced marked deterioration in its natural environment since the period of the Second World War. However, Western capitalism has gone through a number of phases different from those experienced by the East, from an initial phase where the environment was simply seen as a free resource to be used to satisfy the demands of production and to promote economic growth, to a second phase where there is a greater realisation that the environment is not a free resource but, like all factors of production, must itself be costed. This shift stems in part from environmental and consumer pressure and has given rise to a 'greening' of the economy, as seen in the development of green production processes and green consumerism. The second phase of 'green capitalism' has not solved the environmental crisis and capitalism in the West continues to contribute to environmental degradation, especially in underdeveloped regions within the EU, as well as in developing countries (Baker *et al.*, 1994). In comparison to the earlier phase of capitalism, however, this second 'greener' phase can be seen as representing a certain amount of environmental progress, albeit limited. Further, it also gives rise to more environmentally conscious economic behaviour than that hitherto found in the Eastern industrial development model. Whether or not the Eastern European transition economies adopt this modified and environmentally more aware model of economic development remains to be seen, although there is a good deal of initial evidence to suggest that they will rely more heavily upon the older, less environmentally conscious Western path to development.

Third, Western influence has not always been environmentally benign. Increased consumerism has often been accompanied by environmental problems, especially the creation of waste. Indeed, some good practices such as returnable bottles or the emphasis on public transport have been undermined. In the effort to attract investment in a competitive global market economy Eastern European states may sacrifice both jobs and the environment. Efforts to clean up the environment generated by Western influence may be based on existing or outdated technological approaches to clean up rather than an emphasis on pollution prevention, energy conservation and the shift to renewables that is currently being adopted in the West. Thus the shift to the Western model of economic development, away from centrally planned to market-led economies, may not necessarily be good for the environment.

Environmental movements and actors

While communist ideology contributed towards the environmental devastation of East and Central Europe, the attitude of communist regimes, and in particular the Communist Party, towards environmental protection was complicated. In fact, it was difficult for communists not to share the goals that were expressed by environmentalists, as these could be seen as preconditions for a better life for the population – itself a goal of Marxist ideology. Expressing general concerns for environmental protection and indeed in many cases the passing of new environmental protection legislation, however, is not the same thing as implementing sound environmental management policies. Throughout the period of Soviet rule, the quality of the environment in Eastern Europe declined.

Further, it is also important to bear in mind that such regimes could not tolerate criticism, even from environmentalists. Environmental critiques were seen as a threat to the Party's monopoly and to the strong Marxist belief in progress through industrialisation. It is not surprising, therefore, to find that communist regimes did not welcome the growing green movement that developed in the Soviet bloc in the late 1980s (Fisher, 1993).

Despite the weak interest in environmental issues among the ruling elite, environmental consciousness expanded, especially during the 1980s. As the USSR began to loosen its grip on its East and Central European satellites, the public gradually gained exposure to environmental politics in Western Europe. The West German Green Party for example, was influential not only in Western Europe but also in Bulgaria (Jancar-Webster, 1993). The growing support for the green movement has been explained by Vargha by the fact that public opinion in Eastern Europe linked the crisis of the environment with a deeper critique of the political system (Baumgartl, 1993, p.162). Joan DeBardeleben also notes that the unofficial environmental groups of the pre-revolutionary period of the 1980s were in some cases directly, in other cases implicitly, linked to other political tendencies. A prime example, she argues, is the association of ecological concerns with nationalist sentiments, citing, among others, the example of Armenian protests in the Nagorno-Karabakh regions and nationalist pressures in the Baltic states. These contained a strong element of what she terms 'ecological nationalism', that is, 'a protest against the violation of a pristine national environment by *outside* influences' (DeBardeleben, 1991, p.8, emphasis added). Similarly, the unofficial environmental groups were in some cases, as with Charter 77 in Czechoslovakia and ecologists in the Evangelical Church in the German Democratic Republic (GDR), closely linked with dissident thought. Dissident thought posed a challenge to the Stalinist economic and political models, with its priority on heavy industry and its grandiose industrial gigantism (DeBardeleben, 1991, p.8). Thus, as a consequence of the association of environmental concerns with wider political issues, the resolution of environmental disputes ceased to be limited to the implementation of new or stricter environmental management strategies and became instead bound up with the demand for wider, political reform. The rise of the Bulgarian environmental movement, from its humble local origins in the border town of Ruse and the development of its links to wider political protest, which was in turn to contribute to the downfall of the old regime, is a case in point (see Box 2).

The 1989–1990 revolutions in East and Central Europe were followed by high expectations regarding improvements in social, environmental and economic conditions and free expression of political opinion. Within a few short months, however, this enthusiasm was tempered by the harsh reality of increasing unemployment, rising prices and political instability. These have subsequently acted as constraints on the

2

The rise of environmental groups in Eastern Europe: the case of Bulgaria

Ruse is the fourth largest town in Bulgaria, situated on the Northern border of the country. Air pollution in the town reached extremely high levels, mainly caused by a Romanian chlorine factory on the other bank of the Danube in Giurgiu. People in the town began to suffer from an unidentified lung disease for which doctors coined a new term 'Ruse lung'. In 1986, 86,000 children and 62,000 adults (out of a population of approximately 200,000) were outpatients of the hospitals, suffering from respiratory, skin and allergy problems. The number of stillbirths was high and during the periods of highest pollution children were admitted to school only with gas masks. The desire of the population to leave Ruse was so great that a governmental prohibition on moving was passed. During the autumn of 1987 the first protests of the mothers in Ruse occurred and the first national alerts to the dramatic situation in Ruse were announced in cultural journals. The scandal of Ruse became a touchstone of the nation's conscience. Grass-roots protest spread with solidarity committees rising in other towns. In March 1989 the Social Committee for Environmental Protection of the Town of Ruse was established following a meeting in Sofia, with 360 founding members, with a large representation from among the Bulgaria intellectual elite.

A few days after the foundation of the Committee the persecution of its founders started, as non-governmental ecological concern was considered counter-revolutionary activity. After this repression the Committee lost its influence but its members were to reappear later in the Ekoglasnost national umbrella movement and by July 1989 all members seemed to have joined this new group. Ekoglasnost demanded public and democratic control over all environmentally relevant decisions, which was in fact a radical critique of core communist ideology. While presenting itself as solely concerned with environmental issues, members recognised broader political roles and goals. The protests of Ekoglasnost acted as a catalyst for internal fights within the Party and for institutional change. When the opposition forum Union of Democratic Forces was established in December 1989, Ekoglasnost was one of its founding groups. However, Ekoglasnost's most vibrant period and its importance as an ecological umbrella organisation came to an end about this time. From the moment when free political discussion became possible, other issues gained importance. By 1990 most members with political ambition left Ekoglasnost and joined the Green Party.

The rise of the Bulgarian environmental movement

Group	Concern	Power	Extension
Ruse mothers	local	ad hoc protest	local
Committee	local	protect movement	regional
Ekoglasnost	strategic	oppositional	national
Green Party	programmatic	political party	national

Adapted from Baumgartl (1993), p.170.

development of an effective environmental policy. Furthermore, newly emerging democracies faced the sober realisation that they lacked the financial, scientific and technical ability to deal with the environmental devastation inherited from the period of Soviet rule. It is not surprising, therefore, that these countries welcomed outside help, including that offered by the EU.

The impact of the EU

Paradoxically, the involvement of the EU in environmental policy formulation and implementation may serve to weaken the strength of the environmental movement in these countries. The lack of access to the EU policy process may disillusion environmental activists while at the same time the general public may come to believe that the West will aid environmental recovery, especially through the provision of finance and technical assistance, leaving little room or need for their own continued involvement. The political and cultural inheritance from the period of communist rule, where the policy making process was inaccessible to the general public, the space for civil society was severely narrowed, opposition muted, public participation minimal and the expression of political opposition or dissent undertaken only at great personal risk, may reinforce the tendency to withdraw from wider public expression of concern about or involvement in environmental issues. Thus, while EU involvement may provide new opportunities for the development of environmental policy, it may also act as a constraint on the development of the autonomous environmental movement.

Even with outside aid, overcoming the negative environmental legacy of the communist regimes is a major task, requiring as it does new approaches to environmental management. However, this cannot be undertaken without changes in three areas:

1 economic restructuring
2 organisational and institutional changes
3 behavioural, sociocultural and educational changes.

Economic restructuring can act as a powerful tool for dealing with the environmental problems in Eastern and Central Europe by reducing the inefficiencies in the economy, especially those related to production, energy use and recycling. New policy instruments are also needed, including the use of taxation, aimed at promoting pollution-free activities, cleaner products and production. The use of such policy tools is now widespread within the EU and is found, for example, in pricing policies that favour lower taxation on unleaded petrol. Also needed is the introduction of export/import regulation and reductions in subsidies, especially the reduction of state subsidies to environmentally unsustainable economic activity. However, the use of economic incentives is at present restricted by the limited understanding of and experience with the use of market-based instruments for regulating production and consumption patterns. Furthermore, property/use rights with respect to environmental resources also need to be clarified.

Institutional changes are also needed to provide effective systems for environmental management and control. This includes the need for staff retraining and upgrading of monitoring equipment and decentralisation of environmental responsibilities and more co-operation with the key institutions of the transition process, especially the ministries of finance. This co-operation would help to reduce the fragmented policy responses that are typical of environmental management and help to ensure the integration of environmental considerations into all policy areas, steps that are increasingly seen as essential if successful environmental management is to be assured. Strengthening the regulatory mechanism is also of importance but, as we will see below, the implementation capacity of the country has to be taken into account when new legislation is being imposed.

Finally, while the old communist regimes have now collapsed, old attitudes linger and the resolution of environmental issues requires not only clean-up of the environment but also attitudinal changes, especially in relation to the utilisation of environmental resources and the development of a deeper understanding of society's interrelationship with the natural world. Thus, it is important to note that there are a number of constraints operating on the EU stemming from the political, administrative, economic and social situation in the beneficiary countries.

It is clear that in aiding the former Soviet bloc countries to implement more sustainable environmental management strategies, the EU has to undertake a complex variety of tasks. Further, it has to ensure that it helps to meet the expectations of the citizens of the newly emerging democracies and thereby contribute to the stability and legitimacy of the new regimes. Why the EU is interested in undertaking this task and how it goes about achieving its aims is the subject matter of the rest of this chapter.

6.3 EU involvement in East and Central Europe: situating environmental policy in a wider framework of interests

EU interest in East and Central Europe

Since the collapse of the former Soviet bloc, the EU has become involved in helping the countries of East and Central Europe, an involvement that is explicitly aimed at achieving two goals: ensuring a smooth and stable transition to democracy and aiding the establishment of market economies. As part of this task it has also become directly involved in shaping environmental policies in these countries.

The link between the EU economic and political interests on the one hand and its environmental interests on the other cannot be understood without first considering the context within which its wider relationship with East and Central European countries has been framed. There are a number of reasons why the EU is interested in ensuring that the transition to liberal democracy and the market economy is smooth and stable (Pinder, 1991). These include the following.

The potential for trade

The EU believes that market economies, based on the production and consumption of a diverse array of goods and services, are much better adapted to international trade than are centrally planned economies. The former Soviet bloc countries have a vast potential for trade with the EU and, if realised, this trade could benefit the industry of individual member states and contribute to the economic well-being of the Union as a whole.

Mutual reinforcement

It is believed that, although a market economy can function under an authoritarian government, there are tensions between a free economy and a servile polity. The arguments for liberal democracy and the establishment of a market economy in East and Central Europe are intimately linked. A market economy is considered to be the economic expression of a democratic civil society and it is argued that successful transition to market economies needs to be accompanied by pluralist democracy, which in turn will strengthen the new economic liberalism. Under a liberal democracy the market economy is thus considered to be more secure and better able to safeguard the Union's economic interests.

European military security

The Union believes that pluralist democracy can better accommodate the different national and ethnic identities found within the state boundaries of many East and Central European countries. National conflict in some of the Eastern countries, especially in the Balkans, has been shown to be a serious threat to stability and could also threaten the security of Western Europe. There is also a danger of conflict between newly independent states which, it is believed, is less likely to take a violent expression if pluralist democracy is established. As Pinder has argued, 'In so far as the Community can help to strengthen democracy in its eastern neighbours, it will be enhancing its own security' (Pinder, 1991, p.3).

Containing the German problem

Geographically and historically, Germany has the greatest stake in securing good relations with the East as it is more exposed than the other member states to political instability and conflict in the East. It also has economic interests, as the scope for expansion of German trade with Eastern and Central Europe is enormous. At the same time, the EU has always wished to ensure that Germany, all the more so as it is now unified, remains anchored in the Western system and that it does not play an independent role in the East. Stronger Union ties with East and Central Europe are seen as the best way of providing a safer framework for containing German power.

Expanding its sphere of international influence

The collapse of the Soviet empire has left a power vacuum within Europe as well as at the global level. EU involvement in the reconstruction of the countries of the former Soviet bloc has enabled it to expand its sphere of influence. This provides the EU with an ideal opportunity to establish itself as a major international political and economic power.

146

Widening and deepening of the Union

The deepening of the Union, through the creation of another field of policy competence, namely East and Central European policy, has given the Union a greater role in
international affairs. It has also led to pressure for a widening of the EU, that is, the
acceptance of new members, especially those from Eastern Europe. In turn, the
accession of East European countries has became an argument for further deepening.

Forestalling social unrest

Finally, there is the danger that if the countries of the former Soviet bloc do not make
the transition to market economies they are likely to be beset by increased poverty,
social unrest and outward migration to the West and will be more susceptible to
authoritarianism and less likely to continue with the transition to pluralist democracy.

Thus it is clear that the involvement of the EU in East and Central Europe offers it
unique political and economic opportunities, as it also does to the beneficiary countries. Interest in the development of pluralist democracies and market economies in
East and Central Europe has, of course, to be translated into policy. The EU has now
developed a framework within which it provides practical support to the countries in
transition and its support for environmental policy is one component of this wider
policy framework. Such support is particularly important because of the fragility of the

Plate 6.2 Leipzig, East Germany, April 1991. People protest against the slow pace of economic
recovery and the uncertain future that lies ahead of them. Photo: Leo Erken/Hollandse Hoogte

transition process in many of the countries involved. The hardships generated, especially by the economic changes, may easily result in public disillusion with the new experiment in Western-style democracy and capitalist economics and destabilise the entire reform process.

The transition to pluralist democracy and market economy: the reform process

The transition process currently under way in East and Central Europe involves a complex array of adjustments at the social, economic, political, cultural, environmental and administrative levels. Such changes include reform of:

○ the legislative framework, including passing new laws on ownership and property rights, reform of company law and labour law, including their expansion to include workplace protection, external trade and foreign investment and environmental protection
○ enterprise structures away from the domination of the economy by state-owned monopolies to a system based on a mixed economy, with a far greater role for the private sector – this also involves the establishment of appropriate financial institutions, including banks and stock exchanges
○ the physical structure necessary for a competitive economy, including modernisation of industrial plant and equipment, the renewal of physical infrastructure, development of the service sector and the clean-up of the environment and the establishment of new environmental protection measures.

The constraints on the reform process include bureaucratic inertia, financial limitations and social and workplace attitudes which all need to be changed (Hess, 1993). A major constraint as far as EU assistance is concerned is that these countries have weak administrative structures, particularly at the local level. Their administrations generally lack the skills to compile a coherent programme and, as Pinder has found, when the Commission asks for details of programmes to assist, it often receives a mere shopping list of projects (Pinder, 1991, p.91). Also the absorptive capacity of the countries, particularly the capacity to implement projects once funding is received, remains weak and concerns have been expressed about their capacity to provide the long-term maintenance of projects once they have been established. While all experience a common problem in this respect, there are nevertheless sharp variations among the former Eastern bloc countries as to their absorptive capacities. It is generally recognised that Central Europe can absorb more help faster than the countries of Eastern Europe.

The shift to a market economy is difficult in countries where the Communist Party's control over the economy undermined the habits that make for an efficient economy and, as Pinder has argued, the system has deprived economic agents of the necessary juridical and institutional framework (Pinder, 1991, p.46). Further, the centrality of the Party in political life had undermined the basis of civil society, making the transition to pluralist democracy all the more difficult to achieve. Democracy not only involves the establishment of a parliament and a competent legal profession and civil service but:

> Reaching further into society, this principle has to apply to education and to the economy: both must shake free of the habit of domination by a monopoly party. If

the principle's application is widened further again, it becomes that of the civil society, based, within the rule of law, on 'the autonomy of private associations and institutions', including private business firms. Of particular significance for the political process are the independence and quality of the media (Pinder, 1991, p.39).

When we list the profound and many-sided changes that are required of countries moving from a Marxist-Leninist party monopoly to a stable pluralist democracy, we can appreciate the magnitude of the changes involved and can grasp the fragile nature of the transition process in Eastern and Central Europe (see Box 3).

So far in this section we have examined the interests of the EU in shaping the transition process to pluralist democracy and the market economy in East and Central Europe. In doing so we have focused on the constraints operating on and the opportunities arising from EU involvement in the process of reform. As well as its more general interests in reform in East and Central Europe, the EU has more specific interests at stake in the reform process, including the reform in environmental management and the development of more sustainable environmental policies, to which we now turn.

EU interest in the state of the environment in East and Central Europe

Since the 1970s the conventional wisdom that the nation state is the best level at which to deal with environmental policy management has been severely questioned (Weale, 1992). As other chapters in this book have emphasised, environmental policy is considered an international policy area because of the recognition that pollution does not respect artificial, administrative and political boundaries and that many of the major ecological zones requiring environmental protection, such as river systems, straddle national borders. In keeping with this view, the European Commission has, in recent years, advocated stronger involvement of the EU in international environmental affairs. Its involvement in shaping the environmental policy of East and Central Europe is part of this new commitment, which has grown out of the political desire of the Union to acquire a steadily increasing capacity for external action (Jachtenfuchs, 1992, p.24). This not only compensates for the fact that in some cases individual member states are no longer free to act internationally in a given area because they have given legal competence for doing this to the Union, but also the expansion of its international fields of competence heightens the international profile and standing of the EU as a whole.

This explanation, however, only accounts for EU involvement in international environmental policy as a whole. The Union also has specific interests in overcoming the legacy of pollution left behind by the Soviet regime and in ensuring that future economic activity in East and Central Europe is more environmentally sustainable than has hitherto been the case. The Union believes that the state of the environment in Eastern Europe is of direct concern to it for the following reasons.

The environmental and hence the economic resource base and the health of the population of existing member states of the EU can be severely damaged by pollution generated in East and Central Europe and 'imported' into the EU. The effects on the

3

Reforms needed for transition to pluralist democracy and market economy

Political reform
○ *Democratic practices*
Multiparty systems
Holding of elections
Recognition of minorities
Human rights
○ *Development of civil society*
Trade unions
Business interest associations
Chambers of commerce
NGOs
Changes in cultural attitude

Legislative reform
○ *Strengthening of existing laws and establishment of new laws*
Ownership and property rights
Company practice
Labour markets
Environmental protection
Statistics collection
External trade and foreign investment
○ *Reform of the courts*

Economic reform
○ *Reform of enterprise structures*
Privatisation
○ *Establishment of financial institutions*
Banks
Stock exchange

Administrative reform
○ *Establishment of new institutions*
○ *Rationalisation of existing bureaucracy*
○ *New managerial practices*
Financial management
Human resource management and initiative training
○ *Upgrading of statistics collection*
○ *Opening up policy process*
Interest group participation
Public access to information

Physical structure reform
○ *Modernisation of plant and equipment*
○ *Infrastructure development*
Roads, telecommunication, rail
○ *Establishment of private service sector*
○ *Environmental management*
Clean-up
Prevention at source
Ecological modernisation of industry

Social reform
○ *Social welfare provision*
○ *Cultural attitudes*

eastern areas of Germany and the Czech and Polish parts of the 'death triangle' is a case in point, as was the Chernobyl nuclear accident which caused radioactive fall-out well beyond the boundaries of the then USSR.

The Union also has an interest in influencing standards of pollution control for trade reasons. Now that Eastern European imports have penetrated the Union's markets the Commission believes that competition can be undermined by the sale of goods which are low cost because of low environmental standards.

With the opening up of investment opportunities in East and Central Europe, similar environmental standards are needed across Europe as a whole in order to avoid the flight of industry from the West and its relocation in Eastern Europe, which could potentially offer 'polluter havens', enabling industry to avoid the heavy costs of meeting EU pollution abatement standards.

Provision of pollution abatement technology and environmental management skills can provide European industries, especially those that are ecologically modernised, with a new source of profitable business. This is precisely the type of economic spin-off effect of sound environmental management policies envisaged in the EU's Fourth and Fifth Environment Action Programmes (as discussed by Hanf in Chapter 8 of this book).

Reduction of emission standards in East and Central Europe makes economic sense, as in many cases increased ambient quality in Western Europe can be more cheaply achieved this way than by a reduction in pollution originating from within the Union (Jachtenfuchs, 1992, p.29).

There are regional interests that have put pressure on the EU to take an increased role in shaping and funding the environmental policy of East and Central European countries. Many of the member states of the EU share borders with Eastern European countries and have become the victims of transboundary environmental pollution. This is especially so where two or more countries share a common ecological system, such as a river. As a result the EU, through the Phare Programme, is currently funding a number of cross-border co-operation programmes in the field of environ-mental clean-up and management. These include joint projects between Bulgaria and Greece, aimed at water treatment and river protection and monitoring systems; co-operation between the Czech Republic and Germany, including the construction of sewage treatment systems; and between Italy and Slovenia, involving the creation of a natural park in the Karst region that spans the two countries (Commission, 1994c, p.23–35).

EU interest is motivated by the belief that an improvement in the living and working environment and hence in the health of those living in heavily polluted zones, would demonstrate in a tangible and practical way the benefits of reforms and thus help to legitimise the transition to pluralist democracy and the market economy. Box 4 gives a summary of the EU's interests in environmental conditions in Eastern Europe.

It has been argued that much of the expenditure co-ordinated by the EU and intended for dealing with the environmental problems in East and Central Europe will consist of the closure of polluting industrial plants that must anyway be replaced because under the Soviet regime they had depended on unrealistically low energy prices and had become technologically obsolescent. This means that a large part of the spending to improve the environment can be subsumed within the process of regenerating the physical structure as a whole (Pinder, 1991, p.96). This fact can serve to ground further

4

EU interest in the state of the environment of Eastern Europe

EU Interest	Rationale	Example
General	transboundary nature of environmental pollution	importation of air and water pollution
Political	increase EU's international standing	co-ordination of Phare programme
Strategic	demonstrate the benefits of reforms, and legitimise transition	improvement in local living and working environment, and health legitimises reforms
Domestic	protect EU citizens' health and environment quality	Germany, Czech and Polish death black triangle
Trade	low pollution costs in East could undermine free competition	low priced goods from Eastern Europe on EU market
Industry	halt move by industry to relocation to areas of low environmental standards	'polluter havens' as firms relocation to low pollution standard country
Business	opening up business opportunities for transfer of ecological technology	provision of pollution abatement technology and environmental management skills to Eastern Europe
Financial	ambient quality in EU more cheaply achieved through emission reduction in Eastern Europe	relatively lower cost reduction in air pollution in East, improving air quality in EU
Regional	member states share borders resulting in transboundary environmental pollution at regional level	river systems, such as the Danube; ecological zones such as the Mediterranean

EU environmental management in economic, particularly industrial, strategy. Indeed, it could be argued that one of the prime reasons that many of the governments of Eastern European countries are so willing to accept the EU's role in shaping their environmental policy is not that they have a high commitment to environmental protection as such but that EU environmental policy is in fact funding the modernisation of their industry.

Thus, it is clear the EU's interest in environmental policy in East and Central Europe is not limited to concerns with the environment as such, but is rather part of its wider role in shaping political and economic reform. Similarly, the governments of East and Central European countries see this investment as offering the opportunity not only to engage in environmental clean-up but also to bring about economic restructuring and modernisation. The Commission also realised that it cannot rely exclusively on private capital to undertake this environmental clean-up and management, as many of the more urgent needs are for environmental management of public goods, such as transport infrastructure and clean-up of water and air, for which private capital will not be forthcoming. Given this, the EU has not only to co-ordinate but also to contribute towards funding these policies.

By now the general rationale for EU involvement in the transition process in East and Central Europe and its specific interest in shaping environmental policy will have become clear. Attention now needs to be focused on actual policy content. Following the procedure used above, we begin by looking at general EU policy in this area before focusing in detail on EU environmental policy in the former Soviet bloc.

6.4 EU policy towards East and Central Europe

General policy interests

The development by the EU of a foreign policy is legally sanctioned by article 30.1 of the Single European Act (SEA). The Maastricht Treaty further strengthened the EU's commitment to international action. The Community's first trade and co-operation agreement with a Comecon country, Hungary, came into force in December 1988. This was followed by an agreement with Poland in December 1989 and by numerous others, including Bulgaria, in November 1990.

This involvement, however, tended to be both reactive and *ad hoc* and at Rhodes in 1988 the Community argued for the need for a more coherent and effective response to the changes that were occurring in the Soviet bloc. A decision was subsequently made at the 1989 summit of the G7 industrialised countries to sponsor a programme of aid and restructuring in the former Eastern bloc. Later the G7 as well as the World Bank were to commit funding and the European Commission was given responsibility for co-ordinating the actions of the group of 24 OECD countries under a programme called the Phare Programme (Poland and Hungary: Action for Restructuring the Economy). This was initially designed to help Poland and Hungary carry through their reforms. Being given the task of co-ordinating this entire multinational aid programme was a major political success for the Union (see Box 5).

The position of environmental policy in the Phare Programme is ambiguous. On the one hand, the Commission has argued that environmental policy forms a crucial component of its reform package for East and Central Europe. Furthermore, it argues that its aim is to integrate environmental considerations into all aspects of the economic reform package (Commission, 1992b, p.29). On the other hand, it continuously gives priority to economic reform, even if these measures bring negative environmental consequences. The main priority area for funding, for example, has been the restructuring of state enterprises and private sector development, accounting

5

The Phare Programme

Initially the assistance that the European Community co-ordinated was confined to Poland and Hungary, but it was subsequently extended to include Bulgaria, Czechoslovakia, the GDR, Romania and Yugoslavia. Albania and the Baltic states were included in the programme in 1992, bringing the total number of beneficiaries to ten. By 1993 this had been increased to 11 countries.

The aim of the Phare Programme is to support the process of economic restructuring in former Eastern bloc countries and to 'encourage the changes necessary to build a market-orientated economy and to promote private enterprise' (Commission, 1992, p.2). The connection between democratic and market reforms was also explicit in Phare and a second, closely related, concern was to help strengthen the newly forming democracies of Eastern Europe (Commission, 1994d, p.1). In this sense the EU's involvement can be seen as a temporary measure, preparing the ground, politically, economically, socially and environmentally, for subsequent inward investment by European industry. This preparation mainly involves giving technical assistance, start-up aid, infrastructural assistance and skill transfer to the recipient country, as well as some humanitarian aid (Commission, 1994d, p.5). As the recipient countries progress with restructuring, it is intended that the focus of Phare will shift away from the provision of know-how towards investment to support the development of economic, social and physical structures for further integration into the Western European system, in particular full EU membership (Commission, 1994d, p.16).

In the first five years of operation to 1994, Phare has made available 4283 million ECU to 11 partner countries, making Phare the largest assistance programme of its kind (Commission, 1994b, p.5). The money takes the form of grants. The allocation of funds is based on the decision 'to base programmes on a two year perspective whenever possible so as to better concentrate on the long-term infrastructural requirements of economies converting to market principles' (Commission, 1992a, p.42).

After 1991, the Community targeted a small number of core areas on which to focus its assistance, areas identified as key to ensuring the success of the transition process. The first of these is privatisation and restructuring of the economy and the provision of a legislative and regulatory framework within which the market economy can function. The second core area is the modernisation of banking and financial services. The third area is the promotion of small and medium enterprises in the private sector. The fourth area is social, including labour market policy and social security arrangements. Finally, there are policies to deal with the strengthening of civil society and environmental protection.

for 23.5% of Phare funds, with 11.5% going to agricultural restructuring and only 9% to environment and nuclear safety, with a similar 9% to infrastructure, including energy, transport and telecommunications (Commission, 1994d, p.7).

Similar ambiguity surrounds the place of environmental considerations in other EU initiatives. While the Phare initiative is the most important of the EU programmes in the former Soviet bloc, it has also been accompanied by other Union initiatives. These include creating the European Bank for Reconstruction and Development (BERD), which has the specific aim of using Western aid to help develop the private sector in Eastern and Central Europe. The Union and its member states are the largest contributors to BERD and Phare as a whole, although they are joined in it by the USA, Japan and other Western countries as well as by international institutions. Its emphasis is on stimulating private enterprise as well as democracy and the market economy. It is also required to promote in all its activities environmentally sound and sustainable development. However, the shift from declaratory political statements about sustainable development to the integration of environmental consid- erations into the design and implementation of actual policies funded by BERD has yet to be achieved (European Bank for Reconstruction and Development, 1992). When complex policies are implemented in complex settings the result is often a gap between the declared aim of policy and the actual policy outcome and this case is no exception.

Other initiatives are also in operation, including those of a more directly political nature which attempt to rebuild civil society. As well as the introduction of multiparty elections, democratisation also involves the setting up of a whole range of institutions and the introduction of new procedures and practices in most parts of government, the legal system and in representative bodies such as political parties and trade unions (Commission, 1994, p.135). There is also support for non-governmental organisations (NGOs) which contribute to greater participation of individuals and groups in shaping social and economic development and public policy. Helping the development of the voluntary sector is seen as an important component of the social infrastructure of the newly democratising countries. By helping to establish NGOs similar to those found in the West, it is intended to strengthen the ties that hold these new democracies to the Western system, especially at the local level where it is harder for the EU to penetrate directly (Commission, 1994a, p.48–49).

The overall aim is to encourage the development of an open society and encourage open discussion, debate and increased access by interest groups to the policy process. Debate and public participation is considered to be particularly important in the environmental policy arena for the following reasons. First, this policy field is relatively new and the definition of policy problems is open to much controversy, not least among the policy experts. Second, policy solutions remain relatively underdeveloped and a good deal of scientific and technical uncertainty remains. Participation of environmental interest groups in the policy process helps widen the information and evidence available for use in developing policy solutions, while also helping to win acceptance for particular policy solutions. Third, environmental policy does not fit neatly into existing delineations of administrative competencies, but rather straddles traditional administrative boundaries, such as agricul- ture, industry, mining, fishing and forestry as well as urban planning. Thus successful policy outcomes require not only that environmental considerations be integrated into the policy fields, but that open debate take place between interested parties, in order to achieve maximum policy coherence across a wide range of policy areas.

Fourth, environmental management also requires behavioural changes, not only within firms and industry but also at the level of the household and the individual. Thus environmental policy cannot be successful if it is seen only as an imposition from above – it must also emerge as the product of 'bottom-up' input.

Fifth, NGOs, at least in the West, have played a key role in ensuring implementa- tion of environmental policy, acting as watchdogs of the policy process, including informing on member states who fail to implement fully particular policies, raising public awareness of environmental issues, particularly at the local level, providing expertise and policy solutions and in some cases actually taking charge of policy implementation (Baker, 1993). NGO participation in ensuring effective and efficient policy outcomes is, at least in part, dependent upon the openness of the policy process to their interests.

Finally, environmental groups played a key role in destabilising many of the old communist regimes, especially in Czechoslovakia and Bulgaria and the expectation is that the new governments not only acknowledge this but that the reform process will provide environmental interests with access to the policy process, which was long denied them under communism. However, it must also be acknowledged that the influence of local and international NGOs on environmental policy since the revolutions has been relatively weak.

Plate 6.3 Berlin, 10 May 1991. Members of Greenpeace scaled the Brandenburg Gate to protest against the use of nuclear energy. 'Energy for the East – Without Atomic Energy' announced a placard strung across the top of the building. The protest came at a time of growing concern over the safety of nuclear reactors in Eastern Europe and the USSR. Photo: Camera Press, London

EU environmental policy for East and Central Europe

From ad hoc to strategic policy

Current EU environmental policy towards East and Central Europe can be dated from the signing in 1988 of a 'common declaration' between the Community and the Council for Mutual Economic Assistance. Following this, the first special environmental conference was convened by the Conference on Security and Co-operation in Europe held in Sofia, Bulgaria, in 1989. As far as the environmental dimension of EU policy is concerned, the Commission has argued that:

> The basic philosophy is to incorporate ecology into economy and to build on regional initiatives and responsibilities, therefore leading to a totally new strategy based on true energy prices, pollution monitoring systems, new standards for industry and quick action regarding air and water pollution, where efficient techniques should be introduced (Commission, 1992b, p.29).

This statement is in keeping with the current belief of the Commission that effective and efficient environmental management must involve the integration of environmental considerations in all other policy sectors. However, while mentioning that in principle the policies of the Phare Programme have to take account of the environment, little attempt is made to integrate environmental considerations into policy design in specific sectors, giving rise to a gap between expressed intent and policy outcome. Thus, for example, between 1990 and 1993 Phare continued to concentrate its efforts on those sectors that contributed directly to the transition to a market economy and liberal democracy. As the Western experience has shown and as I have argued above, the shift to a market-led economy is no guarantee of increased environmental protection.

The history of the environmental dimension of the Phare Programme can be divided into two phases: an initial phase, characterised by *ad hoc* crisis management and a later, more strategic phase. In the initial phase Phare support covered urgent actions, such as the supply of equipment to monitor air and water pollution, studies on specific problems and help in establishing standards and legislation. The focus was then switched to develop a more strategic approach, based around the development of policies and programmes for specific sectors such as waste treatment. By the second phase, Phare also began to promote environmental investment through co-financing operations with international financial institutions (Commission, 1994d, p.8). Added to this is a sub-programme directed towards nuclear safety to which, after Chernobyl, the international community attaches high priority. In this area, Phare focuses on financing safety studies, improvement of management and control procedures and setting up rapid alert systems and the strengthening of regulatory and safety authorities (Commission, 1994d, p.9). EU management of the safety of nuclear installations outside its own borders protects the Union's own citizens against radiation dangers.

This shift from *ad hoc* responses to strategic involvement in environmental policy reflects more general changes in the nature of the EU response to the collapse of the Soviet bloc. Soon after the initial EU response to the changes in Eastern Europe, the need was felt to move from an *ad hoc* response to a more coherent and secure relationship with its Eastern neighbours. From this developed the policy of establishing 'European

Agreements' with a number of East and Central European countries, specifically those that have made noticeable progress towards pluralist democracy and a market economy. At the Copenhagen Summit in June 1993, the Council offered those countries with European Agreements the prospect of full membership of the European Union, as soon as certain economic and political conditions are met. The European Agreements have now become the main framework within which EU policy is formulated in Bulgaria, the Czech Republic, Hungary, Poland, Romania and the Slovak Republic, with Slovenia and the Baltic countries expected to be offered Association Agreements in the near future.

As a consequence of signing these agreements, there has been a tendency, not least in the environmental policy area, for East and Central European countries to 'import' existing EU policy and apply it in their own domestic policy spheres. Granted many of these countries are in the process of negotiating full membership of the Union and thus will eventually have a say in shaping the content of all EU policy, including environmental policy. For the present, however, the newly forming environmental strategies and policies in these countries are moving in the direction of the EU's policy approach, an approach over which these countries have had effectively no say.

There are a number of problems associated with adopting the pollution standards, practices and policy tools currently in use within the Union and having these form a major component of new environmental management strategies in East and Central European countries. First, many of the EU's environmental policies were formulated when environmental policy required unanimous voting in the Council and as such are the result of compromise. They have therefore been the subject of criticism for being too weak in their standards or too narrow in their focus, criticism levelled in particular by EU member states such as The Netherlands which have a strong commitment to environmental protection. Applying these standards to countries outside the EU, it could be argued, is compounding the problems associated with the adoption of low environmental standards. Second, the relevance of these policies, in particular in relation to the specific environmental problems of peripheral regions, has been questioned (Baker *et al.*, 1994). Third, these policy responses were formulated in relation to specific environmental problems within Western countries and it is not at all evident that they are suitable, possible to implement or the most appropriate responses to the environmental priorities of Eastern Europe. Fourth, many of the policy tools, especially those recently suggested in the Fifth Environment Action Programme, require functioning and effective market systems, which remain as yet underdeveloped in many East and Central European countries.

As well as the particular problems associated with the adoption of EU environmental policies in non-EU member states, the move by many former Soviet bloc countries to full membership of the EU also presents wider difficulties. There are still fears of economic failure and, consequently, of a reversion to authoritarian and nationalistic regimes (Pinder, 1991, p.1). The transition to pluralist democracy and the market economy has had serious negative consequences. Economic liberalisation has resulted in the removal of state subsidies and protectionist control, resulting in sharp increases in unemployment. Outward trade with the West is not easy to establish, given inefficiencies and inadequate quality control in production and the necessity to negotiate trade agreements in the face of import barriers throughout the EU as a whole.

Inflation has decreased the value of the already meagre monthly wage, particularly for those on fixed income such as pensioners and most of the economies are already burdened with heavy debt. In this context, the task of the international communities and in particular the EU, is not merely to aid economic transition but to ensure the continuation of public support for harsh economic policies and to prop up what are in many cases fragile political democracies.

This concern is especially directed towards East Europe, most noticeably the Balkan states, where steps taken towards political and economic reform lag behind those already accomplished in Central Europe. In these countries the prospects of pluralist democracy and a competitive market economy seem more distant and the danger of authoritarian nationalism seems greater than in Central Europe. Since the revolution, economic difficulties have also beset Bulgaria and the net material product of Bulgaria, Poland and Rumania fell by over one-tenth in 1990, cutting already low incomes (Pinder, 1991, p.51). The transition is not helped by the fact that in some countries the revolution has been less complete than in others. For example, in Bulgaria and Rumania, the post-communist elections of 1990 produced governments led by the old communist parties, even if they had adopted new names. Evidence of concern over the fragility of these democracies can be seen by the fact that the Commission still keenly feels the need to monitor the situation in Bulgaria and Rumania and to assess whether the necessary political and economic conditions for transition are being established (Pinder, 1991, p.43).

It should, however, be recognised that Eastern Europe has not simply been a passive recipient of EU environmental initiatives and programmes. For example, there was an attempt to develop a pan-European approach or 'Environment for Europe' process, otherwise known as the 'Dobris' process, after the castle near Prague where the conference of European environmental ministers (and colleagues from the US, Canada and Japan) took place in 1991. Although it has not been pursued it does illustrate that there are potential alternative approaches to environmental protection which deal with Europe as a whole rather than in terms of East–West relationships (see Box 6).

Implementation difficulties

As in other policy areas, the successful implementation of the EU's environmental programme is crucially dependent upon the administrative capacity of the beneficiary states. Recognising this, the EU has specifically given assistance to deal with areas of administrative weaknesses in the policy process, as well as giving funding to deal more directly with pollution control. Approximately 1.5% of the Phare budget has gone towards institutional reform. Examples of help in dealing with administrative weaknesses included helping the establishment of special environmental units within the existing central government administrations and providing advice to local level governments on how to restructure operations, as well as training civil servants in their new roles and responsibilities.

Local government was particularly weak during the period of communist rule, when centralised planning left little room for administrative autonomy at the local or regional levels. The development of local government is considered particularly important for successful environmental policy management, as pollution control policy, including monitoring of pollution levels, is usually implemented at the local

6

The philosophy and objectives of the Dobris Conference 'Environment for Europe', June 1991

Vavrousek states:

'... The basic idea was very simple: to see Europe as a single, very vulnerable ecological unit, afflicted with many severe environmental problems which needed well-co-ordinated national as well as international responses. Unilateral and isolated sectoral activities can be only partially beneficial due to the complexity of human behaviour and interconnected nature of continental as well as planetary ecosystems. So the three long-term objectives proposed for the Dobris conference were derived from these ideas. The first was to upgrade substantially the existing European environmental protection and restoration institutions, national as well as international and to integrate them into a pan-European system of co-ordinated 'mechanisms' of environmental efforts at continental level. This future European Environmental and Protection and Restoration System (EEPRS) has eventually to be established as an integral part of a similar global system.

The second Dobris objective was to develop, implement and then periodically to revise an Environmental Programme for Europe (EPE). This could become the common framework for environmental protection activities on our continent. But the third objective was the least conventional and, in my view, the most important. I wanted the ministers to start to discuss human values and environmental ethics for sustainable development as the basis for such ways of life which can re-establish harmony between humankind and Nature ... .'

Source: Vavrousek, J. *Accepting the Challenge of Environmental Security*. In Prins, G. (ed.) (1993).

level. Governments cannot effectively govern in liberal democracies without a competent civil service, especially at the local level. Therefore the EU regards helping central government decentralise services to local government level as of particular importance and is actively encouraging the provision of local government officials with the range of skills necessary to take on these new responsibilities (Commission, 1994d, p.8). Another important dimension of ensuring policy success is the aid granted towards the establishment of legislative and regulatory frameworks and the development of institutions and organisations adapted towards the new tasks. These developments are especially important in environmental management, as most of the areas in urgent need of policy management are public goods, such as water and air and as such are unlikely to respond to solutions that are exclusively market-led or are unlikely to be provided for by the private sector alone. Some of the difficulties encountered in implementing EU environmental policy have been highlighted in the case study below, dealing with implementation of the Phare Programme.

Problems with EU involvement in East and Central Europe

Involvement in the reconstruction of East and Central Europe is also not without its difficulties for the Union itself. First, this involvement gives rise to institutional and

7

The implementation of EU policies: the case of Phare

The implementation of the Phare Programme involves the establishment of an agreed framework of programmes with the national authorities, within which particular projects are then identified. The tendering and contracts procedures used in the Phare Programme are similar to those used in other Union external aid programmes, such as to developing countries. Participation is open to all within the 15 member states as well as those within the beneficiary country. Major supply contracts are the subject of open tenders, published in the official journal. Monitoring and evaluation is ongoing and for each of the main sector programmes, provision is made for a six-monthly audit of expenditure by independent experts.

The funding of the Phare Programme was initially subject to very severe constraints: the budget had to have full commitment within a year, imposing a very short lead-in time between decision and commitment. This made multi-annual development programmes impossible. Later, the obstacles to multi-annual programmes were removed, although the Phare Programme still maintains end-of-year deadlines for commitments. A review at the end of the first year of the Phare Programme pointed to a number of problems in beneficiary states, including:

○ inappropriate legal and institutional frameworks
○ under-developed institutions, with modernisation of public administration and greater accountability at both local and national level urgently required
○ weakness in civil society and lack of social dialogue.

The Commission thus found that a good deal of flexibility in approach was required, as many of the countries involved had no experience as an aid recipient. For example, the Commission found in the early stages of the Phare Programme, when it applied to Poland and Hungary, that both countries had '[…] difficulties in distinguishing between tied and untied aid, between the programme and project approach, between loan and grant finance'. Furthermore, they found that 'The national authorities did not have much time to work out their own medium term objectives and sectoral adjustment policies, let alone the appropriate institutional structures' (Commission, July 1991, p.5).

Consequently the Phare Programme initially concentrated on the establishment of procedures and relationships. In the light of the magnitude of the political and economic changes facing the countries involved, the Commission has spoken openly about the difficulties of getting the Phare Programme into operation. Within recipient countries:

> Ministers and civil servants were dealing with new concepts, new processes for which little in their previous experience had prepared them. Least of all had they any experience of handling programmes of development assistance. Thus there were inevitable delays in setting up the organisational structures to agree on national priorities for assistance and to co-ordinate on a national basis the offers of a wide range of donors. Further understandable delays occurred as new Parliaments accustomed themselves to tackling the adoption of the necessary legislation for effecting economic reforms (Commission, July 1991, p.18).

administrative problems for the EU. The co-ordination by the EU of Western policy on the former Eastern bloc is a complex process. This is all the more complex given the nature of the EU's own policy-making process and its complex and opaque institutional structures. The Commission has two Directorates-General involved in policy towards the East: DGI, responsible for external relations and hence for trade, for cooperation agreements, for association and in particular for the Phare Programme; and DGII, responsible for economic and financial affairs and thus for the macroeconomic input into Phare, in particular the financial assistance. To this must be added the input of specific Directorates-General, for example, agriculture, environment, etc. The Economic and Social Committee and the European Parliament also play a role in shaping policy, the latter in particular on budgetary matters, relating to Phare expenditure. The Union's capacity to pursue an effective policy towards the East is dependent upon co-ordination and mutual agreement between these institutions. Experience to date in other policy areas has shown that such co-ordination and policy coherence is difficult to achieve.

Implementation of EU-directed policy is dependent upon the conditions and capacity in beneficiary states, especially at the local level. The EU has difficulty penetrating to these levels, a fact not helped by the weakness of local and regional government in East and Central European countries. Further, the Commission's capacity to assess the aid needs of its Eastern neighbours, to disburse aid effectively and to judge economic and political developments, especially those that threaten the new democratisation, can be questioned. It lacks adequate staffing levels, administrative resources and access to feedback and on-the-ground information. This is in contrast to the help it received in shaping its own domestic policies. Here, the Commission can rely on an array of formal as well as informal networks of contacts. DGXI, which is responsible for environmental matters, for example, is in close contact with the European Environmental Bureau (EEB) which is an umbrella group for many European environmental interests; not only does it provide DGXI with scientific information, but also feedback from activists and updates on policy implementation at the local level (Baker, 1993; Mazey and Richardson, 1994). When it comes to formulating policy for East and Central Europe and ensuring effective implementation, this informal policy input is lacking, for two reasons. First, since the revolutions, environmental groups have declined in importance and influence and have few resources and limited experience in gaining access to the EU policy process. Second, within the EU few if any mechanisms are in place to enable it to reach environmental interests from countries that are not member states of the Union.

The second area of difficulty in relation to EU-co-ordinated assistance to East and Central Europe is connected to political issues within the Union. Increased involvement in East and Central European affairs, especially when that involves added financial commitments, runs the risk of generating opposition at home. Economically weaker member states may come to resent the increasing drain that the reforms place on the EU budget, especially given the enormity of the tasks facing the newly democratising economies. The costs involved in environmental clean-up, for example, could be seen as a drain on resources available for dealing with the Union's own severe environmental degradation which, despite over 20 years of policy effort, shows little sign of improvement. The widening of the Union, to allow new membership from East and Central Europe, also exacerbates this concern, especially given the already serious deficit in environmental policy implementation within the existing Union boundaries. This deficit has led to the establishment of a Cohesion Fund to enable peripheral member states to cover the costs of implementation of environmental policy. This fund is financially limited and it is doubtful if the Union can reach agreement on its expansion to enable it to be used to fund the implementation of policy outside the Union.

Third, there are problems relating to the undemocratic nature of EU involvement in shaping the policies, environmental or otherwise, of East and Central Europe. The Commission has argued that its policies, such as those directed through the Phare Programme's activities, are 'demand driven', that is, they are a response to the beneficiary state's own requests (Commission, 1992a, p.40). Thus, for example, it has argued that 'The main priorities of Phare funding reflect the priorities and polices of its partner countries and are adapted to the requirements of the reform in each country' (Commission, 1994d, p.6). However, the Commission goes on to argue that:

> A condition of Phare funding is that each country maintains a commitment to democracy and progress towards a market economy. Subject to this condition, Phare's partner countries decide priority areas for spending the funds, within a framework agreed with the European Union. This joint process results in Indicative Programmes which cover a three year period (Commission, 1994d, p.6).

In other words, while arguing that its policies, such as the Phare Programme, are demand driven, the EU dictates the framework within which the demands are met. The beneficiary states, given that they are outside the Union, can exercise only limited influence over the legislative and policy-making process of the EU. Allowing them to increase their influence without adding to the already cumbersome and opaque nature of the EU policy-making process is a difficult task. Access to the Court of Justice by East and Central European countries is also restricted. Further, there has been very little public discussion about the role that the EU is increasingly playing in shaping the environmental policy of East and Central European countries and in particular those countries that have signed European Association Agreements. Neither, as Pinder has argued, has there been public discussion on the wider issues, such as the political and economic conditions that the EU is laying down for association or about the elements of pluralist democracy that association and aid are intended to encourage (Pinder, 1991, p.38).

Finally, despite the contribution that EU involvement will undoubtedly make to the management of environmental quality in East and Central Europe the irony (as we noted earlier) is that EU policy, including the Phare Programme, is also likely to make a contribution to environmental deterioration. The reasons for this are linked to the failure of the EU to integrate environmental considerations into other policy areas and to continue to give priority to economic restructuring over environmental protection. Developments in the area of transport infrastructure provide a good example. Transport is one of the major contributors to environmental degradation. However, EU funding of transport policy is primarily concerned with road building and improvement. The development of road networks is considered very important by the EU, especially at the regional level, for example in the Balkans, where road building is seen as having an important role to play in opening up trade in the region. However, instead of encouraging this trade to be conducted in an environmentally sustainable manner, the programme aims to encourage more road haulage. For example, currently 86 % of international freight traffic in Bulgaria is by road. It is estimated that by the year 2000, the North–South axis will see a net increase in traffic of some 30% while the East–West axis will see an increase of some 25% (Commission, 1994, p.15). The Phare-funded programme is aimed at realising this growth, through, for example, the rehabilitation of some 800 km of roads and motorways linking Rumania with Greece and those linking the former Yugoslavia with Turkey and the Black Sea and the completion of parts of the trans-European motorway. Public transport or development of the more environmentally efficient rail network, is attracting only limited funding under this project, such as the reconstruction of the Dupnitza-Kulata railway line linking Bulgaria and Greece (Commission, 1994c, p.26).

Concern for the negative environmental consequences that the process of transition may bring and in particular those that may arise as a result of EU involvement, prompts us to ask a set of deeper questions. There is a danger that the shift to a market-led approach, which is very attractive to the new elites seeking to reform the command economies, will result in environmental considerations being placed lower and lower on their priority listing. This approach, based as it is on deregulation and the freeing of market forces, may strengthen the historical tendency of policy makers in these countries to push ahead with economic development whatever the cost, be it environmental or otherwise. This leaves us with an interesting topic for further discussion – what have been the environmental consequences of the collapse of communism and the economic and political reforms that this has unleashed?

6.5 Conclusion

We began this chapter by asking a set of questions surrounding the involvement of the EU in shaping the environmental policies of former Soviet bloc countries. Our initial concern was to enquire into the nature of the environmental problems facing East and Central European countries and to ask why these problems had arisen. Our analysis has shown that under the period of communist rule, environmental problems were by and large ignored, either because of the mistaken belief that only profit-orientated and hence capitalist, economic development could give rise to environmental degradation or because of the overriding centrality of the ideology of industrialisation. We then saw that during the period of transition, environmental issues were not just related to the call for stricter environmental legislation, but became bound up with wider political demands. As a consequence, the environmental problems in many countries became linked with political opposition to the communist state.

We then asked why the EU is interested in ensuring more effective environmental management in these countries. We found that East and Central European environmental policy became an international issue, not only because of the transboundary nature of pollution, but because environmental reform in East and Central Europe became linked with the ending of the Cold War. From the analysis presented in this chapter it has become clear that the EU's involvement in environmental policy formulation and implementation in East and Central Europe is undertaken within the context of aiding these countries to make a smooth and stable transition to market economies and pluralist democracy. EU involvement in shaping the reform process in general and environmental policy in particular, offers it economic, political and environmental opportunities. These include the prospect of increased trade and the opportunity to expand its international standing through involvement in one of the major international political developments of the late 20th century and the chance to improve not only environmental quality in neighbouring countries but also within its own borders. Similar opportunities were also present for East and Central European countries, not least the opportunity to clean up the environmental damage inherited from the period of communist rule, while at the same time allowing them to engage in much needed economic restructuring and modernisation.

However, we also saw that, while there are opportunities, the EU's capacity to bring about an effective environmental management programme is constrained by its own complex policy-making process and by the overriding economic and political priorities of the reform process, as well as fragile democracies, weak administrative capacity, weak local government and undeveloped civil society in the beneficiary states. Further, the EU's dominant role also brings problems for the beneficiary states, not least those connected with the undemocratic nature of the EU's involvement in these countries.

Finally, we asked about the problems associated with the involvement of the EU in playing such a major role in shaping the environmental policy of East and Central European countries. The coupling of environmental policy with the wider process of political and economic transition has brought difficulties. It has meant that environmental policy is limited by and framed within, first, the medium-term goals of transition to pluralist democracy and the market economy and second, the longer term policy goals of widening and deepening of the European integration process. In short, environmental policy management by the EU is not primarily motivated by environmental considerations nor is it primarily directed towards environmental ends.

In conclusion, we have found in this chapter that, while stricter environmental protection strategies have been adopted in the newly emerging democracies of East and Central Europe, environmental policy tends to be reactive, involving by and large the clean-up of the negative environmental legacy of communist rule or the uncritical adoption of EU standards and policy norms; policy effectiveness is hampered by other policy priorities; and implementation is hindered by weakness in administrative capacity, weak local government, the legacy of communist administration, financial constraints and a weakened environmental movement.

7

The scope for North–South co-operation

Colin Sage

7.1 Introduction

This chapter addresses the evolution and development of North–South relations in the context of the emergence and increasing importance attached to international environmental policy making. Its underlying argument is that the root causes of environmental change and resource degradation are to be found in the process of *globalisation*, which is especially influencing patterns of development in countries of the South. By 'South' I mean the developing countries of Africa, Asia and Latin America while the 'North' encompasses the industrialised nations of Europe, Japan, North America and Australasia (Northern in terms of development though Southern in location). There are, of course, many differences within the South, a point I shall return to later in the chapter (for a discussion of the definition of North and South see, for example, Sage, 1996).

Anthony Giddens defines globalisation as 'the intensification of worldwide social relations which link distant localities in such a way that local happenings are shaped by events occurring many miles away and vice versa' (Giddens, 1990, p.64). The most obvious expression of this is the policies of the international agencies which have world-wide consequences that can penetrate down to local level. Examples include the structural adjustment policies of the International Monetary Fund and World Bank; the measures agreed under the Uruguay round of the General Agreement on Tariffs and Trade (GATT) and now regulated by the World Trade Organisation (WTO) (see Chapter 5); and, of course, environmental treaties. While governments may enter into voluntary agreements to protect the environment, such treaties nevertheless bind signatory countries to national policy changes that can have significant social, economic and political repercussions at local level.

Yet underlying the globalisation of policy making is the 'internationalisation of economic, social and cultural forces and models' (Khor, 1995). Transnational corporations, including those working with televisual media, have been responsible for a rapid and dramatic transformation of local societies in the South, especially altering lifestyle aspirations and patterns of consumption. The promotion of infant formula feeds to replace breastfeeding is one of the clearest examples of such change, which occurs to the detriment of the child (lack of sterilisation and use of untreated water) and the family (cost of feed). The notion of globalisation can help to explain such change by revealing the multiple linkages and interconnections that exist between different places and at different levels (local, regional, national) across the world and which operate across all realms of life: political, economic, industrial, military, cultural and environmental.

In the environmental sphere one important consequence of globalisation is that the site of environmental degradation may be far removed from its principal agent. This means that the relationship between cause and effect may not be obvious and, consequently, attributing responsibility is not straightforward. There is also an abundance of evidence demonstrating that globalisation touches on almost every aspect of our daily lives. The

Plate 7.1 A television set powered by solar energy, Niger. Globalisation is transforming local societies in the southern hemisphere. Photo: Mark Edwards/Lineair

concept of globalisation can thus be a useful tool to deepen our understanding of the causes of environmental degradation and constraints on developing effective programmes and policies for sustainable development.

Giddens identifies four dimensions of globalisation: the nation state system; the capitalist world economy; the world military order; and the international division of labour. I shall briefly describe what Giddens means by each of these in turn.

The nation state system has emerged from its European origins to provide a world-wide framework encompassing some 200 or so political units with recognised sovereignty over territory and people. Yet the relative autonomy of each nation state is conditioned by processes of uneven economic development and other factors, not least the legitimacy of the state in the eyes of its citizens or subjects. Clearly those nation states which have been established only during the past 30–40 years following the end of colonial rule have had to work hardest to establish their sovereignty internally, although their autonomy has usually been recognised by other states (see Chapter 1).

The capitalist world economy. Since the demise of the Soviet Union and its East European allies and the market reforms of China, it is effectively the case that a single capitalist economy operates across the entire world. There are major centres of economic power (members of the Group of Seven of industrialised countries) but the main agents are international businesses, principally transnational corporations (TNCs). The largest TNCs today have budgets greater than all but a handful of countries and their influence through trading relations with states brings a global expansion of commodity markets, including labour power.

The world military order. The globalisation of military power is not confined to weaponry and alliances between the armed forces of different states – it also concerns war itself. The involvement of the United States in Indochina and in the Gulf War is a testament to this. Yet many economically weak developing countries are militarily powerful and have long used external development assistance to strengthen their military security. This, of course, has consequences for the *environmental* security of individual countries and of the world community as a whole.

The international division of labour. This fourth dimension of globalisation concerns the expansion of industrial activity and its consequences for the international division of labour. The world-wide distribution of production has created patterns of regional specialisation in terms of type of activity, level of skills, remuneration, profitability and so on. The emergence of the *newly industrialising countries* (NICs) in the South (South Korea, Taiwan, Brazil, Mexico, Thailand, Malaysia, amongst others) has had implications for the old industrialised countries, such as the UK or the United States, which have experienced a decline in their traditional manufacturing base. It has also had a major impact on those industrialising countries themselves, transforming pre-existing forms of social organisation and the relations of local societies with their natural environment. Such transformations take many forms, e.g. the incorporation of young rural women into the factory labour force producing textiles or electronic goods for expor,t or the adoption of modern farming methods including the acquisition of new machinery, which has a major effect on productivity but also on the local resource base.

By employing the notion of globalisation, we can see that contemporary environmental problems are the result of interdependent patterns of development arising from the transfer of industrial technology and market values through the expansion of the international division of labour, reflecting regional specialisation and comparative advantage. The world-wide spread of capitalism and industrialism has penetrated far-flung areas of the world to a degree where even the local state has not brought them wholly under its political control. These forces lie behind the very nature of North–South relations and ultimately determine the prospects for sustainable development.

Yet, in using the notion of globalisation, it is vital to guard against a simplified universalism, in which it is assumed all countries, North and South, share a common threat posed by changes in the global environment and a common destiny of equal restraint. The world is marked by a strongly asymmetrical division in patterns of resource use, both historical and actual and in the relative responsibility for such global problems as ozone depletion and climate change. Consequently, in the many international fora convened to discuss the global environment, from Stockholm in 1972 to Rio de Janeiro in 1992, the countries of the South have continued to emphasise the centrality of economic development and the need to eliminate poverty before they can consider the consequences for natural resources. The North, on the other hand, seeks to urge upon the South a rather different set of priorities. The extract in Box 1 offers an interpretation for this apparent 'dialogue of the deaf'.

Globalisation, then, affords an explanation for the pattern of uneven development that is reflected in the nature of the environmental problems in the South. They are essentially problems of environment and development manifested in such features as land degradation, poor urban environments, bad sanitation, inadequate water quality,

North–South conflict

The essence of the problem (the conflict between North and South) is that the two parts of the world are at different stages of development, so that the South only produces the ingredients for the industry of the North and it sells them at uncertain and fluctuating rates to buy the more expensive finished products. There is an interdependence that locks the two parties into their unequal roles and when the South seeks to share in the industrial role of the North it enters an arena where both the conditions of technology and the rules of competition put it at a disadvantage. Thus, *there is neither equality of present status nor equality of opportunity for the future and the inequality of condition is mirrored and magnified by the inequality of capability to change it.* Not only have the norms and practices of postcolonial international relations trained the new nations to expect something different from their status of economic inferiority, after having emerged from a status of political subjugation, but the problems of economic inferiority within the international economic order keep coming back to the doorstep of the rich, who must keep their debtors alive enough to continue to service their debt, stable enough to continue to export their raw materials and even prosperous enough to continue to buy the exports of the rich. But kept alive to that degree, the South calls for more, demanding the equality that humanitarian norms promise to human beings and that the norms of the United Nations – as part of the current international political order – promise to states. Hence, it is a conflict not only of relations but also of perspectives, for it is primarily seen by both sides in zero-sum terms (Zartman, 1987, p.3).

polluted air and land, gross exploitation of natural resources and the dumping of wastes including toxic and hazardous wastes. This chapter focuses on the component elements of globalisation in North–South relations. It demonstrates the imbalance in these relations of trade, aid, industrialisation and economic growth which result in the North tending to exploit the South. A historical approach is adopted to show how these relations have developed and to indicate the origins of conflicts and the prospects for co-operation between North and South.

In Section 7.2 a historical survey demonstrates how uneven development in the South has been a consequence of the process of economic growth shaped by relations with the North. Section 7.3 discusses the impact of development on the environment and the alternative approaches that have been advanced to try to reconcile the conflicts between development and environmental protection. Section 7.4 examines the lead-up to the Earth Summit and beyond and the conflicts between North and South over the various global agreements that resulted. The conclusion (Section 7.5) considers the opportunities that have emerged for greater co-operation between North and South.

7.2 Tracing the Third World

The development race

According to Wolfgang Sachs, the Third World came into existence on 20 January 1949. This was the day on which President Harry Truman, in his inauguration speech before the United States Congress, identified the poorer countries as 'underdeveloped areas'. Overnight the immeasurable diversity of the South was crammed into a single category – underdeveloped. But, as Sachs argues, such a term was not a matter of accident but the clear expression of a worldview in which 'all the peoples of the world were moving along the same track, some faster, some slower, but all in the same direction' (1993, p.4). Moreover, progress along this track could be measured by gross national product (GNP), and GNP per capita still provides the system of ranking countries in the World Bank's annual World Development Report.

The development process was thus presented as a race in which the task of the stragglers (the poorest countries) was to catch up with the front runners (the rich industrialised countries, led by the United States). The world economic system provided the arena for this competitive process; development aid was the incentive and encouragement to those lagging behind. Truman's vision embodied both the optimism and the arrogance of a country which emerged from the Second World War financially, technologically and politically strengthened and able to take over the mantle of world leader from the European powers exhausted by conflict and without the moral or political capacity to maintain their imperial ambitions. Thus the growing numbers of newly independent countries could look to the United States for their economic and political inspirations and demonstrate allegiance to the West during the height of the Cold War.

The years since Truman's speech have indeed been marked by increasing economic competition, rising levels of agricultural and industrial production and unprecedented levels of material consumption. But this period has also seen a widening of the gap between North and South. In 1960 the richest 20% of the world's countries had incomes 30 times greater than those of the poorest 20% of countries. By 1990 the gap was 60 times greater. There is also the growing belief that the pursuit of economic growth has begun to reach, if not exceed, some biophysical limit.

Despite the emergence of new constellations of economic power, for example comprising the East and South East Asian newly industrialising countries and the capital-rich oil exporting countries of the Middle East, economic dominance still resides in the North, now including Japan. Yet for the majority of people in the South poverty has not been eliminated despite the slogans and rhetoric of successive United Nations' Development Decades and all their efforts at catching up. For example, according to the World Bank, in 1990 an estimated 1.1 billion people were living below the poverty line, of which 50% were in South Asia. Consequently, despite the globalisation of economic life based upon Western values and consumption patterns, the gap between front-runners and stragglers in the economic race is wider than ever (see Figure 7.1). Indeed, for Sachs, not only has the gap 'widened to the extent that it has become inconceivable that it could ever be closed […] it has become evident that the race track leads in the wrong direction' (p.5–6).

The imperative of industrialism

That the world is heading in the wrong direction is, of course, not an uncontroversial conclusion. For many in the South there is a powerful and understandable preoccupation with economic growth and development in the absence of any other obvious remedy for poverty and inequality. The centrality of this concern has been most evident in the context of policy debates around the global environment when the Non-Aligned Movement has invariably expressed in forthright terms the imperative of economic growth and development alongside assertion of the rights of self-determination and national sovereignty. Aspirations for economic growth are inevitably tied to strategies of industrialisation, which offer the only guarantee of breaking out of dependence upon primary commodities. The experience of Latin America is relevant here.

The countries of Latin America gained their independence from Spain and Portugal during the first half of the 19th century. Yet, despite over 100 years of independence by 1945 and the beginning of the end for colonialism in Asia and Africa, there remained in Latin America the persistence of symptoms associated with neocolonialism and underdevelopment. These included high levels of dependence upon external markets for the sale of agricultural products and other raw materials and an internal social structure in which an oligarchical elite exercised control over land and other economic assets. While there were naturally important differences between countries in the social organisation and culture of the majority populations, there were strong similarities in the position of the political elites and in economic structures. These circumstances gradually gave rise in the late 1940s to analysis by the UN Economic Commission for Latin America (ECLA) on the causes of economic stagnation and ways of overcoming it.

The analysis of ECLA demonstrated a deterioration in the terms of trade for Latin America's raw material exports as against the import of manufactured goods from the North. Their evidence thus flew in the face of theories of comparative advantage which emphasise the benefits of each country performing roles to which it is best suited. In Latin America's case it was always argued by neoclassical economists that development

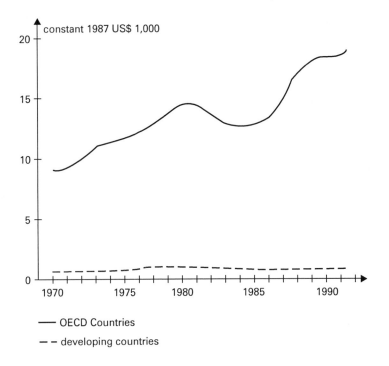

Fig. 7.1 Trends in GNP per capita, 1970–1992. Source: World Resources Institute, World Resources 1994–1995, p.5.

would follow on the exports of coffee, tin, copper, beef, etc. What such theories had not foreseen was the collapse of world trade in the 1930s following the 'crash' of 1929, when Brazilian coffee beans stockpiled on the dockside were eventually burnt for lack of a market. Or that the war of 1939–1945 would mean that the suppliers of manufactured goods stopped exports as industry was retooled to meet the need for armaments and other means of military conflict.

ECLA's analysis of external bottlenecks on trade led inevitably to consideration of strategies that would overcome such dependence on foreign markets. *Import substituting industrialisation* (ISI) became the slogan as the larger Latin American economies – Brazil, Argentina, Mexico – followed later by Chile, Colombia and Peru, as well as by India, Taiwan, South Korea and Hong Kong, began their own manufacturing activities to meet domestic demand. The main characteristic of ISI involves a relatively high degree of state intervention in the economy, principally through strategic direct investment in infrastructural and other projects and encouraging the inflow of private sector funds and concessional development assistance. The state sought to protect this incipient process of endogenous industrialisation by establishing high tariff barriers which imposed heavy taxes on cheaper foreign imports. As the process of industrialisation proceeded from the initial stage, where the manufacture of consumer goods (textiles, household items, foodstuffs) prevails, to the stage marked by the production of capital goods (e.g. iron and steel making, motor vehicle assembly, chemical plant) the role of foreign capital is increased. In seeking to develop an independent, modern, diversified industrial economy via a strategy of ISI, the countries of Latin America in particular increasingly came to depend upon the technology, scientific and managerial expertise and capital of transnational corporations (TNCs).

The consequences of industrialisation

During the 1950s and 1960s economic growth in the South, according to Brett, was 'uneven but not unimpressive'. The middle-income countries grew at a slightly faster rate (5.7%) than the developed countries (4.7%) which in turn outperformed the low-income countries (3.6%), although this was sufficient to produce improvements in per capita income. Between 1956 and 1970 total foreign private investment from the Organization for Economic Co-operation and Development (OECD) countries approached $58 billion, of which 50% originated in the USA, more than half was invested in raw material production, over a quarter in manufacturing and the rest in public utilities and services. Inflows of official development assistance over the same period was half the size again of private investment at just over $86 billion. Yet by the late 1960s these generally favourable developments could not disguise the serious structural dislocations and uneven process of development that was occurring. Brett identifies several key problems that became apparent during this period.

First was the continuing failure to narrow the gap between North and South even during a period of growth within the world economy. Indeed, the persistence of relative deprivation was associated with increasing internal inequality and of absolute impoverishment of the poorest in many countries.

Secondly, the 1950s and 1960s also saw increasing differentiation within the South as the newly industrialising countries (the NICs) and the oil exporters outperformed the rest. Moreover, the role of TNCs strongly reinforced this tendency towards uneven development, concentrating resources in a few developing countries. Brett cites a UN document which reports that 43% of the stock of direct foreign investment was concentrated in seven countries and a further 30% in another 13.

Thirdly, by the late 1960s serious structural problems had begun to appear in national strategies of ISI. The high levels of protection and subsidisation of capital-intensive industrialization drained the surpluses from the traditional export sectors and created major problems for national balance of payments. Meanwhile employment growth was constrained by the adoption of new, labour-saving technologies and further increased inequalities, which also worsened as chronic inflation took hold. The popular disillusionment with ruling bureaucratic elites and the political process which inevitably followed finally led to the wide-spread intervention of the military in politics. Throughout the 1960s and 1970s there were few countries in Latin America which escaped the seizure of power by the generals.

However, one group of countries escaped this particular set of outcomes associated with ISI. In Taiwan, South Korea, Hong Kong and Singapore the initial period of growth with non-durable consumer goods for the domestic market was followed by an expansion of manufacturing output for the export market. Taking advantage of their low-cost labour, these countries set out on a strategy of *export-oriented industrialisation* (EOI), in which manufactured output increased dramatically, as did levels of industrial employment. Once full employment had been achieved wages also began to grow, improving the distribution of national income and increasing domestic demand. Moreover, because TNCs were not the leading actors in export promotion during the early period, national investment adopted more appropriate labour-intensive technologies and sought greater domestic sourcing of inputs, leading to more balanced growth. Consequently, the experience of the four 'Asian Tigers' offered the most successful development model to other NICs, most especially those in the region such as Malaysia, the Philippines and Indonesia.

Yet it is important to recognise how development has become equated with industrialisation. Far from freeing society from the constraints of Nature as Marxists once argued, industrialism has arguably enslaved us to an obsessive pursuit of growth, continuous technological innovation and a belief in the right to spiralling levels of material consumption. The chief characteristic of industrialism for Giddens is 'the use of inanimate sources of material power in the production of goods, coupled to the central role of machinery in the production process' (1990, p.55–56). Industrialism consequently presupposes regularised social organisation in which old ways of

Plate 7.2 The Dutch-based multinational Philips uses cheap labour in Zambia to produce televisions. Photo: Ron Giling/Lineair

production and systems of work are shattered and the balance of economic power irreversibly shifts in favour of a new social class. It also, echoing Giddens, involves a transformation of the capacity to harness energy which powers production.

The degree to which the success of industrialism is entirely contingent upon unlimited supplies of cheap energy is, of course, borne out by the Gulf War, when the industrial countries went to war to protect a source of non-renewable fossil fuel resources. Moreover, our unreflexive dependence upon the tools of industrialism, such as the use of even simple electrical appliances, means that little thought is given to its social and environmental consequences. The implications of industrialism for every-day life are illustrated by the example in Box 2. Finally, the hazards of large-scale energy production are illustrated by the case of Chernobyl, where explosions in the nuclear reactor resulted in radioactive fallout across much of Europe.

2

The impact of technology

To demonstrate how Western technology in the South is a Trojan horse of Western economic values, Wolfgang Sachs uses the seemingly innocuous example of the electric mixer:

> Whirring and slightly vibrating, it makes juice from solid fruit in next to no time. A wonderful tool! So it seems. But a quick look at cord and wall socket shows that what we have before us is rather the domestic terminal of a national, indeed worldwide system.
>
> The electricity arrives via a network of cables and overhead utility lines, which are fed by power stations that depend on water pressures, pipelines or tanker consign-ments, which in turn require dams, off-shore platforms or derricks in distant deserts. The whole chain only guarantees an adequate and prompt delivery if every one of its parts is staffed by armies of engineers, planners and financial experts, who themselves can fall back on administrations, universities, indeed entire industries (and sometimes even the military) [...] Whoever flicks a switch on is not using a tool. He or she is plugging into a combine of functioning systems. Between the use of simple techniques and that of modern equipment lies the reorganisation of a whole society (Sachs, 1990, cited and extracted from McCully, 1991, p.249).

Downturn, divergence and debt

The relatively positive performance of the developing countries during the 1950s and 1960s was, of course, closely associated with the sustained period of growth in the world economy from 1945. However, by the mid-1970s a new phase of structural dislocation occurred which caused further differentiation and uneven development amongst the countries of the South. This was triggered, first, by US repudiation of the gold standard and the collapse of the fixed exchange rate system and second, by the fourfold increase in oil prices. This latter development was to push the balance of payments of oil importers into deficit and while the industrialised countries were able to restore economic equilibrium within a short period – albeit with significantly higher energy costs – the South sought to make increased use of borrowing. Members of the Organisation of Petroleum Exporting Countries (OPEC, of which more below) found themselves with more revenue than they were generally able to use and naturally deposited surplus capital with the international banks. These petrodollar deposits were then recirculated by the banks as loans, primarily to non-oil, middle-income countries whose industrialisation programmes had been interrupted by higher import prices. Between 1973 and 1981, the private banks increased their lending to the South sixfold to $220 billion. By 1981 70% of developing country debt was to the commercial banking sector (as opposed to the official development agencies such as the World Bank).

It is at this point worth emphasising once again that the collective nouns such as the 'Third World', the 'South', the 'developing countries' mask increasingly divergent economic performances, structures and interests. As Ravenhill observes:

> [...] the newly industrialising countries are worlds apart from sub-Saharan Africa: their interest in inexpensive raw materials inputs for their burgeoning industries sets them at odds with the latter's enthusiasm for higher prices; similarly, the dependence on imported oil of the north-east Asian NICs and Brazil gives rise to a sustained conflict of interests with OPEC and other LDC oil-exporters (1990, p.732; 'LDC' stands for 'least developed countries').

This divergence was to increase throughout the 1970s and 1980s. In the least developed countries production barely kept ahead of population growth, while in sub-Saharan Africa per capita food production actually began to decline. The non-oil, middle-income industrialising countries, meanwhile, borrowed heavily on the international financial markets and by the late 1970s were achieving high rates of growth of GDP and manufactured exports. In 1979, however, OPEC played its hand again, raising oil prices and this time the consequences were even more far-reaching, coinciding with the beginnings of the monetarist experiment in the UK and USA. Here, interest rates were the principal tool for controlling inflation in their domestic economies and as these rose across the financial markets, the world economy moved into deep recession. Demand for raw materials fell, as did prices, so that by 1982 they were at their lowest level since 1945. This decline, together with high interest rates on heavy borrowings, put many of the middle-income countries under intense financial pressure. Finally, in August 1982 the announcement that Mexico could not meet its debt-service commitments sent shock waves throughout the international banking system. The International Monetary Fund (IMF) stepped in to co-ordinate a series of rescue packages for countries (Brazil and Venezuela amongst them) caught in the debt crisis. This involved a rescheduling of the debt but also imposed a programme of structural adjustment designed to reorient the economies away from domestic concerns with employment generation and poverty alleviation and towards the needs of the world market and the dictates of world market prices.

The consequences of the 'debt crisis' and the structural adjustment remedy have been written about extensively and there is not the space to go into detail here. However, we should note that the main elements of *structural adjustment programmes* (SAPs) include exchange rate devaluation, restraints on government spending, controls on wages, liberalisation of trade and the encouragement of export-oriented activity: in other words, a widespread intervention in the commanding heights of a nation's economy. UNICEF, amongst others, have highlighted the consequences of

SAPs in deepening impoverishment, especially amongst the most vulnerable sections of the community and in undermining the legitimacy and authority of governments. It has also been widely argued that SAPs have caused widespread environmental destruction. The proponents of economic liberalisation, on the other hand, have either refuted the evidence deployed by critics of SAPs or have argued that the medicine may have had unpleasant side-effects but was necessary to restore full health in the long term. However, even the most orthodox economist seems unable to refute the scale of the financial transfer from South to North, which is described in Box 3. There is also general agreement that the process of development in the South has resulted in environmental degradation, the subject to which I now turn.

3

The Southern debt crisis

If the goals of official debt managers were to squeeze the debtors dry, to transfer enormous resources from South to North and to wage undeclared war on the poor continents and their people, then their policies have been an unqualified success ...

From the onset of the debt crisis in 1982 through 1990 ... each and every month, for 108 months, debtor countries of the South remitted to their creditors in the North an average six billion five hundred million dollars in interest payments alone. If payments of principal are included in the tally, then each of the 108 months from January 1982 through December 1990 witnessed payments from debtors to creditors averaging twelve billion four hundred and fifty million dollars.

Theoretically, the Third World's interest payments alone could have provided every man, woman and child in North America and Europe with over $1,000 during this nine year period.

According to the OECD, between 1982 and 1990, total resource flows to developing countries amounted to $927 billion. This sum includes ... all official bilateral and multilateral aid, grants by private charities, trade credits plus direct private investment and bank loans. Much of this inflow was not in the form of grants but was rather new debt, on which dividends or interest will naturally come due in the future.

During the same 1982–90 period, developing countries remitted *in debt service alone* $1,345 billion (interest and principal) to the creditor countries. For a true picture of resource flows, one would have to add many other South-to-North outflows such as royalties, dividends, repatriated profits, underpaid raw materials and the like. The income-outflow difference between $1,345 and $927 billion is thus a much understated $418 billion in the rich countries' favour. For purposes of comparison, the US Marshall Plan transferred $14 billion 1948 dollars to war-ravaged Europe, about $70 billion in 1991 dollars. Thus in the eight years from 1982–90 the poor have financed six Marshall Plans for the rich through debt service alone.

Have these extraordinary outflows at least served to reduce the absolute size of the debt burden? Unfortunately not: in spite of total debt service ... of more than 1.3 trillion dollars from 1982–90, the debtor countries as a group began the 1990s *fully 61 per cent more in debt than they were in 1982.* Sub-Saharan Africa's debt increased by 113 per cent during this period; the debt burden of the very poorest – the 'least developed' countries – was up by 110 per cent.

Source: George (1992), p.xiii–xvi.

7.3 Development versus environment

North and South – conflicting objectives

In the early 1970s there was a growing chorus of disquiet about the pace and extent of environmental destruction resulting from the continuing horizontal expansion of economic growth and rising levels of material consumption. The publication of the Club of Rome's report, *Limits to Growth* (Meadows *et al.* 1972), was a benchmark study that raised serious questions about the future supply of finite stocks of minerals and fossil fuels given the apparent unlimited capacity for consumption. Although the methods, assumptions and conclusions of this report were systematically attacked by development economists, *Limits to Growth* was nevertheless a highly influential publication that coincided with other signs of the gathering crisis. In 1971 the Man and the Biosphere Programme was launched by UNESCO to monitor human impacts on natural ecosystems while in the following year the United Nations Conference on the Human Environment was held in Stockholm.

The Stockholm conference marked a first step in dialogue between North and South in which the environment was a primary focus. Yet it was the rich industrialised countries which had the greatest need for the Conference to be a success, given rising public concern over pollution and 'the effluence of affluence'. For these countries it was necessary to agree some common environmental standards to which all subscribed and contributed in order that 'free riders' did not benefit from lower costs and thereby gain the advantage of producing cheaper goods for the global market. For the South, however, Stockholm represented an opportunity to talk about increased resource transfers to speed up the pace of development. Environmental pollution was seen as a necessary by-product of economic growth and only growth could help to eliminate the worst pollutant: poverty. As Enzensberger observed in 1974, all 'the brotherly rhetoric of Spaceship Earth conveniently overlooks the difference between the bridge and the engine room'. Consequently, Stockholm witnessed the first discordant note in what became a cacophonous and strident exchange between North and South during the 1970s and beyond as the United Nations became a battleground in setting an international agenda.

The aspirations for a united 'Third World'

The early 1970s represented the pinnacle of collective Southern leverage over the global development agenda. This was a time of a gradual thawing in the Cold War, a period of détente between the First and Second Worlds and the opening of a political space which allowed the countries of the South to promote their demands for a more equitable share of global resources under the banner of a so-called New International Economic Order. As mentioned earlier, the 1950s and 1960s had been a period of steady growth in the world economy which had brought rising demand for raw materials from the South. It was also a period of state building as a mass of countries emerged from the last gasps of an old colonialism to establish new national identities and join the development race; it was also a period of growing international solidarity between developing countries. Professing non-alignment with either of the two superpowers, the number of members grew steadily during the 1960s so that by the time of the Algiers meeting in September 1973, the Non-Aligned Movement formally established the Group of 77 as an operating caucus within the United Nations system.

By the end of 1974 the UN General Assembly had approved the Charter of Rights and Duties of States as well as the declaration of a New International Economic Order. These raised the profile of several issues relating to the environment, such as the sovereignty of states over their natural resources, the need for indexation of commodity prices and the right of countries to regulate the activities of transnational corporations, amongst others. But it was the attempt to create a new international trade regime in primary commodities that was the central issue of North–South relations throughout the 1970s. Taking the lead from OPEC's considerable success in agreeing to regulate the supply of oil to the industrialised countries and, consequently, reaping the rewards with higher prices, the South sought to establish other commodity agreements between producers. These were then to be made operational with the North through the Integrated Programme for Commodities under the auspices of the United Nations Conference on Trade and Development (UNCTAD).

The response of the North to the proposal to establish a series of linked international commodity agreements with the purpose of raising prices was predictably hostile. However, its strategy was principally one of foot-dragging; avoiding actions that would encourage greater co-operation between Southern countries and referring items for further negotiation. Meanwhile, individual producers sought to expand their output of primary commodities, with the encouragement of the World Bank and of the importing countries, with the consequences of aggregate oversupply relative to demand. Once recession began in the North in 1979, commodity prices began to plummet. This was exacerbated by a change in systems of production and types of industrial technology that sought greater efficiency in the use of energy and raw materials and in the development of synthetic substitutes. Consequently, today there are few effective international commodity agreements, UNCTAD has been entirely marginalised by the GATT and now the World Trade Organisation (see Chapter 4) and the power of OPEC has waned as its share of world oil production has diminished. Moreover, there are few new potential areas for greater Southern leverage in securing improvements in its terms of trade with the North, although the environment may still represent one. However, this will depend on whether the South is able to speak in any coherent fashion on behalf of the poor. As Saravanamuttu observes, 'Success ... in agenda setting is quite a different matter from success in agenda implementation, as the North–South balance of power has shown' (Saravanamuttu, 1994, p.228).

Aid and development

There have been, however, important initiatives led by Northern representatives which have sought improvements in the conditions of trade, aid and international development. The first of these was the Pearson Commission, led by an ex-Prime Minister of Canada, which was directed to examine overseas aid policies and find ways of improving the quality of development assistance. Arising out of the Pearson Commission came the UN recommendation that the developed countries should commit at least 0.7% of their GNP to overseas aid. In 1991 only five countries had reached and exceeded this target figure: Norway, Denmark, Sweden, The Netherlands and Finland. The contributions of the OECD donor countries are shown in Figure 7.2 (see also Middleton *et al.*, 1993).

The main concern of the Independent Commission on International Development Issues, established in 1977 under the chairmanship of the former chancellor of West Germany, Willy Brandt, was similarly with increasing the quantity of aid and international finance available to the South. In its first report published in 1980, the Commission recommended *inter alia*: an increase in the aid budgets of wealthy nations to a minimum of 1% of GNP; a system of international taxation to finance support for the poor; least developed countries having more say in the World Bank and the International Monetary Fund; more concessionary and preferential funds and so on. In light of the figures for aid budgets listed above and the fact that none of the other recommendations has been acted upon, it seems appropriate to dismiss the Brandt Commission as a failure. Whether its failure was due to timing or because its recommendations were politically unacceptable, or perhaps both, is largely inconsequential. Ekins favours the first explanation, noting that the international climate for development co-operation in the 1980s was not encouraging. The rise of a neo-liberal conservative orthodoxy, exemplified by the 'special relationship' between US President Reagan and British Prime Minister Thatcher, was certainly hostile to anything other than tight fiscal restraint and free market economics. The idea of concessionary terms was thus anathema to those in control of the reins of power. Middleton and colleagues believe that Northern governments as a whole were unsettled by the Brandt agenda which might have seriously challenged power relationships throughout the world. Not only do such governments owe their existence, at least in part, to the enormous financial interests of the North but, given the existence of the Cold War, 'Poor countries could not necessarily be relied upon to support the right side' (Middleton *et al.*, 1993, p.14).

However, it is Brandt's argument for mutual self-interest which lies at the heart of the Commission's thinking which is its great weakness. The North should help the South to greater prosperity, so the argument goes, not only on the grounds of equity but because Southern prosperity would produce more demand for Northern goods. As Ekins argues, this is very unconvincing:

At present powerful Northern (creditor) institutions are reaping handsome returns on loans that never get any smaller; Northern industry and consumers are getting Southern commodities at rock bottom prices; Northern arms manufacturers are selling nervous Third World elites large quantities of weapons; and, perhaps most important, Third World countries are being effectively tied in to Western models of development, with Western countries guaranteed a permanent technological lead. The old economic order is doing industrial countries very nicely economically and politically (Ekins, 1992, p.28–29).

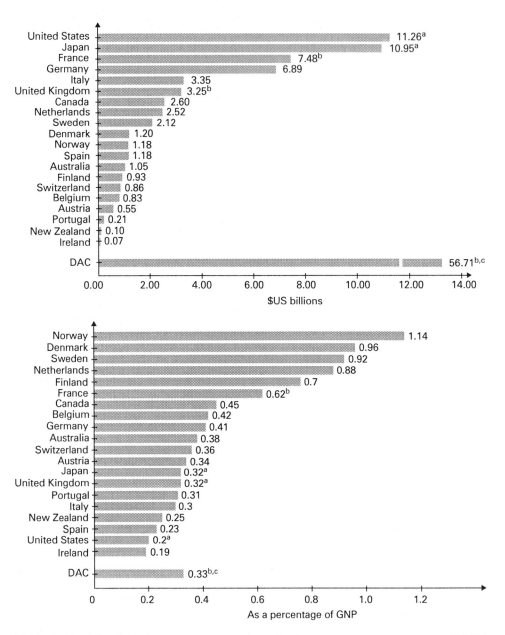

Fig. 7.2 Net official development assistance from development assistance countries (DACs), 1991. Top: in billions, U.S. dollars. Bottom: as a percentage of GNP. Source: Organisation for Economic Co-operation and Development (OECD), Development Co-operation: 1992 Report (OECD, Paris, 1992), Chart 2, p.24,
Notes: a. Includes forgiveness of non-official development assistance debt. b. Includes overseas territories but excludes overseas departments. c. Excludes forgiveness of non-official development assistance debt. Source: World Resources Institute, World Resources 1994–1995, p.227.

Plate 7.3 An African white elephant: an unsuccessful project in Tanzania. Dutch funding was used to pay for the construction of an aircraft hangar at Kilimanjaro Airport, so that aircraft maintenance could be carried out on the spot. The only piece of equipment which has been maintained so far, however, is a lawn-mower. Photo: Ron Giling/Lineair

Thus, for Ekins, the Brandt Reports, for all their insight, expertise and commitment to Third World development, remain flawed:

○ They fail to recognise the main cause of development failure contributed by corruption, bureaucratic mismanagement and inappropriate development models. Increased financial flows resulting from Brandt's recommendations would be more likely to repeat development failure than initiate success.
○ They propose a mutual self-interest in reform where none in fact exists. This means that their recommendations are most unlikely to be implemented.
○ They fail to identify the real *reforming agenda* which could break the development deadlock, including strategies of participation, community organisation, democratisation, etc. However, this agenda comes from the grassroots, from the bottom up, whereas 'The Brandt Commission [...] was composed of top people, thinking top-down, as such people normally do' (Ekins, 1992).

An example of a 'reforming agenda'

It is important to emphasise, however, that thinking in the North need not only be characterised by a top-down, bureaucratic agenda. For example, one might compare the Brandt agenda with another appraisal of the existing global order which produced a radically different set of conclusions. The Dag Hammarskjöld Foundation, established in memory of an eminent Swedish diplomat and UN Secretary-General, published its alternative agenda in 1975 under the label of 'Another Development'. It was a stock-taking exercise which argued that there would be no genuine development if some key questions were not asked and concretely answered: development *how, of what, by whom and for whom*?

'Another Development' comprised five organically linked components:

1 *Need-oriented* – to begin with the satisfaction of the basic needs of the majority of the world's inhabitants.
2 *Endogenous* – since development is not a linear process with a single universal model, each society must define its own values and vision of the future.
3 *Self-reliant* – where each society relies upon its own strength and resources. While it must be exercised at national and international levels, it acquires its full meaning only if rooted at local level, in the praxis of each community.
4 *Ecologically sound* – utilising rationally the resources of the biosphere in full awareness of the potential of local ecosystems and the limits imposed on present and future generations.
5 *Based on structural transformations* – required in social relations, economic activities and their spatial distribution and in the structure of power, so as to realise the conditions of self-management and participation in decision making by all those affected by it.

All five of these components remain as relevant today as when they first appeared 20 years ago and together they are a testimony to a clear, coherent and remarkably visionary programme for a new world order. The Dag Hammarskjöld Foundation was fully behind the aspirations of the Non-Aligned Movement for a New International Economic Order which would support an endogenous and self-reliant national development throughout the South. Yet it also saw the need for the application of another development to the advanced industrialised countries in order to create more environmentally sound societies and individual lifestyles. Such a visionary approach contrasts sharply with the rather time-worn agenda of the South Commission.

The South Commission

The South Commission was established in 1987 by the Non-Aligned Movement and headed by Julius Nyerere, former President of Tanzania. Its objectives were to investigate the common problems facing the South and to find ways of working together to solve them and to develop a new dialogue with the North. The South Commission might be seen as yet another group of eminent people – principally diplomats – to get development onto the international agenda, but this time without the hindrances of the language of environmental conservation. The motivation was right: the 1980s were seen as a lost decade for development in the South, caused by the slowing down of economic activity in the North, which in turn led to a deterioration in commodity prices. The 'debt crisis' of 1982 also initiated a drain of capital as the level of debt-service payments outstripped direct foreign investment and lending to the South for the rest of the decade, as Box 3 clearly demonstrated. Countries of the South, most especially in sub-Saharan Africa but also in Latin America, were consequently experiencing a loss of illusions associated with the prospect of future development. This has become ever more apparent as the process of economic reconstruction in Eastern Europe has attracted the technical and financial interest of the Western countries and thereby diverted attention from the countries of the South.

From the perspective of the Commission, North–South relations are portrayed in terms of conflict. It calls for the cancellation of debt to Northern multilateral and private banks but also more loans to build up infrastructure for development in the South. It seems self-evident that more loans will lead to more debt and more environmental destruction, just as the call for more multinational investment to acquire new business and technological skills will likely result in more dependency. Notwithstanding the sense of conflict, the South Commission shares precisely the same aspirations and ideology of industrial development as the North and seeks to use its collective leverage in the interests of expanding its industrial capacity. The environment is, consequently, of little immediate concern beyond a 'space' for further industrial development: 'Only rapid industrial development can create the resources to satisfy the basic requirements of (the South's) growing population'. Moreover, this will be achieved through the adoption of 'modern science and technology' from the North, hopefully, no doubt, to be acquired on concessionary terms. At the same time, 'The needs of the North should be met in ways that do not compromise the satisfaction of the present and future needs of the South'. In other words, while the North is facilitating the transfer of technologies that contribute to global environmental change, it should itself be substantially reducing production and practising compensatory restraint. This is unrealistic and suggests that the Commission, a 'Southern elite', had little vision beyond the notion of 'replicable development'.

Reconciling development and environment? The Brundtland Commission

The World Commission on Environment and Development, or Brundtland Commission as it became known under the chairmanship of Norwegian ex-Premier Gro Harlem Brundtland, was established by the United Nations General Assembly in 1983 with three broad objectives:

1 to re-examine the critical environment and development issues and to formulate realistic proposals for dealing with them
2 to propose new forms of international co-operation on these issues that will influence policies and events in the direction of needed changes
3 to raise the levels of understanding and commitment to action of individuals voluntary organisations, businesses, institutes and governments.

The Commission's Report was published under the title, *Our Common Future* in 1987. The Commission focused its deliberations within six broad policy areas: population and human resources; food security; species and ecosystems; energy; industry; and urbanisation. It also considered the management of the global commons, peace and security and institutional reform. The Commission held a series of public hearings across the world to take individual testimonies in an attempt to reflect the circumstances in which increasing numbers of people experience poverty and vulnerability. The Report captured the public imagination because of its central concern with sustainable development, which was defined in its most simplified and oft-repeated form as 'development that meets the needs of the present without compromising the ability of future generations to meet their own needs'. (For a more rigorous interpretation of the meaning and application of 'sustainable development', see Blowers and Glasbergen, 1995.) It also acknowledges the contribution of Brundtland in ensuring that this term has become the most important within the international environmental lexicon. Here, however, I want to look more critically at the impact of *Our Common Future* for North–South environmental agenda setting and policy-making in the lead-up to the United Nations Conference on Environment and Development held in Rio de Janeiro in 1992.

In the first place it is important to note that the Brundtland Commission appeared to support a new political agenda in which the imperative of greater co-operation between governments would also be complemented by recognition of the need for more effective participation by people in decision making. Yet, notwithstanding the hopes for a more thorough-going critique of the existing social and economic order, the Commission produced a Report in which a single, universal solution was proposed: more economic growth.

> If large parts of the developing world are to avert economic, social and environmental catastrophes, it is essential that global economic growth be revitalised. In practical terms, this means more rapid economic growth in both industrial and developing countries, freer market access for the products of developing countries, lower interest rates, greater technology transfer and significantly larger capital flows, both concessional and commercial (WCED, 1987, p.89).

As Ekins observes, 'This is pure, conventional developmentalism of the Brandt variety' but more dangerous still given Brundtland's concern with sustainability. He goes on:

> The problem with calling for more economic growth in this way is that nowhere in the Brundtland Report is there a clear statement of how 'sustainable economic growth' can be recognised and distinguished from the patently unsustainable variety which is all the industrial world has so far known and which was largely responsible, by the Commission's own analysis, for the environmental destruction which led to it being convened (Ekins, 1992, p.31).

The Report simply believes that the international economy must speed up world growth while 'respecting the environmental constraints'. While more growth may be necessary in developing countries in order to uplift the living standards of the poorest, this should be done as far as possible on the basis of sustainable production. It is difficult, however, to justify continued growth in the North given the existing disparities in levels of resource consumption (Sage, 1996).

The Report appears not to recognise the simple truth that economic growth leads to more consumption and that more consumption puts greater pressure on renewable and non-renewable resources and the earth's capacity to absorb waste. Moreover, as Middleton and colleagues argue, the Report fails to 'operationalise' a number of important development issues such as local participation and social justice which have been subsumed into economic and environmental imperatives. While it cements the relationship between environment and development, it does not question the role of the world's dominant governments and institutions in preserving the conditions in which environmental and developmental problems arise. So in the end the Report, while raising hopes and expectations for deep and meaningful change, reinforces the *status quo* and the hegemony of the market.

The various approaches to the problems of development have each in their different ways revealed the contradictions between the process of growth and the capacity of the environment for sustaining that growth. These contradictions and the means of resolving them were the focus of the deliberations leading up to and including the UNCED Conference in Rio de Janeiro in 1992.

Plate 7.4 Political instability has a tremendous impact on both society and the environment. On 17 July 1995, a makeshift camp 10 km north of the eastern Zairean border town of Goma was packed with some 160,000 Rwandan refugees. According to the UN High Commission for Refugees (UNHCR), at least 600,000 Rwandans have sought refuge in Goma. Photo: ANP Foto

7.4 The road to Rio

The Earth Summit

The original purpose of the United Nations Conference on Environment and Development (UNCED, or the Earth Summit as it became known) was to examine the world's progress in meeting the demands made by the Brundtland Commission. In the event, UNCED placed greater emphasis upon the global environment than upon development considerations and people's livelihoods. It invited the nations of the world to shoulder their global responsibilities but failed to address issues of poverty and equity or guarantee the necessary redistribution of resources. Yet UNCED was not just a conference or a series of intergovernmental negotiations but a catalyst for a wide range of activities, both before June 1992 and since.

The conference itself was scheduled for June 1992 in order to mark the 20th anniversary of the Stockholm conference and the Brazilian government offered to act as hosts. This was a calculated move on the part of President Sarney in responding to the international outcry over the burning of the Amazonian forest. This outcry had been triggered in the North by the long, hot summer of 1988 which recorded sustained high temperatures and which, in the public mind, appeared to validate the concerns of scientists over global warming. Together with the murder of Chico Mendez, the leader of the Brazilian rubber tappers union who had defended an alternative model for the sustainable use of the forest, the images of burning forests brought further media attention to the region. Suddenly, the violence and lawlessness of the frontier became a global threat in the popular imagination as forest clearance was seen as the principal cause of climate change. This was an issue which created strong lines of cleavage between North and South.

As Grubb and colleagues note, UNCED was not just a conference or a series of negotiations, but a springboard for a wide range of activities. Governments were invited to submit national reports on their environment and development and, by the time of the Summit, 172 countries had done so. Many countries had established regional committees to co-ordinate activities, consult with non-governmental organisations (NGOs) and across government departments and foster interest in the process. Many other countries, of course, did not. Besides the Preparatory Committees (PrepComs) which met over the preceding year in advance of Rio in order to draw up the documents for signing by the heads of government, there were a number of other international conferences held to discuss sectoral priorities. These covered such topics as sustainable agriculture and rural development, water and the environment, industry, etc. and included expert meetings convened by such bodies as the International Council of Scientific Unions and the International Union for the Conservation of Nature and regional gatherings of government leaders under the auspices of the United Nations Regional Commissions and so on. Consequently, UNCED embodied a process in which politicians, business leaders and NGOs representing the environment and the interests of the poor began to co-ordinate their positions.

The main agreements reached in Rio are summarised in Box 4. A more critical view of UNCED is summarised in Box 5. Agenda 21 and the Rio Declaration are not central to the concerns of this chapter. Here we shall look in a little more detail, first, at the

4

The UNCED agreements

The *Framework Convention on Climate Change* establishes principles that climate change is a serious problem; that action cannot wait upon the resolution of scientific uncertainties; that developed countries should take the lead; and, that they should compensate developing countries for any additional costs incurred in taking measures under the Convention. The Convention lacks bindng policy commitments but indicates that industrialised countries should aim as a first step to return greenhouse gas emissions to 1990 levels by 2000. It establishes a strong process by which governments must submit reports on their relevant policies and projections and meet regularly to evaluate progress and if necessary amend the commitments. The Convention will enter into force with unusual rapidity.

The *Convention on Biological Diversity* aims to preserve the biological diversity of the planet, through the protection of species and ecosystems and to establish terms for the associated uses of biological resources and technology. It affirms that states have 'sovereign rights' over biological resources on their territory, the fruits of which should, however, be shared in a 'fair and equitable' way on 'mutually agreed terms'. Countries must develop plans to protect biodiversity and submit some information on them. The Convention may enter into force rapidly, but key developed countries may delay or refuse to ratify it primarily because of concerns over control of funding.

Agenda 21 is an immense document of 40 chapters outlining an 'action plan' for sustainable development, covering a wide range of specific natural resources and the role of different groups, as well as issues of social and economic development and implementation. It effectively integrates environment and development concerns; it is strongly oriented towards 'bottom-up', participatory and community-based approaches in many areas, including population policy and it shows more acceptance of market principles, within appropriate regulatory frameworks, than previous UN agreements. Performance targets are mostly limited to those previously agreed elsewhere. Agenda 21 will form the key intergovernmental guiding and reference document on the issues for the rest of the decade.

The *Rio Declaration* comprises 27 principles for guiding action on environment and development. Many address development concerns, stressing the right to and need for development and poverty alleviation. Some principles concerning trade and environment are ambiguous; others concern the rights and roles of special groups.

The *Forest Principles* form the rump of blocked attempts to negotiate a convention on forests. It emphasises the sovereign right to exploit forest resources along with various general principles of forest protection and management.

development of a Framework Convention on Climate Change, then at the Convention on Biological Diversity, and, finally, at the steps leading towards a Convention on Desertification.

Climate change and the South

The growing scientific consensus regarding atmospheric change had already begun to find a degree of commitment within the diplomatic arena. The discovery of the 'hole' in the ozone layer over Antarctica concentrated the minds of politicians, enabling them to develop agreement around the Montreal Protocol on Substances that Deplete the Ozone Layer in 1987 and then a process of regime strengthening in which a phasing out of ozone-depleting chemicals was accelerated. The mounting concern about human interference with the Earth's atmospheric heat balance and the prospects of climate change led to the establishment of the Intergovernmental Panel on Climate Change (IPCC) in 1988. This brought together over 400 scientists organised into three working groups (Scientific Processes, Impacts and Responses) in the preparation of the First Assessment Report launched in 1990. The Report predicted that if states continue 'business as usual' the global average surface temperature will rise during the next century by an estimated average of 0.3°C per decade, a rate of change unprecedented in human history. It was a call for prompt action to stabilise emissions of greenhouse gases (see Beukering and Vellinga, 1996, for a fuller discussion).

However, the substantive issue dividing international opinion along North–South lines is that the industrialized countries account for the lion's share of carbon dioxide emissions arising from the combustion of fossil fuels – some 75% in the mid-1980s – and therefore are primarily responsible for causing global warming. Yet the consequences of this are expected to be felt especially severely in the South, particularly in low-lying coastal areas such as small islands and river deltas. Perhaps surprisingly, the IPCC process had been established without anticipating a role for developing countries and Brazil and Mexico, amongst others, had to work strenuously to increase their level of participation.

The Earth Summit – an alternative view

For the major players, the Earth Summit was a phenomenal success. The World Bank not only emerged with its development policies intact but with control of an expanded Global Environmental Facility (GEF), a prize that it had worked for two years to achieve. The US got the biodiversity convention it sought simply by not signing the convention on offer. The corporate sector, which throughout the UNCED process enjoyed special access to the Secretariat, also got what it wanted: the final documents not only treated TNCs with kid gloves but extolled them as key actors in the 'battle to save the planet'. Free-market environmentalism – the philosophy that TNCs brought to Rio through the Business Council on Sustainable Development – has become the order of the day, uniting Southern and Northern leaders alike …

In brief, the Summit went according to plan. The net outcome was to minimise change to the status quo, an outcome that was inevitable from the outset of the UNCED process three years ago. Unwilling to question the desirability of economic growth, the market economy or the development process itself, UNCED never had a chance of addressing the real problems of 'environment and development'. Its Secretariat provided delegates with materials for a convention on biodiversity but not on free trade; on forests but not on agribusiness; on climate but not on automobiles. Agenda 21 – the Summit's 'action plan' – featured clauses on 'enabling the poor to achieve sustainable livelihoods' but none on enabling the rich to do so; a section on women but none on men. By such deliberate evasion of the central issues which economic expansion poses for human societies, UNCED condemned itself to irrelevance even before the first preparatory meeting got underway. (Hildyard, 1994, p.22–23).

By the time the Second World Climate Conference was convened in 1990, many of the developing countries were better prepared and ready to thwart the control of the industrialised countries over the IPCC process. Already facing uncomfortable scientific 'truths', the North wished to proceed to negotiations on a possible climate change convention under the auspices of the United Nations Environment Programme (UNEP) and the World Meteorological Organisation (WMO). The South, however, saw the issue in developmental as well as environmental terms, with implications for all sectors of national economies – energy, industry, transport, forests and agriculture. Moreover, the developing countries were concerned with procedures involving the universality of representation and transparency of decision-making processes. Consequently, through their collective efforts, they were able to ensure that it was the United Nations General Assembly, rather than UNEP and the WMO, which was the body responsible for establishing the Intergovernmental Negotiating Committee (INC) for a Framework Convention on Climate Change. Under the auspices of the General Assembly, the INC was given a mandate to negotiate a convention containing appropriate commitments which would be ready for signing at the United Nations Conference on Environment and Development (UNCED). The INC held five sessions between February 1991 and May 1992 and came through some extremely tough bargaining to produce an agreed text that was taken forward to Rio for signing by heads of state.

Negotiations in preparing the Framework Convention on Climate Change and, since Rio, in developing an agreed protocol have revealed considerable schisms within the bloc of Southern countries. The Group of 77, the operating caucus of the Non-Aligned Movement, was joined by China to present a common front in defence of the South, but their positions and demands tended to reiterate the language of the 1970s in emphasising:

○ the historical responsibility of the North in causing climate change;
○ the need for new and additional resources to be provided to the South before it was able to consider abatement measures;
○ the transfer of technology on concessionary and preferential terms, etc.

Inevitably, as negotiations proceeded to map out the commitments of individual countries, contrasting positions began to emerge between different groups of countries within the G77. For Ahmed Djoghlef, leader of the Algerian delegation and vice-chair of the INC, it was a matter of regret that the climate issue caused a fracturing of the G77 and that it was unable to play a leading role in the negotiations (Djoghlef, 1994). The most important group of developing countries which emerged in the INC was the Alliance of Small Island States (AOSIS) chaired by Vanuatu. This group comprised low-lying member states and territories most at risk from global warming, rising sea levels and a predicted increase in tropical storms. It tabled a proposal containing the most far-reaching set of commitments, including a CO_2 stabilisation target for developed countries of 1990 emission levels to be achieved by 1995, with a further programme of reductions thereafter.

The Kuala Lumpur Group emerged as a second cluster of developing countries from within the ranks of the G77. It comprised 43 states, including some of the larger countries with important forest resources, which viewed the climate change negotiations as an attempt by the North to dictate the use of forests in the South. Throughout the UNCED process, this group adopted a largely defensive posture, rejecting any such attempts as a violation of their national sovereignty, but otherwise awaited agreement from the developed countries on a set of commitments to reduce emissions.

The INC process also gave the member states of OPEC an opportunity, according to Djoghlef, to renew the tradition of holding periodic consultations in conjunction with major international events. This process had been suspended since the early 1980s and the intervening period had been marked by acrimony and worse, between member countries. Reconvening as a group with shared interests was motivated by concerns about the potential impact of a Climate Change Convention on the future international oil market, especially given proposals for an international carbon tax that would be imposed on all sales of petroleum products.

The influence of self-interest in forming attitudes to global warming is apparent in the positions taken by each of these three groups. For the small island states immediate and drastic measures are needed to cut greenhouse gas emissions and halt the apparent trends of global warming which threaten their survival. The newly industrialising countries, on the other hand, can afford to 'wait and see' and refuse to forego economic development unless the North offers sufficient inducements of finance and technology. Finally, the OPEC countries would surely prefer to believe that global warming was unrelated to the burning of fossil fuels. However, a revealing anecdote is provided by Bodansky to demonstrate how far self-interest influences scientific understanding. Discussing the Noordwijk Ministerial Conference on Atmospheric Pollution and Climate Change held in November 1989 Bodansky notes the statement made by the Saudi Arabian delegation:

> In this statement, Saudi Arabia characterised global warming as 'a life or death issue for considerable areas of the earth', acknowledged that there is 'no argument' that the 'main culprit' for global warming is carbon dioxide and recognised the need to move to non-greenhouse emission energy production and consumption systems and to stabilise and reduce emissions of greenhouse gases. In contrast, by the end of 1990, Saudi Arabia was stressing the uncertainty of climate change and strongly opposed establishing targets and timetables to reduce carbon dioxide emissions (Bodansky, 1994, p.72).

The Convention on Biological Diversity

The Biodiversity Convention has arguably become the most difficult and intractable of the agreements under the UNCED process although negotiations began long before plans were laid for signing ceremonies in June 1992 (for a full description, see Barnes, 1996). Indeed, it was in 1987 that UNEP called upon governments to consider establishing international legislation on the conservation and sustainable use of biodiversity. An Expert Working Group was established which later became the INC for a Convention on Biological Diversity, paralleling the climate change negotiation process. Indeed, the development of an agreement experienced comparable fundamental disagreements between North and South, particularly on the exchange of biological resources in return for access to biotechnology. Essentially, it is the developing countries which possess the greatest diversity of species and they have asserted their sovereign rights over genetic resources within their territories. The industrialised countries, on the other hand, view biodiversity as a common heritage of humankind and seek to draw upon the universal 'gene pool' for their biotechnology industries which produce genetically manipulated organisms that can benefit agriculture world-wide. While the South seeks access to such benefits of biotechnology, the industry itself is preoccupied with patents, profits and the control of gene banks. The resulting Convention may thus attempt to address 'the conservation of biological diversity and the equitable sharing of the benefits arising from the use of genetic resources' (article 1), but it offers no solution to the ongoing destruction of biodiversity.

Indeed, despite 155 governments signing the Convention in Rio, progress towards its implementation has become bogged down. One of the many problem areas

Plate 7.5 Rwandan refugees taking firewood back to the Benaco refugee camp in Ngara district, Tanzania. Since the countryside near the camp is already woodless, those wishing to gather firewood have to walk longer and longer distances every day. The ongoing deforestation in the area has also greatly exacerbated the problem of soil erosion. Photo: Heldur Netocny/Lineair

concerns the role of *ex situ* gene banks or the conservation of species outside their natural habitats and countries of origin. It must be remembered that the countries of the North have benefited from the 'collection' (some would say 'plunder') of genetic materials from the South over several centuries. Botanical gardens, such as Kew in London, are essentially gene banks with an enormous variety of plants brought from the tropics not simply for the curiosity of botanists. The smuggling of seeds of *Hevea brasiliensis* from Amazonia in the late 19th century ended Brazil's monopoly in the supply of rubber once the seeds had been transplanted via Kew to plantations in colonial Ceylon and Malaya. By 1910 almost 1 million acres were given over to *Hevea* plantations in Malaya and proved of enormous benefit to the British economy at the expense of Brazil (Hecht and Cockburn, 1990).

However, botanical gardens and other forms of storage of genetic material (many in the hands of pharmaceutical and agro-industry companies) representing past collection are currently excluded from the jurisdiction of the Convention. Consequently, the South is unable to secure any rights to compensation for this material previously taken. Yet the Convention legitimises the patenting of genetically modified organisms which have been derived from genes originally taken from the South. This means that a country such as Ethiopia, let us say, would be forced to purchase from the United States seeds of wheat or barley resistant to a particular virus, even though the gene responsible for such resistance was originally found in Ethiopia. While this gene may not have been isolated and named in that country because of Ethiopia's lack of DNA-profiling technology and expertise, it is likely that many poor and illiterate peasants had recognised the properties and characteristics of the variety containing the gene and ensured its conservation for future generations by maintaining crop and varietal diversity.

It is this kind of inequity which has made progress toward ratification of the Convention so difficult. At the first meeting of the Conference of the Parties held in the Bahamas at the end of 1994 few important decisions were made beyond the symbolic declaration of December 29th as the International Day for Biological Diversity. Meanwhile, the United States pressed for the free movement of genetically modified organisms in order to test its biotechnological products in developing countries, while some voices in the South demanded that existing *ex situ* collections be brought under the jurisdictional scope of the Convention. There were likely to be prolonged negotiations to resolve the conflicting views of intellectual property rights and the system of establishing patents which threatens to privatise new combinations of genetic material hitherto maintained by many generations of poor farmers and forest dwellers.

The Convention on Desertification

It was precisely because of the North's view of the environment that African delegates at the Earth Summit lobbied hard for a desertification convention to address their most pressing problems. Yet there was little interest among the non-African countries at Rio in desertification and even some objection to the issue being addressed as a global problem despite an estimated 35% of the Earth's land surface being threatened and 900 million people affected by desertification worldwide (Chatterjee and Finger, 1994;

Toulmin, 1994). Nevertheless, it was agreed at Rio to establish an intergovernmental group and in turn the UN General Assembly commissioned the formation of an intergovernmental negotiating committee (INC) to develop a convention on desertification. An agreed text was adopted at the fifth meeting of the INC in Paris in June 1994 for signature and eventual ratification by the participating countries.

However, how far can a global Convention to Combat Desertification overcome the problems of dryland degradation? As Toulmin observes, unlike other environmental issues (such as ozone depletion or greenhouse gas emissions), desertification lacks clearly identifiable linkages at global level in which levels of resource use in individual countries have consequences for the world as a whole. Upon such linkages can be based global agreements that attempt to regulate behaviour of individual countries for the global good. In the case of desertification, however, there is no clear scientific agreement about the global climatic consequences of dryland degradation. Indeed, some researchers have begun to challenge the way in which desertification has been assessed and presented, creating, from inadequate and insufficient data, the myth of the rapidly advancing desert. According to Thomas and Middleton (1994) the United Nations has played a major role in creating the desertification myth with little reliable scientific foundation. Moreover, its anti-desertification measures have yet to be proven effective and appear to have little relevance to affected peoples. Consequently, while the UN has managed to get desertification on the global environmental agenda, it is at local and subnational level where efforts to combat it need to be concentrated. As Toulmin argues:

> Local people need an economic, social, technical and institutional framework within which to develop appropriate methods of resource use and management. Such measures are probably not best dealt with by global conventions. Experience .. has demonstrated the very limited value of drawing up plans at global, regional, or national levels, since they rarely bear much resemblance to reality and are usually impossible to implement (Toulmin, 1994, p.87).

Small-scale, participatory projects are increasingly recognised as the only really effective way of improving local resource management and reducing the threat of dryland degradation and desertification. Such projects are usually relatively low-cost and the main achievement of the Convention could be to harness donor funds to support such projects. It remains to be seen whether the Convention will do this given the anticipated disagreements in future meetings of the INC over funding mechanisms, especially whether desertification control would be supported by the Global Environmental Facility. On the more positive side the Convention has emphasised the importance of national environmental frameworks and the part that NGOs can play in implementation at the grassroots. Indeed, the stress on mobilising the resources of the people at local level is one of the innovatory features of the Convention.

7.5 Conclusion: the scope for North–South co-operation

Throughout this chapter there has been an emphasis on the constraints on North–South co-operation. The conflicts of interests between North and South – and indeed those conflicts that occur between the countries of the South – appear to place formidable obstacles in the way of achieving agreements on policies to deal with environmental problems, let alone agreements over the means of implementing them. Such agreements as there are, notably the conventions that have emerged from the Rio process, are still in their early stages with little immediate prospect of making an impact on the problems they seek to address. Indeed, it is generally acknowledged that the problems are likely to get worse before they begin to get better.

8

Implementing international environmental policies

Kenneth Hanf

8.1 Introduction

Earlier chapters in this book have shown that environmental problems do not respect national borders. It is also clear that the condition of the environment in any given country is not the result of the policies of the national government alone. To an increasing extent the quality of life in one country is affected by the impact on its environment of the activities of citizens of other countries. Consequently, in dealing with these kinds of environmental problems, some way must be found of gaining the co-operation of the governments of those other countries so as to influence the behaviour of the members of those societies who cause the discomfort of others.

However, although co-operation is essential in order to deal with these types of problems, it may be difficult to achieve. Indeed, in some cases, it may not happen at all. For, although international ecological interdependence has grown, sovereign states continue to be the primary actors on the stage of world politics. As a result, the interests that determine the willingness to co-operate and, ultimately, the shape of whatever collective policies and measures of implementation are decided upon tend to be defined by national rather than international or global concerns. Despite the pressures from different directions for some form of collaboration to serve mutual interests in environmental protection, international co-operation in dealing with these problems is not a foregone conclusion. On the contrary, governments 'may respond paradoxically to the erosion of their influence by clinging even more tightly to their powers' (Mathews, 1991, p.32–33).

This chapter focuses on the problem of implementing international regimes for environmental protection. In particular I shall discuss implementation as a complex process involving different stages and relationships between many different actors. In doing so I shall examine the constraints which must be overcome in order to achieve necessary co-operation among the various interests involved. The next section (8.2) considers the central role of the nation state in ensuring the success or failure of international environmental regimes. It stresses the importance of the domestic social and political context both in shaping the nature of the regime and in influencing the course of implementation. Section 8.3, using the example of environmental programmes in the European Union, illustrates the problems and prospects for integrating environmental protection and economic performance in the process called 'ecological modernisation'. Continuing this general theme, Section 8.4 shows how implementation will be affected by the culture of the individual countries and the different levels of government within them. Another major actor is the business community which influences the balance between regulation and the market as means of policy implementation. The concluding section (8.5) argues that it is in the mutual interest of states to surrender some sovereignty to achieve the level of international co-operation necessary for environmental protection.

8.2 International regimes and the nation state

Institutional arrangements and international order

Nation states continue to be the most important actors in world affairs in a highly decentralised international system. Still, the absence of a central government at the international level does not necessarily rule out the possibility of creating international environmental regimes and the organisations needed to implement and administer them. The term 'anarchy', as traditionally used to characterise international society, does not mean that the international community is 'entirely without institutions and orderly procedures' (Keohane, 1989, p.1). As Keohane reminds us, if we want to understand world politics, 'we must keep in mind both decentralisation and institutionalisation' (ibid., 1989, p.5).

Institutional arrangements for international co-operation are now so numerous and so important that they have become a defining feature of the global political system of the second half of the 20th century (Jacobson, 1984). Many kinds of international institutions now exist that influence and guide the behaviour of individual governments and the interactions between individual actors. When the international community confronts a problem demanding the pooling of resources and common purpose, there are institutions to organise the specific arrangements to achieve the necessary co-operation between nation states. Such institutions help define the incentives states need in order to engage in co-operative efforts and make it possible for them to act in ways which they otherwise would not find attractive. Institutional arrangements affect the costs of alternative courses of actions as well as the way states view their own roles and the assumptions they make regarding the behaviour of others. In this way, international institutions fulfil the following functions. They:

○ provide both a context and sets of procedures through which representatives of national governments can arrive at common understandings of environmental problems
○ define shared meanings regarding the situation they face
○ develop procedures to facilitate negotiations and decision making

○ ensure the necessary measures to monitor compliance and guard against defection.

In these ways international institutions play an important role in facilitating mutually beneficial policy co-ordination among governments.

Domestic factors in international environmental co-operation

International co-operation is not something that is achieved (or missed) at a single given point in time. On the contrary, it tends to emerge from a long, often arduous process during which individual states come to realise, against the background of national demands and priorities, the need and advantages of joining forces with others. This international co-operation consists of a series of separate but interrelated activities extending over time. Young has suggested that the overall sequence or process of *regime formation* can be divided into three stages: prenegotiation, negotiation ('institutional bargaining') and postnegotiation (Young, 1994, p.83).

The phenomenon of international co-operation has been an object of concern to a good many scholars for some time. However, most studies have concentrated on the negotiations and interactions among states at the international level. Clearly, the outcome of efforts to generate international co-operation for the protection of the environment will not depend only on the availability and use of such international institutions. What happens in the international arena is important for determining the success of efforts to mobilise joint action to deal with transboundary environmental problems. However, such co-operation must be viewed as a complex process of multi-level problem solving which links decisions and developments taking place at both the domestic and the international levels. Yet, with some notable exceptions, international relations research has paid only limited attention to linkages between domestic and international politics.

Two points need to be emphasised when talking about international environmental co-operation. Firstly, the interests that shape collective measures for dealing with environmental degradation are national rather than international in character. This is also true of the institutional context within which national preferences are formulated and the resultant negotiated agreements are carried out. Secondly, in order to understand the processes of international co-operation and the role played by institutions in facilitating and structuring efforts to mobilise joint or co-ordinated action on environmental problems, we need to examine the developments that precede any decision by a particular country to join in searching for a mutually acceptable way of dealing with an international problem as well as those that follow, once the agreement has been signed, in carrying out the obligations or commitments entered into.

Each phase of this co-operative process has both an international and domestic dimension. For example, while the pre-negotiation stage will involve international meetings – of scientists, representatives of concerned governments and working parties – there will also be parallel activities at the national level. Indeed, the decision by the national governments (the 'states') to enter into negotiations on some kind of formal agreement, regulating the scope and content of co-operative action to deal with a particular problem, will be a product of the interaction of domestic and international decision-making processes. Likewise, the national position that the representatives of

199

a given country take to these international negotiations will also be shaped by this same set of processes.

For this reason, when looking for the factors that determine success and failure in attempts to find and apply co-operative solutions to international environmental problems, we must consider the domestic setting of decision making and not only in the interstate game. If we wish to understand what is likely to happen at the international level, it is necessary to examine the processes, structures and values at the national unit level which determine the manner in which national positions on negotiating international agreements are arrived at and the ultimate agreements are then carried out (see Box 1).

The effectiveness of international regimes

It is the implementation of agreements that is the area *par excellence* for examining the impact of domestic processes and structures on the ultimate effectiveness of international co-operation. International environmental agreements are designed to have an effect on different categories of (societal) activities which are perceived as harming the environment. Even if agreement can be reached regarding the nature of the problem and the actions that should be undertaken by the various parties in dealing with it, there still remains the challenge of translating this international agreement into the necessary national programmes and then applying them to bring about the kinds of behavioural changes required to 'solve' the problem. The effectiveness of these accords depends upon the actions taken by the states to effect these behavioural changes *within* their societies.

Ultimately, it is national decisions that affect environmental quality, even though international measures may be necessary to harmonise national measures. Needless to

Domestic underpinnings of international co-operation

> State priorities and policies are determined by politicians at the head of national government, who are 'embedded in domestic and transnational civil society, which decisively constrains their identities and purposes'. Events and decisions at the international level '... create patterns of societal interests that influence governments via the "transmission belt" of domestic politics ...' (Moravcsik, 1993, p.483).

It is through domestic institutions and modes of political representation that national interests or goals emerge that states then bring to international negotiations. It would seem to follow, then, that if international organisations are to be effective in mobilising 'pressures for international regulation that enhances environmental protection', they will need to promote sufficient political concern for such measures within societies (Keohane, 1994, p.28). It is the combination of international pressure and domestic environmentalism that is crucial for putting pressure on national governments to participate in international environmental regimes.

Plate 8.1 The UN Summit on Climate Change, Berlin, 1 April 1995. Holding home-made posters proclaiming 'When will you start to think?' and 'Rio, Berlin – what are you going to fob us off with this time?', two girls take part in a children's demonstration on the sidelines of the Summit. Several hundred demonstrators called on the delegates to take more rapid action. Photo: ANP Foto

say, although states have signed many agreements, compliance is far from perfect and violations abound. Non-compliance continues to be an issue of broad concern in that many states lack the resources to implement accords or choose not to abide by them because the international system lacks a strong mechanism for enforcement. In this sense, effectiveness of international agreements is limited by the fact that monitoring and verification of domestic implementation of international accords are carried out predominantly by the states themselves.

The effectiveness of international agreements and the regimes that embody them, will depend on the extent to which national policy efforts actually comply with the new international obligations. For this reason, we will now look more closely at what happens when international environmental agreements are implemented by the countries that have signed them. This post-negotiation phase covers all those steps needed to transform an international agreement signed by the parties who have agreed to its terms into an actual institutional arrangement. It encompasses those administrative actions at the national level which are intended to bring about the behavioural changes on the part of the relevant target groups and, thereby, to realise the objectives of the agreements.

The relative neglect of the implementation phase of international co-operation

The international 'policy' process does not end with the signing of a convention (unless we are dealing with a case of purely symbolic politics). Post-agreement activity for the realisation of the objectives of international co-operation is most important. It is, therefore, surprising how often this aspect is neglected in studies of international co-operation. The issue here is the ultimate effectiveness of the agreement (measured in terms of the impact of the agreement on the environmental problem to be dealt with): if there is no implementation, there is no 'real' policy. Nor is implementation merely a matter of 'compliance' in the narrow sense. On the contrary, it represents a complex political process that deserves attention in its own right (Hanf and Underdal, 1995).

This relative neglect of the implementation phase of international co-operation can, in part, be attributed to the fact that traditional foreign policy and security issues did not raise the same kinds of questions as those concerning international environmental agreements. The behavioural prescriptions or proscriptions such treaties contained were addressed in the first instance to the *state* itself (i.e. to the national government) and, in terms of the domestic forces involved, to a limited set of actors (even though the issues themselves could be of great importance to the society as a whole). International environmental problems and the agreements drawn up to deal with them tend to penetrate societies in a more pervasive and direct way and carry potentially high costs for important interests, such as producers and/or consumers of particular goods and services.

A second reason for the lack of attention to the implementation of international environmental agreements seems to be a misconception of what implementation is all about. Implementation must be seen as a distinct policy 'game', leaving its own imprint on the actual thrust of environmental policies. This approach places a different perspective on the problems faced in meeting international obligations; more specifically, it leads us to conceive of implementation 'failure' and 'success' as not only a matter of 'will' (deliberate choice) but also as a matter of *ability* and capacity to govern. Already, in deciding whether or not to join or conclude an agreement, decision makers will have made their calculations with an eye to the domestic interests that support or oppose the agreement. Indeed, whether or not a problem requiring international agreement even exists may be viewed differently by countries, in part as a function of their economic structure and the political power of different economic interests. For example, the unwillingness of the US government to agree on reductions of CO_2 emissions is due to its reluctance to bear the economic and political costs that would result from the impact that controls would have upon important societal interests. Likewise, different types of agreements on the measures to be taken will affect domestic interests in different ways. The regulation of emissions of CFCs involves a limited, more or less clearly visible, set of emitters; substitutes for these (or many of these) chemical compounds are available, at economically acceptable costs. On the other hand, significant reductions of CO_2 emissions, involving a multitude of different kinds of emitters, would entail substantial costs for important segments of the population, some of which are of crucial economic (and political) importance.

Factors affecting domestic implementation of international treaties

It is important, therefore, to note that these international agreements are not formulated and certainly not implemented, in a vacuum. They enter a 'regulatory space' already occupied by a set of problem definitions and policy strategies. They must be fitted into ongoing programmes and preferences for particular policy instruments. The national programmes through which international obligations are to be met will be shaped within a set of institutional arrangements favouring particular actors and interests over others.

In the case of The Netherlands, for example, the measures taken to implement the CFC reduction goals of the Montreal Protocol have taken the form of a programme of co-operative regulation between government and industry, consistent with the overall national policy strategy of the country. Here, the bottom line of implementation involves actions by the Environmental Inspectorate of the national government to make sure that companies installing refrigeration employ at least one technician with the appropriate diploma, who has undergone training in the approved techniques for working with CFCs. Having one such employee is then a precondition for being recognised as a firm that can do business in this area. Such a 'strategy' for implementing international obligations also introduces new, in this case non-governmental, actors into the regulatory system: the STEK (Stichting Erkenningsregeling voor de Uitoefening van het Koeltechnisch Installatiebedrijf, roughly, the foundation for the certification of cooling equipment installing companies), an institute to which refrigeration firms must apply for certification that they possess the requisite competence to install and service installations containing CFCs. On the other hand, the US government has set up a marketable permit system consistent with the regulatory ideology and legal framework already in place. What a given country seeks through international negotiations and what commitments it ultimately finds acceptable, along with the way in which the agreements reached are translated into national action, will be a function of this ongoing political dialogue among domestic interests.

The implementation of an international environmental regime is thus a very complex process. There are, clearly, many points at which things can go wrong despite the best intentions of the actors involved. Given this complexity, what are some of the factors that ultimately determine how effective a regime will be in successfully carrying out its programme of activities? Which factors shape the capacity of members of international regimes to meet their obligations and responsibilities?

An important component of this implementation capacity will be the *vertical unity* of government, i.e. the division of authority and labour between different levels of government (Weale, 1992). To the extent that the authority to do what is required to implement an international agreement is in the hands of sub-national bodies and officials, one can easily imagine that environmental agencies at the national level will have to bargain with these sub-national actors over the conditions of implementation.

Such bargaining can, at a minimum, delay implementation but it may even thwart the efforts of the national government to honour commitments undertaken in international agreements. This is so particularly when we are dealing with environmental problems that are not strictly local in their ramifications. Whenever an activity located in one local government area imposes costs on another local government area, calculations of costs and benefits are likely to differ significantly from those of the nation at large. Everything else being equal, the greater the external costs imposed, the more the policy preferences of local government will deviate from those of central government. In such cases local actors in areas deriving economic benefits but bearing few environmental costs from an activity can be expected to be less favourable towards strict environmental measures than the national government. Conversely, local areas experiencing environmental costs created by activities elsewhere will favour strict regulation (see Box 2).

Whether or not such bargaining between national authorities and sub-national actors becomes necessary will also depend on the overall *policy strategy* selected at the national level for the implementation of the international agreement. The formal vertical division of labour does not, by itself, make a decentralised implementation inevitable. If a country, as in the case of the United States, chooses to implement the Montreal Protocol by means of a nationally organised and administered system of marketable emission rights, national decision makers will retain direct control and not be dependent on sub-national actors. On the other hand, an implementation programme based on emission reductions negotiated between industry and government, as we find in The Netherlands, means that national environmental officials have less direct control. However, in both cases national decision makers will have to depend on other sub-national public and private actors to supply important informational inputs

---

Institutional fragmentation and effective policy co-ordination |2|

The notion of 'vertical unity' gives the impression that the problems encountered in implementing international environmental agreements could be reduced – if not solved completely – if central decision makers were given more effective control over the actions of the sub-national actors on whom the execution of national programmes depends. This 'top-down' perspective means that the fact that national officials share responsibility for carrying out international agreements with other sub-national governmental – and, increasingly, non-governmental – actors makes it difficult to implement international obligations. This view implies that more centralised countries, such as France or the United Kingdom, should have less difficulty in this regard than federal countries, such as Germany or the United States. It is, however, doubtful that this will necessarily be the case. The structural differentiation that characterises the modern state, irrespective of its formal constitutional order, leads to varying degrees of *de facto* autonomy of the different actors involved in the various phases of the policy process. Consequently, effective implementation will require a variety of arrangements through which these actors are joined together.

Plate 8.2 Japanese graphic artists protest against French nuclear tests in the South Pacific, August 1995. Photo: ANP Foto

or services needed to carry out the implementation strategy chosen. In this sense, the implementation of international environmental agreements at the national level will always remain a multi-actor and multi-level process.

Although the interactions between negotiators at the international and domestic levels are likely to include estimations of the feasibility of implementing any eventual agreement, the implementation process has its own political logic and dynamic. This means that, even though the agreement was concluded in the belief that adequate political support would be forthcoming (and that the agreement would, therefore, be ratified), it may still prove difficult, if not impossible, to deliver the commitments made; or the measures designed to implement the accord may look quite different from what was intended before the agreement was negotiated. An appreciation of the difficulties involved in moving from international agreement to national action and, ultimately, on to the required behavioural changes on the part of society's members suggests that instances of *in*voluntary defection may be at least as frequent and interesting as 'cheating' by deliberate choice.

What emerges from this description of the way environmental regimes operate is a picture of a *multi-level complex* of norm-setting and rule-implementing activities, performed by different sets of actors at both the national and international levels.

205

Approached in terms of a series of interrelated national and international activities, regime implementation is more than a matter of national compliance with specific obligations. A number of separate, yet linked, networks join public and private actors in the performance of these different functions. Together they determine to what extent a regime will achieve the intended behavioural changes within the individual countries concerned.

8.3 Environmental problem solving in the context of the European Union

In the structure of international environmental co-operation, the European Union occupies a particularly important position. Observers have long wrestled with questions regarding the nature of the 'European Union' (EU) and how it is likely to develop further and with what consequences for the national governments of its member states. Whatever it may become, the environmental policy of the EU is already an extremely important source of constraints on business and other kinds of activities within its member states. In addition, the EU, acting through the European Commission, participates in international environmental negotiations in other institutional arenas with considerable consequences for both its own member states and the world community at large.

As far as business and government within the member states are concerned, the EU has become a key source of environmental legislation. It sets important parameters within which national policy takes shape. It has had its own environmental policy since 1973, the year in which the First Environment Action Programme of what was then still the European Community was approved (Hildebrand, 1992; Lefferink, *et al.*, 1994). For our purposes, the details of the specific regulatory programmes are less important than the strategic concepts which have guided the overall development of the Union's policy. In particular, what is interesting for us is the emerging redefinition of the relations between economic activity within the Community (the promotion of which was initially and still is the primary concern of the EU) and the management of environmental quality. In order to suggest the way in which the notion of sustainability has come to occupy a central place in this strategic concept, we will look a bit more closely at the more recent Environment Action Programmes. These will indicate the kinds of demands that Community policy is making on its member states. In particular, it will be of interest to note the adjustments these countries need to make in the way they manage the relationships between environmental quality and economic development and the kinds of institutional changes necessary to meet these demands (Weale, 1992 and 1993, provide an overall discussion of the environmental strategy of the EU; see also Chapter 5 of this book, for an historical overview).

Redefining the relation between environment and economy

In 1992 the Commission presented its proposal for a Fifth Environment Action Programme for approval to the Council of Ministers. This programme was intended to serve as the framework for dealing with what was seen as 'one of the most important tasks of the Community in the 1990s', to wit the 'reconciliation of social-economic development with the maintenance and protection of the environment' (Commission, 1992, p.19). In pursuit of this objective, the programme offered a fundamentally different approach to those of the other four programmes. The emphasis now lies upon the actors and activities that cause the exhaustion (exploitation) of natural resources and other forms of disturbances in the environment, the so-called 'target groups'.

Although this action programme has been touted as a significant 'break' or 'turning point' in Community policy, it represents a 'logical' development of a policy line that had been gradually evolving. Whereas the initial action programme in 1973 was primarily concerned with the problems different national environmental regulations might cause for the creation of a single European market (Hildebrand, 1992, p.25), the Third Programme (1982–1986) was already informed by the conviction that resources of the environment were the basis – and limits – of further economic and social development and improvement of the working situation. In adopting the Third Programme, the Council of Ministers explicitly recognised the benefits that environmental protection could offer the EU in terms of greater competitiveness. This theme was picked up and developed further in the Fourth Programme (1987–1992) in which it was argued that the measures taken to protect the quality of the environment would be an important stimulus to economic growth and would, consequently, work to facilitate creation of employment opportunities (Weale, 1993, p. 207). Just how far the traditional growth ethos of the Community has been 'greened' can be seen in the preamble to the Maastricht Treaty which speaks of 'balanced and sustainable economic and social progress' as the overall objective of the Community.

It has been argued for some time, then, that the increased economic growth, anticipated as a consequence of the completion of the internal market, cannot be sustained unless environmental considerations are taken into account. These must no longer be viewed as a potential limiting factor but rather as an incentive to greater efficiency and competitiveness of European industry. Instead of being seen as a burden on the economy, environmental protection is now to be considered a potential source of future growth. If a country intends to acquire or maintain a secure position in the international market place it will need the technical and production capability to respond to the increasing demand for environmental quality; it will need to manufacture goods whose production minimises pollution and to produce pollution control technology. Such a capability has become necessary because in the emerging global markets, the standards of acceptability of products will more and more be determined by the country with the most stringent pollution control standards. As Weale puts it: 'The future development of a postindustrial economy will depend upon (a country's) ability to produce high value, high quality products with stringent environmental standards enforced' (Weale, 1992, p.77).

In this sense, the ideology of 'ecological modernisation' (see Box 3) underlying the environmental quality management strategies of the Community and individual member states directly links the 'prospects for future economic development in an era of global markets with higher standards of pollution control and environmentally safe products and processes' (Weale, 1992, p.77).

A review of its Action Programmes reveals how the European Community attempted to reconcile its growing concern with environmental protection with its earlier and stronger, historic commitment to economic growth. By the Fifth Programme

207

3

Different dimensions of ecological modernisation

With its reconceptualisation of the relationship between economy and environment, the ideology of ecological modernisation marks a decisive break with the basic tenets of the first wave of environmental policy. This 'new belief system' has, according to Weale, '... challenged the fundamental assumption of the conventional wisdom ... that there was a zero-sum trade-off between economic prosperity and environmental concern'. On the contrary:

> Instead of there being a conflict between concern for the economy and concern for the environment, the argument emerged ... that environmental protection to a high level was a precondition of long-term economic development. Without the maintenance of a healthy environment, the economy would be threatened, partly because environmental degradation threatened, partly because cleanup costs would inevitably expand and partly because environmental degradation threatened the social and physical resources upon which economic prosperity depended (Weale, 1992, p.31).

Furthermore, the redefinition of the relationship between the environment and the economy has affected other elements of the older belief systems: 'The challenge of ecological modernisation extends ... beyond the economic point that a sound environment is a necessary condition for long-term prosperity and it comes to embrace changes in the relationship between the state, its citizens and private corporations, as well as changes in the relationship between states' (Weale, 1992, p.31–32). It also leads to realignments – potential and actual – in the more traditional economic-feasibility coalition and the clean environment coalition. It is in this sense that 'ecological modernisation suggests a plural and variegated set of interests, with competing and different interpretations of what values are at stake in matters of environmental policy' (Weale, 1992, p.32).

The various strands out of which this ideology has been woven provide opportunities for different groups to give somewhat different interpretations and set different accents regarding what measures are specifically required. At the same time, the idea of 'ecological modernisation' does provide a common frame of reference or mode of discourse for a meeting of the minds – and interests – of actors who had, under earlier problem definitions, been on opposing sides of the debate. It suggests a way of finding win-win solutions to problems of integrating or balancing economic rationality and environmental quality. It provides a legitimising device for reframing public policy debate and development. By setting new accents and points of reference, the concept can potentially serve as an important source of policy ideas and principles. In this way it can be used to define new strategies of action which will call new actors on to the political scene, thereby laying the basis for the formation of new policy coalitions (Weale, 1992, p.78–79).

Community policy had evolved to a point where the twin imperatives of economic development and environmental protection were linked in a new way. At least at the level of official programmes, the earlier tension between these different sets of objectives had given way to the view that they were compatible and mutually reinforcing aims of policy.

The regulatory strategy of the Fifth Environment Action Programme

According to figures presented in the Fifth Environment Action Programme, the industrial sector accounts for approximately 25% of the wealth of the European Union. Not surprisingly, then, industrialisation is a key element of the economic development strategy of the Union. In this connection, one of the primary goals of the industrial policy of the EU is to create 'the framework and conditions for a strong, innovative industrial sector' (Commission, 1992, p.28). Ensuring the optimum conditions for the continued economic growth of the member states requires identifying the necessary long-term strategies to remain economically competitive in the global economic order. The further development of the internal market among the member countries of the European Union is the cornerstone of this policy.

At the same time, with regard to the exploitation of natural resources, consumption of energy and the generation of pollution and wastes, the industrial sector is one of the principal causes of environmental deterioration. All economic enterprises, although in varying combinations and degrees, ultimately use natural resources for processes and products, create wastes and contribute to the pollution of the air, water and soil. However, until now, these long-term social costs have been effectively internalised only to a limited extent in the costs of operating or the final products. The Fifth Action Programme states unequivocally that 'The perpetuation of this situation is not viable on either economic or environmental grounds' (Commission, 1992, p.27).

As the title of the Action Programme indicates, the policy strategy for the coming years is intended to transform 'the patterns of economic growth in the Community in such a way as to reach a sustainable development path' (Commission, 1992, p.25). The programme recognises that the implementation of such a strategy will require considerable change in almost all major policy areas in which the Community is involved; it will mean that environmental protection will have to be integrated into the definition and implementation of these Community policies, not just for the sake of the environment but also for the sake of the continued efficiency of other policy areas as well.

A policy focused on the agents and activities which damage the environment and deplete natural resources will require 'significant changes in current patterns of human consumption and behaviour' (Commission, 1992, p.19). Any attempt to get at the causes of environmental problems (e.g. excessive resource use and pollution) means that current trends and practices will have to be modified. In turn, these behavioural changes can only be realised if policy makers, at both the European and member state levels, make use of a broader range of policy instruments. Until now European environmental policy has largely been based on legislation and controls in the tradition of direct regulation. Of course, there will be a continuing need for legislative instruments to define the fundamentally desirable levels of environmental care and protection, as well as for setting the common standards compatible with the internal market. Still, as the Fifth Action Programme observes, it is '... not feasible to adopt a Directive or Regulation which says: "Thou shalt act in a sustainable manner" ' (Commission, 1992, p.64).

While juridical (or legislative) instruments will remain an important element in the arsenal, a second set of instruments, the so-called market-orientated instruments, is intended to play an increasingly important role. By means of these instruments, both producers and consumers are to be motivated to a sustainable use of natural resources by being forced to calculate the external environmental costs in the prices of the product. In this way the market must ensure that environmentally friendly goods and services have a competitive advantage over those that cause pollution and waste. Examples of such instruments are: fiscal stimulation measures or charges; the environmental audit; the eco-label; and liability for environmental damage caused. Further measures are also being planned and in some cases have already been introduced, to give a new direction and thrust to the environment and industrial policy interface. This package of measures is intended to:

1 induce action designed to improve the management and control of the production processes
2 develop EU-wide product standards
3 promote the integration of effective waste management into the general management of firms
4 improve the capacity of consumers for making environmentally informed choices
5 provide the information necessary for the effective monitoring of both public and private activities and for making them more transparent.

Sustainable development through government regulation and market forces

The redefinition of the relation of economic growth and environmental protection, which underlies the notion of ecological modernisation, will have important consequences for the types of instruments deemed appropriate for effecting the necessary behavioural changes. In contrast to the earlier approach of building policy around a restrictive regulatory framework, the European Union has now embarked on the more positive task of constructing a balanced relationship between the use of environmental resources and economic activity within the member states. Box 4 quotes the relevant passage from the EC's Fifth Environment Action Programme.

In terms of policy it has been shown that the EC intends to use both legislative controls and market-orientated mechanisms to ensure that industry maintains an environmentally sound economic performance. The overall objective is to achieve sustainability of resources while, at the same time, providing for continued economic growth in Europe. In specific terms policies will be directed at reducing environmental impacts at different points in the product lifecycle which extends from product design through production and marketing to consumer use and waste management.

Such an approach requires that government play a more supportive and facilitating role. It is not expected that ecological modernisation will be realised by spontaneous adjustment by economic actors in response to moral imperatives or market forces. Public intervention (regulation) will be essential for ensuring that the relation between industry and the environment as posited by the notion of ecological modernisation in fact comes about. There is, therefore, a positive role for government to play – at both the national and the European level – in raising standards of environmental regulation as a spur to industrial innovation. It is in this connection that former Director General Brinkhorst argued that the right kind of government action, in the form of 'an effective environmental policy', will be required for 'our industrial survival in many areas'

The EU's search for sustainable development

4

One of the primary goals of the Community's industrial policy is to create the framework and conditions for a strong, innovative and competitive industrial sector, thereby ensuring the competitiveness and sustainability of Europe's industries .... Previous environment measures have tended to be proscriptive in character, with an emphasis on the 'thou shalt not' rather than the 'let's work together' approach. As a consequence, there has been a tendency to view industrialisation or economic development and environmental concern as being mutually hostile .... It is now clear that environmentally sound industry is no longer a matter of luxury but rather a matter of necessity ....In order to ensure that optimum conditions exist for continued economic growth within the Community ... it is essential to view environmental quality and economic growth as mutually dependent .... Under this Programme the dual approach of high environmental standards combined with positive incentives to even better performance should be applied in a co-ordinated manner to the different points in the *research-process-production-marketing-use-disposal chain* where industry and industrial products, may impact upon the Community's environmental resource base ... (Commission of the European Communities, *Towards Sustainability*, 1992, p.28).

Legislatively-based rules, standards and procedures will be used to provide incentives for environmentally friendly decisions on product design, investment and production. Measures are also to be taken to strengthen consumer awareness and to provide opportunities for consumer choice. Together these two different, but complementary pressures are supposed to create a market-driven and self-regulatory cycle that will encourage industry to move towards environmentally responsible production processes and products.

(quoted in Weale, 1992, p.78). However, while government policy and regulation will continue to play an essential role in shaping the conditions under which ecological modernisation can be achieved, it will not be a system of government intervention modelled on traditional direct regulation. The relationships between government (public authorities) and economic actors will also need to be adjusted to reflect the logic underlying the ideology defining both the objectives of this policy and the means for its achievement. The nature and role of Community environmental policy will, in turn, reflect processes already underway in many member states and provide a Community-wide framework to channel further developments.

While it will remain the task of the Community and the member states to determine the framework for and the conditions under which sustainable development is to be realised, it is expected that industrial enterprises, the ultimate targets of these policies, will participate actively in the efforts to move toward sustainability. The involvement of these industrial enterprises is but one aspect of the basic strategy which aims at the full integration of environmental and other relevant policies through the active participation of all the main actors in society (administrators, enterprises, general public). This is to be achieved through a broadening and deepening of the instruments for control and behavioural change. In particular, this will mean, as we have seen, that greater emphasis will be placed on market-based instruments.

Redefining the relationships between government and economic actors

The Fifth Environment Action Programme does not deal only with the critical substantive issues of European environmental protection. Even more importantly, it is designed to create a new interplay between the main groups of governmental and societal actors and the principal economic sectors, through the use of an extended and integrated range of instruments. The realisation of the objective of sustainable development requires a Union-wide framework within which other actors can work together. The framework can provide scope for co-ordinating and integrating the actions of individual member states in order to generate cumulative impact and to protect the integrity of other policy actions of EU, especially those relating to the internal market. These policy objectives cannot, however, be met by actions taken on the European level alone. On the contrary, successful policy will require a sharing of responsibility at all levels of society including governments, regional and local authorities, non-governmental organisations, financial institutions, production, distribution and retail enterprises and individual citizens (Commission, 1992, p.19).

Underlying the policy strategy of the Fifth Programme is the assumption that the general objective of sustainable development, as well as the various specific objectives included in the programme, can only be achieved by means of a joint effort by all parties in the form of 'partnership' (Brinkhorst and Klatte, 1993, p.73). In line with the 'subsidiarity principle' the Community is only supposed to come into action whenever and insofar as the objectives to be pursued cannot adequately be achieved by the member states alone and therefore, given the nature and scope of the problem, can better be realised by action at the Community level. The Fifth Programme, however, links the notion of subsidiarity with the idea of partnership or, as it is often referred to, joint responsibility. According to Brinkhorst and Klatte: 'Partnership does not so much mean a choice of the most suitable level of action to the exclusion of other levels' (Brinkhorst and Klatte, 1993, p.74). Rather, the issue is to find the most appropriate combination of different environmental instruments and 'actors' within the boundaries set by the existing allocation of tasks and powers between the Community, the member states, regional and local authorities.

Traditionally, EU environmental policy has relied heavily on legislation (a 'top-down' approach). The new strategy is based upon the 'active participation of all social-economic partners in the joint search for solutions for environmental problems and the realisation of sustainable development' (Brinkhorst and Klatte, 1993, p.74). Crucial for the success of this approach is the level and quality of the dialogue between the different actors in the context of active partnership. For its part, the Commission intends to promote and structure such a dialogue by providing a number of formally institutionalised arenas or fora (Commission, 1992, p.82–83). One such body will channel contacts between the various social-economic and governmental partners by establishing a general advisory body on environmental issues. This Advisory Council is supposed to function as a platform for consultation and information exchange on environmental matters between representatives of the diverse sectors and target groups from the member states. In addition, two other discussion groups or advisory bodies at EU level are intended to provide the framework for an effective dialogue of the kind envisaged as part of a strategy of shared responsibility or partnership: an Implementation Network and a Policy Review Group. The Implementation Network, made up of representatives from the national and community authorities, will be charged with the practical application of the Community environmental regulations. It is expected to provide a vehicle for the exchange of practical experience in enforcing these programmes at the national level. The Policy Review Group is made up of representatives from the member states at the level of Director General and will facilitate co-ordination between the national policies of the 12 members and the policy of the Community.

In setting up these groups the Commission hopes it will be possible to create an institutional framework within which there can be 'better preparation of measures, including improved consultation arrangements, more effective integration with complementary measures, better practical follow up to legislative measures … and stricter compliance checking and enforcement' (Commission, 1992, p.75). And, perhaps most important of all, these three groups can serve to promote, in an active way, a greater sense of responsibility among the principal actors involved in the formulation and implementation of European environmental policy.

8.4 Ecological modernisation and regulatory change in the member states of the European Union

Implementing EU policy in the member states

Through the various institutions, linking decision makers at the national and European levels, the European Union plays a central role in defining the normative context within which national environmental policy decisions are to be taken. However, it can only influence the implementation of this policy indirectly. Direct and final responsibility for carrying out EU environmental policy lies in the hands of the member states. Consequently, although the executive agent of the EU, the European Commission (EC), is formally responsible for the execution and enforcement of European policies, its powers and resources for doing so are limited. It is dependent on the willingness and the ability, of national administrative actors in the member states for the realisation of EU policy objectives. Based on previous experience, the record of the member states in carrying out environmental policy has left much to be desired. This is the case with regard to both the phase of 'formal implementation', i.e. the incorporation of EU directives into national law, and the phase of 'practical implementation', i.e. the application of these national programmes to effect the required changes in the behaviour of groups targeted by the directives.

For this reason, improving policy implementation has become an issue of top priority within the European Union. However, despite attempts to improve implementation and ensure compliance, the EU, acting through the Commission, cannot penetrate directly to the sub-national administrative structures of local and regional government, where much of the implementation of environmental policy actually takes place. Consequently, when it comes to the implementation stage, national factors, such as policy style, level of economic development and political culture, play a key role in shaping the nature of the protection afforded to the environment. Therefore, in order to appreciate what is going on with regard to the implementation of EU policy, it is necessary to look at the interplay of politics and administration at the different levels of government in the member states.

Changing relations between government and business: regulatory strategies in the member states

In our earlier discussion of the implementation of international agreements we noted that 'implementation capacity' is a function of the properties of government itself (including the administrative system) as well as its relationship to society in general and the social groups directly affected by the regime in particular. Furthermore, implementation capacity is also related to 'implementation strategies'. The strategy needed to meet policy objectives – and how well 'equipped' a country is at a given point in time – will depend on the country's overall 'policy' which guides the selection of instruments and the division of labour between governmental and other actors required to carry it out. For example, The Netherlands has opted for the so-called 'target group approach' as a key element in its attempt to translate its general strategic commitment to sustainable development into specific reduction objectives for different groups of economic activities. Its capacity to implement its strategy can be judged by the extent to which institutional arrangements exist to 'organise' the collaboration between government and target groups and the extent to which actors involved are able to manage the relationships on which the success of this strategy ultimately will depend.

Plate 8.3 Mercedes-Benz: the symbol of the power exerted by business in contemporary society. Photo: Mercedes-Benz

In the overview of developments with regard to the environmental policy 'strategy' of the EU we observed that the strategic line laid out in the Fifth Action Programme leads on from developments already underway in a number of member states. In these countries the nature of public intervention in the economy is also undergoing significant change through which the regulatory relationship between government and economic actors is being redefined. Since the EU is dependent upon the member states to implement its environmental policy, a brief look at some of the main features of regulatory change within these countries can suggest the extent to which they are 'capable' of participating in the policy dialogue between member states and the Community and of implementing the environmental strategy of the EU.

In most countries in Western Europe, reducing the regulatory burden on business has occupied a central place on the political agenda. As an important element of governmental interventions under the heading of 'social regulation', environmental policies have been a prime target of these deregulation measures. However, deregulation in Western European countries has not lead to the abolition of, or even a fundamental alteration in, the basic set of regulatory constraints on economic activity through which the country's commitment to environmental quality has been defined. Nor has it brought about any significant changes in the mechanisms that hold the existing system of environmental regulation in place. The underlying regulatory impulse carrying these environmental policy measures remains operative and, therefore, continues to legitimate and give direction to regulatory intervention 'shaping' market behaviour in an environmentally friendly manner. For example, the deregulation programme in The Netherlands has resulted in a restructuring of regulatory space by creating the preconditions for (a particular kind of) self-regulation as an integral part of a larger system of government 'regulation' of environmentally relevant activities. This is a redefinition of the traditional regulatory relationship between government and the economy to create something that could be called 'co-operative self-regulation'. This involves, on the one hand, the freeing up of certain kinds of restraints so as to expose economic actors to the discipline of the market and on the other hand, 'creating' a market for environmental quality to which these actors can respond when making product and investment decisions.

Deregulation, re-regulation and self-regulation

Thus, in the last analysis, regulatory reform has been designed to provide increasing leeway for economic actors ('deregulation') in order to improve their ability to respond to market signals and developments. At the same time they have had to take responsibility for the development of pollution prevention strategies within the parameters set by the government's environmental policy objectives ('re-regulation'). Such a system of co-operative self-regulation not only provides economic actors with substantial freedom in deciding for themselves how they will meet these quality objectives; it also guarantees them an active role in co-determining what the general policy goals will mean for particular industrial branches and, ultimately, the individual firms. Both policy making and more specific rule making become processes of joint decision making based on extensive consultation and bargaining between government and target groups affected by governmental intervention.

In these countries, therefore, the renegotiation of the agreements governing the relations between government and economic actors has resulted in the restructuring of regulatory space around a point of equilibrium between concern for environmental quality on the part of economic actors and improved economic competitiveness of firms as a result of increased responsiveness to market forces. Both in response to political pressures from voters and action groups – forces at work in the traditional political market – and as a result of direct consultation and bargaining between government and representatives of economic sector(s), a regulatory framework has been created that in turn generates the 'market' forces which discipline the calculations of individual economic actors.

In order to understand how government intervention has worked to create such a regulated market for environmental quality, the following points should be kept in mind. At the ideological or programmatic level, deregulation has been carried by the call to unshackle business from 'bureaucratic regulations' and free it to respond to market forces. To the extent that society wishes to promote certain collective environmental quality objectives, it should be left to the firms themselves to decide the ways in which their activities can be brought into conformity with these objectives; they should be allowed to respond to the same kinds of market considerations that guide their decisions on investment and production. However, there is an important difference between deregulation in the area of economic regulation and deregulation with regard to social regulation. It is difficult to imagine what it would mean to determine environmental quality decisions on the basis of the free play of 'market forces'. The original problem giving rise to government intervention in the first place was – and remains – that the market alone cannot deal adequately with the problem of the negative externalities of production which we experience as pollution. Consequently, there are no market forces to rely on or return to, once regulations have been lifted, to promote the politically defined objectives of socially acceptable environmental conditions (see Box 5).

On the other hand, as we have seen, deregulation is less about leaving environmental quality at the mercy of free market forces and more about the relation between the instruments to be used in pursuing these objectives and the impact of these policy

---

5

The limits to deregulation

Neither in the United States nor in Europe has deregulation meant an end to all regulation. Airlines have not been deregulated with respect to safety and newly deregulated or privatised industries are subject to national antitrust laws or to the competition rules of the European Community ... Deregulation often means less restrictive or rigid regulation, rather than no regulation ... In the field of (environmental) regulation ... the real issue is not deregulation but how to achieve the regulatory objectives by less burdensome methods ... Again, in Europe deregulation at the national level is often followed by re-regulation at the Community level, as in the case of Community-wide harmonisation of essential health and safety (as well as environmental) regulations (Majone, 1994, p.54).

constraints on the ability of the affected firm to act efficiently in the market place. Government intervention in private decision making to correct shortcomings of the market is not to be abolished by deregulation. Public authority is still to be used to influence economic behaviour in an environmentally 'friendly' direction. What is to be changed, within these continuing policy parameters, is the mix of instruments through which behaviour is affected. Both by rationalising the instruments of direct regulation and by making greater use of economic incentives, as well as by institutionalising self-regulation into the daily operations of the firm, more leeway is to be given to the firm to select its own response to the constraints of environmental regulation in making its market calculations. By simultaneously retaining the objectives of environmental regulation and increasing the firm's ability to adapt to the market, it is assumed that the goals of economic development and a socially efficient environmental protection can be achieved together.

Co-operative regulation: government policy and the market for environmental quality

All well and good, as long as we keep in mind that government regulation continues to be the basis on which the effectiveness of these alternative instruments of environmental policy depends. Consequently, if 'care of the environment' is to become 'good business' (practice), there will have to be some kind of 'market' (economic bottom line) conditions or incentives to stimulate and carry this commitment. It would, clearly, be unrealistic to expect industrial managers to take actions that undermine or are at odds with the well-understood economic interests of their firm. Their commitment to environmental responsibility needs to be 'carried' by its consistency with market logic. At the same time, however, if the fundamental 'economic' cause of environmental pollution is the failure of the market (under 'normal conditions') to provide the signals that would force economic decision makers to internalise all the relevant costs of production/consumption, then these 'signals' (prices) have to be introduced by government (external) action. In this important sense, then, it is the regulatory activity of government (in response to the politically articulated will of the community) that creates the 'market' situation in terms of which firms calculate the cost/benefit ratios of responses to economic incentives for environmentally sound behaviour or to the attractiveness of governmental initiatives on pollution prevention. While industrial managers may indeed be moved by notions of moral responsibility and personal feelings regarding environmental quality, they will, in the last analysis, act on the basis of economic rationality (Hanf, 1994). If pollution prevention is to pay (i.e. be in the long-term economic interest of firms in the broadest sense, not just in terms of 'short-term, immediate profit'), government policy must help structure the market so that it provides appropriate signals for calculating these payoffs (see Box 6).

Co-operative self-regulation within such a regulated market for environmental quality has also led to the enlargement of the community of relevant actors, involved both in negotiating the regulatory agreements and in the functioning of the markets these measures create. A number of actors in addition to national government participate in the translation of general objectives into operative goals and procedures. These include representatives from sub-national governmental authorities, the target groups

> # The Dutch implementation strategy for environmental policy
>
> The final responsibility for implementing policy lies with the target groups. In an ideal situation the target groups would modify their behaviour so as to realise sustainable development. Although there is broad collective support for the principle, there are often conflicts with the particular interests of individuals and enterprises. Implementation will be pursued and instruments chosen so as to achieve a better coincidence of collective and individual interests .... The scope given to target groups, provinces and municipalities and intermediary organisations, to make their own choices can be enlarged, within a clear framework. The targets set for target groups, an essential component of this framework, are fixed in an open planning process in consultation with each group, such that the overall theme objectives are achieved. It is the responsibility of the target groups to achieve their targets.
>
> It is up to each group to indicate how it will achieve its own targets and regulate its own conduct. Monitoring and reporting will show the efforts being made ... and the results being achieved (Ministry of the Environment, 1994, p.42).

themselves and other interested groups in society. Once in place, the market creates both new opportunities and risks which, in turn, mobilise new and old actors. For example, legislation defining the legal liability of firms for environmental pollution affects the market for liability insurance. This then leads insurance companies to evaluate a particular company's risk and thus the premium it must pay, in terms of the in-house capacity of the firm to manage its environmental affairs effectively. Likewise, the loan and investment policies of financial institutions, including banks and financial markets, can be geared to the perceived 'greenness' of the firm in question. And of course, government programmes regarding product information and labelling reinforce the position of consumers 'demanding' environmentally friendly products. In this way, private market actors perform important functions within the overall system of public regulation.

These, then, are some of the ways in which government policy creates the foundation on which this particular social market economy is based and also generates the incentives (both positive and negative) which ensure that economic actors will remain sensitive to the market forces so created. This combination of market incentives and regulatory constraints provides the material basis for a system of self-regulation that is not just a question of good will and admirable intentions. Co-operative self-regulation requires the discipline of both a publicly structured market and the ultimate threat of the regulatory stick to keep things honest.

Ecological modernisation and the reordering of regulatory space

The emerging strategy of environmental regulation in Western Europe and the EU is part of the process of redefining the relations between society and its governmental authorities and the working out of a new division of labour and pattern of collaboration between them. Students of alternative regulatory schemes for promoting new environmental protection strategies stress that efforts to prevent pollution will need to become a joint responsibility – in an important sense, a co-produced result. The character of the regulatory relationship between business and government will need to shift from confrontation to collaboration. At the heart of their vision is the belief that socially responsible self-interest can be mobilised in support of long-term adjustments towards pollution prevention. Supporting this faith is the already visible growing awareness on the part of some large corporations that continued corporate existence depends on the environmental performance of firms and enterprises and the continued support of public and government.

A serious commitment to the policy strategy of sustainable development with its promise of a mutually supportive integration of economic development and environmental quality makes necessary a new 'regulatory framework' for market activity. In an important sense it is not a question of regulation or no regulation but rather one of finding the appropriate kinds of governmental interventions, intended to shape and steer economic activity in socially desirable (as defined through the political process) ways. This clearly means that traditional forms of direct intervention will be replaced or supplemented by various modes of more indirect guidance. In other words, it means that 'hard' instruments of direct regulation will give way to 'soft' intervention modes of indirect and self-regulation. In any case, it is important to keep in mind the need for various governmental initiatives – jointly conceived with target groups – to stimulate and encourage, but also to 'keep socially honest' the market-orientated decision making of economic actors.

A commitment to a strategy of ecological modernisation as a central element of environmental policy involves a reordering of regulatory space in a search for a balance between market forces and government regulation of a new type. By creating the kind of regulated market described above, the objectives of sustainable development are to be achieved by introducing considerations of environmental quality and care as parameters for the decisions of economic actors. There are at least three levels of institutional adaptation to market economies which should be distinguished in this connection:

1 There is the need to create the conditions for a new macrosystem, based on relatively free play of market forces; this is the main focus for deregulation and privatisation measures.
2 At an intermediate or meso-level, an associational infrastructure must be created, either by adapting existing social and economic organisations or by creating new ones to perform various functions required by a capitalist economy. This will include redefining the working relationship between government and the different economic actors.
3 The development of such a market system will require adjustments on the part of managers of industrial firms since managing a firm in a market situation is different from performing the same tasks in a planned economy in which the disciplining effects of market exchanges are absent. The same holds true for government officials whose job it has been to 'regulate' this economic activity in one way or another.

The nature of the regulatory role of the state, the instruments employed and the relationships between regulatory agencies and their target groups will need to be adapted to the requirements of the institutional context of the particular market economy. These kinds of adjustments in the role conceptions and management skills of both public and private actors are important preconditions for the transition to an effectively working market order.

8.5 Conclusion: co-governance and the problem-solving capacity of the nation state

At the beginning of the chapter we noted that environmental interdependence restricts the ability of national governments to attain their (quality) objectives unilaterally. In light of this situation, there are those who conclude that such interdependence constitutes a threat to state sovereignty in the sense that the state is no longer able to perform its basic function of meeting the demands of its citizens. Moreover, satisfactory solutions to problems of ecological interdependence will require some kind of institutional arrangement that supplants or significantly limits the nation state, so as to bring about the necessary co-operation among these separate actors.

But, formal sovereignty (defined as a situation where the state is subject to no other state and has full and exclusive power within its own jurisdiction) does not appear to have been seriously threatened by interdependence and international agreements. Indeed, as we have seen, all forms of international co-operation are based on the fundamental fact of international life: sovereign nation states continue to be the basic actors in international relations. On the other hand, the governments of these 'formally sovereign states' increasingly find it in their interest (as a result of domestic political pressures) to undertake collective action to deal with problems that are perceived as presenting a shared threat.

If such collaboration is to be achieved, the individual states will have to accept that their 'operational sovereignty' (their legal freedom to act under international law) will be 'eroded' or constrained to one degree or another, as a precondition for finding mutually beneficial solutions to problems of joint concern. International agreements do, indeed, restrict a country's freedom to do as it pleases. In this sense then, ecological interdependence does change the relationship between operational sovereignty and effective action: under conditions of close interdependence, attempts to maintain unlimited sovereignty may make it impossible for anyone to take any effective action.

Taking all this into consideration, the modern state at the end of the 20th century may very well have lost a good deal of its traditionally imputed ability to act 'alone' – as a 'sovereign authority' – in ordering its relations with other members of the international community and in dealing with the problems of its citizens. At the same time, it has gained through various arrangements for collaborative or joint decision making a capacity to tackle problems requiring the concerted inputs or action capabilities of a number of separate actors. Consequently, what we are seeing is not a 'leaking away' of state sovereignty toward international or supranational bodies but (keeping with the hydraulic metaphor) a 'pooling' of sovereignties to create institutional arrangements for joint decision making and problem solving on the basis of the continued independence and formal autonomy of the constituent units. It should be noted that the logic of joint action holds for all players, not just public authorities: all lose (relatively speaking) their capacity for unilateral action and steering while gaining, in return, partners who commit themselves with their own resources and potential for action to engage in joint problem-solving activity. It has been the argument of this chapter that these 'negotiated orders' for joint action are 'repeated' at each of the different levels of collective decision making and social action – ranging from international treaty making down to relations between individual firms and sub-national governmental authorities. Together they constitute a set of more or less tightly interlinked networks of actors through which the various 'functions of international governance' are performed.

The number of international environmental agreements has grown rapidly in recent years. Although they vary greatly in their individual features, they all establish some form of international regime through which the processes of international governance take place. Increasingly, the attention of those concerned with international environmental management is shifting from issues relating to regime formation ('Is international co-operation possible?') to questions concerning the results of such arrangements ('What are the impacts of such regimes?').

With this shift in interest toward the consequences of international environmental regimes, questions of implementation come to the fore. What happens within the signatory states will determine how successful these efforts to institutionalise international co-operation will be. As we have seen, implementation of international environmental agreements is a complex process. It involves multiple channels of interaction between agents of public authorities and those subject to the regime rules and the regulations promulgated to enforce them. In the last analysis, regime effectiveness will depend on the legislation and regulations national governments pass to put them into operation and on the actions taken to ensure compliance. In this sense, 'running' regimes, once the treaty is concluded and adjusting them to changes within national and international society is as difficult and daunting a task as reaching the initial agreement itself.

9

Policy scenarios for sustainable development

Henk van Latesteijn and Jan Schoonenboom

9.1 Introduction

Environmental policies have been through a distinct process of evolution over the past two decades. The 1970s were dominated by problem-solving policies. Problems such as summer smog or water pollution (e.g. of the River Thames, the River Rhine and Love Canal) were addressed through a range of policies.

The 1980s saw the advent of environmental policies with a more structural approach. New products and processes were forced to comply with certain environmental standards. The purpose of this shift was to avoid future environmental damage by imposing standards that resulted from the identification of earlier pollution problems.

Although this approach was continued into the 1990s, calls have now begun for more general preventive policies. New terms have emerged that suggest a shift in thinking: 'proactive policies', 'no-regret policies', 'precautionary principles', etc. The basic idea is very simple: we can prevent the occurrence of new environmental problems by taking account of the environmental impacts of all products and processes from the outset. In theory, this would seem to provide a promising opportunity for changing the current trends. In practice, however, the situation is much more complicated. If preventive policies are to encompass more than a statement of good intentions, it must be clear for all parties what action is permissible and what is not. It is here that the relatively new concept of sustainable development comes into play.

This chapter discusses the efforts which have been made to operationalise the concept of sustainable development in the form of policies that are capable of implementation. The analysis presented here is based on a study by the Dutch Scientific Council for Government Policy (known in Dutch as the WRR), which was designed to assess the usefulness of sustainable development in terms of policy making (Dutch Scientific Council for Government Policy, 1995). The chapter begins (Section 9.2) with a discussion of the concept of sustainable development from the viewpoints of ecology and economics and suggests that the right balance must be found for the purposes of policy making. Section 9.3 considers the problem of assessing indicators for sustainable development and the constraints imposed on policy making by scientific uncertainty and varying perceptions of risk. This is followed in Section 9.4 by an analysis of policy scenario building using case studies relating to the world food supply and Nature conservation in order to evaluate four action perspectives for sustainable development. Finally, in Section 9.5, the problems facing decision makers in choosing between alternative strategies are described.

9.2 Environmental policy and sustainable development

The nature of the concept

The concepts of sustainability and sustainable development arose in response to the still present feeling that the environment is being increasingly harmed by human activity. The fear is that if things go on as they are, an untenable situation will arise. There is a strong feeling that people will not only degrade the physical environment by their actions, but will ultimately also threaten human existence itself. This untenability manifests itself in the waste of finite raw materials, the utilisation of natural resources in excess of their regenerative capacity and the damage caused by human activity to the conditions required to enable the existence of all manner of plant and animal species. Such damage may be regarded as reprehensible enough in itself, but is particularly calamitous if potentially vital information for human survival is lost. This sense of unease promotes the reasoning that this untenable relationship with the environment must be moulded into a tenable, sustainable relationship.

The general feeling of the imminent approach of an unstoppable catastrophe has undoubtedly been fed by numerous scientific publications on all sorts of environmental problems. These include the deteriorating condition of forests and agricultural soils, the carcinogenic properties of various chemicals, the depletion of the ozone layer and the threatened extinction of species as well as highly prominent incidents such as algae plagues, oil spills, the Chernobyl nuclear disaster and floods caused by soil erosion.

Cumulative negative information, however, may sometimes also evoke simplistic generalisations, which underestimate the massive degree of uncertainty surrounding the scientifically based 'evidence' of impending disaster. Most notably, a few hot summers in Northern Europe may easily be looked upon as evidence of an anthropogenically enhanced greenhouse effect. At the same time, it is easy to overlook the fact that, although human endeavours have negative implications for the environment, they have also brought prosperity and quality to people's lives. For example, it is tempting to forget that agriculture has been able to feed the sharp rise in the world population, that life expectancies have increased substantially, that people's health has improved significantly and that average standards of living have increased on a worldwide scale. At the same time, this recognition should not automatically deny the fact that these achievements are also associated with the exhaustion of natural resources and with damage to the natural environment.

So, in order to assess the value of developments, we need to understand fully both aspects of human activities. Although human endeavours have led to the fulfilment of many needs, this positive outcome is sometimes overshadowed by various undesirable side-effects on the environment. The destruction of the environment is not an intentional goal, but springs from an urge to meet the growing needs and demands of people. The notion of sustainable development was introduced so as to encourage a two-sided appraisal of human activities and thus create a more balanced relationship.

Although the idea of sustainability was formulated as far back as the 1970s, it was the work of the World Commission for Environment and Development (WCED), usually called the Brundtland Commission that placed the concept firmly on the political agenda of national governments and international fora. By way of a follow-up, a wide range of slightly differing definitions have since been given for the term. The problem of defining sustainable development has been discussed at various points in the three volumes of this series, most notably by Blowers and Glasbergen (1995; see also Section 7.3 of the present volume). We do not intend to repeat the debate here, but rather merely to observe that the concept embraces both a scientific conception of 'sustainability' and a social conception of 'development'. It is an elusive concept that is difficult to pin down in operational terms. The latter is what this chapter attempts to do.

In its report entitled *Our Common Future*, the Brundtland Commission gave a formulation of the concept of sustainable development that leaves a good deal of room for individual interpretation (WCED, 1987). The underlying tenor of the report that 'sustainable development' is under threat from both wealth (in the form of overexploitation) and poverty (neglect) has, however, been broadly adopted. The report states that:

> In essence, sustainable development is a process of change in which the exploitation of resources, the direction of investments, the orientation of technological development and institutional change are all in harmony and enhance both current and future potential to meet human needs and aspirations.

This definition underlines the fact that sustainable development is concerned with at least two aspects: the continued existence and well-being of humankind and that of the environment. In doing so, harmony must be established between all the activities required in order to meet human needs. This does not, however, suggest anything about the extent to which human needs should be met. In addition, attitudes will vary towards which human needs or environmental values are acceptable or not. The Brundtland Report does not elaborate on what is meant by the harmonious treatment of the environment or the point at which human activities will result in unacceptable damage to the environment. The fact that these questions can elicit divergent responses is evident from the differing measures used to determine these factors. In other words, the two aspects of sustainable development (i.e. scientific and human) require some further consideration.

Ecological and economic sustainability

The differences in definitions and interpretations make clear that sustainable development is not an objective feature of a process, but instead involves assigning the

Plate 9.1 Deadwood: this sculpture on Paseo de la Reforma in Mexico City is made from the trunk of a huge tree and symbolises the alarming rate at which the city is falling prey to environmental degradation. Photo: ANP Foto

label of sustainable or non-sustainable to human activities and their effects on the environment. Sustainable development is a two-sided relationship, since the well-being of both society and the environment plays a role in the evaluation of these activities. Social well-being can be measured in terms of the extent to which needs are satisfied, whilst environmental well-being can be measured in terms of the extent to which environmental functions and assets are left intact. In defining these needs, we are dealing with a broad concept which covers the needs not just of the present generation, but also of future generations. However, the needs of future generations must be defined as those felt by the present generation on behalf of future generations. The decision as to whether human activities deserve to be labelled as 'sustainable' must consequently be based on two fundamentally different approaches to developments which are deemed to be desirable.

Figure 9.1 indicates how the satisfaction of social needs and the quality of the environment are interrelated. In fact, there are two separate 'boxes'. In the economic box, activities affect society via the satisfaction of existing needs. In the ecological box, activities affect environmental functions and values via the inevitable emissions of polluting substances, for example. The burden imposed on the environment by a

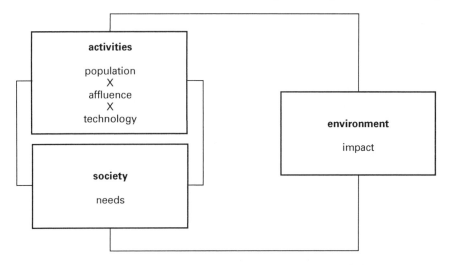

Fig. 9.1 Interrelationships between activities, needs and the environment in the economic and ecological systems. For an explanation, see text in this chapter.

particular activity may take many different forms. Apart from emissions, the effect may be disruption, fragmentation, exhaustion, etc. Together, these influences are known as an 'impact'. In other words, besides having a positive effect on the satisfaction of needs, an activity may also have a negative impact on the environment. Moreover, there may also be a causal link with the economic system if the impact causes damage to an environmental function or asset that helps meet an identified need in the economic system.

The impact of a human activity on the environment bears a relationship to the number of people involved in the activity in question and the way in which the activity is carried out. Take, for example, the environmental impact of the production and use of paper. The impact on the environment depends on:

○ the number of people using paper
○ the amount of paper each person uses
○ the way in which the paper is manufactured and consumed, i.e. the way in which wood fibres are processed into pulp, whether or not the paper is bleached, whether or not the waste paper is recycled, etc.

The relationship between the impact on the environment and the fulfilment of economic needs by human activities is illustrated in Figure 9.1. All activities originate primarily in the economic domain; some activities, however, will have a negative impact on the environment. The magnitude of the impact is related to the number of people involved in the activity, the level of affluence of society and the technologies used.

Many interpretations of sustainable development take just one of the two boxes into consideration, either as a condition of the ecological system to be defined in isolation (i.e. the larger box) or the economic system (i.e. the smaller box). In the former case, a standard is assigned to elements of the environment that may not be exceeded. In the latter case, it is the satisfaction of defined needs which is the central feature. Both cases view sustainable development from their own particular vantage points.

Ecology prevails

Where the emphasis is on giving greater priority to 'environmental criteria' than to human needs (Daly, 1990), 'ecological constraints' are determined in terms of absolute values. The advocates of this position, sometimes referred to as *strong sustainability*, argue that the natural resource base should be kept intact, despite the effect which this will have on society. Limits are therefore defined within which human activity must take place if it is to be sustainable (Daly, 1995). The maximum permissible impact on the environment is determined by specifying criteria for environmental values and functions. Generally speaking, this means that the impact must decline in relation to the present situation. This decline is to be realised either through an adjustment of the number of people involved, or through a decline in the level of affluence, or else through an alteration of the technologies involved in production and consumption.

We have now identified the three steering policy variables. The first and most far-reaching of these, involves proposals for population control. This is generally prompted by the anticipated growth of the population in developing countries. Combined with a rise in living standards, this is regarded as being likely to impose an unacceptable burden on the ecological system. The view may therefore be taken that environmental criteria necessitate an active population policy. In his farewell lecture as Professor of Atmospheric Hygiene and Pollution at Wageningen Agricultural University, The Netherlands, Professor Adema referred to evolutionary development, which '[…] as long as human beings do not get in the way, in my view […] is the purest form of sustainable development.' On the basis of a postulated maximum permissible burden on the environment and a desired level of prosperity, he calculated that the maximum sustainable global population by the year 2040 would be 2 billion (Adema, 1992).

Secondly, proposals may relate to the adjustment of material welfare or affluence. Viewed from this perspective, per capita income should be reduced so as to relieve the burden imposed on the environment. This should not be confused with a variant proposing that consumption, especially in the rich West, should be 'de-materialised'. The underlying principle in the latter case is that the impact on the environment will be reduced if average human wants assume a less material nature. For example, the consumption of 'culture' (by attending a concert, for example) is less harmful to the environment than the procurement and use of a speedboat. With this approach, policy does not impinge on living standards, but affects the level of technology applied in the process of consumption.

Thirdly, it may be urged that the technology of production should be modified. This would involve investments in new, substitute technology which is capable of reversing the negative impact on the environment.

If the sole focus is on the assets and functions of the environment, a significant element of the social satisfaction of wants is either left out of account or becomes a derivative factor. Proponents of environmental interests may, for example, adopt the

228

uncompromising standpoint that any use of chlorinated hydrocarbons is unacceptable on account of its environmental consequences, without taking into account the effects on human activities and other interests. Such a position is justified by those concerned because of their view that environmental risks are exceptionally great and that the environment must not therefore be exposed to a 'corrupting' process of trade-offs. This ignores the fact that others may have a totally different, though equally justifiable attitude towards the use of these substances, in which the environmental risks are kept within acceptable limits.

'Hard' environmental requirements, then, come into conflict with the 'hard' require-ments of society, with, in the background, a difference of interpretation concerning the risks involved. If the required standard of living, the environmental intensity of production and consumption or the population size cannot be regulated, or only with difficulty, we will find ourselves in a stalemate. The most common response to an absolutist but unattainable norm is to find a way of escaping the burden imposed by that norm. In these circumstances, there is a risk that, when concrete choices have to be made, charity will begin at home and priority will be given on grounds of necessity to employment, economic growth, the improvement of the infrastructure and so on – in brief, to more 'worldly' needs.

The economy prevails

Alternatively, confidence in the ecological system may be so robust that emphasis is placed lopsidedly on the economic system. In such circumstances, activities are evaluated entirely against the background of social needs. The satisfaction of these wants is given primacy and any effects on the environment are justified in terms of the express desire of meeting these needs. In this view, the risks of undermining these social needs are regarded as excessive.

This approach does not primarily examine whether needs can be satisfied in an 'environmentally friendlier' manner. Environmental interests, however, automatically come into focus if the perceived social needs which the environment is required to facilitate can no longer be achieved. If the impact on the environment should prove too great, the scope can then be examined for improving the 'ecological performance' of technologies used in production and consumption. In some cases, even an adjustment to the level of affluence with respect to this problem or an effort to bring down population growth might be considered. This 'learning by doing' approach implies that there are sufficient response mechanisms in society and that there is enough time in which to respond. One of the prime exponents of this vision is Wildavsky: 'Formerly people always needed a justification for doing nothing. These days we need a justification for doing something. Progress is based on trial and error, but now we suddenly want a trial without error. We want a free lunch. Unfortunately, there's no such thing' (Rozendaal, 1992).

Balancing subjective preferences

Both one-sided approaches discussed above fail to do justice to the complexity of society. In the first case, environmental requirements are imposed and the rest of the social system simply has to fit in as well as possible. In the second case, economic requirements prevail and the resulting quality of the environment is accepted as an inevitable factor. These partial approaches cloak a risk of an imperative denial of other potential approaches.

In the case of sustainable development, there is a danger of reducing the debate to the views of proponents and opponents. It is, however, critically important to acknowledge that there are a number of highly divergent and in some cases conflicting, perceptions of sustainability that exist side by side. Each of these perceptions provides its own interpretation of the two most important aspects of sustainable development: the ecological norms and values which must be respected on the one hand and the socio-economic norms and values which must be respected on the other.

A failure to take all the relevant aspects into account when elaborating the concept of sustainable development tends to be the rule rather than the exception. It is therefore essential for both the broadly interpreted socio-economic and the ecological dimension to be incorporated in the analysis for the purpose of rendering sustainable development operational. Choices in favour of certain environmental values or certain human needs must be determined in the light of the consequences of these choices. Although it is not in itself a new notion, this 'double goal' is not always equally clear in the present policies aimed at bringing about sustainable development.

9.3 Sustainable development as a policy tool
Carrying capacity and indicators of sustainable development

There is a clear dichotomy in current policy. Economic and socio-economic policies have traditionally been geared towards the attainment of economic goals. At best, these policies sometimes take the environment into account as a marginal limiting factor. As a reaction to this one-dimensional thinking, environmental policies have often been based on the same attitude. Again, at best, the economic situation is regarded as a marginal limiting factor. Those environmental policies that seek to attain sustainable development do not usually incorporate any notion of limiting factors outside the environmental domain. Here, the sole focus is on environmental conditions, as is reflected by the concept of the carrying or absorbent capacity of the environment which underpins these policies. The possibility that a scientific concept might lead to an impartial appraisal of sustainability is very tempting indeed. Tempting as it may be, this type of decision support tool for policy making presupposes scientific information that is capable of distinguishing between the sustainable and the unsustainable in a way convincing enough to overcome political differences of opinion.

The idea behind the notion of an *ecological carrying capacity* in this context is that the environment will be damaged if it is excessively burdened. Serious and possibly even insuperable environmental problems may arise, as a result of which people will die or fall ill, suffer serious inconvenience or loss of well-being and animal and plant species will die out, ecosystems will be ruined, water supplies, soil fertility and the agricultural heritage will be damaged and physical and economic development may be held back. If the absorbent capacity of the environment is known, constraints can be defined for the various activities that impose a burden on the environment. These constraints can in turn be used to determine the behavioural changes which are needed in order to achieve sustainable development.

A particular branch of the literature which was published in the wake of the Brundtland Report addressed the problems in assessing the 'right' constraints with respect to the environment's absorbent capacity. The idea was that, once these were identified, then sustainable development would come within reach. Daly suggested that the carrying capacity of the environment could be represented as a set of Plimsoll lines drawn on the hull of a ship. Plimsoll lines are used to indicate a ship's maximum loading capacity and there are different Plimsoll lines for different weather conditions and for different types of water (i.e. different degrees of salinity). Daly used this metaphor to illustrate the environment's limited absorbent capacity (Daly, 1973).

Various researchers and groups started a quest to identify a number of environmental Plimsoll lines in the guise of indicators of sustainable development. This search for indicators is a logical extension of the same line of thought. The notion of an indicator is based on the assumption that the system as a whole can be monitored efficiently by studying a limited set of key organisms or state variables (Keurs and Meelis, 1987). The results of this quest so far have shown that there are still many difficulties to be overcome before indicators can be used in practical situations (Kuik and Verbruggen, 1991). Nevertheless, a number of authors remain firmly committed to the need for such tools, notwithstanding the problems that have been encountered (Arrow *et al.*, 1995).

Other attempts have recognised that sustainability must be considered in terms of the multi-dimensional nature of environmental space. In this case, two problems arise if we try to identify indicators and establish the target values which need to be met in order to bring about a sustainable environment (van Latesteijn *et al.*, 1994). The first is the problem of assessing the right dimensions of the environmental space. This is the same question as: *What* exactly are the indicators of sustainable development? Or, in more general terms, what exactly does sustainability encompass? The second problem is how to assess the values on each axis that bound the multidimensional environmental space. This is the same question as: *Which* levels are critical for the indicators of sustainability? Or, in more general terms, how can one discriminate between the sustainable and the unsustainable?

Scientific uncertainties and conflicts of interest

The notion that scientific information can be used objectively and unequivocally to indicate the margins within which human activities should take place is, to begin with, at variance with the observation made earlier that sustainable development relates to the quality of both the environment and society. If the 'demands' of the environment do not cut across social desiderata, there is of course no problem. In practice, we find that the greatest progress is made in 'win-win' situations of this kind. Where ecological and social desiderata come into conflict with one another, however, problems arise. If a criterion that is laid down as absolute proves to be unattainable, the policy in question will cease to provide a guiding framework.

Even if an abstract consensus has been reached on the need to strive for sustainable development, it can suddenly prove paper-thin once the consequences become visible

231

and tangible. This is evident from the conflicts that arise, such as following attempts to reduce human dependence on cars or to curb industrial production. In such situations, it becomes apparent that fundamental changes in behaviour are required, often in circumstances when the public fail to accept the need for such changes. Instead of providing clarity, the application of the concept then simply encounters problems of political feasibility.

The concept of sustainable development suggests that definitive knowledge is achievable in principle, i.e. knowledge that enables the limits to and the criteria for behaviour to be determined. This is what makes the whole idea so attractive to governments: hard, scientifically formulated constraints and parameters can render all sorts of political debates superfluous.

This denies, however, the dynamic nature of science. New knowledge is constantly generated that qualifies or tightens previously formulated 'demands' on society. What was previously regarded as incontrovertible knowledge then proves to have been no more than provisional knowledge. This is a consequence of the fact that the accumulation of knowledge is an ongoing process. Many areas of scientific investigation are still in their infancy, particularly in the environmental field. In addition, relevant knowledge also derives from action itself or, in other words, from experience. Every experience gained with the use of new technologies in dealing with certain environmental problems leads to the gathering of new scientific information and knowledge. (The role of scientific knowledge in the conceptualisation of environmental problems and the relationship of this knowledge to the problems of policy making are fully explored in Sloep and van Dam, 1995; Liberatore, 1995; Blowers and Glasbergen, 1995.)

The main scientific problem in distinguishing the sustainable from the unsustainable is the lack of the information which is needed for a complete and coherent analysis. In many cases, knowledge of environmental trends and the impact of human activities on these trends is no more than fragmentary. There are two problems in particular: inherent ignorance and uncertainty.

Inherent ignorance

In order to assess the sustainability of a given development, information is needed on the extent to which the development exceeds the critical limits of both the ecological and the economic system. But even if we restrict ourselves to the physical environment alone, we are still dealing with a highly complex system. The environment does not exist as a unit or entity, but as a system of differing ecosystems (such as forests, fenlands and river deltas) supplemented by abiotic elements (e.g. a supply of raw materials). Ecology is concerned with the analysis of ecosystems and could therefore provide the most important building blocks for setting quality standards for the environment. To date, however, it has proved all but impossible to determine unambiguously which elements are vital for the sustainable functioning of an ecosystem. Ecology is not ready for questions of this type and will probably never be able to come up with definitive answers to such questions.

This may be clarified by drawing a distinction between repeatable and unique systems. Repeatable agro-ecosystems, such as a field of potatoes or wheat, can be identified and the mechanisms of their functioning explained. The time-scale of the system is known and the number of elements in the system is limited. Hypotheses on its functioning are testable and can be experimentally falsified, because the object of the system is clear, i.e. to produce potatoes or wheat. All non-productive elements of the original natural ecosystems, such as weeds and vermin, are therefore eliminated as far as possible in the development of this agro-ecosystem. All other external influences on the system are related to the ultimate goal. In a productive sense, this knowledge is used in order to respond to changing influences. If, for example, the density of a plague organism exceeds an experimentally determined threshold, a decision may be taken to take certain counteractions. To a great extent, therefore, scientific information can be used to identify the characteristics of these comparatively simple systems. This does not imply that there is no ambiguity concerning the relevant indicators of sustainable development. The concepts of stability, resilience, productivity and tenability are employed side by side and attention is given to the use of both renewable and non-renewable resources.

The majority of natural ecosystems, however, form part of unique systems in which the time-scale is in fact infinite. Unique systems are characterised by a large number of unknown positive and negative feedbacks, so that the characteristics of the system cannot be described. In contrast to repeatable agro-ecosystems, the most important goal of the system and consequently the most important elements in it, are less clear in the case of natural ecosystems. Numerous qualitative standards are therefore imposed on ecosystems that are highly constrained in space and time. They therefore draw for their frame of reference on the state of Nature in the past. One such standard might be based, for example, on the goal of encouraging salmon to return to the Rhine. Various indicators of sustainable development can coexist, without it being possible to assign priority to them on scientific grounds. For example, a range of indicators might be used in order to establish the ecological value of the Wadden Sea, such as the state of feeding grounds for birds of passage, the number of seals, the size of the region and the wealth of lower organisms.

If quality standards relate to the entire system, the characteristics of the system become important. In the case of more complex natural ecosystems, however, our knowledge of the resilience, robustness and persistence of the system is highly limited. On the other hand, much may be known about individual elements of such systems and the consequences of disruption can therefore be estimated. The consequences of such disruption for the system as a whole, however, remain largely confined to speculation. The tropical rainforest, for example, is known especially for its abundance of species but their precise numbers, their frequencies and the situation concerning persistence are unknown.

Whereas science is at best able to provide a partial and conditional insight into positive and negative feedbacks, policy, by contrast, is interested in the net result and seeks to find answers to absolute questions, such as 'Is the earth warming up or not?'. Especially in the case of unique systems, science is unable to identify all the determinants of the functioning of ecosystems. In the absence of such knowledge, it is impossible, especially in relation to these unique systems, to determine the quality of the environment. Similarly, it is also often impossible to provide a response to questions about ecological disruption. An inherent ignorance of the consequences of change is more or less characteristic of unique systems. In other words, it is not possible to come up with clear-cut, non-controversial definitions of sustainable development.

Uncertainty

The debate on sustainable development is also hampered by statistical and fundamental uncertainty. The statistical uncertainty stems from the lack of knowledge of human intervention and its effects on the environment, while the fundamental uncertainty stems from a partial knowledge of complex relationships that may lead to differences in insight about them.

It is sometimes possible – within reasonable limits – to predict the effect of a certain intensity of human activity on the quality of the environment. This applies, for example, to the relationship between urbanisation and Nature conservation. Clearly, nature must give way where urban development takes place. In many cases, however, this relationship is surrounded by uncertainties and ambiguities. Although industrial activities result in the emission of acidifying substances, such as nitrogen oxides and sulphur dioxide, their effects on the vitality of forests can be determined only by averaging a large number of observations of the reduced vitality of trees. Causal relationships can sometimes be established at the level of the component elements. This applies, for example, to the effects of acidification on the biochemical process that forms part of photosynthesis. The extrapolation of these relationships is controversial and it is difficult to draw direct conclusions with respect to the growth and production of forests. In this case, therefore, we have to make do with a statistical estimate of the average effect of acidifying deposition on the vitality of forests. The relationship between the dose and the effect may then be portrayed in the form of a scatter diagram indicating that a number of effects have been observed for a particular intervention. The relationship between the intervention and the effect is evidently disrupted by background interference that cannot be screened out.

In many dose–effect relationships, it is not even possible to provide an indication of the size of the background interference and there is total uncertainty about the precise position of the points. The reason for this is not only that much scientific research into these relationships reveals statistical uncertainties, but also that more fundamental uncertainties prove unbridgeable. A good example is provided by the theoretical basis of measures in the field of climate control. Far-reaching statements have been made about climatic changes due to the greenhouse effect, all of varying reliability. These statements range from the belief that the next ice age will be brought forward to a claim that there will be no effect and to the more prevalent conviction that there will be an acceleration in the process of global warming. (A full account of the relationship between scientific knowledge and policy making in relation to climate change is presented by Beukering and Vellinga, 1996.)

A study conducted by the IPCC, however, has examined the status of the various data and has classified them into three categories: facts, suppositions and guesses (Houghton *et al.*, 1990). For example, it is a scientifically established *fact* that human activity (i.e. the combustion of fossil fuels and deforestation) has caused the CO_2 content of the atmosphere to increase at an accelerating rate. It is *suspected* that the increase in CO_2 levels will enhance the greenhouse effect and result in higher average temperatures on Earth. This supposition is based on calculations using incomplete models of the 'unique' climate system, embracing all the problems mentioned above. Tests can be conducted on the component elements of these models, but not on the models as a whole. This means that, depending on the feedbacks for which allowance is made, the results may vary considerably. For this reason, it is necessary to speak of estimates and suppositions and not of probabilities and facts. Finally, there are *guesses* that the greenhouse effect will result in a rise in the sea level; these are not based on hydrological models of the world and are generally no more than speculative in nature and therefore highly controversial (Böttcher, 1992).

However, even if the relationship between, for example, the use of fossil fuels and the rise in the sea level is unknown, choices still have to be made for policy purposes. In these circumstances, the *potential risk* becomes the determining factor in the choice. In the case of statistical uncertainties, this risk can be estimated and both the distinguishing capacity and the reliability of the statements can then be assessed. In the case of fundamental uncertainties, we cannot do anything beyond make a subjective estimate of the risks. In fact, we are therefore concerned here with the *perception of risks*, with respect to both the environment (i.e. can the environment cope with a particular impact?) and the socio-economic order (can society, with its needs, wishes and institutions, adapt to new activities without problems?).

These perceptions of risk come into play when a decision has to be made in a specific instance to adapt certain economic activities in order to reduce the burden imposed on the environment. Generally speaking, this will then mean that environmental investments have to be made. If the relationship between environmental investments and environmental quality is a diffuse one, it will not be clear how great the investment will need to be in order to achieve a given level of environmental quality and conversely it will be unclear what level of environmental improvement will be achieved by a given investment. The recent debate on the cost imposed on the agricultural industry by the Dutch government's manure abatement policy (see Bolsius and Frouws, 1996) and the supposed benefits in the form of vital forests provides one example. Although many farmers are by definition well disposed towards the natural environment, they are not all convinced of the need to eliminate every last emission of ammonia from animal pens at high cost, given that the benefits are not immediately apparent to them. For Nature conservationists wishing to conserve the Peel region in the Dutch province of Brabant from negative external influences, the benefits in the form of an unspoiled natural environment are clear. The estimation of risks therefore invariably comes with a price tag.

It is, however, by no means always the case that life as we know it will cease to exist if a set critical value or an indicator is exceeded. Accordingly, it is virtually impossible to base policy decisions on scientifically established facts. An attempt has been made to draw up sustainability indicators in the case of copper and aluminium (Van Egmond *et al.*, 1992). The researchers in question compared the present level of consumption with the 'permitted level of consumption' as derived from a calculation based on the exhaustion of reserves in 50 years' time. The concept of 'permitted consumption' is subject to highly different interpretations, however. Taking the case of aluminium, there is an enormous difference (by a factor of 400 million) between the present commercially exploitable reserves and the actual geological reserves. On the basis of what is considered technically feasible at present, the technically extractable reserves are estimated at roughly 700 times the current commercial reserves. Differing assumptions about technological progress may lead to lower, but equally to substantially

Limits to scientific analysis

Uncertainty, ignorance and risk impose limits on the applicability of scientific analysis in a policy context. Funtowicz and Ravetz (1991) identify three different stages in scientific policy-oriented analyses. In a context of *applied science*, the normal scientific quality standards hold true. The policy problem is translated into a standard scientific puzzle that is solved using the standard methodologies and the standard quality control in the guise of a peer review. This is applicable to small-scale problems that need a policy decision.

Most policy problems are not that simple, however. There is much more uncertainty involved in most cases and there is much at stake which may be affected by the policy decision. This means that stakeholders no longer comply with the scientific analysis and instead seek their solution in *professional consultancy*. Experts are consulted who give their opinion, based on lengthy scientific experience. This expert judgement is no longer subject to a peer review. On the contrary, different stakeholders employ different experts to give different advice.

Over time, the uncertainties and interests involved in policy decisions show a tendency to increase. Most environmental problems are characterised by huge uncertainties and huge stakes. In these situations, people do not even rely on the judgement of professional consultants. There is a feeling that, because of the uncertainties and stakes involved, a personal opinion is equally relevant. We still lack a sound methodology for this sort of policy problem. Funtowicz and Ravetz propose the term *'postnormal science'* for this area. The different stages are summarised below.

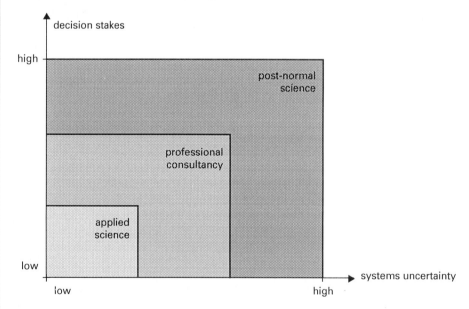

Source: Funtowicz, S.O. and Ravetz, J.R. (1990) *Uncertainty and Quality in Science for Policy.* Dordecht: Kluwer Academic Publishers.

higher estimates of these technical reserves. Reducing all these uncertainties to a 'safe' margin of 50 years is therefore, at the very least, a gross simplification of reality. The length of the critical reserve period is in fact determined by the uncertainty surrounding the volume of the reserves and the development of suitable substitutes. If that uncertainty is assessed differently, the result is a different indicator. The problem of relating scientific uncertainty to policy analysis is examined in Box 1.

Perceptions of risks and sustainable development

The problems surrounding the determination of indicators of sustainable development arise at both scientific and ethical levels (Opschoor and Reijnders, 1991). For example, the question of whether species and quality characteristics need to be taken into account in order to determine the functioning of an ecosystem lends itself only partially to a scientific answer. Subjective arguments also enter into the debate: which elements of the environment may be regarded as vital for the quality of the environment? Opinions on this aspect tend to differ very widely. All this indicates that there is no single definition of sustainable development, but a range of subjective value judgements leading to different opinions on what the term 'sustainable development' should encompass.

9.4 Exploring sustainable developments

Scenarios for future developments

Potential sustainable developments can be explored first by examining the trade-offs in terms of current environmental and societal values. Next, the trade-offs with respect to time (i.e. future generations) can be examined. The needs of future generations – at least beyond trivial statements such as that they have to be fed – are by definition unknown. In other words, the time trade-off is our perception of the needs that future generations may have. This implies a method that refrains from quantitative or qualitative assessments of current and future needs, but points to the use of scenarios that visualise the consequences of positions that we might take in the debate on the values that are at stake.

The starting point for this type of analysis is an identification of the different positions that exist in the perceptions of risks involved. If we feel that the environment is very vulnerable and that society should be willing and able to accept fairly drastic changes, we should be able to conceive some idea of the sustainable developments that go with this point of view. This notion of what is sustainable will then differ considerably from a view that considers the environment to be highly flexible and society as very reluctant to accept changes. In the next step, these different positions can be used to sketch possible future developments in a number of scenarios that point to the consequences of current policy decisions for future generations.

The Dutch Scientific Council for Government Policy (1995) has proposed four different paradigms of sustainability. They can be considered as defining the corners of the playing field of most of the debates on sustainability. The paradigms are denoted as *utilising*, *saving*, *managing* and *preserving*.

1 In the *utilising* paradigm, the environment is thought to revert to its original state after a disturbance has taken place. Although human activities do have an effect on the environment, the environment can generally absorb the impacts. This does not imply that there are no risks for the environment, but rather that these risks are relatively small and, moreover, that timely adjustments in technology can be made if major problems occur in connection with the environment. In other words, technology is assumed to be self-regulatory to a certain extent.

2 The *saving* paradigm accepts that the environment has a limited absorbing capacity. However, the risks involved where the productive structures have to adapt to a new situation are considered to be prohibitive. Technology is very difficult to steer in a certain direction and forced shifts in economic production systems will cause massive societal obstruction. The solution must therefore lie in reducing the levels of consumption. Although this is not an easy task, the consumer society will prove to be malleable in the long run.

3 The *managing* paradigm also regards the environment as a vulnerable entity. The solution must lie in adapting technologies to environmental conditions. While there are no major limitations to transforming technology, changing the level of consumption is viewed as leading to unacceptable societal risks.

4 The *preserving* paradigm considers the environment as being highly fragile. Human activities are thought to entail very great risks for the environment. In other words, all possible adaptations of society that we can think of should be put into effect. The risks for society emanating from these drastic changes are acceptable. Society is very flexible and, with the right measures and proper efforts, changes can be initiated before major damage is caused to the environment.

These four paradigms hardly represent all the possible courses of action. In reality, the number of possible paradigms is far greater than four. For example, some people hold the view that any environmental risk should be avoided, regardless of the consequences for society. However, we have not taken this position into account, nor the opposite one that states that socio-economic needs deserve absolute priority whatever the environmental consequences. The reason for this is that these extreme positions have little to do with sustainability, given that the latter concept always involves a weighing up of ecological and socio-economic needs. In other words, any standpoint should at least give some hint as to how the position in one dimension (e.g. safeguarding the environment) affects the other dimension (society). Both extreme positions fail to do this.

All four paradigms aim at sustainability, however different their underlying assumptions may be. These assumptions may be considered as inputs or motivations for behaviour. Whether this behaviour will result in a sustainable situation cannot be assessed *a priori*, but should be judged by its effects in the long term. Scenarios can help by shedding some light on the long-term effects of the initial behaviour. To this end, these paradigms can be translated into action perspectives by considering concrete examples in relation to the environment. Two such examples are now considered: world food production and nature conservation.

Sustainable development and world food production

The most elementary prior condition for sustainable development is an undisrupted food supply, as the continued survival of the human race obviously depends critically on the presence of a guaranteed food supply. At the same time, agriculture poses a threat to the conservation of Nature and environment in many places. This forms the essence of the trade-off problem.

The explosive growth of the world population has been accompanied by an enormous expansion in food production. Although part of the increase has been due to an expansion of the area under cultivation, the bulk comes from an increase in agricultural productivity. Sharp increases in agricultural productivity have been the result of a combination of improved operational technological know-how, coupled with an ability to apply this knowledge. In particular, the hefty increases in output per hectare have been due to the ability to overcome poor soil fertility and water shortages by using fertilisers and irrigation techniques. The increase in labour productivity has been even more impressive. During the course of this century, labour productivity in agriculture has risen in the industrialised world from 4 kg of wheat per man hour to 600 kg per man hour. This is reflected in a reverse effect: an enormous decline in employment in agriculture.

According to the FAO, the growth in food production in the rich countries is falling sharply to less than 1% a year due to the large production surpluses, the virtual stagnation of exports and a limited rise in the demand for food. The FAO expects that food production will continue to increase in many poor countries until the year 2010, at a rate of just under 3% a year. Compared with the period from 1970 to 1989, this

Plate 9.2 Large-scale food production. Combines unload harvested wheat 'on the run' in central Oregon, USA. Photo: UPI/Bettmann

represents a fall in growth (Alexandratos, 1988). Nearly two-thirds of the increase in food production in the poor countries has been achieved by higher yields per hectare and around a third by an expansion of the cultivated area. The latter creates enormous problems, because it means using increasingly marginal agricultural land and environmentally highly vulnerable land.

Ranged against this growth in agricultural output has been a growth in the population which needs to be fed. The most recent FAO projections suggest that the growth in food production will outstrip population growth in virtually every region in the world. The overall conclusion reached by the FAO is that the availability of food in developing countries may rise from 10.5 kJ to 11.5 kJ in the year 2010. This will not eliminate the problem of continuing malnutrition in numerous developing countries, especially in southern Africa and southern Asia. Of the 800 million people who are

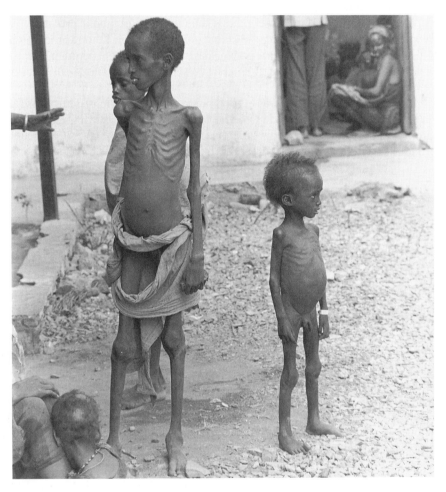

Plate 9.3 Somalia, August 1992. Starving Somali children in a feeding centre run by the International Red Cross in Baidoha, one of the many Somali towns accommodating thousands of people affected by the famine that hit Somalia after 18 months of civil war. Photo: ANP Foto

currently beset by hunger and malnutrition, 650 million will still be in the same situation in 2010 (FAO, 1993).

Other institutes have put forward somewhat different figures and, more particularly, have reached different conclusions. According to the Worldwatch Institute, for example, per capita food production has not increased throughout the world since 1984 (Brown *et al.*, 1993). According to these figures, the average growth in production from that point on has been less than 1% a year, while the population has continued to increase at over 2% a year. The Worldwatch Institute concludes on this basis that a major problem is looming. The 6% fall in per capita food production between 1984 and 1992 cannot be viewed in isolation. The degradation of the environment and the threat of a growing greenhouse effect combined with a loss of momentum in food production and an inability to check the growth of the world population will ultimately result in growing hunger throughout the world (for a more extensive discussion of this topic, see Sage, 1996.)

Whatever interpretation is chosen, the distribution of food is a source of major concern. The main causes of the distribution problems are war, natural disasters and poverty. The disastrous food situation in a number of African countries is largely attributable to the consequences of war, poor government and the self-perpetuating effect of the poverty spiral. Healthy agriculture requires investment in the means of production. The lack (due to poor harvests) of the financial resources which are needed in order to undertake such investment results in a further decline in agricultural yields. This, in turn, reduces the chance of the necessary investments being made in the following season.

Environmental problems associated with the supply of food

For all the benefits that agricultural production has brought, humankind has been aware for many centuries that certain forms of agriculture also come at a cost. The exhaustion of soils and the overutilisation of irrigation systems have resulted in erosion and the irreversible loss of good soils. The bare hills in the Mediterranean, especially in Greece, are evidence of this tragedy. Although these problems have been recognised for centuries, newly eroded areas continue to appear. Soil degradation due to erosion occurs primarily on less fertile soils. Farming on excessively steep slopes or shallow soils or in semiarid areas is inviting difficulties. In many cases, however, the local population is forced to put these less fertile soils to productive use as a result of population pressures and poverty. Farmers lack the capital to maintain the soil fertility, so that the soils become overfarmed and soil degradation continues.

In sharp contrast to the environmental problems in agriculture caused by poverty are those arising from prosperity. In certain parts of the industrialised world and, increasingly, also in the *newly industrialised countries* (NICs), fertilisers and pesticides have been overused in both environmental and agricultural terms. This has caused major environmental problems. The same applies to large-scale irrigation projects that use water in an uncontrolled manner.

Environmental problems arising from poverty and wealth are endangering the continuity of food production. Food security is not, therefore, wholly guaranteed.

The current trends in the world food supply cannot be characterised as sustainable. The issue of the world food supply is, however, subject to numerous uncertainties when it comes to describing possible trends. There is also a great dearth of knowledge about the relevant relationships: is the environment suffering more from over-input or from under-input? Can erosion be countered by changes in agriculture or do all activities result in a loss of soil quality? These uncertainties and questions have resulted not only in differences in attitudes towards the present situation, but also in major differences of opinion as to how agriculture could develop.

A universal starting point for any analysis of the possibilities for sustainable food production is the *potential* for agricultural production. This potential is restricted only by the quality of the soil, climate conditions and the properties of the crop. In addition, sustainable production is also affected by the assumptions which are made about production techniques and consumption patterns.

Production techniques

The first assumption concerns the possibility of closing all the material cycles in the production system as effectively as possible. Agriculture makes use of nature's productive capacity, tapping outputs from the system in the form of products. If agriculture is to be maintained over a lengthier period, inputs need to be added to the system in order to compensate for the outputs which have been tapped off. By definition, it is never possible to convert 100% of inputs into outputs; this implies that some of the inputs will inevitably be lost to the environment in the form of leakages.

Various strategies may be pursued so as to minimise these losses. Attempts can be made to close the cycles at either a global or a regional level. At a global level, sustainability may be achieved by trying to maximise agricultural efficiency on a global scale. This then makes it possible for comparatively high local leakages to the environment to be accepted with a view to reducing the overall burden on the environment. If we make use of efficiently produced fertiliser and transport it to places where such nutrients can be converted as efficiently as possible into agricultural products, we can attempt to limit the aggregate losses as much as possible. Sustainability may be achieved at a regional level by aiming at the lowest possible rate of input loss *per hectare*. This principle results in the deployment of techniques that avoid the use of external, alien substances such as fertilisers and pesticides wherever possible. Efficiency is therefore defined at a totally different level of scale.

Consumption patterns

Opinions on sustainable food production differ not only in relation to the potential agricultural techniques, but also as to the amount of food which the average world citizen should consume in the future. The choice in favour of either a *luxury* or a *moderate* diet is prompted by differing estimates of the environmental consequences. The choice of a moderate diet is based on the view that, in the long term, the world population cannot be fed at the present level of Western consumption, as this would impose an undue strain on the environment. In the case of a Western diet, by contrast, the environmental risks are deemed acceptable. It may be noted that neither of these two diets is extreme; the moderate diet is substantially higher than the present world average, while the luxury diet is lower than the present level of consumption in, for example, the United States.

	'Luxury' diet	'Moderate' diet
Globally oriented agriculture	Utilising	Saving
Locally oriented agriculture	Managing	Preserving

Table 9.1 Action perspectives for the sustainable development of the world food supply

Action perspectives

The four action perspectives introduced earlier can be related to the different combinations of diet and production techniques, as is shown in Table 9.1.

The *utilising perspective* aims at the provision of a luxury diet on a world-wide scale as quickly as possible. It assumes that this level of consumption is consistent with people's aspirations in large parts of the world. Potential environmental problems are regarded as not being insuperable. In addition, there is marked confidence in technological solutions to environmental problems. In particular, increasing agricultural output on good soils is thought to result in the highly efficient utilisation of physical inputs such as fertilisers and pesticides, to the benefit of the environment. This agricultural technique requires a minimum level of physical inputs per unit of product. Furthermore, comparatively little land is taken up at maximum levels of production. The utilising perspective regards the social risks associated with the introduction of a globally oriented agricultural system that is required to meet a sharply increasing demand for food as being acceptable. The relevant know-how is also increasingly exploited by food producers throughout the world.

The *saving perspective* considers that major environmental risks are attached to feeding a rapidly rising world population. Locally oriented agriculture would, however, involve an excessive change in relation to the present forms of agriculture, for which reason the system seeks to minimise the risks for the environment by limiting the demand for food. This would involve a substantial reduction in the pressure exerted by the agricultural system on the environment. The aim is a moderate diet for each world citizen both now and in the future. This situation is to be realised by the redistribution of the food output. Residual environmental problems that could arise under the globally oriented system are regarded as soluble. The system can be fine-tuned to the point that alien substances such as fertilisers and pesticides need not be released in large quantities into the environment.

The *managing perspective* departs from the aim of a moderate diet on account of the social risks that are associated with it. This may not, however, be at the expense of subsequent generations. The risks to the environment of a globally oriented agricultural system are therefore regarded as excessive. The environment faces threats not so much from the losses per unit of product as from the local losses to the various environmental compartments. Water, soil and air must be of high quality and energy and resources must be used sparingly. The comparatively high uptake of land that may be expected under a locally oriented agricultural system is regarded as less of a problem, as are the necessary adjustments in the structure of production.

The *preserving perspective* regards the risks to the environment as so grave that the demand for food needs to be limited and local material cycles optimised by the development of modified agricultural systems. The introduction of alien substances and the long-range transportation of potentially harmful substances (e.g. fertilisers) are considered to pose an undue risk to the environment. The social risks of 'adjusting' the demand to a moderate diet are regarded as acceptable. The reduction in demand combined with careful chain-management on a local scale would guarantee a sustainable world food supply. Here too, the emphasis is on achieving an equitable distribution of a supply of food which is by no means overabundant.

Self-sufficiency is realisable at a global level in all four scenarios. However, only in the saving scenario (i.e. based on a moderate diet, produced by a globally oriented agricultural system) can self-sufficiency be achieved in each region. This implies that, in all the other scenarios, certain regions suffer from shortages and that interregional trade is required in order to meet food needs.

A self-sufficiency index does not of course tell us much about the absolute quantities. The potential surplus production can be estimated by comparing the maximum production per region with the regional demand, which is set equal to a self-sufficiency index of 1.1. This calculation shows that the managing scenario is unattainable. The combination of locally oriented agriculture and the wish to provide a luxury diet is therefore not a practical proposition. At world level, there remains a shortfall of around 1.5 billion tonnes of grain equivalent.

The other scenarios show a surplus. The imposed rate of 110% self-sufficiency can therefore be achieved. In all three of these scenarios, however, there remain regions with a shortfall, especially Asia (East, Southeast, South and, to a lesser extent, West Asia in particular). Food supplies in these regions will need to be supplemented by supplies from other regions with a food surplus.

The biggest trade flow is required under the utilising scenario and amounts to around 5.5 billion tonnes. This is followed by the preserving scenario, with around 4 billion tonnes and finally the saving scenario with around 1 billion tonnes. The figures also reveal that the impact of a change in the diet is greater than that of the production technique applied.

Evaluation

Enough food can be produced to feed the entire world in almost any of the scenarios. Depending on the level of consumption selected, the agricultural system in question and the availability of water, between 11 billion (in the managing scenario) and 44 billion (in the saving scenario) people can be fed world-wide. A sustainable food supply does not therefore run up against physical limits for the world as a whole. The extent to which the world population can be fed depends rather on political and socioeconomic factors.

The results indicate that sufficient food can always be produced in South America, North America, Central Africa and Oceania to meet the demand, irrespective of the preferred diet. In East and South Asia, however, this is only the case given a moderate diet and a globally oriented agricultural system. Problems may arise in various regions. In a limited number of regions (i.e. North and South America and Europe), the luxury of a Western diet combined with locally oriented agriculture can be afforded, but this is an exception. For the rest of the world, the distribution of food is a possibility. This presupposes an economic climate that is conducive to international trade, adequate purchasing power in the deficit regions and a high degree of international solidarity. In terms of the present world community, these are extremely exacting conditions.

In all cases, the scenarios outlined above will involve enormous changes in the agricultural system in comparison with the present structure. These adjustments will require across the board co-operation among all concerned. In a system either aimed at self-sufficiency or based on international trade, considerable demands will be made on international co-operation and solidarity. Just how likely this is to succeed will be judged differently by different people.

Sustainable development and Nature conservation

Humankind has never been particularly careful with the natural environment. It is only in recent decades that a general awareness has arisen that current human practices are a threat to Nature. Direct exploitation for the purposes of food production, timber and other raw materials is resulting in the withdrawal of large areas of land from the natural environment. In addition, considerable damage is being caused indirectly by the pollution of the soil, water and the air. The result is a substantial change in natural conditions, in turn reflected by changes in the flora and fauna (Bink *et al.*, 1994). The scale and severity of the damage has led to a realisation that a halt must be called to these developments, both nationally and internationally.

Global concern for the quality of the natural environment has increased in recent decades. Since 1970, the amount of land surface officially designated as 'Nature conservation areas' has increased sharply from 5 to 7.5 million km^2. More than a sixth of the total land surface of the world now consists of protected Nature conservation areas. These protected areas are intended not only to preserve wildlife, but also to conserve landscapes that are deemed to be 'characteristic' in terms of what the World Conservation Union (IUCN) calls the 'harmonious interaction between inhabitants and land'. In recent years, this attitude towards conservation has not merely been a response to acute problems. More and more emphasis is now being placed on the prevention of problems; it is no longer a matter of waiting until a particular species is threatened with extinction, but rather of preventing threatening situations from arising in the first place. In The Netherlands, this preventive strategy has been translated into a network of protection areas, in which the government envisages considerable expansion (Nature Policy Plan, 1990).

In the present situation, a limited part of the global wildlife area is afforded protection against direct harm, but not against indirect disturbance. Once again, the question arises as to what the concept of 'sustainability' in the relationship between people and Nature actually implies. In order to decide which natural areas need to be protected from the viewpoint of sustainability, one first of all needs to define what 'natural' means. This is a matter of considerable ambiguity and attitudes vary widely. What is regarded as natural may on further reflection in fact be a feature that has arisen as a result of human activity, such as excavated peatland or an artificial lake. Furthermore, the frame of reference may vary from one person to another: a city

245

Plate 9.4 Eco-tourism in Thailand. Photo: Ron Giling/Lineair

dweller may regard a trip through farmland as a venture into 'Nature', whereas a biologist may regard the same farmland as being short on natural features. From both perspectives, however, 'Nature' is defined here as the occurrence of interesting natural assets in an area and the latter also includes areas or landscapes affected by human activity. The extent to which one considers that an area contains certain natural assets is determined on historical, aesthetic, educational and recreational grounds. As the example of the city dweller and the biologist indicates, these are all subjective variables. For this reason, it is not possible to assign an objective, universally valid substance to this category of 'Nature'. (The problem of defining landscape quality is discussed in Blunden and Curry, 1996 of this series.)

For the purpose of this section, a distinction is made between 'primary' and 'secondary' Nature' (van der Meij *et al.*, 1995). Primary nature consists of wildlife areas, i.e. areas largely untouched by human activities. Secondary Nature consists of highly visible animal species (such as seals, beavers and black-tailed godwits) or valued natural features (such as peatlands, sand drifts and reed beds) within a cultivated area influenced by mankind. Although this is often assumed, there is no correlation between the distinction between primary and secondary Nature and the distinction between ecocentric and anthropocentric views of Nature. When it comes to the protection of unspoilt areas, some people argue that this is in the interests of Nature itself, in that Nature has intrinsic assets and deserves to be protected on these grounds. However, it is of course once again human beings who form a judgement on the intrinsic value of Nature. Since we are concerned in both cases with the assignment of a value, anthropocentric motives apply.

The distinction between primary and secondary Nature is also open to debate for other reasons. Ultimately, natural assets (i.e. secondary Nature) also form part of the goal of Nature conservation in wildlife areas (i.e. primary Nature). If human activity constitutes a threat to the maintenance of natural assets, a system of limiting conditions may be imposed on the activity in question. This is the case with the EC Regulation on hill farming, which imposes a number of conditions on agricultural activities in order to give natural assets, such as meadow birds and hedgerows, an opportunity for continued existence in the areas in question. With this type of regulation, there is no longer a clear distinction between Nature conservation aimed at wildlife areas (i.e. primary Nature) and Nature conservation aimed at natural assets (i.e. secondary Nature); indeed the difference is somewhat blurred. Nevertheless, for the sake of the analysis, the two categories will be treated as distinct types of Nature conservation.

Lack of knowledge and structural uncertainties

If we wish to form a picture of developments in the natural environment, we run into major gaps in our knowledge. Global evaluations do not, for example, pay any systematic attention to the occurrence of natural assets in urbanised areas. This can result in a distorted picture of the state of Nature, at least in the eyes of someone who includes these assets in the definition of Nature. Similarly, our knowledge of the species living in large natural areas and of past developments is no more than fragmentary. The total number of plant and animal species on Earth has not even been remotely established; estimates range from 5 to 80 million. Only some 1.7 million species have actually been described (see Barnes, 1996).

Significant differences in definition also interfere with the comparison and interpretation of research findings. How unspoiled must a wildlife area be in order to qualify as such? What is meant by tropical rainforest? What precisely is a species and which organisms belong to it? For how long must there have been no sightings of a particular species for it to be regarded as extinct and how intensively should it have been looked for? In other words, estimates of declining natural assets differ widely, as may be seen from Table 9.2. This makes it difficult to make any precise judgements about the current state of affairs.

Against the background of the deterioration of the natural environment, the question arises of what a sustainable relationship with Nature would involve. The notion of sustainability means that account needs to be taken not just of the general or specific natural features that *currently* need to be safeguarded or realised, but also of what general or specific natural features need to be passed on to future generations. Opponents may argue that natural conditions are always dynamic and have always been changed by human activity. The present generation does not miss the dinosaur or those species which are associated with the cultivated landscape which existed in the last century. This argument is based on an assumption that adjustments will always be made to changes in specific natural features and the amount of unspoiled Nature; why,

	1990			1992		
	Extinct	*Threatened*	*Known*	*Extinct*	*Threatened*	*Known*
Plants	384	19.078	294.650	595	23.078	400.000
Mammals	83	497	4.170	60	507	4.170
Birds	113	1.037	9.198	116	1.029	8.715
Fish	23	343	19.056	29	713	21.000
Reptiles	21	170	6.300	23	169	5.115
Amphibians	2	50	4.184	2	57	3.125
Invert.	98	1.355	1.046.361	252	1.977	1.300.000

Source: WRR, 1995

Table 9.2 Different estimates of globally extinct and endangered species, since 1600. Source: van der Meij, T., Hendriks, J.H.W. and Musters, C.J.M. *et al.* (1994) *Ontwikkelingen in de natuur; visies op de levende natuur in de wereld en scenario's voor het behoud daarvan.* Leiden: Milieubiologie Rijksuniversiteit Leiden.

therefore, could not future generations in turn adjust to an environment with less 'Nature' or fewer specific natural features? The question is, however, whether the present generation actually wants this. The perspective also takes on a different complexion if it is borne in mind that the processes of decline have increased sharply throughout the world in recent decades as a result of population growth and economic activity.

Action perspectives

The action perspectives for future developments differ primarily in their definition of what should be aimed for in terms of Nature. The aim of the preserving and saving action perspectives is the preservation of an unspoiled natural environment, while the managing and utilising action perspectives seek to sustain specific natural features. Clearly, the responsibility *vis-à-vis* future generations is given widely differing interpretations in these two pairs of action perspectives. Both pairs are designed to combat irreversible trends, though in the case of one pair this attempt is *non-selective* (i.e. involving all primary Nature), whilst in the case of the other pair it is *selective* (i.e. concentrating on various valued natural assets).

An attempt can be made to translate these basic principles into claims on an area of countryside which is in need of protection. This gives rise to a difference within each of the pairs of action perspectives because, although the aim is to preserve as large an area as possible of unspoiled Nature, the actual extent of that area depends greatly on whether this basic principle means 'the total area which is still unspoiled' (i.e. under the preserving perspective) or 'all current options for the natural environment must be kept open' (i.e. under the saving perspective). The same distinction can be made between an action perspective which seeks to realise natural assets primarily in cultivated areas (i.e. the utilising perspective) and one which is focused mainly on natural areas (i.e. the managing perspective) (see Table 9.3).

The *utilising action perspective* is based on the principle that humans have a need not only for natural products, but also for green spaces and contact with interesting, attractive, fascinating and appealing plants and animals which deserve their care. In order to satisfy the need for these natural resources, however, it is not considered necessary to set aside separate areas on a large scale. It is perfectly possible to enjoy and study Nature within built-up and non-built-up cultivated areas, zoos, botanical gardens and parks and to maintain species in cultivated settings, if necessary through breeding and cultivation programmes. The creation of separate spaces in the form of Nature reserves is therefore only necessary if certain valuable species or ecosystems cannot be sustained in a cultivated setting. The population size of these species and the extent of these ecosystems must be large enough to enable samples to be taken from them at intervals in order to enable the populations of botanical gardens, zoos, etc. to be supplemented.

The *saving perspective* is based on the principle that natural areas must be safe-guarded. Moreover, the opportunities for using these areas must also be retained for the future. At least one representative section of each type of ecosystem must be protected in as complete a form as possible. The size of the systems must be such that they are self-sustaining, possibly supported by a certain amount of management aimed at maintaining important parameters for the system. This supportive management must then be focused on important environmental factors, such as the supply of clean water and the maintenance of the soil structure and/or key species, such as the most important producers, consumers, predators and reducers. The knowledge required for this is already available or should be made available in the short term. Nature management using 'large grazers' is an example of the application of this approach.

In the *managing action perspective*, the need for contact with Nature can be satisfied only by observing plants and animals in natural conditions. Space has to be created for this and Nature conservation therefore has to concentrate on preserving and develop-ing plants and animals and their respective biotopes. Opportunities must also be created for the recreational and educational use of these natural areas, though this must take place in such a way that the species concerned and their biotopes are disrupted or eroded as little as possible. National parks may be regarded as an example of the application of this approach.

The *preserving perspective* is based on the view that all the Earth's existing unspoiled Nature must as far as possible be allowed to develop freely. In places where this Nature has been eroded or has become extinct, the natural conditions should be restored as far as possible. This is the only way to keep all the options open for future generations. It is acceptable for the preservation and restoration of wildlife to take up

	Natural features	Unspoiled nature
Minimum space	Utilising: Interesting nature in cultivated areas and towns	Saving: Preservation of representative ecosystems
Maximum space	Managing: Interesting nature in natural areas	Preserving: Preservation of all unspoiled nature

Table 9.3 Action perspectives for the sustainable development of nature.

a lot of space, though this should not be at the expense of all else. This view is based on the idea that each component in an ecosystem has a function which cannot be substituted. Systems cannot be sustained by simply protecting a typical part of them, because this brings with it the risk of the system becoming isolated and thus impoverished. A Nature policy which allows Nature a completely free hand to develop in a given area is typical of this view. This does not mean, however, that areas which are currently not used by humans are by definition areas of unspoiled Nature; the natural environment in these areas may have been indirectly disrupted or may not yet have recovered from severe disruption in the past.

Scenarios

Habitat destruction, i.e. a reduction in the amount of space available for Nature, is the most important threat to many specific natural features and valuable natural areas. The various solutions have therefore been translated into claims on that space. Although this is a rough criterion, it does give an indication of what the concept of sustainability could entail, if taken seriously. The question is whether science can help in explicating the subjective action perspectives. For example, what area would be needed in order to sustain the present wealth of species?

Clearly, the amount of space needed in the utilising scenario is limited. In this scenario, it is perfectly possible to study and enjoy Nature within agricultural areas, productive forests, the urban environment and in museums, although some protected Nature reserves will be needed in addition to this in order to sustain species which cannot as yet be bred or cultivated. In this scenario, the existing acreage of protected areas, which adds up to at least 5% of the total land area, is assumed to suffice. This would appear to be a realistic option for the preservation of some species. In Africa, for example, it has been estimated that the present acreage of protected areas is the minimum needed to preserve the large mammals (Soulé *et al.*, 1979). What will be necessary is a relocation of the protected areas in order to ensure that sufficient space is created for Nature conservation. This will involve an expansion of the protected areas in Asia and Africa and, to a lesser extent, in Europe and the former USSR; the existing acreage in North and South America is more than adequate.

There is a greater need for space in the managing scenario. The assumption is that 10% of the total land area will be required, i.e. twice the size of the present protected areas. This choice is relatively arbitrary, since the information that is needed in order to carry out a precise determination is not available. What is clear, however, is that the present protected area is too small, so much so that many attractive species are already facing extinction.

The saving scenario also opts for a total protected area covering 10% of the overall land area, though here again a great deal of research is needed in order to confirm this figure more precisely. This estimate is based on calculations by Wolf, who produced a figure of 1.3 billion hectares as a minimum requirement for the preservation of at least one representative ecosystem (Wolf, 1987). The location of this 10% is not identical to that in the previous scenario, since the saving scenario covers all possible ecosystems.

The preserving scenario designates all presently uncultivated areas – totalling 60% of the total land mass – as worthy of protection.

Obviously, the size of the areas chosen is open to debate; there is no hard scientific proof of either the minimum or the maximum area required. Nonetheless, the choices appear defensible. It is plausible, for example, that the preservation of the existing wealth of species and ecosystems will not permit further domestication and a resultant reduction in the present area of unspoiled Nature. The 'hardest' consequences of the scenarios relate to the use of space. The amount of space available on Earth is fixed and if part of it is reserved for Nature, the question arises as to how much space will be left for other purposes, in particular for the other activity which demands large amounts of space, namely agriculture. In addition, other 'softer' factors are equally relevant, including the cost of establishing protective measures or refraining from the exploitation of Nature for other purposes. Whether there is a willingness to pay the price this will demand depends on the priorities set, the physical scarcity of raw materials, etc.

Each scenario has its own specific measures and costs. In the utilising scenario, for example, it will be necessary to relocate a number of protected areas in order to ensure that sufficient space for Nature conservation can be realised in areas where many attractive species originate; these are principally the relatively warm and wet regions on land and the coastal areas in warm regions. The area needing to be protected in Africa and Asia and to a lesser extent in Europe and the former USSR, will have to increase, while a slight reduction will be feasible in North and South America.

The utilising scenario demands certain changes, particularly in the way in which agriculture, forestry and urban development interact with Nature. Rural areas will have to sustain a varied landscape and use of land, while urban areas will have to contain extensive green spaces. The present decline in specific interesting natural features due to overexploitation and cultivation must be stopped. The space needed for forestry and agriculture will thus have to increase still further in this scenario. Many plants and animals will benefit from smaller scale agriculture and forestry, although these will mainly be 'culture followers'. The remodelling of urban areas will also demand more space for parks, zoos, botanical gardens, museums, etc. and substantial financial investments will be needed to achieve this. Moreover, this scenario relies strongly on the knowledge which is needed in order to determine which species can be cultivated and in which areas they can be preserved. This knowledge will have to be accumulated in the short term.

In the managing scenario, interesting plants and animals will be preserved in natural conditions. The risk of extinction is regarded as lower where natural populations are preserved. No requirements are set in terms of natural features in cultivated areas, since the occurrence of plant and animal species in these areas is not the result of natural processes. It is not necessary to protect the entire population of the species selected in designated natural areas; instead, only sufficient subpopulations need protection so as to guarantee the continued existence of the species in conditions which are accessible to humans. Natural areas can also be used for other purposes in this scenario, such as for timber harvesting and fishing, as long as the continued existence of the population is not placed in danger.

The doubling of the size of the protected areas envisaged by the managing scenario will demand a considerable international effort in order to reach sound agreements on

251

locations, the degree of protection and the funding of purchases and management. Recreational facilities will have to be introduced in the protected natural areas and supervision will be necessary to limit the pressure on the natural environment and the populations within it. A great deal of knowledge will have to be acquired for this purpose: how large must a population be in order to be able to survive? How much space is needed for this? What quality standards will that space have to meet? The establishment of designated natural areas, their organisation, management and maintenance, as well as the provision of more information on the conservation of species in these areas, will all have to be financed. On the other hand, money will also flow in from Nature tourism which, under this scenario, should go through a boom. It is even feasible that this economic interest will offer a certain degree of guarantee for the preservation of natural areas.

The saving scenario seeks to preserve at least one characteristic part or example of each ecosystem. This does not mean that all species of plants and animals would automatically be protected. In order to achieve this, several examples of each ecosystem would have to be protected or supportive conservation techniques such as zoos and gene banks would be needed. A large body of information would also be needed on ecosystems and their limitations. Given the very patchy state of our current knowledge, a safety strategy which takes the objectives of this scenario seriously could mean that protected areas would initially demand even more space. All of this carries a substantial price tag. Due to the minimal area which is set aside for Nature in this scenario, natural areas could easily be disrupted. The harvesting of products such as timber, minerals and energy, as well as recreational activities, would accordingly have to take place almost exclusively outside the natural areas, unless it can be demonstrated that no damage would be caused to the ecosystem.

In the preserving scenario, a great deal will be invested in protecting natural areas to preserve as much of the natural environment as possible. A very large area will have to be protected and this will be very expensive. Not only will the initial costs be high, but monitoring and maintenance of the protected status – a very weak point at the moment – will also cost a great deal of money. Moreover, it will be possible to meet the demand for agricultural products and timber only by means of a large-scale shift to high-production agriculture and plantation forestry.

Clearly, this scenario demands great advances in knowledge. Not only will the productivity of agriculture and forestry have to be radically increased, but solutions will also have to be found to the problems of harvesting raw materials and energy from the protected areas. This can only be achieved through the use of highly advanced, environmentally friendly techniques. The availability of water in the natural areas must be left essentially intact; this means it will not be possible to draw water on a large scale from nature reserves, for example for irrigation purposes. This limitation alone may lead to major conflicts with agriculture and other human activities.

Evaluation

The concept of sustainability in the relationship between humanity and Nature can be interpreted in a variety of ways, each of which is value driven. In other words, the adoption of a given position means other positions are perceived as unsustainable.

For example, if sustainability is interpreted as the preservation of the existing unspoiled Nature and the diversity of species, the utilising and managing scenarios will be seen as 'blasphemous' in view of their acceptance of the loss of certain species. Conversely, supporters of the other positions will see the preserving perspective as unsustainable, because of the high social price that must be paid in order to preserve natural areas.

At the same time, these scenarios highlight important directions for choices. The continuing impoverishment of both Nature in general and specific natural features creates an obligation to take a stand on whether this process should be allowed to continue unchecked. If not, the question unavoidably arises as to what sort of protection is needed, i.e. selective or non-selective. If it is felt that non-selective protection is not desirable or is no longer possible, the question of the selection criteria then arises. What sort of plants and animals should be protected, why and at what cost?

The debate on sustainability in relation to Nature also depends on the temporal context. It is still possible at the moment to consider the various sustainability options alongside each other. As domestication and the concomitant impoverishment of Nature progress, however, in tandem with ever-increasing competition between claims made on the available space, the need to make a choice becomes more and more urgent.

9.5 Sustainable development – the challenge to environmental policy in an international context

Sustainability is not a magic stone which, once found through scientific effort, automatically produces answers. Although scientists can elucidate the choices which have to be made, the final decision is of a political nature. The choices are not self-evident. Even if agreement can be reached on the choice dimensions, at what levels must efforts be made in order to be able to talk of sustainability? The measures currently being taken – through international agreements amongst other channels – are necessarily just the first steps. But how far must the following steps go? If the discussion of sustainability is to become more substantive, greater clarity on this question is essential. The scenarios presented here show that there are no firm foundations at present for producing clear results. Nonetheless, such provisional choices can pave the way for continued discussion.

The two examples given in the previous section illustrate the fact that any attempts to specify the abstract concept of sustainable development end in wildly differing and far-reaching outcomes. Food can be produced around the world in different ways; each method can be labelled as 'sustainable' from a different point of view. The same is true of global Nature conservation. The various scenarios also make clear that the distribution of benefits and costs is not always equal. Efficient agriculture will not ultimately lead to a situation of local self-sufficiency. This shows the need for co-operation between nations to balance out the inequalities through trade. If one looks at the major environmental threats of tomorrow, international solutions to the problems will be needed in order to arrive at practical solutions.

The same conclusion can be drawn from the case of Nature conservation. Though this topic is surrounded by pitfalls and traps, the general impression is that an internationally co-ordinated effort to safeguard elements of our natural environment is vital. The combination of the value-driven political choices that have to be made and the necessity of operating at an international level places a heavy weight on the international environmental policy agenda for the next decades. First, different governments will have to agree on the 'right' values that should be pursued in terms of environmental policy. What is equally important, however, is the recognition that the burden of resolving major environmental problems will be unevenly distributed.

The same combination of aspects may also be looked upon as a challenge for further international co-operation. The analysis of the scope of sustainable development shows clearly that there is no single 'best' solution. This creates room for manoeuvre for governments, so that they can produce a commonly agreed agenda. The challenge for the next generations of policy makers is to find the vocabulary and mechanisms in order to translate words into action.

Numerous doomsday predictions have been made with respect to sustainable development. The analysis given in this chapter represents an attempt to go beyond the point of surrender to inevitable developments. The examples show that the concept of sustainable development can – in one way or another – lead to the identification of intervention points for policy. They also show that these policy tasks are tremendous and that most of them are not even within sight. The results of the various scenarios illustrate that a careful scrutiny of the objectives of sustainable development can lead to the formulation of a research agenda. This may be of the utmost importance as a first step towards more comprehensive international environmental policies.

10

Environment and society: shaping the future

Andrew Blowers and Pieter Leroy

10.1 A transforming moment?

As we approach the end of the millennium we may be experiencing a transforming
moment in the relationship between society and the environment. Awareness of an
impending environmental crisis has been gathering for the last three decades. Evidence of environmental deterioration has been uncovered by scientists, analysed in
expert publications and publicised in the media; it has also stimulated the growth of
environmental movements lobbying for environmental conservation. We have become
familiar with such problems as depletion of the stratospheric ozone layer, the enhanced
greenhouse effect, acid rain, the destruction of species and habitats, deforestation,
desertification and resource depletion. From time to time the destructive power and
environmental impact of modern technology are brought home by individual events
such as the *Exxon Valdez* oil spill off Alaska in 1989, the explosion of the pesticide
plant at Bhopal in 1984 and, most defining of all, the Chernobyl disaster of 1986.

Growing awareness of environmental problems has been paralleled by increasing
political and governmental activity at all levels to confront them. There have been
major assessments of the scale of problems and potential solutions. Among them have
been *The Limits to Growth* (Meadows *et al.*, 1972) and *Beyond the Limits* by
substantially the same authors two decades later (Meadows *et al.*, 1992); analyses of
specific issues such as the problem of pesticides in *Silent Spring* (Carson, 1965); as
well as reports drawn up by global commissions, of which the Brundtland Report, *Our
Common Future* (WCED, 1987), which focuses on the concept of 'sustainable
development', is by far the most influential. Sustainable development has become a
leitmotiv of environmental policy at the national level (for example, the Dutch
National Environmental Policy Plan (NEPP, 1989, summarised in Weale, 1992) or the
UK environmental White Paper *This Common Inheritance* (HMSO, 1990) and at the
international level (the European Commission's Fifth Environment Action Programme,

Towards Sustainability, 1992). The global interest reached an apotheosis in the panoply of reports, principles, conventions, programmes and policies generated by the UNCED Earth Summit at Rio in 1992 and it has continued through implementation plans and the Agenda 21 process. A point has been reached where sustainable development has become, at once, a goal, a strategy and a policy. Yet, for all its potency as a watchword, it remains an elusive, even enigmatic notion combining a scientific principle ('natural' standards and goals for sustainability), a moral guideline (an appeal to bring human behaviour within these 'natural' limits), a political goal (a starting point and final aim of a whole series of policy reports and measures) and a social practice (social development and change towards a more environmentally sound society).

There have been myriad attempts to define sustainable development. The concept is fully discussed in Blowers and Glasbergen (1995) of this series and the same ground will not be covered here. However, for the purposes of the following analysis, it is appropriate to provide a definition. This is taken from a Report of the Town and Country Planning Association of the UK and is essentially an elaboration of the Brundtland definition. Sustainable development is 'development that enhances the natural and built environment in ways that are compatible with:

○ the requirement to conserve the stock of natural assets, wherever possible offsetting any unavoidable reduction by a compensating increase so that the total is left undiminished
○ the need to avoid damaging the regenerative capacity of the world's natural ecosystems
○ the need to achieve greater social equality
○ the avoidance of the imposition of added costs or risks on succeeding generations (Blowers, ed., 1993).

This is, of course, a contentious definition. In its emphasis on human needs it reflects an anthropocentric perspective and its implicit recognition that natural assets may be diminished or substituted signals the optimising criteria of the more pragmatic approach often designated 'weak sustainability'. It represents a more practical approach than strong sustainability with its ecocentric view and uncompromising and unrealistic stance on maintaining the resource base intact.

Some critics consider the debate to be too indulgent. Beckerman, for example, argues that 'too much time and effort is [...] being devoted to developing the implications of the sustainable development concept' (1994, p.206). But, the concept of sustainable development goes far beyond such economic criteria as welfare, optimality, substitutability and thus refers to more than the scientific elaboration and economic quantification of the concept. It embraces a broader moral, social and political domain. The above definition and approaches contained in it recognise the importance of greater social equality as both a social condition and an ethical basis for sustainability.

The introduction of these moral and social aspects of the concept of sustainability places environmental politics and policy making in a much broader ecopolitical context. The so-called environmental crisis can be seen as a (possible) starting point for a fundamental change of view which challenges most of the contemporary

Plate 10.1 Traffic jams in Manila illustrate the growing problem of pollution in rapidly developing countries. Photo: Open University, BBC programming

assumptions (in the industrialised West) about growth, capitalism and lifestyle, associated with what sociologists call 'modern' society. As ecopolitical thought has developed so has a new ethic emerged, characterised, according to Eckersley, by its 'emphasis on cultural renewal, the emphasis on developing an ecological consciousness and the critique of industrialism' (1992, p.27). Berger *et al.*, back in 1973, characterised the ecological rhetoric, ideology and programmes of the early environmental movement as a typical part of the 'de-modernising consciousness'. By using the word 'de-modernising' they aimed to make clear that the protests of the new social movements were not against modernisation as such (and therefore, not 'anti-modernist'). They were against the specific 'external effects' of the processes of technological and economic modernisation on the one hand and the relative lack of modernisation in the political and social areas on the other. Environmental damage was one of these external effects, along with, inter alia, the tendency towards big scale technologies and the dependence upon technocratic expertise, autocratic styles of decision making and exploitation of the Third World. Therefore, Berger *et al.* suspected this de-modernising consciousness to be a basic feature of different so-called 'new' social movements (from the civil rights via students and women's to environmental and Third World movements), protesting against basic mechanisms of modern industrial society. Their protests call for a fundamental change, for a fundamental shift in values. Since the early 1970s, the motivation for such change is even more imperative as the environmental consequences of modern industrial society become more apparent. This leads, in short, to the prospect of change, embracing sustainable development not only as a scientific concept, but in its fullest social, moral and political sense.

In this chapter we shall examine the prospects for significant social change related to and motivated by environmental change. We shall emphasise the *opportunities* for social change, but also the *constraints* which combine to resist or prevent it. Our argument proceeds as follows. It is possible to perceive the opportunity for social change especially as established patterns of industrialisation, employment, class and social organisation are disturbed and fragment. But we also have to pay attention to the constraints. These constraints are, first, encountered in the individual person and entrenched in the attitudes of the general public *vis-à-vis* the environment. People have been seduced by the values of consumer society such as growth, individualism, competition and self-interest which have become ascendant through the 1980s and 1990s in Western societies. A second constraint is an institutional one, namely that attitudes cannot be regarded separately, rooted as they are in political, economic and social institutions which were not designed or developed to implement sustainability goals. Such institutions (e.g. the organisations for energy production and supply, for drinking water supply, for waste disposal, etc.) aim to produce, sell and turn over more and more energy, resources and money. Sustainable development thus needs dramatic institutional change. Any attempt for such change, however, will have to deal with a third constraint, which is inherent in the authority of the nation state, the political and economic competition between national states and the relative weakness of recently developing international regimes. These constraints at the individual, institutional and the state level are closely interrelated. It is clear that change is needed at all these levels.

However speculative it might be, it is possible to argue that we may now have reached the point where environmental imperatives coincide with conditions of both individual, social and institutional uncertainty that can nurture social and political movements able to encourage policy change in the direction of sustainable development. These changes would be accompanied by a shift from a modern to a postmodern society, an industrial to a postindustrial economy and individualistic to communitarian values, which would involve a social willingness to tackle inequalities and a political system more concerned with long-term developments on a global level.

The argument is fairly abstract, although it will be supported by examples from time to time. The discussion is derived largely from observation of Western societies and we are conscious that it will often be inapplicable to developing countries. At times, also, the argument will be based on untested assumptions and even assertions. It is, therefore, provisional, speculative and tentative but it does attempt to look forward, to foresee a future society, different from the present, in which social and environmental change are compatible rather than in conflict. But, the analysis also examines the constraints (some might say the realities) that may prevent change. The argument must be viewed as an examination of possibilities, not as a forecast of the future.

We shall begin by examining the main characteristics of contemporary environmental problems (section 10.2), followed by an overview of some characteristics of contemporary society, starting from the concept of the 'risk society' (section 10.3).

This will demonstrate that the uncertainty of environmental risks is paralleled by increasing uncertainty and insecurity among individuals in (mainly Western) society. The interaction of environmental and social risks may pave the way for a shift in social values and for the emergence of new solidarities. The possibility of such a shift in values towards sustainable development and the political potential for achieving the necessary change are tackled in the next two sections. Section 10.4 examines the social conditions for change by drawing lessons from local environmental conflicts. Section 10.5 discusses the political conditions for change by analysing the actual influence of the environmental movement in precipitating both shifts in values and political changes. Although there is some evidence for a probable change, major political constraints are blocking the path to sustainable development, as we will discuss in the concluding section.

This conclusion and the chapter as a whole inevitably leave the question of what direction change is likely to take unanswered. It is in the speculative nature of a chapter that attempts to look into the future that questions are raised, but not answered. The argument is structured around some key questions on the relationship between environment and society, questions we hope will remain in the mind long after the book has been read.

10.2 Some characteristics of contemporary environmental problems

The key question for this section is: What are international environmental problems and what characteristics do they have in common? From the analysis provided throughout this book and its companion volumes it is possible to make some general statements about the distinctive nature of contemporary environmental problems and in particular about the relationship between environment and society.

First of all, except for some natural events, environmental problems are *anthropogenic in origin*, which means that they are created by human intervention in natural systems. Volcanoes, earthquakes and some climatic events are 'natural' events, which become social problems or disasters when they impact on human societies. But some events, apparently 'natural' at first sight, are seen to be anthropogenic on closer examination (e.g. floods caused by deforestation). However, the causal mechanisms of some environmental problems are not yet clear and this uncertainty calls for for the application of the precautionary principle. In short, environmental problems, generally speaking, are anthropogenic: some, such as deforestation and soil erosion, are centuries old but they and others are also the product of modern society, an outcome of the processes of industrialisation, agricultural development, economic growth and technological development.

Secondly, contemporary environmental problems are *global in reach*. It is, of course, true that in the past some natural disasters such as floods, famine and plague were widespread, sometimes threatening large areas of continental proportions. But in the late 20th century some environmental problems have become truly global. With Turner *et al.* (1990), we can distinguish between two types of globalisation of environmental problems. The first kind of globalisation is anthropogenic and has to do with the 'diffusion of sources', for example, the transfer and diffusion of modern agricultural techniques, the spread of polluting industries and transport technologies to developing countries, the export of hazardous substances or the proliferation of nuclear weapons all over the world. The second type of globalisation is 'natural' and involves the 'diffusion of impacts'. It is 'natural', for these processes of globalisation are caused by natural media such as water, air and the atmosphere. Examples include global warming, ozone layer depletion, acid rain and radioactive fallout, which are problems which spread all over the world irrespective of their actual sources.

This leads on to the third characteristic of contemporary environmental problems which is their *unevenness of impact*. The globalisation of environmental problems, by one mechanism or another, implies that their impacts and costs are transferred, both socially and spatially. This in turn implies that those within our society and those nations of the world which are less able than others to protest successfully tend to bear a greater part of the environmental burden. Two questions follow from this: who is responsible for environmental problems and who are the victims? In the case of environmental problems caused by the 'diffusion of sources', co-operation, collaboration or corruption are involved and the benefits and impacts will be unevenly distributed. In the case of the 'diffusion of impacts', they are universal and unavoidable and many areas will bear the impacts without benefiting from the industrial and economic growth which caused them. Moreover, the latter kind of environmental

Plate 10.2 The human consequences of natural disasters — Mt. Pinatubo, Philippines — shows how environmental risks are a familiar feature in developing societies. Photo: Andrew Blowers

problem tends to be irreversible, thereby having an impact on future generations. Inequalities are likely to persist in so far as impacts will be uneven and wealthy countries can take preventative action (e.g. by building flood defences). Ultimately, of course, no one can escape.

This introduces a fourth characteristic, the fact that global environmental problems are *constituted in terms of survival*. Although health, amenity and resource depletion are also issues of concern (Goodin, 1976), survival of the natural processes which support human and other forms of life has become the key issue. The destruction of forests, loss of biodiversity, climate change, ozone depletion and desertification are now viewed in terms of the survival of human beings and other species.

A fifth characteristic is *the dependence upon experts and expert systems*, both for the identification of environmental problems and for the means of solution. The role of scientists has been crucial in identifying such problems as the enhanced greenhouse effect or ozone depletion, problems which are invisible but incremental and cumulative and thus of high consequence. But scientific expertise is not unequivocal; there are many uncertainties, models are imperfect, theories controversial, evidence incomplete and forecasts speculative. As Boehmer-Christiansen and Skea (1991) and Boehmer-Christiansen (1994) make clear, science not only retains enormous influence in revealing problems, but also plays a major role in the processes of agenda setting and decision making on environmental issues.

Conflict of interests is a sixth characteristic which becomes prominent in the setting of the international environmental agenda. The scientific community is but one such interest, which depends upon many other, obviously conflicting interests. Business corporations, especially multinationally organised banks, holdings and firms, involved in natural resources, agriculture and food, energy production, transport and basic industrial products all play a major role in constructing the issues for attention. Their interests are often in conflict with each other and also with the interests of competing nation states who may also be in conflict with supranational or even (sub)continental economic regimes such as the EU, NAFTA, etc. Moreover, international organisations such as the World Bank or the International Monetary Fund also play their role in international agenda setting and decision making. Against the overwhelming strength of these economic and political powers, the influence of the international environmental movement seems rather limited (see Box 1).

A seventh characteristic is *the ethical dimension* of environmental problems which arises as the logical outcome of the characteristics enumerated above. In general, environmental problems have stimulated a major debate about the relationship between society and its environment; more specifically, the debate centres on people's responsibility for the environment in a context of scientific knowledge and uncertainty and of short-term advantages and long-term risk. This debate extends into consideration of a range of issues such as the rights of individuals and the nature of participation in decision making, the rights of future generations, the problem of social inequality and so on. As we have seen, this debate is to an extent encapsulated in the concept and goal of sustainable development which links together the natural and the social, science and moral values, principles and policies.

These seven characteristics help to define the nature of contemporary global environmental problems. We turn now to our analysis of the main characteristics of

---

Conflicting interests over international environmental issues

At the Rio Earth Summit, the conflicts between the rich and poor became evident. The Northern countries, which felt vulnerable to global environmental problems such as climate change and biodiversity loss, attempted to extract commitments on environmental conservation from the South. However, the South, which felt more vulnerable to perceived underdevelopment, was concerned with extracting transfers from the North. For example, the South resisted demands from the North for a Global Forests Convention, arguing that the North should agree to large-scale financial and technology transfers to the South to compensate the latter if it was to agree to conserve its forests. It was also noticeable at the Earth Summit that environmental issues peculiar to the South did not receive high level attention from the North, although agreement was reached that a Convention to Combat Desertification should be negotiated. The negotiations for this convention were concluded in 1994.

---

contemporary society in order to understand the societal and political context of the environmental problems mentioned above.

10.3 Some characteristics of contemporary society

The question for this section is, 'What are the main characteristics of contemporary society and what are their implications for environmental problems?' Depending upon one's scientific point of view or upon one's scientific interest, contemporary society can be characterised in many different ways. The seriousness and globalisation of environmental problems, however, has led some authors to link up the typical characteristics of environmental problems with some basic features of contemporary society. One of these authors is the German sociologist Ulrich Beck (Beck, 1992; Beck *et al.*, 1994). He has introduced the term 'risk society' to describe contemporary uncertainty and insecurity at both the individual and social level. This uncertainty does not refer only to the globalisation of environmental problems but also to another important aspect, the changing nature of environmental problems, especially their threatening character and their possibly far-reaching impacts and consequences. These characteristics are combined in the concept of 'high consequence risks', characterised by a low probability of occurrence but having great impacts if they ever do occur. The concept of 'high consequence risks' has long been recognised in both nuclear and chemical industries and has given rise to a lot of rather theoretical discussion and exercises on risk analysis. The meaning of the concept became obvious to everyone with the 1986 Chernobyl accident.

Apart from these high consequence risks, Beck's concept of risk society refers to the fact that the significance of contemporary environmental problems can be put in a social context. Certain problems, such as global warming, nuclear proliferation, ozone depletion and species destruction, pose risks that are indiscriminate, unpredictable and, in some cases, unavoidable and irreversible. They are risks from which no one can escape but, since individual actions in themselves cannot affect the system, everyone can evade responsibility. Harm to the environment cannot be prevented since 'one can do something and continue doing it without having to take personal responsibility for it' (Beck, 1992, p.33). In the terminal case, a nuclear war, 'the effect only exists when it occurs and when it occurs, it no longer exists, because nothing exists any more' (p.38). Moreover, since the creation of risks, the identification of global environmental problems and the protection from risks are all in the realm of scientific expertise, people feel incapable of dealing with such problems and resigned to leaving them to the experts. The tendency to evade individual responsibility, to adopt a kind of fatalism, is confirmed.

We shall deal in more detail with the 'risk society' concept below. Here we should take note of the context in which the concept has been developed. Though useful in linking up contemporary environmental and societal problems as we shall see, we have to be aware of the typical Western and contemporary bias of the notion itself. Indeed,

Plate 10.3 A residential area in the middle of heavy industrial plants, Chorzów, Poland. Photo: Wim Oskam/Hollandse Hoogte

some of the features of 'risk society' are not particularly new, novel or even modern. In the distant past there have been risks such as plague and famine which also had continental reach. And even in our times, the concept of a risk society is, for many different reasons such as authoritarian political systems, poverty, war, etc., nothing new to an average citizen of Iran or Iraq, of some South Asian and Latin American countries, or for citizens in Ethiopia and Zaire, let alone Rwanda.

Beck does not deny the Western bias of the concept when he links it up with the typical kinds of both individual and social uncertainty Western citizens have to deal with. Individual uncertainty, in Beck's view, has to do, first, with 'individualisation' in Western societies. Individualisation is the outcome of two processes: (a) the emancipation of some sections of society such as women, workers, students and ethnic minorities from traditional, often somewhat authoritarian institutions (families, industries, universities, etc.) where they have been victimised or discriminated against; (b) the weakening of both traditional and modern patterns of societal integration. By 'traditional' we refer to patterns of integration based upon family, kinship, neighbourhood or religion, whereas 'modern' refers to the mechanisms of integration based upon profession or socio-economic status, such as trade unions or political parties. The fragmentation and sometimes even the breakdown of some integrative networks and structures from traditional and modern society is well documented empirically by reports on the waning influence of traditional communities and neighbourhood networks or on the weakening of loyalty to religion, trade unions and political parties.

Emancipation on the one hand and weakening integrative capacity on the other are of course mirror images of each other. Beck conceives the situation thus: people 'are *set free* from the *apparently naturally ordained* ways of life and certainties of industrial society …' and: 'Traditional forms of coping with anxiety and insecurity in socio-moral milieus, families, marriage and male–female roles are failing. To the same degree, coping with anxiety and insecurity is demanded of individuals themselves' (Beck, 1992, p.153). Individualisation and its underlying processes of emancipation and weakening integrative capacity have both created and reinforced the uncertainty for the personal life of the individual. Basic decisions, such as those involving education, relationships, marriage, ideology and career, which were formerly more or less automatically decided by group culture, institutional tradition and social context, now call for a 'personal decision', corresponding to a highly personal 'lifestyle'. This greater personal responsibility and insecurity are evident from, among other things, tension over the role and the relationship between the sexes, the tendency towards higher divorce, lower fertility, the lack of job security and the risk of poverty, loneliness or isolation. In short, individualisation requires the individual to be responsible for his or her destiny and therefore leads individuals to believe that 'everything revolves around the axis of one's personal ego and personal life' (Beck, 1992, p.135).

These processes of individualisation have been set in train by such things as the emergence and spread of modern techniques for transport and travelling and by electronic communication. Along with creating more chances for emancipation, these techniques have been weakening the former, locality-based patterns of social interaction and integration. But the personal uncertainty resulting from the (social) processes of individualisation has been increased by changing economic circumstances. Not only has economic growth been lower than in the 1960s, thereby making a whole generation uncertain about their economic future. Their professional future has been endangered also by reorganisation of the industrial sector; by processes of deindustrialisation and automisation of the economy; by economic liberalisation and the ideology of the market which have penetrated into areas such as health, education, welfare and transport and changed functions formerly performed by the state on a universal basis; and by deregulation and privatisation of important parts of the public sector which were considered formerly as relatively safe for a career. The combination of these processes has led to greater unemployment and to an increasing dependence upon welfare payments, which have themselves been reduced by governments forced to cut public expenditure in order to be able to cut taxes in the hope of stimulating the economy again. Indeed, although economic growth has increased over the last years, it has become clear that employment has not grown likewise. Therefore, these technological, organisational and economic changes seem to make flexibility the only sustaining quality required on the labour market.

The implications of this analysis for environmental politics and policy making are complex. On the one hand, the fatalism induced by the scale, uncertainty and elusiveness of environmental risk combined with the insecurity experienced at the individual level suggests a focus on the immediate, the short term and a tendency to ignore possible but distant future perils. And indeed, there is some evidence of greater emphasis, at both the individual and the social levels, on short-term interests, on immediate and local interests. In some cases, personal, social and economic uncertainty even leads to the emergence and success of social movements and political parties exploiting the feelings of insecurity by blaming minority groups, especially foreign workers, for it. In any case, the processes of individualisation have weakened the basis for organised 'classical' solidarity and may seem to make the emergence of new solidarity movements rather unlikely. Yet, on the political level, the emphasis of policy making in Western countries remains firmly on the economic sphere, with environmental protection as an important but secondary consideration in the face of economic imperatives of production, employment, profit and growth.

On the other hand, the urgency of the environmental problems combined with the fragmentation of classical social institutions has led to new forms of environmental action and solidarity. Action groups in different countries have been protesting successfully against various kinds of environmental threat, thereby sometimes expressing and organising solidarity with overseas regions and countries. Furthermore, the communication techniques introduced recently enable NGOs to communicate, exchange expertise and organise lobbying all over the world. Greenpeace which is based upon a small group of highly motivated 'professional militants', supported morally and financially by an almost global audience, is one of the best known examples of such a postmodern social movement.

These examples give rise to such questions as, 'What are the actual social conditions for a social change towards sustainable development' and 'What political circumstances do we need for environmental management and planning to become central activities in contemporary society'? We shall look at each of these in turn in the subsequent sections of this chapter.

10.4 The social conditions for environmental change

Environmental problems, whether at local, national or international level, arouse social conflicts which engage a variety of interests. Examples have been provided throughout this Environmental Policy series of books, but especially in Sloep and Blowers (1996). The key question in this section is: What are the typical features of the social conflicts surrounding environmental problems, the definition of these conflicts and their potential solution? Paradoxically, we shall start by focusing on local conflicts, intending though to draw out some of the implications for problems at the international level also.

Environmental quality and social (in)equality: the processes of peripheralisation

Environmental problems, as a result of their globalisation, need not be characterised as 'indiscriminate' as Beck does. It is true that the globalisation of the economy causes the transfer of the sources of environmental damage from the richer, Northern countries to the South and politics and technology make possible the transfer of some environmental impacts. But the question arises as to who is responsible for the sources and the impacts and who is suffering from them? In our view, environmental problems and their impacts are still to be characterised by their unevenness. Hence, the association between social inequality and environmental inequality: they are mutually reinforcing processes. Conflicts between rich and poor are resolved by the rich, exercising power in order to sustain their interest in a clean environment, whereas the poor become spatially segregated in areas of greater environmental degradation. While the demarcation is nowhere and never precise or complete, the general tendency towards spatial/social segregation may be observed historically. During the 19th century fear of cholera and other epidemics stimulated both the movement of the rich to the suburbs and the development of clean water supplies and sewerage systems spreading from the rich districts eventually to the poor (De Swaan, 1988). During the 20th century, the wealthy have often managed to defend their territory against public access on grounds of amenity and environmental conservation. And the fear of environmental risks to health, amenity or survival has provided the basis for social conflicts over the siting of a whole range of polluting industries or facilities, sometimes known as Locally Unwanted Land Uses (LULUs). Among these are chemical plants, toxic waste incinerators, radioactive waste repositories, nuclear power stations and transportation infrastructures, such as roads, railways and airports.

These social conflicts over the location of locally unwanted facilities more often than not result in the polluting activities ending up in already environmentally degraded or economically depressed areas. These areas are sometimes called 'pollution havens' or specifically 'nuclear oases' (Blowers *et al.*, 1991) or 'national sacrifice areas' (Davis, 1993). They may also be defined as 'peripheral communities' which share certain specific characteristics (Blowers and Leroy, 1994). These are, first, remoteness defined as either physical distance or relative inaccessibility from metropolitan centres.

Plate 10.4 The Waste Isolation Pilot Plant near Carlsbad, New Mexico, a nuclear repository in a remote area of the United States. Photo: Andrew Blowers

Second, such communities tend to be economically on the margins, either dominated by one industry (often with its headquarters elsewhere) or victims of industrial decline and high unemployment. A third characteristic is their relative powerlessness, their inability to mobilise socially and politically against decisions taken elsewhere. This is reinforced by a fourth characteristic, a culture in which acceptance, cynicism and defensiveness against external influence are mixed, thereby reinforcing the situation of isolation and powerlessness. The fifth characteristic is both cause and effect, it is the condition of environmental degradation associated with polluting and risk-creating activities (see Box 2).

These peripheral communities are, in a sense, the victims of a process, a process of 'peripheralisation'. Unwanted activities gravitate towards them because of the condition of powerlessness, acceptance and marginality – it is in their economic interest to gain the employment and wealth that is offered. By contrast, other areas are able to resist such activities by exercising their power and influence. These communities stand in contrast to peripheral areas in terms of their greater accessibility, their social and economic variety and the ability to mobilise effectively against external threats. The process of peripheralisation, therefore, is one of push and pull, a mutually reinforcing process reflecting inequalities in wealth and power between communities.

Conflicts over the allocation of LULUs reveal some fascinating social features. Alliances and coalitions are mobilised which cut right across the conventional social and political divides of modern society. Peripheral communities often manifest

Examples of 'peripheral communities'

2

Large-scale industrial activities, involving pollution and risk, tend to be found in locations that are 'peripheral' in a geographical, social or economic sense. Geographical remoteness is particularly characteristic of the nuclear industry, especially of those activities connected with nuclear weapons, reprocessing or waste management. In the United States, as the nuclear military complex developed vast reservations were created at Hanford in the semidesert of Washington state in the Pacific North West, in Idaho, in the Texas Panhandle and at the Savannah River plant in South Carolina. A nuclear waste repository for military wastes has been developed in the Chihuahua Desert of South Eastern New Mexico (Plate 10.4), the state where the first atomic bomb was exploded, and a repository for high level wastes from the civil nuclear programme is proposed at Yucca Mountain in the desert of Nevada about 100 miles North of Las Vegas.

In writing about Hanford, Paul Loeb described its society as a 'nuclear culture', a combination of isolation, acceptance and defensiveness about a complex responsible for the production of nuclear weapons. Geographically, he encountered 'a model for the "nuclear parks" which, by concentrating all atomic operations in a few scattered sites, distanced them geographically from any opposition. The Area, as it is called by most employees, included 570 fenced and guarded square miles through which 13,000 workers travelled daily to their jobs …' (Loeb, 1986, p.28).

Even in the smaller, more densely populated countries, nuclear facilities are found in relatively remote locations. In the UK, Sellafield on the coast of West Cumbria and Dounreay on the Northern tip of the Scottish mainland are the locations for reprocessing and nuclear waste projects. Wynne *et al.* encountered in West Cumbria 'a widely expressed feeling of being a subservient and somewhat marginal population' (Zonabend, 1993, p.38) that led to a sense of stigma, dependency and disempowerment. In France, the major reprocessing complex is located at the tip of the Cotentin peninsula in Normandy, an area described as follows by Françoise Zonabend:

> Cut off, windswept, ringed by powerful ocean currents, unfit for any kind of economic development in terms of farming or fishing, doomed to depopulation – that was how geographers and historians used to describe La Hague up until the beginning of the 1960s. The selfsame reasons, however, made this the ideal site for an industrial complex, dedicated to the reprocessing and stockpiling of spent nuclear fuel (1993, p.15).

In Germany, too, the location for spent fuel storage and a potential waste repository is in a relatively isolated rural area, at Gorleben in the Wendland, in Lower Saxony. Until reunification it was on the border of the country bounded on three sides by East Germany.

In other industries locations may be characterised by social and economic peripherality rather than geographical isolation. For example, in Belgium, Tessenderlo, the centre of a polluting and hazardous petrochemicals complex, though not far from Liège and Antwerp, is in an area of economic stagnation heavily dependent on one economic sector. Whether they are geographically remote or not, all peripheral communities experience some degree of isolation.

alliances between workers and management, linked together in mutual defence. In communities resisting LULUs successfully, local elites combine with groups right across the political and class spectrum in a united front to defend their territory against external threat. Occasionally, where more than one community is earmarked for a possible LULU, a coalition of threatened communities may develop. Often these communities will be joined by environmental activists who perceive that a local conflict will enhance their broader objectives.

These conflicts over the (al)location of LULUs are not merely evidence of NIMBYism (Not In My Backyard) (Wolsink, 1992). Defence of territory is, indeed, a key objective of many participants who will not be much troubled if the activity ends up somewhere else. Other participants, marching to a different drum, may be against the activity altogether or arguing for further justification, review or delay while necessary research establishes the justification. Such conflicts are inherently complex expressing in a single cause a multitude of different objectives, values, interests and preferences. Environmental conflicts, especially over activities which pollute or degrade the environment, give rise to cross-cutting coalitions of interests united (at least temporarily) in defending their community. But, if successful, they also reinforce patterns of location which ensure the perpetuation of environmental inequalities.

Some qualifications need to be made about this thesis of peripheralisation. Firstly, conflicts of this kind are not inevitable. In some cases it is possible to achieve locations of LULUs through negotiation, a process which will often include some trade-offs in the form of improved facilities, modifications to the proposals, environmental enhancement, detailed emergency planning procedures and so on. Secondly, the coalitions of interest may be fragile and subject to internal conflicts. For example, opponents of a LULU may be divided over whether it is acceptable in modified form or not at all. Similarly supporters may be opposed by business interests elsewhere who see the proposal as a threat. For example, under privatisation a nuclear power station might be opposed by other suppliers of electricity, coal or oil. And, thirdly, attitudes to LULUs will vary over time. For instance, whereas 30 years ago there was virtually no opposition to the construction of nuclear plants, today resistance can be almost guaranteed. The likelihood and intensity of conflict also varies in response to the salience of the environment as an issue. Its importance varies over time as a result of a number of interlinked factors such as the level of prosperity (the environment has a higher priority in prosperous times), the aftermath of an environmental disaster (Chernobyl heightened fears and environmental consciousness) and in response to changing social values or cultural differences.

Global peripheralisation?

The analysis above is based on the observation of conflicts over LULUs in Western countries. Therefore it is partial and limited in a number of respects. It focuses on local problems and conflicts, particularly on the siting and (al)location aspects of these conflicts and their possible political solutions. As the scope is limited to issues of siting and locating, both broader diffused *sources*, such as agricultural or traffic pollution, and broader diffused *impacts*, such as air and water pollution, tend to be neglected.

Having said that, the thesis of peripheralisation intuitively seems to be applicable also to some international environmental problems, conflicts and their solution. The transfer of both sources and impacts to developing countries may be seen as part of a comprehensive process of global peripheralisation. The transfer of sources includes hazardous products and industries to Third World countries highly dependent on them for their development, the export of hazardous waste to countries with a less developed system of environmental law and protection and the exploitation by Northern firms and countries of the natural resources in some Southern countries (examples of these are discussed in Sage, 1996 and Blowers, 1996). Though we should not push the analogy too far, the emergence of different kinds of protest movements in countries of the South, varying from traditional or religious via ethnic or nationalistic to very modern, can be regarded as a social and political reaction to the intrusion of this threatening Western technology. These coalitions, like the local ones, are fragile and often temporary, whereas others deviate from the original goals and purposes, ending up in a national or religious (contra)revolution. Nevertheless, these movements, sometimes supported by Western NGOs, basically try to overcome their countries' dependence upon Western economics and culture. Their success, like that of local coalitions anywhere, depends greatly upon their ability to mobilise enough social, political and economic support, thereby cutting across the ethnic, national, religious and political divides of their developing society. The support and power they are able to build up can change the international power balance and thereby explain the actual outcome of most negotiation processes on international environmental issues (the development of environmental movements and their impact in developing countries is discussed in Chapter 2 of this volume and in Potter, 1995).

Changing values

As we stated earlier, focusing on the environmental problems of LULUs may lead to some premature conclusions on the social conditions for environmental change. Whereas LULUs often provoke fierce reactions, that is not so for the vast majority of environmental problems. The impact on people's actual lives may be barely perceptible or it may be transferred either in time (to future generations) or in space (to other places). One of the typical features of LULUs is that the environmental risks they pose are very visible, specific and nearby, which enhances the possibilities for societal and political mobilisation and protest. Environmental problems related, for instance, to high levels of energy consumption and car use have more diffuse sources and impacts, which provide the excuse and opportunities to evade responsibility.

However, environmental conflicts over LULUs have a common characteristic that may be of general importance. Although related to specific issues and proposals, they manifest a clash between environmental and economic interests. In more general terms they represent a clash between value systems concerned with economic growth and material development on the one hand and values concerning the locality, the environment and (participation in) decision making on the other. Those holding vastly different interests and values can be brought together in a temporary coalition based upon apparently similar objectives. For instance, those opposing nuclear energy may link up with those who support it, combining forces to prevent a nuclear facility in a specific location.

During the course of the conflict these contrasting value systems become co-mingled, united in the common cause of defending the local environment and trying to influence decision makers. We can distinguish broadly two sets of values engaged in these coalitions: one more conservative, the other more radical. As both may nurture value systems which are more aligned to sustainable living, they may be important social conditions for an environmental change. Conservative values engage in environmental protest for they emphasise continuity and the status quo. These are defensive values, defending property, territory, amenity, heritage. They espouse policies of conservation and environmental protection. They do not challenge the existing economic or political system, but intend to work within it. In a more ethical perspective, they emphasise *stewardship*, the 'moral duty to look after our planet and to hand it on in good order to future generations' (HMSO, 1990, p.10). They may also take a utilitarian approach to the evaluation of the relationship between interests or between society and Nature. Basically, this is an anthropocentric position devoted to human needs, which requires the balancing of costs and benefits, advantages and disadvantages, pleasure and pain so that the positive qualities are maximised. Supporters of this conservative value system may be prepared to accept some minor changes for the sake of the environment, but they are not prepared to alter the basic structure of society or the dominating world-views and paradigms.

Radical value systems provide some obvious points of contrast. These perspectives recognise the interaction of human and natural systems; they seek to protect the global commons, biodiversity, the rights of future generations, animal rights and so on. They articulate the need for fundamental changes in economic and political systems. They campaign against such activities as the trade in hazardous wastes or the nuclear industry which they claim are the cause of environmental degradation. Instead they advocate *communitarian principles*, the need for sustainable lifestyles and policies enabling long-term environmental management. They have developed an ecocentric philosophy and have motivated the emergence of green politics and a range of environmentalist perspectives during the past three decades. In short, they advocate a so-called 'New Environmental Paradigm' (NEP), contrasting with the 'Human Exemptionalism Paradigm' (HEP) (see Box 3).

Radical approaches stand in sharp contrast to conservative values in that they are 'concerned to challenge and ultimately transform existing power relations, such as those based on class, gender, race and nationality, to ensure an equitable transition towards an ecologically sustainable society' (Eckersley, 1992, p.22). This is an idealistic approach compared to the more pragmatic, conservative position with its emphasis on established order and resistance to change. But at the level of both environmental action and policy making, there are interesting convergences between the different positions. 'The most significant of these are an emphasis on prudence or caution in innovation (especially with respect to technology), the desire to conserve existing things (old buildings, Nature reserves, endangered values) to maintain continuity with the past, the use of organic political metaphors and the rejection of totalitarianism' (*ibid.*, p.21). Hence, the *precautionary principle* is readily endorsed by conservatives and radicals alike. This was expressed in the Rio Declaration on Environment and Development as principle 15: 'Where there are threats of serious or irreversible damage, lack of full scientific certainty shall not be used as a reason for postponing cost-effective measures to prevent environmental degradation' (UN, 1993, p.10).

3

The identification of environmental perspectives

Since the emergence of environmental concerns in the early 1970s, many authors have tried to identify the basic ideas and features of the environmentalist world-view. Parallel to and elaborating the anthropocentric–ecocentric dichotomy, Catton and Dunlap (1978, 1980) distinguished between HEP and NEP.

The argument is as follows. Environmental problems are caused by the dominance of a world-view in which human beings are different from and superior to all other creatures, apparently giving them the right to exploit Nature for their own sake. In this clearly anthropocentric view, human society has unlimited opportunities to progress, as its technical skills are superior, enabling it to tackle every single problem. Nature and natural resources also give human beings unlimited possibilities. In short, these are the basic features of the predominant world-view, represented in the so-called 'Human Exemptionalism Paradigm'. It is important to stress that HEP is not just an isolated part of our world-view. This paradigm and the values corresponding with it are deeply rooted in our attitudes and behaviour, institutionalised in our societal organisation and our economy and organised into and legitimised by the concept of the nation state and its policies.

Social change for a more sustainable development implies a dramatic change in our world-view and thus in our basic thoughts and values, our attitudes, institutions and policies. Catton and Dunlap signalled the emergence of a new value system, the so-called 'New Ecological Paradigm' or NEP. From this perspective, human beings, though exceptional creatures, are perceived as highly involved in and dependent upon the rather autonomous laws and mechanisms of the (global) ecosystem. They cannot, therefore, afford to ignore these laws and mechanisms and will have to tailor their attitudes and behaviour to the limits and uncertainties these mechanisms set out. NEP clearly has moral implications, such as the need for human restraint *vis-à-vis* the environment. The precautionary principle is one of the moral and political outcomes of this radical environmental paradigm.

Despite their differences in world-view, ideologies and objectives, the conservative and the radical perspectives can motivate unified action, not only over specific environmental issues and in isolated conflicts, but also in formulating environmental policy principles. We should not be too optimistic here, for the links between a shift in values manifested during some local environmental conflicts and a major shift towards sustainable development are tenuous and partial. Nevertheless, as the notion of risk society makes clear, we can expect environmental problems to be more and more perceived as nearby and visible, having specific impacts on people's lives. Parallel to local environmental conflicts forging new, albeit temporary coalitions and revitalising traditional community solidarity, we can expect environmental threats at a more general level in a context of general uncertainty to increase the demand for new or revitalised forms of coalition. Thus a risk society may exert increasing influence in that it opens up some new forms of solidarity and has the potential for shifting values, two necessary social conditions for a possible political change. The potential for shifting values is the main subject of the next section.

10.5 The political conditions for environmental change

In the previous sections, we have tackled three key questions: the first on the nature of contemporary global environmental problems, the second on the characteristics of contemporary society and the third on some possible prospects for a social change. We now turn to a fourth question: What are the constraints and opportunities that influence environmental policy making in an international context? Here we focus on the political conditions favouring or preventing the social changes that are necessary. Those conditions are partly concerned with the opportunities a political system offers, for example, the degree of political openness and participation it allows; on the other hand they are also concerned with those political conditions concerning the strength and effectiveness of the countervailing powers which are challenging the political system to effect change.

Political openness and participation

The opportunities for political changes in a society depend upon the emergence of new political ideas and movements, but also on the openness of the political system itself. Typically in the local environmental conflicts mentioned above, local interests are pitted against government or major industries which possess economic and social resources, professional information and expertise and political power. These powerful economic interests are able to exercise their power in two ways. One is through the privileged access they enjoy to the decision-making centres. Business has routine representation on advisory committees and enjoys both institutionalised and informal access to political decision makers. The other way of deploying power has been called non-decision making (Bachrach and Baratz, 1970; Crenson, 1971). In other words, business does not have to assert its power because its needs are already assumed and understood by political decision makers. There is, therefore, a political culture in which the reciprocal needs of business and government are fully understood by each side. Business provides economic growth and resources and its ability to withdraw or transfer these elsewhere is implicitly acknowledged. As Lindblom, reflecting on the power of industry to influence environmental policies, has put it, 'Yet ordinarily as new conditions or problems arise – for example, public demands for restriction on air pollution – businessmen know that government officials will understand their wishes – in this case their unwillingness or incapacity to bear without help the costs of stopping industrial discharges into the air' (Lindblom, 1977, p.184). Decision making is relatively closed and secretive with limited participation by the general public.

By contrast, environmentalist interests rely for their influence and power on their ability to prise open the political process. They emphasise the need for openness in terms of information and decision making; they use the media to publicise their cause and they seek to influence decision makers through lobbying; they try to mobilise a wider public through campaigning, demonstrations and various forms of protest including, occasionally, direct action, thereby increasing again media attention and political strength. Though the environmental movement applies pressure on decision makers at all levels, the level of local government (which needs to reflect local interests and which is responsible for the local environment) is particularly susceptible to the influence of local action groups.

Environmentalist groups appear to have achieved some successes. There are numerous examples of projects (e.g. road schemes, nuclear repositories, incinerators, housing developments) that have been withdrawn, deferred or revised, though in some cases it is doubtful whether withdrawal or postponing was caused by environmental action. Very often the cause is the government failing or being unwilling to find enough funds to finance projects such as new motorways, airports, etc. Once the pressure on cutting back public spending has diminished, formerly postponed projects reappear on the agenda. On the other hand, it is clear that environmental movements, by using a variety of strategies (mobilisation, consultation, lobbying, communication, organising counter-expertise, etc.) have influenced policy making in general and environmentally relevant plans in particular at a formative stage. In recent years their arguments have achieved greater credibility, since they frequently employ experts to challenge and counter the expertise of their opponents. In some cases environmental movements have succeeded in provoking new and often specific procedures for decision making – especially referenda, both at national and local level – thereby not only increasing, albeit temporarily, the openness of the political system but also, to some extent, altering the balance of power.

The dichotomy presented here between a closed and elitist decision-making process for business and an open and participative process for environmental movements should not be pressed too far. Certainly in recent years business and government have proved more susceptible to the pressures and arguments of environmental groups, especially of those which command expertise and can claim to speak for influential constituencies. At the same time, some environmental groups, notably the big nationally based NGOs, have themselves gained direct access to decision makers through routine consultation, membership of advisory bodies and even privileged access. They have achieved greater potential influence over the policy-making process. But this raises some important questions for them as to how far they may become co-opted and compromised by the need to negotiate solutions. There may well develop a conflict between their accountability to their constituency and their legitimacy in the political process.

These are complex questions about the openness of a political system and the nature of democracies, particularly of the role of formal political representation, which sometimes conflicts with actual societal claims and protests. These questions have been considered from time to time in this series of books (see, for example, Chapter 4 and Chapters 1 and 2 in this volume and Potter, 1996). It does appear that the environmental movement, at least in the Northern world, has developed a greater influence over policy making because of the ability of organisations to engage in greater political participation. This influence has been further developed as the links between the local and the global, in the context of global environmental change, have become more evident. This raises questions about the possible and actual role of the environmental movement and its allies as countervailing powers in what may be called the globalisation of environmental politics.

The environmental movement and the globalisation of environmental politics

Environmental ideologies challenge classical political ideologies for they do not fit into the traditional left–right or labour–capital distinctions. Similarly, environmental organisations cannot easily be sorted along classical political party divides and environmental politics for different reasons challenges conventional politics. Thus, environmental politics and policies, to a greater or lesser degree, both stand outside and cut across the political party system and the traditional division of policy fields and public management tasks; furthermore, they are not confined to any specific political level. Environmental conflicts may be conducted at local, national and global levels at one and the same time. Environmental politics, in fact, links the local to the global just as environmental problems do.

In addition environmental issues are also linked to other global issues, such as peace and development. This globalisation of political issues is one of the most typical features of the so-called 'new social movements', such as the contemporary international peace movement, the human rights movement, the Third World organisations as well as the environmental movement. They are called 'new' social movements to distinguish them from both classical social movements, such as the labour movement which emerged in the 19th century and from previous waves of societal concern about environmental issues such as the early Nature conservation movement, which emerged at the end of the 19th and the beginning of the 20th century. As stated earlier in this chapter, the new social movements can be differentiated as the more or less organised expressions of the so-called demodernising consciousness which emerged in the early 1970s.

These 'new' social movements, like their predecessors, are characterised by a concern to achieve social and political change through collective action. They constitute a form of 'new politics', operating within but also beyond the traditional political system. They combine a variety of values, comprise a multiplicity of organisations (from local activists, via nationally operating green parties, to globally organised NGOs), seek a variety of goals and operate both to shift public opinion and to affect specific decision-making processes. Although generally accepted, it is clear that the concept 'movement' fails to reveal the differences, sometimes even the fragmentation within and between these movements, as they differ in specific objectives, strategies and organisational forms. Though most of them emerged only in the early 1970s, their goals and strategies have since changed, influenced by, among other things, modern communication techniques and the process of globalisation itself. Therefore the concept 'environmental movement' in itself is a broad concept and embraces at least three types of organisation.

First and operating at the local level, are citizens' action groups or citizen-based organisations (CBOs). These may be evanescent, spontaneously arising in response to a perceived threat to local environmental interests and dying as soon as the threat is removed. Or they may develop into a broader movement taking on other issues and reflecting local concerns. The Burgerinitiativen (citizen action groups) in Germany are a good example. Such groups seek to mobilise and reflect local opinion although they are not formally accountable.

Second, at the national level, there are the more formally organised environmental groups which are a form of non-governmental or voluntary organisation. These include the major national bodies concerned with preservation issues and the protection of species, some of which are part of the classical Nature conservation movement which emerged in the early 20th century. Examples of these voluntary associations in the UK are the Council for the Protection of Rural England (CPRE) and the Royal Society for the Protection of Birds (RSPB) and the major campaigning groups based in many countries and having both national and international organisational structures (e.g. World Wildlife Fund, Friends of the Earth and Greenpeace). These groups focus on specific environmental concerns and claim support from their membership and a wider public for their actions (see Chapter 2 for a more detailed discussion of NGOs).

Thirdly, there are the green political parties which seek access to the formal representative political system. Their emergence in different Western countries in the late 1970s and early 1980s resulted from long and fundamental strategic debates within the environmental movement. Although successful from time to time at the local level and despite a certain recognition of their national organisations by governmental authorities, some members and groups within the environmental movement felt the political system was still not open enough to be able to influence political

Plate 10.5 Police presence at a protest against the shipment of spent nuclear fuel flasks into Gorleben in the rural Wendland, Germany. Photo: Andrew Blowers

agenda setting successfully. Consultation and lobbying were not sufficient and therefore part of the environmental movement wanted to enter the political arena itself. This, of course, raises the problem of a possible contradiction between their radical agenda for transforming the political system and their seeking to participate in it. This contradiction has been reflected in the debates and conflicts within the green movement between realist and fundamentalist perspectives, the 'realos' versus the 'fundis' which especially in Germany has aroused great interest. It reflects a principal question for green parties, namely, 'whether a sustainable society can be brought about through the use of existing state institutions' (Dobson, 1990, p.134). In the context of the globalisation of environmental politics, two basic strategic questions for green parties arise: how effective can nationally based strategies be and how can they link these national strategies at a continental and global level?

The environmental movement in its widest definition represents a general societal and political tendency which aims to preserve resources and prevent pollution and thereby seek a more sustainable form of social development. Earlier in this chapter we argued that both the opportunities and the constraints for a comprehensive social change towards sustainability embrace three different but interrelated levels: the individual, the institutional and the political or state level. We can use this distinction here, in order to regroup the strategies of the environmental movement into its three 'target groups': first, the attitudes and values of the general public (the citizen, the consumer, the household, the car driver or the tourist); second, the attitudes and behaviour of institutions (private firms, banks, waste management, water or energy supply companies, etc.); and thirdly, politics in general. As 'politics in general' is too abstract to be a specific aim of action, we see the environmental movement actually operating in two distinctive ways: first, at the level of the values of the general public and second, at the level of specific policies, plans, proposals and projects. The first strategy aims not only to shift the value systems as such, but indirectly to influence both institutional and political changes. The second strategy aims, by focusing on specific decision-making processes, to provoke subsequent changes on a more institutional and structural level. Here it is intended that action against specific decisions will be the lever for more fundamental social and political changes.

Shifts in values

As stated earlier, a shift in values is imperative in order to achieve long-term sustainable development. Such shifts are subtle, often conflicting with other deeply implanted values, but to be effective in creating social change, they must be pervasive and long lasting. There is little evidence that such a situation has yet been reached with respect to the environment. Although 'sustainable development' is universally acknowledged at the level of governments, big business and among environmental movements, neither the idea nor its implications have yet penetrated into the consciousness of the majority of people. Indeed, it is extremely difficult to apprehend, let alone measure, changes in values and their social and political impact.

Yet, there are signs of change. The very fact that sustainable development is now a policy pronouncement at all levels of government and that the Rio process through Agenda 21 and the various conventions is continuing demonstrates how far an

277

international environmental agenda has been established in a short time. It may be argued that the effective agenda is still dominated by Northern interests in terms of climate change and biodiversity, but the desertification convention developed in the aftermath of Rio shows that Southern interests are being recognised, even if they are not backed by sufficient resources or effective action. As mentioned earlier, most observers discern a convergence at the broader level among the new social movements and NGOs (on environment, peace, human rights, women's rights and Third World development) in their radical critique of modern society. 'This new theoretical project is concerned to find ways of overcoming the destructive logic of capital accumulation, the acquisitive values of consumer society, and, more generally, all systems of domination (including class domination, patriarchy, imperialism, racism, totalitarianism and the domination of nature)' (Eckersley, 1992, pp.20–21). At the more specific level it is undoubtedly the case that the anti-nuclear, the environmental and the peace movements have had a major influence on public attitudes towards nuclear weapons, nuclear energy and, more recently, nuclear reprocessing and waste management.

Impact on policy making

Both at the general and at the more specific level of policy making 'more and more people question whether the global environmental crisis can actually be managed along the lines of the development spiral and the corresponding problem-solving strategies, such as more science and technology, better nation state politics, more efficient economic growth and better education' (Finger, 1994, p.62). Policies aiming at sustainable development in principle are being increasingly articulated and countries are producing their national strategies partly as a follow-up to Rio.

But there is no evidence that fundamental conflicts between growth and environmental conservation are being recognised. For example, the UK's strategy states its basic aims and principles thus:

> Sustainable development does not mean having less economic development: on the contrary, a healthy economy is better able to generate the resources to meet people's needs and new investment and environmental improvement often go hand in hand. Nor does it mean that every aspect of the present environment should be preserved at all costs. What it requires is that decisions throughout society are taken with proper regard to their environmental impact' (HMSO, 1994, p.7).

At this stage it is the idea rather than the practical application of policy that is seeping into governmental statements. Perhaps more progress is being made at the local level as some local authorities try to grasp the practical implications in terms of resource inventories, formulating policy targets and monitoring. But, as environmental values become more pervasive, the fundamental conflicts between contemporary sectoral policies for energy, transportation, agriculture and industry on the one hand and the need for a comprehensive restraint to conserve the environment on the other will be revealed. But, before changes can be achieved at the policy level, shifts in attitudes and behaviour are necessary.

Such shifts are already becoming apparent at the level of specific proposals and projects. We discussed earlier how local communities have been mobilised to resist polluting or dangerous industries. On a more positive side there are many instances of communities acting to defend environmental values in the form of specific landscapes, areas of natural interest or cultural significance. At this project level, again radical and conservative values intersect to create an environmental consciousness that embraces a wide community of interest.

The political conditions of increasing participation and globalisation have been substantially developed by the emergence of increasingly influential and coherent environmental movements. The fact that they have flourished is the result of changes in Western society and the opening up of areas of influence both outside and within the formal political system.

10.6 Conclusion: major political constraints on achieving sustainability

The analysis in previous sections of the social and political conditions needed for a change towards a more sustainable development seems to lead to an optimistic conclusion. In this last section we do not aim to reverse our arguments and set out a a pessimistic view. We will examine, however, some final questions about the actual role and influence of the environmental movement as an agent for change affecting values and politics and end with an overall assessment of the direction which social and political changes are likely to take.

Changes in public concern and political decision making

At first sight the influence of the environmental movement seems considerable. Operating in different organisational forms and using a variety of strategies and methods, these groups seem to be able to mobilise resources and people, to apply expertise and, by doing so, to influence values and political decisions from local to global. We will consider some of these aspects critically, starting with the presumed changes in values and decision making.

It would be imprudent to overstate the actual impact of environmental movements. While their influence is important, it is not all-pervasive. At the superficial level of public awareness and public concern as measured in opinion polls in the early 1990s, the environment ranks well below other issues such as (un)employment, health, criminality and education. Other issues obviously cause more unease among the general public than the environmental issue. The idea of 'sustainable development' may have excited environmental groups and even governments, but it has hardly penetrated the public consciousness.

At the level of specific policy, plans and projects, environmental protest has sometimes succeeded in preventing an unwanted project or at least in delaying its development or implementation. Different states have introduced particular political procedures or methods, such as cost–benefit analysis and environmental impact assessments to guarantee that environmental aspects of the plans and projects concerned are seriously taken into account. In some cases these methods and procedures imply an extra, sometimes almost an institutionalised opportunity for the environmental movement to exercise its influence, by bringing in counter-expertise. But, as we stated earlier, it is hard to get empirical evidence that this influence was successful in that it led to substantial changes in the design or implementation of a plan or proposal. And even if substantial changes occurred or if a plan was delayed or cancelled, it is almost impossible to judge whether this was caused by the environmental movements' action or by other political or economic factors. The fast development of the nuclear industry in Western Europe in the 1970s, for instance, was not stopped by environmental protest, whereas its standstill in the 1980s was due to economic factors, such as cost and (lack of) competitiveness.

If the actual influence of the environmental movement on decision making has been somewhat exaggerated, it is also questionable if its influence on agenda setting is as considerable as some observers presume. The environmental movement may have been most influential with respect to agenda setting back in the 1970s, when environmental problems were barely recogniseed as important political issues. Drawing attention to these problems and formulating them was then one of the main tasks of the environmental movement. Nowadays problem formulation on environmental issues is institutionalised as a primary activity of government, with a plethora of departments, inspectorates and other organisations undertaking routine environmental monitoring, regulation and control. If there is a signal function left, it has been taken over largely by environmental scientists, working at universities or in state department laboratories and institutes.

Environmental science as a countervailing power?

This brings us to the role of science and scientists, more specifically to their possible role as a countervailing power against the predominant problem definitions. The environmental movement has been successful in challenging the monopoly of expertise held by the state and business. By deploying counter-expertise, the assumptions, methods and conclusions of experts have been opened up to questioning by both environmental activists and society as a whole. Some commentators have even observed an interdependence, a 'symbiotic relationship', between environmental sciences and environmental movements. 'On the one hand, increased public concern with environmental issues over the past three decades has contributed to expansion of the environmental sciences. On the other hand, environmental groups depend heavily on scientific justifications' (Buttel *et al.*, 1990, p.61).

The scientific community remains of fundamental importance in setting the agenda, while scientific information becomes more important in shaping environmental policy measures. The former is particularly the case with those issues that have been 'discovered' by scientists (acid rain, ozone depletion and global warming) or which require the collection of scientific evidence and careful evaluation (e.g. biodiversity). But as we stated earlier, the role of science in the monitoring of environmental problems and in the designing of environmental policy is not unproblematic (Boehmer-Christiansen, 1994). First of all, there are basic disagreements within the scientific community over the explanation of phenomena and the meaning to be attributed to evidence (which is often incomplete and contested). Society and politics often look for certainty which the scientific community is not (yet) able to provide. And secondly, environmental problems are socially constituted (a subject that is fully discussed by Liberatore, 1995). As scientists themselves are an interest group seeking power, prestige and resources, they are engaged in a process of problem definition and priority setting which is not disinterested but which also reflects their interests and those of their sponsors. That is not to say that the problems presented by science are no less real, merely to acknowledge that scientific endeavour is itself constrained and influenced by resources, priorities and judgements that are socially conditioned. Therefore the advancement of environmental issues into large-scale and internationally organised research programmes of the UNEP, OECD, EU and other organisations can be seen as a positive result and a symbol of changing values within the scientific community. On the other hand, this concentration of scientific resources and expertise can endanger the scientific independence of those working within such programmes.

The relative openness of the political system threatened?

Since the 1970s, as part of a process of political modernisation in which traditional, often somewhat authoritarian structures were broken down, political systems in the Western world seem to be more open for different kinds of citizens' participation. This process resulted partly from the tremendous efforts of a variety of new social movements, claiming more public participation in politics. It has also enabled environmental concerns to be brought into decision-making processes.

However, the nation state and the formal political system are not the only, perhaps not even the most important form of politics in Western societies. A zone of what Beck calls 'sub-politics' can be identified, which is becoming increasingly significant (Beck, 1992; Beck *et al.*, 1994). This area includes the decision-making areas of business, but also the realm of social movements, including the environmental movement and a whole range of regional and local interest groups. They have developed as the state has retreated. According to Beck, it is a process whereby 'political modernisation disempowers and unbinds politics and politicises society' (1992, p.194). Other political scientists have made similar observations. Like Beck, they suggest that the relative political vacuum left has become populated by groups and organisations which purport to represent a variety of interests, including those with environmental interests. They become engaged in the process of 'shaping society from below' (Beck *et al.*, 1994, p.23).

This seems paradoxical, when there is so much evidence of the increasing centralisation of state power and the decline of local government in the UK and of the increasing dominance of the executive over Parliament in almost all European countries. But at the same time there have been processes of decentralisation and deconcentration in almost all Western states, accomplished by deregulation and privatisation. One of the results of these operations is the growing number of quangos (quasi-autonomous non-governmental organisations) set up to administer a range of former state functions such as public transport, welfare, health, waste management, drinking water supply and education. This combination of centralisation and decentralisation has created an important political area where formal representative politics no longer exist. Quangos are responsible in economic terms rather than in political

Plate 10.6 Igloo in Labrador, Canada. A harmonious fusion of nature and artifice.
Photo: ZEFA

ones, in that they have to meet fixed goals and output figures, rather than function as
a public service. It also means that the accessibility and responsibility of these
functions and services for citizens is now almost similar to that of private firms.
Unfortunately, consumer rights seem to be even weaker than political rights. Therefore, instead of the political system being broken down to give way to a political
modernisation process from below, it appears that deregulation and privatisation
threaten the hard-won openness of the political system.

10.7 A sustainable future?

Looking back over the various debates in the three volumes of *Environmental Policy
in an International Context*, the barriers to a sustainable future on the individual, the
institutional and the political level seem enormous. The constraints appear, at the
present time, overwhelming. Although dominant value systems may be challenged by
the value shifts outlined earlier in this chapter, the challenge may prove too limited and
too feeble to bring about any fundamental changes. Inequalities in education and in
access to communications media will prevent the diffusion of new ideas. Instead of
greater co-operation, social uncertainty and political fragmentation may prevent the
development, adoption and implementation of sustainable development policies.
Policy development thus may prove too slow to match the pace and scale of global
environmental change. Environmental degradation will continue to occur as a product
of poverty, inefficiency and exploitation. Although dominant power structures, such as

the nation state and multinational companies, have accommodated some changes in the direction of environmental sustainability, their priorities continue to lie in economic growth. And the form of that growth may continue to be environmentally damaging.

Nevertheless, some of the necessary conditions for change are emerging. They include encouraging the shift towards value systems which support sustainable practices; they imply an effort to overcome inequalities by redistribution of resources or compensation to encourage co-operation; and they urge the development of more democratic and open societies in which participation can flourish, enabling people to influence and be responsible for policies. Although the constraints seem formidable, some of the opportunities for a change have been created and others are still being created. Though slowly, value systems are influenced and power is mobilised to affect policy making. In the context of global environmental politics, the development of the Rio process itself seems to be hopeful, in that it implies the creation of elaborated, institutionalised and monitored international environmental policy regimes. This development, together with the increasing importance of international networks of environmental movements and environmental scientists, establishing the international environmental agenda, provides some grounds for tentative optimism about the prospects for shifting international policy making towards the goals of sustainable development.

References

ADEMA, E.H. (1992) *Boeren tussen hemel en aarde, hoe lang nog?* (Farming between heaven and earth: how much longer?). Farewell lecture as Professor of Atmospheric Hygiene and Pollution at Wageningen Agricultural University, 28 April 1992.

AGARWAL, A. (1994) What Cairo did not discuss. *Down to Earth*, 15 October, 3.

ALEXANDRATOS, N. (ed.) (1988) *World Agriculture: Toward 2000*. London: Belhaven Press.

ANDERSON, K. (1992) The standard welfare economics of policies affecting trade and the environment. In Anderson, K. and Blackhurst, R (eds), *The Greening of World Trade Issues*, New York: Harvester Wheatsheaf, Ch.2.

ANDERSON, W.T. (1987) *To Govern Evolution: Further Adventures of the Political Animal*. Boston: Harcourt Brace.

ARATO, A. and COHEN, J. (1992) *Civil Society and Democratic Theory*. Cambridge, Mass: MIT Press.

ARROW, K., BOLIN, B., CONSTANZA, R. *et al.*(1995) Economic growth, carrying capacity, and the environment. *Science*, **268**, 520–521.

BACHRACH, P. and BARATZ, M. (1970) *Power and Poverty*. New York: Oxford University Press.

BAKER, S. (1993) Environmental policy of the European Community: a critical review. *Kent Journal of International Relations*, **7**(1), 8–29.

BAKER, S. (1993a) *The Principles and Practice of Ecofeminism: A Review*. Rotterdam: Erasmus University RISBO Press.

BAKER, S., MILTON, K. and YEARLEY, S. (eds) (1994) *Protecting the Periphery: Environmental Policy in Peripheral Regions of the EU*. London: Frank Cass.

BARBIER, E.B., BURGESS, J., SWANSON, T. and PEARCE, D.W. (1990) *Elephants, Economies and Ivory*. London: Earthscan.

BARNES, N. (1996) Conflicts over biodiversity. In Sloep, P.B. and Blowers, A. (eds), *Environmental Problems as Conflicts of Interest*. London: Arnold, pp. 217–241.

BAUMGARTL, B. (1993) Environmental protest as a vehicle for transition: the case of Ekoglasnost in Bulgaria. In Vari, A. and Tamas, P. (eds), *Environment and Democratic Transition: Policy and Politics in Central and Eastern Europe*. Dordrecht: Kluwer.

BECK, U. (1992) *Risk Society: Towards a New Modernity*. London: Sage Publications.

BECK, U., GIDDENS, A. and LASH, S. (1994) *Reflexive Modernization: Politics, Tradition and Aesthetics in the Modern Social Order*. Cambridge: Polity Press.

BECKERMAN, W. (1994), Sustainable development. *Environmental Values*, **3**(3),191–210.

BENNET, G. (ed.) (1991) *EECONET: Towards a European Ecological Network*. Arnhem: Institute for European Environmental Policy.

BERGER, P., BERGER, B. and KELLNER, H. (1973) *The Homeless Mind.* Harmondsworth: Penguin.

BERGESEN, H. *et al.* (eds) (1992) *Green Globe Yearbook 1992.* Oxford: Oxford University Press.

BEUKERING, P. AND VELLINGA, P. (1996) Climate change: from science to global politics. In Sloep, P.B. and Blowers, A. (eds), *Environmental Problems as Conflicts of Interest.* London: Arnold, pp. 187–215.

BINK, R.J., BAL, D., VAN DER BERK, V.M. *et al.* (1994) *De toestand van de natuur 2* (The state of nature 2). Wageningen: Centre for Information and Knowledge on Nature, Forestry, Landscape and Fauna.

BLOWERS, A. (ed.) (1993) *Planning for a Sustainable Environment.* London: Earthscan.

BLOWERS, A. and GLASBERGEN, P. (1995) The search for sustainable development. In Glasbergen, P. and Blowers, A. (eds) *Perspectives on Environmental Problems.* London: Arnold, pp. 163–183.

BLOWERS, A. (1996) Transboundary transfers of hazardous and radioactive wastes. In Sloep, P.B. and Blowers, A. (eds), *Environmental Problems as Conflicts of Interest.* London: Arnold, pp. 151–186.

BLOWERS, A. and LEROY, P. (1994) Power, politics and environmental inequality: a theoretical and empirical analysis of the process of 'peripheralisation'. *Environmental Politics,* **3**(2), 197–228.

BLOWERS, A., LOWRY, D. and SOLOMON, B. (1991) *The International Politics of Nuclear Waste.* London: Macmillan.

BLUNDEN, J. AND CURRY, N. (1996) Analysing amenity and scientific problems: the Broadlands, England. In Sloep, P.B. and Blowers, A. (eds), *Environmental Problems as Conflicts of Interest.* London: Arnold, pp. 37–66.

BODANSKY, D. (1994) Prologue to the Climate Change Convention. In Mintzer, I. and Leonard, J. (eds), *Negotiating Climate Change: The Inside Story of the Rio Convention.* Cambridge: Cambridge University Press.

BOEHMER-CHRISTIANSEN, S. (1994) Politics and environmental management. *Journal of Environmental Planning and Management,* **37**(1), 69–85.

BOEHMER-CHRISTIANSEN, S. and SKEA, J. (1991) *Acid Politics: Energy and Environmental Policies in Britain and Germany.* London: Belhaven Press.

BOLSIUS, E. and FROUWS, J. (1996) Agricultural intensification: livestock farming in The Netherlands. In Sloep, P.B. and Blowers, A. (eds), *Environmental Problems as Conflicts of Interest.* London: Arnold, pp. 11–36.

BÖTTCHER, C.J.F. (1992) *Science and Fiction of the Greenhouse Effect and Carbon Dioxide.* The Hague: Global Institute for the Study of Natural Resources.

BRAMBLE, B. and PORTER, G. (1992) Non-governmental organizations and the making of US international environmental policy. In Hurrell, A and Kingsbury, B. (eds), *The International Politics of the Environment.* Oxford: Clarendon Press.

BRETT, E.A. (1985) *The World Economy Since the War.* London: Macmillan.

BRINKHORST, L.J. and KLATTE, E.R. (1993) EC Environmental policy. Evolution and perspective. In Spaargaren, G. *et al.* (eds), *Internationaal Environmental Policy.* The Hague: pp.59–86.

BROWN, L.R. (1991) The new world order. In Brown, L.R. *et al.*(eds), *State of the World 1991.* London: Earthscan.

BROWN, L.R., DURNING, A., FLAVIN, C. *et al.* (1993) *State of the World 1993.* New York: W.W. Norton.

BUSINESS COUNCIL FOR SUSTAINABLE DEVELOPMENT (1992) *Changing Course: The Global Business Perspective on Development and the Environment.* Cambridge, Mass: MIT Press.

285

BUTTEL, F., HAWKINS, A. and POWER, G. (1990) From limits to growth to global change: constraints and contradictions in the evolution of environmental science and ideology. *Global Environmental Change, Human and Policy Dimensions,* **1**(1), 57–66.

CARLEY, M. and CHRISTIE, I. (1992) *Managing Sustainable Development.* London: Earthscan.

CARSON, R. (1965) *Silent Spring.* Harmondsworth: Penguin.

CARTER, N. and TURNOCK, D. (1993) *Environmental Problems in Eastern Europe.* London: Routledge.

CATTON, W. and DUNLAP, R. (1978) Environmental sociology: a new paradigm. *American Sociologist,* **13**, 41–49.

CATTON, W. and DUNLAP, R. (1980) A new ecological paradigm for post-exuberant sociology. *American Behavioral Scientist,* **24**, 15–47.

CHARNOVITZ, S. (1993) Environmentalism confronts GATT rules. Recent developments and new opportunities. *Journal of World Trade,* **27**(2),

CHATTERJEE, P. and FINGER, M. (1994) *The Earth Brokers: Power, Politics and World Development.* London: Routledge.

CLARK, J. (1991) *Democratizing Development: The Role of Voluntary Organizations.* London: Earthscan.

CLARK, M. (1994) The Antarctic environmental protocol: NGOs in the protection of Antarctica. In Princen T. and Finger, M. (eds), *Environmental NGOs in World Politics.* London: Routledge, pp.160–185.

COLCHESTER, M. (1993) to Dr B. Eccleston and Ms A. Taylor in an interview. Chedlington, Oxfordshire, 6 July.

COMMISSION (1992a) *The PHARE Indicative Programme, 1992.* Brussels: Commission, PHARE Documentation, 1/673/92 - EN.

COMMISSION (1992b) *General Guidelines.* Brussels: Commission, PHARE Documentation, 1/673/92 - EN.

COMMISSION (1994) *PHARE: Compendium of Operational Programmes 1993.* Brussels: Commission, June.

COMMISSION (1994a) *PHARE: Operational Programmes 1994, Update No. 3.* Brussels: Commission, August.

COMMISSION (1994b) *PHARE: Infocontract No. 1 1994.* Brussels: Commission, July.

COMMISSION (1994c) *PHARE: Infocontract No. 2 1994.* Brussels: Commission, August.

COMMISSION (1994d) *What is PHARE? A European Union Initiative for Economic Integration with Central and Eastern European Countries.* Brussels: Commission, June.

COMMISSION (July 1991) *First Annual Report from the Commission to the Council and the European Parliament on the Implementation of Economic Aid to the Countries of East and Central Europe as of 31 December 1990.* Brussels: Commission, SEC (91) 1354 Final.

COMMISSION (June 1992) *EC-East Europe: Relations with Central and Eastern Europe and the Commonwealth of Independent States.* Brussels: Commission, Background Brief, BB/12.

COMMISSION OF THE EUROPEAN COMMUNITIES (1986) *Fourth Environmental Action Program* COM (86) 485 final.

COMMISSION OF THE EUROPEAN COMMUNITIES (1992) *Fifth Environmental Action Program.* COM(92) 23 final.

COMMISSION OF THE EUROPEAN COMMUNITIES (1992) *The State of the Environment in the European Community. COM* (92) 23, Vol. III, 27 March 1992.

COMMONER, B. (1990) Can capitalists be environmentalists? *Business and Society Review*, **75**, 31–35.

CRENSON, M. (1971) *The Un-Politics of Air Pollution: A Study of Non-Decisionmaking in the Cities*. Baltimore: Johns Hopkins University Press.

DAHL, R. (1961) *Who Governs?* New Haven: Yale University Press.

DALY, H.E. (1973) *Steady-State Economics*. San Francisco: Freeman.

DALY, H.E. (1990) Towards some operational principles of sustainable development. *Ecological Economics*, **2**(1), 6.

DALY, H.E. (1995) On Wilfred Beckerman – critique of sustainable development. *Environmental Values*, **4**, 49–55.

DAVIS, M. (1993) Dead West: ecocide in Marlboro County. *New Left Review,* **200**.

DEBARDELEBEN, J. (ed.) (1991) *To Breathe Free: Eastern Europe's Environmental Crisis*. Baltimore: Johns Hopkins University Press.

DE SWAAN, A. (1988) *In Care of the State*. Cambridge: Polity Press.

DEVOS, J.M. (1991) Industrial liability – the future in Europe. In Richardson, M.L. (ed.), *Risk Management of Chemicals*. London: Royal Society of Chemistry.

DJOGHLAF, A. (1994) The beginnings of an international climate lLaw. In Mintzer, I. and Leonard, J. (eds), *Negotiating Climate Change: The Inside Story of the Rio Convention*. Cambridge: Cambridge University Press.

DONALDSON J. (1989) *Key Issues in Business Ethics*. San Diego: Academic Press.

DONALDSON, J. and WALLER, M. (1980) Ethics and organisation. *Journal of Management Studies*, **17**, 1.

DUTCH SCIENTIFIC COUNCIL FOR GOVERNMENT POLICY (WRR) (1995) *Sustained risks, a lasting phenomenon*. Reports to the Government, No. 44, Sdu, The Hague.

ECCLESTON, B. (1996) Does North-South collaboration enhance NGO influence on deforestation policies in Malaysia and Indonesia? *Journal of Commonwealth and Comparative Politics*, **1**, in press.

ECKERSLEY, R. (1992) *Environmentalism and Political Theory: Towards and Ecocentric Approach*. London: UCL Press.

EDWARDS, M. (1993) Interest group behaviour in Britain: continuity and change. In Richardson, J. (ed.), *Pressure Groups*. Oxford: Oxford University Press.

EKINS, P. (1992) *A New World Order: Grassroots Movements for Global Change*. London: Routledge.

ENVIRONMENTAL DATA SERVICES (ENDS) (1993) Jury still out on responsible care. *Industry Report No. 55*, ENDS, **222**, July.

ETZIONI-HALEVY, E. (1993) *The Elite Connection. Problems and Potential of Western Democracy*. Cambridge: Polity Press.

EUROPEAN BANK FOR RECONSTRUCTION AND DEVELOPMENT (1992) *Environmental Procedures*. London: European Bank for Reconstruction and Development.

EUROPEAN COMMISSION (1985) *White Paper on the Completion of the Internal Market*. Brussels: EC.

EUROPEAN COMMISSION (1992) *Towards Sustainability: A European Community Programme of Policy and Action in Relation to the Environment and Sustainable Development*. Brussels: EC.

EUROPEAN COMMISSION, (1993) *White Paper on Growth, Competitiveness and Employment*. Brussels: EC.

EUROPEAN ENVIRONMENTAL BUREAU (ed.) (1994) *Your Rights under the European Unions' Legislation*. Brussels: EEB.

EYERMAN, R. and JAMISON, A. (1991) *Social Movements: A Cognitive Approach*. Cambridge: Polity Press.

FABER, G. (1990) Trade and economic development. In Faber, G (ed.), *Trade Policy and Development. The Role of Europe in North-South trade: A Multidisciplinary Approach*. Rotterdam: Universitaire Pers, pp.11–39.

FABER, G. (1993) Combatting the greenhouse effect: options for Indo-EC initiative. In Ahuja,K., Coppens, H. and van der Wusten, H. (eds), *Regime Transformations and Global Realignments*. New Delhi: pp.355–367

FARRINGTON, J. and LEWIS, D. (eds) (1993) *Non-Governmental Organizations and the State in Asia*. London: Routledge.

FINGER, M. (1994) NGOs and transformation: beyond social movement theory, In Princen, T. and Finger, M. (eds), *Environmental NGOs in World Politics*. London: Routledge.

FISHER, D. (1993) The emergence of the environmental movement in Eastern Europe and its role in the revolutions of 1989. In Jancar-Webster, B. (ed.), *Environmental Action in Eastern Europe: Responses to Crisis*. New York: Sharpe.

FRENCH, H. F. (1993) *Costly Tradeoffs: Reconciling Trade and the Environment*. Worldwatch Paper 113. Washington: Worldwatch Institute.

GADGIL, M. and GUHA, R. (1994) Ecological conflicts and the environmental movement in India. In Ghai, D. (ed.), *Development and Environment: Sustaining People and Nature*. Oxford: Blackwell, pp. 101–136.

GATT (1992) *Trade and Environment*. Geneva: GATT.

GEHRING, T. (1994) *Dynamic International Regimes. Institutions for International Environmental Governance*. Frankfurt: P. Lang.

GEORGE, S. (1992) *The Debt Boomerang: How Third World Debt Harms Us All*. London: Pluto Press.

GEORGIEVA, K. (1993) Environmental policy in a transition economy: the Bulgarian example. In Vari, A. and Tamas, P. (eds), *Environment and Democratic Transition: Policy and Politics in Central and Eastern Europe*. Dordrecht: Kluwer.

GIDDENS, A. (1990) *The Consequences of Modernity*. Cambridge: Polity Press.

GOODIN, R. (1976) *The Politics of Rational Man*. London: Wiley.

GRINDLE, M. and THOMAS, J. (1991) *Public Choices and Policy Change: The Political Economy of Reform in Developing Countries*. Baltimore: Johns Hopkins University Press.

GRUBB, M., KOCH, M., MUNSON, A., SULLIVAN, F. and THOMSON, K. (1993) *The Earth Summit Agreements: A Guide and Assessment*. London: Earthscan.

HAAS, P. (1989) Do regimes matter? Epistemic communities and Mediterranean pollution control. *International Organization*, **43**(3), 377–403.

HAAS, P. (ed.)(1992), Knowledge, power and international policy coordination. *International Organization,* **46**(4)

HAAS, P., KEOHANE, R.O. and LEVY, M.A. (eds) (1993) *Institutions for the Earth. Sources of Effective International Environmental Protection*. Cambridge, Mass: MIT Press.

HAAVELO, T. and HANSEN, S. (1992) On the strategy of trying to reduce economic inequality. In Goodland, R., Daly, H., El Sarafy, S. and von Droste, B. (eds), *Environmentally Sustainable Economic Development: Building on Brundtland*. Paris: Unesco.

HANF, K. (1994) The political economy of ecological modernization. Creating a regulated market for environmental quality. In Moran, M. and Prosser, T. (eds), *Privatisation and Regulatory Change*. Buckingham: Open University Press, pp.126–44.

HANF, K. and UNDERDAL, A. (1995) Domesticating international agreements. The problem of implementation and compliance. In Underdal, A. (ed.), *The International Politics of Environmental Management*. Dordrecht: Kluwer Academic Publishers.

HAWKEN, P. (1993) *The Ecology of Commerce*. New York: Harper.

HECHT, S. and COCKBURN, A. (1990) *The Fate of the Forest: Developers, Destroyers and Defenders of the Amazon*. Harmondsworth: Penguin Books.

HEERINK, N.B.M. and KUYVENHOVEN, A. (1993) Macro-economic policy reform and sustainable agriculture in West Africa. In Huijsman, A. and van Tilburg, A. (eds), *Agriculture, Economics and Sustainability in the Sahel*. Amsterdam: Royal Tropical Institute.

HESS, J.J. (1993) Introduction. *Public Administration*. Special Issue on Administrative Transformation of Central and Eastern Europe, **71**, Spring/Summer.

HILDEBRAND, P.M. (1992) The European Community's environmental policy, 1957–1992. From incidental measures to an international regime? *Environmental Politics,* **1**(4), 13–44.

HILDYARD, N. (1993) Foxes in charge of the chickens. In Sachs, S. (ed.), *Global Ecology: A New Arena of Political Conflict*. London: Zed Books.

HMSO (1990) *This Common Inheritance*. Cmd 1200. London: HMSO.

HMSO (1994) *Sustainable Development: The UK Strategy.*Cmd 2426. London: HMSO.

HOUGHTON, J.T., JENKINS, G.J. and EPHRAUMS, J.J. (eds) (1990) *Climate Change: The IPCC Scientific Assessment*. Cambridge: Cambridge University Press.

HUETING, R. (1990) Correcting national income for environmental losses: a practical solution for a theoretical dilemma. In Constanza, R. (ed.) *Ecological Economics. The Science and Management of Ssustainability*. New York: Columbia University Press.

HUPPES, G., VAN DER VOET, E., VAN DER NAALD, W.G.H., VONKEMAN, G.H. and MAXSON, P. (1992) *New Market-oriented Instruments for Environmental Policies*. London: Graham and Trotman.

INDEPENDENT COMMISSION ON INTERNATIONAL DEVELOPMENT ISSUES (1980) *North-South: A Programme for Survival*. London: Pan Books.

INTERNATIONAL CHAMBER OF COMMERCE (1990) *The Business Charter for Sustainable Development*. Paris: ICC.

INTERNATIONAL CHAMBER OF COMMERCE (1991) *The Business Charter for Sustainable Development – Principles for Environmental Management*. Paris: ICC.

IUCN, UNEP, WWF (1980) *World Conservation Strategy*.

JACHTENFUCHS, M. (1992) EC foreign environmental policy and Eastern Europe. In Jachtenfuchs, M. and Strübel, M. (eds), *Environmental Policy in Europe: Assessment, Challenges and Perspectives*. Baden-Baden: Nomos.

JACOBSON, H.K. (1984) *Networks of Interdependence. International Organizations and the Global Political System*, 2nd edn. New York: Alfred A. Knopf.

JANCAR-WEBSTER, B. (1993) The Eastern European environmental movement and the transformation of Eastern European society. In Jancar-Webster, B. (ed.), *Environmental Action in Eastern Europe: Responses to Crisis*. New York: Sharpe.

JÄNICKE, M. (1992) Conditions for environmental policy success. An international comparison. In Jachtenfuchs, M. and Strübel, M. (eds), *Environmental Policy in Europe. Assessment, Challenges and Perspectives*. Baden-Baden: Nomos, pp. 71–97.

KEANE, J. (ed.) (1988) *Civil Society and the State. New European Perspectives*. London: Verso.

KEOHANE, R.O. (1989) *International institutions and state power. Essays in International Relations Theory*. Boulder: Westview Press.

KEOHANE, R.O. (1993) Sovereignty, interdependence, and international institutions. In Miller, L. and Smith, M.J. (eds), *Ideas and Ideals. Essays on Politics in Honor of Stanley Hoffmann*. Boulder: Westview Press, pp.91–107.

KEOHANE, R.O. (1994) Against hierarchy: an institutional approach to international environmental protection. In Haas, P.M. *et al.* (eds), *Complex Co-operation. Institutions and Processes in Intenational Resource Management*. Oslo: Scandinavian University Press, pp.13–34.

KEOHANE, R.O. (1996) *Institutions for Environmental Aid: Pitfalls and Promise*. Cambridge, Mass: MIT Press.

KEOHANE, R.O. and NYE, J. (1989) *Power and Interdependence. World Politics in Transition*, 2nd edn. Boston: Little, Brown.

KEURS, W.J. and MEELIS, E. (1986) Monitoring the biotic aspects of our environment. *Environmental Monitoring and Assessment*, **7**, 161–168.

KHOR, M. (1995) Globalization and the need for coordinated Southern policy responses. *Cooperation South* (UNDP), May.

KITSCHELT, H. (1993) Social movements, political parties and democratic theory. *The Annals*, **528**, 13–29.

KNOKE, D. (1990) *Political Networks: the Structural Perspective*. Cambridge: Cambridge University Press.

KOX, H.L.M. (1991) *The "non-polluter gets paid" principle for Third World commodity exports*. Research Memorandum of the Department of Economics and Econometrics. Amsterdam: Free University.

KOX, H.L.M. (1993) *International commodity-related environmental agreements and the GATT system of trade rules*. Research Memorandum of the Department of Economics and Econometrics. Amsterdam: Free University.

KRASNER, S. (ed.)(1983) *International Regimes*. Ithaca: Cornell University Press.

KUIK, O. and VERBRUGGEN, H. (1991) *In search of indicators of sustainable development*. Dordrecht: Kluwer.

LIBERATORE, A. (1996) The social construction of environmental problems. In Glasbergen, P. and Blowers, A. (eds), *Perspectives on Environmental Problems*. London, Arnold, pp.59–83.

LIEFFERINK, J.D., LOWE, P.D. and MOL, A.P.J. (eds) (1993) *European Integration and Environmental Policy*. London: Belhaven Press.

LINDBLOM, C. (1977) *Politics and Markets: The World's Political-Economic Systems*. New York: Basic Books.

LINDERT, P.H. (1991) *International Economics*. Homewood, Ill: Irwin.

LIST, M. (1990) Cleaning up the Baltic. In Rittberger, V. (ed.), *International Regimes in East-West Politics*. London: Pinter, pp.90–116.

LIST, M. and RITTBERGER, V. (1992) Regime theory and international environmental management. In Hurrell, A. and Kingsbury, B. (eds), *The International Politics of the Environment*. Oxford: Clarendon Press, pp.85–109.

LOEB, P. (1986) *Nuclear Culture: Living and Working in the World's Largest Atomic Complex*. Philadelphia: New Society Publishers.

MAJONE, G. (1994) Paradoxes of privatization and deregulation. *Journal of European Public Policy*, **1**(1), 53–69.

MANNO, J. (1994) Advocacy and diplomacy: NGOs and the Great Lakes Water Quality Agreement. In Princen, T. and Finger, M. (eds) *Environmental NGOs in World Politics*. London: Routledge, pp.69–120.

MATHEWS, J.T. (ed.) (1991) *Preserving the Global Environment. The Challenge of Shared Leadership*. New York: Norton.

MAZEY, S. and RICHARDSON, J. (1992) British pressure groups in the European Community: the challenge of Brussels. *Parliamentary Affairs*, **45**(1), 92–107.

MAZEY, S. and RICHARDSON, J. (1994) Policy co-ordination in Brussels: environmental and regional policy. In Baker, S., Milton, K. and Yearley, S. (eds), *Protecting the Periphery: Environmental Policy in Peripheral Regions of the EU*. London: Frank Cass.

MCCORMICK, J. (1993) Environmental politics. In Dunleavy, P. *et al.* (eds), *Developments in British Politics*, *4*. London: Macmillan, pp.267–284.

MCCULLY, P. (1991) The case against climate aid. *Ecologist*, **21**(6), 244–251.

MCNEELY, J., MILLER, K.R., REED, W.V., MITTERMEIER, R.A. and WERNER, T.B. (1990) *Conserving the World's Biological Diversity*. Gland, Switzerland: IUCN/WRI/CI/WWF-US/World Bank.

MEADOWS, D.H., MEADOWS, D.L., RANDERS, J, and BEHRENS, W. (1972) *The Limits to Growth: A Report for the Club of Rome Project on the Predicament of Mankind*. London: Earth Island Press.

MEADOWS, D.H., MEADOWS, D.L. and RANDERS, J. (1992) *Beyond the Limits*. London: Earthscan.

MIDDLETON, N., O'KEEFE, P., MOYO, S. (1993) *The Tears of the Crocodile: From Rio to Reality in the Developing World*. London: Pluto Press.

MIGDAL, J. (1988) *Strong Societies and Weak States. State-Society Relations and State Capabilities in the Third World*. Princeton: Princeton University Press.

MINISTRY OF HOUSING, PHYSICAL PLANNING AND ENVIRONMENT OF THE NETHERLANDS (1988) *To choose or to lose – National Environmental Policy Plan. Second Chamber of the States-General*, session 1988–1989, 21 137, Nos. 1 and 2. The Hague: SDU Publishers.

MINISTRY OF HOUSING, PHYSICAL PLANNING AND ENVIRONMENT OF THE NETHERLANDS (1991) *Environmental Resources Limited. The Structure and Functions of Environmental Enforcement Organisations in EC Member States*. The Hague.

MINISTRY OF HOUSING, PHYSICAL PLANNING AND ENVIRONMENT OF THE NETHERLANDS (1992) Environment and development of the Republic of Bulgaria. In *Nations of the Earth Report*, Vol. 2. Geneva: United Nations.

MINISTRY OF HOUSING, PHYSICAL PLANNING AND ENVIRONMENT OF THE NETHERLANDS (1994) *The Netherlands' National Environmental Policy Plan 2*. The Hague.

MITCHELL, R. (1995), Heterogeneities at two levels: states, non-state actors and intentional oil pollution. In Keohane, R.O. and Ostrom, E. (eds), *Local Commons and Global Interdependence: Heterogeneity and Cooperation in Two Domains*. Thousand Oaks: Sage Publications.

MORAVCSIK, A. (1993) Preferences and power in the European Community: a liberal intergovernmentalist approach. *Journal of Common Market Studies,* **31**(4), 473–524.

NATIONAL INSTITUTE OF PUBLIC HEALTH AND ENVIRONMENTAL PROTECTION (1988) *Concern for Tomorrow, National Environmental Survey 1985–2010*. Alphen aan den Rijn: Samsom H.D. Tjeenk Willink.

NATURE POLICY PLAN (1990) Lower House, 1989/1990 session, 21 149, Nos. 2 and 3.

OECD (1995) *OECD Employment Outlook*. Paris: OECD.

OPSCHOOR, J.B. (1987) *Duurzaamheid en verandering; over de ecologische inpasbaarheid van economische activiteiten (Sustainability and change: on the ecological compatibility of economic activities).* Oration, Amsterdam: VU Uitgeverij.

OPSCHOOR, J.B. and REIJNDERS, L. (1991) Towards sustainable development indicators. In Kuik, O. and Verbruggen, H. (eds), *In Search of Indicators of Sustainable Development.* Dordrecht: Kluwer.

PELUSO, N. (1993), Coercive conservation: the politics of state resource control. In Lipschutz, R. and Conca, K. (eds), *The State and Social Power in Global Environmental Politics.* New York: Columbia University Press, pp.46–70.

PERELET, R. (1994) The environment as a security issue. In CLTM (ed.), *The Environment: Towards a Sustainable Future.* Dordrecht: Kluwer, pp.147–174.

PEREZ-DIAZ, V. (1993), *The Return of Civil Society. The Emergence of Democratic Spain.* Cambridge, Mass: Harvard University Press.

PINDER, J. (1991) *The European Community and Eastern Europe.* London: Royal Institute of International Affairs.

POTTER, D. (1995) Environmental problems in their political context. In Glasbergen, P. and Blowers, A. (eds), *Perspectives on Environmental Problems.* London: Arnold, pp.85–110.

PRINCEN, T. and FINGER, M. (1994) *Environmental NGOs in World Politics.* London: Routledge.

PRINS, G. (ed.) (1993) *Threats Without Enemies: Institutions for Environmental Security.* London: Earthscan.

PUTNAM, R. D. (1993), *Making Democracy Work. Civic Traditions in Modern Italy.* Princeton: Princeton University Press.

RAN (Rainforest Action Network) (1993) Logging company looks for investors. *World Rainforest Report,* **X**(4).

RAVENHILL, J. (1990) The North-South balance of power. *International Affairs,* **66**(4), 731–748.

RICH, B. (1994), *Mortgaging the Earth. The World Bank, Environmental Impoverishment, and the Crisis of Development.* Boston: Beacon Press.

RICHARDSON, J. (1993) Interest group behaviour in Britain: continuity and change. In Richardson, J. (ed.), *Pressure Groups.* Oxford: Oxford University Press.

RITCHIE, M. (1990) *The Environmental Implications of the GATT Negotiations.* Discussion paper. Minneapolis: Institute for Agriculture and Trade Policy.

ROBERTS, L. and WHEALE, A. (1991) *Innovation and Environmental Risk.* London: Belhaven.

ROCHON, T. and MAZMANIAN, D. (1993) Social movements and the policy process. *The Annals,* **528**, 75–87.

ROZENDAAL, S. (1992) Milieubeleid is geldverspilling: De tegendraadse opvattingen van politicoloog Aaron Wildavsky (Environmental policy is a waste of money: The heretical views of the political scientist Aaron Wildavsky). *Elsevier,* 12 December 1992.

SACHS, W. (1993) Global ecology and the shadow of 'development'. In Sachs, W. (ed.), *Global Ecology: A New Arena of Political Conflict.* London: Zed Books.

SAGE, C. (1996) Population, poverty and land in the South. In Sloep, P. and Blowers, A. (eds), *Environmental Problems as Conflicts of Interest.* London: Arnold, pp.97–125.

SANDS, P. (1992) The role of environmental NGOs in international environmental law. *Development* (Journal of SID), **2**, 28–31.

SARAVANAMUTTU, P. (1994) Environment, development and security. In Thomas, C. (ed.), *Rio: Unravelling the Consequences.* London: Frank Cass.

SCHMIDHEINY, S. (1992) *Changing Course: A Global Business Perspective on Development and the Environment.* Cambridge, Mass: MIT Press.

SEBENIUS, J.K. (1991) Designing negotiations towards a new regime: the case of global warming. *International Security*, **15**(4).

SHAYLER, M., WELFORD, R.J. and SHAYLER, G. (1994) BS7750: panacea or palliative? *Eco-management and Auditing*, **1**, 2.

SHRYBMAN, S. (1990) International trade and the environment: an environmental assessment of the General Agreement on Tariffs and Trade. *Ecologist*, **20**(1).

SHRYBMAN, S. (1991) Trading away the environment. *World Policy Journal*, **9**(1),

SLOEP, P. and BLOWERS, A. (eds) (1996) *Environmental Problems as Conflicts of Interest.* Environmental Policy in an International Context series. London: Arnold.

SLOEP, P. and VAN DAM-MIERAS, M. (1995) Science on environmental problems. In Glassbergen, P. and Blowers, A. (eds), *Perspectives on Environmental Problems*. London: Arnold, pp.31–58.

SMITH, M. (1993) *Pressure, Power and Policy: State Autonomy and Policy Networks in Britain and the United States*. New York: Harvester Wheatsheaf.

SORSA, P. (1992a) GATT and environment. *World Economy*, **15**(1).

SORSA, P. (1992b) *The Environment: A New Challenge to GATT?* Washington: World Bank Policy Research Papers.

SOULÉ, M.I., WILCOX, B.A. and HOLTBY, C. (1979) Benign neglect: a model of formal collapse in the game reserves of East Africa. *Biological Conservation*, **15**, 259–271.

SOUTH COMMISSION (1990) *The Challenge to the South: The Report of the South Commission.* Oxford: Oxford University.

STORTENBEKER, C. (1990) Op weg naar het Paaseilandscenario (On the way to the Easter Island scenario). In Long-Term Environmental Policy committee of the Central Council for Environmental Protection, *Het milieu: denkbeelden voor de 21ste eeuw*. Zeist: Kerkebosch.

SUSSKIND, L. (1994) *Environmental Diplomacy. Negotiating More Effective Global Agreements.* New York: Oxford University Press.

TASK FORCE ENVIRONMENT AND THE INTERNAL MARKET (1990) '*1992*' – *The Environmental Dimension*. Bonn: Economica Verlag GmbH.

TELLEGEN, E. (1995) Environmental conflicts in transforming economies: Central and Eastern Europe. In Sloep, P. and Blowers, A. (eds), *Environmental Problems as Conflicts of Interest*. London: Edward Arnold.

THOMAS, D. and MIDDLETON, N. (1994) *Desertification: Exploding the Myth*. Chichester: John Wiley.

TODARO, M. P. (1981) *Economic Development in the Third World*. Harlow: Longman.

TOLBA, M. (1992) *Saving our Future: Challenges and Hopes*. London: Chapman and Hall.

TOLBA, M. *et al.* (1992) *The World Environment 1972–1992*. London: Chapman and Hall.

TOULMIN, C. (1994) Combatting desertification: encouraging local action within a global framework. In Bergesen, H.O. and Parmann, G. (eds), *Green Globe Yearbook 1994*. Oxford: Oxford University Press.

TOYE, J. (1993) *Dilemmas of Development*, 2nd edn. Oxford: Blackwell.

TURNER, B. *et al.* (1990) Two types of global environmental change: definitional and space-scale issues in their human dimensions. *Global Environmental Change: Human and Policy Dimensions,* **1**(1), 14–22.

US COUNCIL ON ENVIRONMENTAL POLICY AND DEPARTMENT OF STATE (1981) *Global Future: Time to Act. Report to the President on Global Resources, Environment and Population.* Washington DC: Government Printing Office.

293

US COUNCIL ON ENVIRONMENTAL QUALITY AND DEPARTMENT OF STATE (1980) *Global 2000 Report to the President of the United States – Entering the Twenty-First Century.* Washington DC: Government Printing Office.

UNITED NATIONS (1993) *Earth Summit Agenda 21: The United Nations Programme of Action from Rio.* New York: United Nations Department of Public Information.

VAN DEN NOORT, P.C. (1993) Groei als voorwaarde voor duurzaamheid (Growth as a precondition for sustainability). *Economisch Statistische Berichten*, **78**(3922).

VAN DER MEIJ, T., HENDRIKS, J.H.W., MUSTERS, C.J.M. *et al.* (1995) *Ontwikkelingen in de natuur; visies op de levende natuur in de wereld en scenario's voor het behoud daarvan* (Developments in nature; views of living nature in the world and scenarios for its preservation), Voorstudies en achtergronden V87. The Hague: Wetenschappelijke Raad voor het Regeringsbeleid (Scientific Council for Government Policy).

VAN EGMOND, P., GRAAFLAND, F., HANEKAMP, E. *et al.* (1992) Is een duurzaamheidsindicator (al) een betrouwbare barometer? (Is a sustainability indicator (already) a reliable barometer?). *Milieu*, **4**, 120–128.

VAN LATESTEIJN, H.C., SCHEELE, D. and SCHOONENBOOM, I.J. (1994) Paradigms of sustainability and perceptions of environmental utilisation space. *Milieu*, **9**, 244–252.

VERHOEVE, B., BENNET, G. and WILKINSON, D. (1992) *Maastricht and the Environment.* Arnhem: Institute for European Environmental Policy.

VONKEMAN, G.H. (1989) *Budgets for environmental research.* Seminar on Research and Environment. Brussels: EEB.

VONKEMAN, G.H. (1992) *After Rio: Perspectives for the XXIst Century. Third European Seminar on Environment.* Île de Berder (Morbihan, Bretagne), 12 September.

VONKEMAN, G.H. (1995a) *International environmental policy: laws of the earth, laws for the world.* Inaugural address Utrecht State University. English version – Brussels: Institute for European Environmental Policy.

VONKEMAN, G.H. (1995b) Arbeit in einer nachhaltigen Wirtschaft (Work in a sustainable economy). In Graz Technical University (ed.), *Arbeit in einer nachhaltigen Wirtschaft* (Series: Strategien der Nachhaltigkeit).

VONKEMAN, G.H. and. MAXSON, P.A. (1991) *Environmental Research in the Member States. Volume I Public Environmental and Climatic Research of the Member States of the European Community. Volume II Country Reports.* Brussels: European Commission, DG XII.

VONKEMAN, G.H. and MAXSON, P.A. (1994) International views on long-term environmental policy. In CLTM (ed.), *The Environment: Towards a Sustainable Future.* Dordrecht: Kluwer, p.235.

VORLAT, K. (1993) The international ozone regime: concessions and loopholes? *Fletcher Forum of World Affairs*, **17**(1).

WEALE, A. (1992) *The New Politics of Pollution.* Manchester: Manchester University Press.

WEALE, A. (1993) Ecological modernization and the integration of European environmental policy. In Liefferink, J.D., Lowe, P.D. and Mol, A.P.J. (eds), *European Integration and Environmental Policy.* London: Belhaven Press, pp. 196–216.

WELFORD, R.J. (1995) *Environmental Strategy and Sustainable Development: The Corporate Challenge for the 21st Century.* London: Routledge.

WELFORD, R.J. and PRESCOTT, C.E. (1994) *European Business: An Issue Based Approach*, 2nd edn. London: Pitman Publishing.

WETERINGS, R.A.P.M. and OPSCHOOR, J.B. (1992) *The Ecocapacity as a Challenge to Technological Development.* Rijswijk: RMNO publ. 74a.

WHEELER, D. (1993) Auditing for sustainability: philosophy and practice of The Body Shop International. *Eco-management and Auditing*, **1**, 1.

WILLETTS, P. (1982) The impact of promotional pressure groups on global politics. In Willetts, P. (ed.), *Pressure Groups in the Global System: The Transnational Relations of Issue-Oriented Non-Governmental Organisations*. London: Pinter.

WITOELAR, E. (1984) NGO networking in Indonesia. *Environment, Development and Natural Resource Crisis in Asia: Proceedings of Symposium Organized by SAM, 22–25 October 1993*. Penang: Sahabat Alam Malaysia.

WOLF, E.C. (1987) *On the Brink of Extinction: Conserving the Diversity of Life*. Worldwatch Paper 78. Washington DC: Worldwatch Institute.

WOLSINK, M. (1993) Entanglement of interests and motives in facility siting: the not-in-my-backyard 'theory'. Unpublished paper.

WORCESTER, R. (1994) European attitudes to the environment. *European Environment*, **4**, 6.

WORLD BANK (1992) *World Development Report 1992*. Oxford: Oxford University Press.

WORLD BANK (1993) *The World Bank and the Environment: Fiscal 1993*. Oxford: Oxford University Press.

WORLD BANK (1993) *World Development Report 1993*. Oxford: Oxford University Press.

WORLD BANK (1994) *Environment Bulletin*, **6**(3).

WORLD COMMISSION ON ENVIRONMENT AND DEVELOPMENT (WCED) (1987) *Our Common Future*. Oxford: Oxford University Press.

WORLD RESOURCES INSTITUTE (WRI) in collaboration with The United Nations Environment Programme and The United Nations Development Programme (1992) *World Resources 1992–93: A Guide to the Global Environment*. New York: Oxford University Press.

WORLD RESOURCES INSTITUTE (WRI) (1994) *World Resources 1994–5*. Oxford: Oxford University Press.

WUYTS, M. *et al.* (eds) (1992) *Development Policy and Public Action*. Oxford: Oxford University Press.

WYNNE, B., WATERTON, C. and GROVE-WHITE, R. (1993) *Public Perceptions and the Nuclear Industry in West Cumbria*. Lancaster: Centre for the Study of Environmental Change.

YOUNG, O. (1991) Political leadership and regime formation. On the development of institutions in international society. *International Organization,* **45**(3), 281–308.

YOUNG, O.R. (1994) *International Governance. Protecting the Environment in a Stateless Society*. Ithaca, New York: Cornell University Press.

ZARTMAN, I.W. (1987) Introduction: explaining North-South negotiations. In Zartman, I.W. (ed.), *Positive Sum: Improving North-South Negotiations*. New Brunswick: Transaction Books.

ZONABEND, F. (1993) *The Nuclear Peninsula*. Cambridge: Cambridge University Press.

Index